The Student's Guide to Canadian Universities

Edited by Christine Ibarra
and Blair Trudell

Illustrations by George A. Walker

KEY PORTER BOOKS

Canadian Cataloguing in Publication Data

Ibarra, Christine, 1977–
    The student's guide to Canadian universities

ISBN 1-55263-105-2

1. Universities and colleges – Canada – Handbooks, manuals, etc. 2. Universities and colleges – Canada – Directories. I. Trudell, Blair, 1977– . II. Title.

L905.T78 1999   378.71   C99-932530-2

The publisher gratefully acknowledges the assistance of the Canada Council and the Ontario Arts Council.

Canadä

We acknowledge the financial support of the Government of Canada through the Book Publishing Industry Development Program (BPIDP) for our publishing activities.

Key Porter Books Limited
70 The Esplanade
Toronto, Ontario
Canada M5E 1R2

www.keyporter.com

Illustrations: George A. Walker

Electronic formatting: Jean Peters

Design: Peter Maher

Printed and bound in Canada

99 00 01 02 6 5 4 3 2 1

What's Inside . . .

Quebec

Nova Scotia

New Brunswick

Prince Edward Island

Newfoundland

Acknowledgements . . .

A book like this wouldn't have come together without the participation and support of many people, and we would like to extend our appreciation and express our gratitude to them. We would like to thank Anna Porter, whose accomplishments in her career and motherhood are true testament to her character. We are grateful for her belief in us, for her generosity, and for giving us the opportunity to take on this mammoth task. We would also like to thank our editor, Andrea Bock, for her ability and direction, and for swimming through a sea of paper. Of course, we cannot offer enough thanks to all the writers for their hard work and reliability—we hope to meet each of you in the future.

From Christine Ibarra: I wish to thank my parents, whose love, constant support, and encouragement for this book and for all my endeavours have meant so much to me. I love you, Mom and Dad. A special thanks to my wonderful sister, Kimberley, for her patience, thoughtful suggestions, and research. Love ya, Bebe. A huge thanks to my friends, especially to Brenda Wong for her friendship, smile, words of wisdom, and timely feedback; to Melissa Johnson for her super ideas and anecdotes over coffee, bagels, and the occasional cherry cheesecake; to Charmaine D'Silva for listening and

rooting me on; to Maria Gallo for her valuable suggestions; to David McAlduff for tapping into his "X-family" connections; to my cousin Joseph Talavera for his Mac know-how and for coming to the rescue during those late-night computer emergencies; and to Ibraheim Seif for his cool ideas. I also wish to dedicate this book to the memory of my grandma "Lola," who nurtured me into the person I am today and instilled in me the love of reading.

From Blair Trudell: I would like to thank all of my friends and family who supplied me with the resources to finish this book. To my mother, who dealt with the paper wasteland that became my office, and to my father, who supplied the transportation to get me from A to B. And to my sister Eryn, who listened to all of my breakdowns. I love you all very much. I would also like to acknowledge John H., Jer D., Gubby, Trainor, Chris O., Bianca, Steph, Cara, Pete, Don, Trish, and the rest of the Dal crew, who offered both support and escape throughout the summer, especially Juls for her love, shoulder, and ear, without which this book would never have been completed. All of you make me feel as though I am the luckiest puma cat in the world. I would also like to dedicate this book to the memory of my grandfather.

Introduction

Okay. You're finally about to enter university life. You've made it. Adolescence is close to over and soon you'll be out on your own. All the freedom you've been dreaming about is now at your fingertips. Soon, very soon, you'll be able to come and go as you please, and make as many late-night phone calls as you want; you can eat cereal with marshmallows, leave your clothes on the floor, eat in front of the television, get drunk on a school night, do your homework (or not)…whatever you want. All you have to do is decide where you're going to do these things. Aaah, freedom. The one nagging thing, though, is that with all this freedom comes the great paradox—responsibility. The more freedom you have, the more responsibility goes with it.

It wasn't too long ago that we were in the very same place—sitting knee deep in university pamphlets, sleuthing through university websites, reading endless magazine rankings, and scheduling countless ultimately useless appointments with guidance counsellors. If you are anything like us, right about now you're probably feeling a bit overwhelmed, a bit confused, and still pretty much in the dark about where you're going to spend the next four years of your life.

That's where we come in. With this guide we are going to shine the proverbial light into the dark and show you exactly how to make the right decision for you. You see, the reason you're probably feeling unsatisfied with the pamphlets, the interviews, and the university rankings is because they don't give you the "real" picture. Finding out what programs are offered where and which are reputable is only a small part of choosing a university. What you also need to know is which university environment is going to make you feel the most comfortable. After all, university is going to be your home away from home for the next four years—wouldn't you like to make sure it's going to be as fun and rewarding as possible? If you're not happy with the scene, not only will you miss out on the full university experience (which you'll be paying for anyway), but you'll be unhappy and then it'll be harder to focus on your academics—which is the real reason you're there. Remember: University is much more than a school; it's a lifestyle.

The idea behind *The Student's Guide to Canadian Universities* is to create a comprehensive source book that will give you one-stop shopping to some of the more interesting questions about universities that you may have. *The Student's Guide to Canadian Universities* isn't about rank. It simply gives you a candid look at what it's really like to attend Bishop's, Queen's, UBC, Simon Fraser, St. Mary's, St. FX, or the University of Toronto. The truth is: We're all different. Luckily, so are the universities. With the help of this book, we're sure we can help you choose the right school for you. Certainly class size and student–professor contact are important, but so is social environment. You also need to think about whether you want to live at home or move out; whether you'd prefer the anonymity of a big university or the familiarity of a smaller one. Do you want to attend a school with a lively social scene, one that's more academic, or something in between? The best thing you can do is to choose a university that suits your personality, your goals, and your pocketbook.

Atmosphere is therefore the major focus of this book. We've designed this guide so that you can get an insider's look at the reputation, campus life, academics, culture, and lifestyle of the universities from the perspective of those who know them best—the students themselves. We've included information on everything from class size to rez life; from library facilities to party palaces; from social clubs to life in the university town or city, and everything in between. It is our hope that this book will not only address all of your pre-university concerns, but help you make the right choice in what is one of the most important decisions of your life.

Oh, and if you want some advice from a couple of people who've been through this, just remember: University can and should be much more than a learning institution. Not only will it help shape who you are, how you think, and how you perceive the world, it will teach you about life. Your university years are the time to expand your ideas, develop a new philosophy, and experience a whole new side of your personality. If you use them wisely, you can reap the rewards for the rest of your life. This is, after all, the first step into the real world. After all the partying is done, the people you meet at university could become lifelong contacts. They could help you with a job or even a career. They can be your friends for years. It's all up to you.

If there is any other advice we can give, it's this: Be adventurous. Exploit your university's possibilities. After all, a university education is one of the most expensive things that you (or your parents) will ever invest in, so be sure to take advantage of all the resources your tuition money pays for: participate in exchange programs, join a weird club, enroll in a society, write for the paper, be a radio DJ, run for office in student politics, join your favourite sports team—above all, get involved. Many universities will even give you the money to start your own club—at one university someone started a beer drinking society, at another a friend started a surfing club—both of the clubs were completely funded by the university. A last piece of advice is to dig deep into the world of financial aid. Universities are willing to give out big bursaries for seemingly obscure reasons. The key is only that you must ask. You'd be amazed at the amount of money that just sits in bank accounts, waiting for students to come and collect it (kinda like the free refills at McDonald's: no one seems to know that they exist, but they do).

That last bit of advice is so important we are going to repeat it. The key to survival and success at university is to *ask*.

Do not be afraid to find out about things like societies, clubs, bursaries, and programmes. Don't be afraid to make yourself visible; talk to your professors, seek help from counsellors and especially T.A.s. The better your relationship is with these people, the more successful you will be in your studies, and the more opportunities will become available to you.

Our own university years have been rewarding, challenging, stressful, but, most of all, they've been a whole lot of fun. Some students will never experience the real university experience because when they first stick in their toes to test the water, they quickly pull them back out. They never end up jumping in. Now, after experiencing the very wide limits of our own $40,000 university education, we can honestly say, "Go ahead, jump in. The water's fine."

NOTE: All statistics and figures that appear in this book are the most up-to-date at the time of publication. Numbers vary from semester to semester, particularly those dealing with average entrance grades and tuition fees.

Canadian Universities

University of British Columbia

By Amy Patterson

Contrary to popular belief, UBC is not home to one single counter-culture. And the campus is not teeming with long-haired pseudo-hippies living in tents. Nor is there a constant stream of student uprisings and rebellions. And no, not all students are vegetarian environmentalists out to change the world, nor do all UBC students have pepper-sprayed eyes and are awaiting a court hearing. The truth is UBC is an urban campus with quite a diverse student population. UBC is, above and beyond, a means to an end for most students. Like all urban campuses, it lacks the intimacy of a Mount Allison or Acadia, and is representative of the paradox that exists in most urban campuses—that is to say that despite its population of some 30,000 students, most are independent and generally alienated from campus culture. After classes, most students hurry off campus into the city to rejoin their personal lives, or they are off to the surrounding mountains and trails for some climbing, hiking, and biking.

One student, in fact, cynically remarked that UBC is like a factory, where students are made to feel like "another brick in the wall." Having said this, UBC does regularly manufacture top students and maintains a highly competitive atmosphere. It is, therefore, one of Canada's most prestigious universities and thus has high entrance requirements.

Perhaps one of UBC's most positive attributes is its location. Set in Point Grey, at the edge of a forested provincial park and right by English Bay, UBC is beautiful—you'll even admit this after weeks of pouring rain and grey skies. The gorgeous landscape emphasizes the campus's natural aesthetics. The Rose Garden at the north end of the campus is the perfect venue for a spectacular view of the inlet and the local North Shore Mountains. Wide pedestrian boulevards are lined with trees; long strips of green grass and flowering shrubs provide the perfect spot to contemplate your studies or to gossip with friends. You can even see nature in all its naked (literally) splendour: Just take a hike down to Wrek Beach—the only nude beach in Vancouver.

Whether it's the long walk from B-lot, or the sheer size of the lecture halls in the Institutional Resource Centre, open space is what most characterizes the layout of this campus. In other words, be prepared to do lots of walking, because it's all about the outdoors at UBC.

CAMPUS CULTURE

UBC's student body evades generalizations. It is diverse because of ethnicity, sexual orientation, age, religion, nationality, politics, and ability, among a host of other things. To some the typical undergrad may be perceived as a white Vancouverite still living at home—but that's a misconception. UBC is a dynamic place because of the differences that each student contributes. In general, students can find their own niche and are at UBC mostly to achieve a set goal. This gives them the ability to mosey through university life without much of a ripple. Despite the recent hoopla surrounding UBC students protesting APEC, most students are quite apathetic, conservative, and far from radical.

UBC does provide, however, the ability to escape the boredom and complacency of everyday life through its endless supply of events, societies, and clubs. Run in a student society election. Volunteer. Write for the *Ubysey*. Join one of over 200 student-run clubs for martial arts, dancing, fly-fishing, pottery, skiing, or anything else you have an affinity for. Whatever it is, make sure it's something. Merely studying at UBC can be a bore and will ultimately strengthen feelings of alienation. Remember: There's more to a university education than just academics. And quite simply, life at UBC is what you make of it—drab or exciting, you choose. It is important to get involved at UBC, especially if you are from out of town and do not have the friends or networks to sustain your interest and sanity. UBC is not the most "touchy feely" campus that Canada has to offer and it is possible to become lost in the shuffle, but the most important thing is to get involved.

ACADEMIC ISSUES

UBC is the largest and oldest university in BC. It's a prestigious institution with an excellent academic reputation. Eighty percent of all research done in BC is conducted here. UBC boasts a prize-winning faculty and offers innovative programs. Numerous research centres, hundreds of faculty members, thousands of support staff, and more than 32,000 students make UBC what it is—a huge bureaucratic institution. Undergrads are often left feeling isolated, disoriented, and overwhelmed. To combat being reduced to a lonely little number, students must make a point of building a smaller community within the bigger one. See profs during office hours. Join undergrad societies. Study with classmates. And keep in mind that smaller faculties, like Applied Science and Human Kinetics, foster a sense of community more than do the larger faculties, like Arts and Science. To feel more at home in the two big faculties, and to get a great start in your academic career, take Arts or Science One, a course that is available to all first-year students accepted into either arts, commerce, or science programs. Arts or Science One consists of a reading list of political, philosophical, and sociological works by authors such as Plato, Mao Zedong, and even Mozart and is taught in an informal and intimate manner, with group work and open discussions. Another option providing similar benefits is Foundations—a soon to be available Arts program that will be interdisciplinary but have a social science bent. Co-op programs are another way to establish

contacts and receive a well-rounded education. Other programs, like International Relations and Women's Studies, are known to be a bit challenging. The Engineering faculty is notorious for its silly pranks—a VW bug has been squeezed inside the Student Union Building and hung from the downtown public library. At UBC you can take innovative genetics courses, major in Gay and Lesbian Studies, or choose to build a robot and get credit for it. UBC is a leader in establishing new and innovative programs.

Overall, most of the faculty at UBC are preoccupied with their own research, committee meetings, and academic writing—not teaching, calming the fears of eager students, or keeping long office hours. For the most part, the profs are reputable and adequate. Tutoring services are available and often free, provided you look. Numbers are another concern. UBC is known to have horribly large class sizes, particularly in faculties and programs like Biology and Psychology. Expect to be in classes numbering 500 students or more, though this phenomenon is more true for the sciences than the arts. Arts lectures tend to be smaller. Most lower-level survey courses will range from 25 to 100 students. Class size usually decreases as you progress in your studies.

Vital Statistics

Address: Undergraduate Admissions Office, 2016-1874 East Mall, Vancouver, B.C., V6T 1Z1

Admissions office: (604) 822-3014

Website: www.ubc.ca

Total enrollment: 33,447

Male-female ratio: 45 to 55

Average entrance grades: Arts: 75%; Science: 82%; Commerce: 78%; Engineering: 82%

Tuition fees: $2,563

Residence fees: $4,222–$5,405 in residence (including meals); off-campus bachelor rentals range from $500–$650/month; one bedrooms from $600–$900; two bedrooms from $800–$1400; the more roommates, the cheaper it gets.

Percentage of students in residence: 24%

Percentage of out-of-province first-year students: 9%

Financial aid: Unless you're a super high achiever or are in considerable need, the Awards and Financial Aid Office expects you to plan for your finances yourself. But if you do need help, they don't bite and might be able to offer a hand. Ask questions and be sure to look into bursaries—many go unused.

Co-op programs: Applied Science, Arts, Atmospheric Science, Biology, Biotechnology in Microbiology and Immunology, Chemistry, Commerce, Computer Science, Mathematics, Pharmacology, Physics, Science, Statistics, Wood Products Processing.

Services for students with disabilities: The Disability Resource Centre provides a range of services and support. Lack of accessibility is an issue. Things are changing, but much more improvement is needed. Questions? Contact an advisor; they're helpful.

Student services: A spectrum of services is available. The trick is knowing what is out there and taking advantage of it. Services include the Equity Office, the Women Student's Office, Student Health, Counselling Services, the First Nations House of Learning, Career Services, and a slew of student-run services through the Alma Mater Society (a.k.a. the student union). Important tip: Take AMS orientations to figure out UBC before classes start. Otherwise third year rolls around and you still don't know where to go for stress management (and you'll need it!).

Despite the incredibly long line-ups at the bookstore and the high number of underpaid and stressed-out sessional profs, earning a degree at UBC is a worthwhile and rewarding experience. Also, it's a lot more affordable place to study (about $2,500) than other places in Canada. Wondering how to weasel your way into UBC? Want to make the system work for you? Breaking out in hives over questions about UBC? Tips: Contact Student Recruitment—the friendliest and most helpful resource available to UBC hopefuls—and don't expect your faculty of interest or the Registrar's Office to hold your hand.

REZ LIFE

Living in rez is a blast. It's super for your social life, but potentially damaging to academic performance—good time-management skills are a must in order to ensure that your grades don't suffer. Frosh can choose between Totem and Vanier residences. Totem is more of a party house, Vanier is more low-key. Both have small but liveable rooms that scream for space organizers, a wide selection of quasi-edible foods, and lots to do—broom-ball at midnight, bonfires at Wrek beach, and pyjama sessions with fellow co-eds. However, residence life is never without its pitfalls: the nasty roommate and 4:00 a.m. fire alarms the night before your Physics exam.

Once you're over the age of 20, there are more options for housing that are cheaper as well. Gage is an apartment-style building located near the Student Union Building. Each floor has four quads in which six students share a kitchen and a bathroom, but have their own rooms. Fairview is a townhouse complex in which two to six students share a living space. Out near B-lot, Thunderbird is a mix of separate apartments and townhouses.

After living in rez for a year or two, venture off campus. Live in Vancouver. Make the city your home. There are several great neighbourhoods that are close to campus. Point Grey is quiet, like a suburb, and is the closest to campus. Kerrisdale has a similar feel—cute shops and is on the bus route—but is not too exciting. Kits, especially down by the beach, is a more happening location: tree-lined streets, good shopping, neighbourhood pubs, and, of course, coffee houses. (Coffee? In Vancouver?...Nah.) For similar amenities, close proximity to Stanley Park, and a cosier feel, try the west end. The north end of Cambie Street is a little less pricey, features an independent theatre, and has good restaurants. Even less expensive is the area around Broadway and Granville. Located near Granville Island Market, False Creek has lots of green space and is right on the water. Commercial Drive is a trendy neighbourhood that is busy in an offbeat kind of way and diverse in population (it is much less yuppyish than other areas). Be sure to take advantage of housing boards in the Student Union Building and the Rentsline, a student-run service that helps you find a place to call home.

> "The reason universities are so full of knowledge is that students come with so much and they leave with so little."
>
> Marshall McLuhan, communications theorist, quoted by Fred Thompson in "Monday Night Sessions," *Antigonish Review*, 1989.

A Word to the Wise:

1. Learn to love the rain and don't whine about the grey sky. Vancouver's still green in January because of the weeks and weeks of endless rain...so, appreciate it!
2. Get to know Vancouver. Hang out. Do stuff. Don't be one of those students from back east who don't know where the Drive is because they've never left campus!
3. Get active on campus.
4. Take advantage of Vancouver's proximity to local mountains, the ocean, and the islands.
5. The infamous campus legends about Main Library are only myths. Sure the stacks are a little creepy, but silly stories are not a good enough excuse for neglecting research.

NIGHT LIFE

Campus night life hits its peak on Wednesday's for Pit Night. The student-owned and -operated Pit Pub is located in the basement of the SUB (Student Union Building). On Wednesdays, line-ups start early. Show your student card for free admission and bring ID. If you're hungry for a greasy burger, pop into the Pit—it's open for lunch. This is also the place to guzzle beer and watch Monday night hockey. If you're looking for a more subdued spot, go to the Gallery. It's not an art gallery; it's a smoke-filled drinking den on the main floor of the SUB. Grab a booth and cram for your exam or celebrate here with friends. For an older crowd, go to Thea's Lounge in the Grad Studies Centre. If you want to support fellow students while simultaneously drinking large quantities of inexpensive beer, attend the beer gardens that are held at various locations around campus and generally start at 4:30 p.m. Keep an eye peeled for posters advertising the upcoming events. If you're really keen, join the beer gardening club.

After a long week of studying, eating, and sleeping at UBC, get off campus and head downtown. Vancouver has great places to party. If you want to dance, go to Luv-Affair. For Top 40 music and a meat market, try the Roxy. Go to Kits Pub on Broadway for a young, casual crowd. If flannel

In a Nut Shell

The university in a phrase: Big, beautiful, and plentiful—*Tuum est* (it's up to you).

Best thing about the university: The city and location.

Worst thing about the university: How the overwhelming size can be isolating at first.

Favourite professors: Sneja Gunew (English), Becky Ross (Sociology), Sherill Grace (English), Valerie Raoul (French), Marlee Kline (Law). Want the lowdown on UBC profs? Get a copy of the *YardStick*—it's a student review of profs that the AMS produces.

Most popular bird courses: Your usuals. Any science course catering to Arts students, i.e., Geology 101, or any language course with an "in translation" suffix (it's where foreign literature is studied in English).

Hot spot to study on campus: Conversation Pit in the SUB.

Quietest spot to study on campus: Koerner Library or, for women, the Women Student's Lounge in Brock Hall.

Need for a car and parking availability: A car in Vancouver is a bonus. Useful and convenient, but not absolutely necessary. Transit is okay—especially if you live near easily accessible routes like Broadway and take the B-line. If you drive, be warned: Parking at UBC can be a nightmare! The trek in from B-lot ("B" for budget—about $4 per day) sucks! To the main area of campus, it's a good 15 to 20 minute walk. Other, more convenient options are costly ($15+ per day). Parkade passes are tricky to snag. To get one, students must enter a lottery. If selected, you then have the chance to pay almost $600 for a spot. Tip: Ride your bike, bus it, or live on campus.

Sexually speaking: The ocean view is not the only good looking thing on campus. Overall, the student body is quite attractive. To meet prospective romantic interests, participate in intramural sports or join the student society. Note: Pride UBC is an excellent way to meet same-sex friends and is a great resource for queer students and those wanting to learn more about heterosexism and homophobia.

Fraternities/sororities: A few frats and sororities do exist, but they seem to resemble the run-down frat houses.

Athletic facilities: UBC's sporting facilities satisfy the needs of students who range from super sporty to somewhat athletically inclined. The Bird Coop—the gym in the Student Rec Centre—is new, affordable, and a great place to meet people. Take advantage of free student swims and skating. Participate in intramural sports or join an athletic club. Year round, at UBC and in Vancouver, you can take part in kayaking, dragon boat racing, cycling, martial arts, skiing, hiking, and more!

Library facilities: UBC has 13 libraries. Different libraries are for different areas of study. Most first years use Koerner—a new, centrally located facility. The library system can be incredibly daunting! To save yourself hours of grief and madness, sign up for the library workshops that are offered.

Weather: Vancouver is wet! Be prepared for rain year-round. An umbrella and a sturdy rain jacket are a must. Despite the chill of dampness, the climate is mild—not too cold, not too hot. The changing of the seasons is gradual, but beautiful. Daytime temperatures below freezing are an oddity, meaning that snow is very unusual. In the late spring and summer, expect temperatures in the low to mid twenties.

Safety on campus: Be sure to use campus safety services like Safewalk and Campus Security. Don't walk alone at night. Report anything suspicious. Use a buddy system when partying. Do what it takes to make you feel safe.

Alumni: Allan Fotheringham, Pierre Berton, Judith Frost, John Turner.

shirts are your thing, drink at Fred's Uptown Tavern. Dance at Celebrities—one of many local gay bars. For a night of Celtic music and a laugh at west coasters trying to do the River Dance, go to the Blarney Stone. For something a little trendier, try Bar None for dancing and a girlie drink. For an older, mellower atmosphere, sip martinis at the Urban Well or dance to funky music at Babaloo's. Stop by the Star Fish Room to catch a glimpse of the local music scene. Vancouver is home to many more pubs, clubs, and bars than this. Check out *The Georgia Straight* newspaper for the latest on live shows and what's happening and where.

Besides the drinking thing, there's plenty to do. Frankly, life at UBC need not resemble your average drunken party scene. Eat out—the restaurants are fabulous. For Mexican food go to Tapangas; for great pad thai try Sala Thai; for mouth-watering cheesecake go to True Confections. If you've been out partying, it's late, and you're starving for vegetarian food, go to the Naam; it's open 24 hours, seven days a week and the food is excellent. Once you've stuffed yourself, catch a movie at one of the many independent theatres or retreat back to UBC and see one for three bucks, courtesy of the Film Society. Go bowling. Take dance lessons. For the cheapest pool rates in the city, play pool in the SUB Arcade. Join a club—fun social events are planned regularly.

After a night out, a tasty brunch is in order. For fabulous eggs Benny and the best French toast in town, go to Café Zen. Pop across the street to King's Head if you're in the mood for a cheap, basic breakfast. If you're looking for a spot that isn't filled with young white professionals, go to Café Deux Soleil on Commercial. It's easy to see that Vancouver offers it all.

ON VANCOUVER

Vancouver is a fabulous city. According to many, it's the most beautiful city in Canada. Located on the west coast, Vancouver is at the edge of the ocean and is a short drive from local mountains and the acclaimed Whistler Ski Resort. On a clear day, you can go ocean kayaking, shop on Robson, and even go skiing. The city is young, vibrant, and green year-round, with a wet and mild climate. The population is diverse. It is home to many lively ethnic communities and a range of social classes. A definite negative, which might be due to the calm weather or the fact that the social system has failed many, is that the homeless population, squeegee kids, and panhandlers are abundant and visible throughout the city. On a happier note, there's plenty to do and see. Picnic at Spanish Banks; grab a coffee and watch the sunset from Kits Beach; go for dim sum in China Town; shop for produce at Granville Island market; walk the Stanley Park sea wall; and see and be seen on Robson Street. Also, Vancouver is the venue for many events like the Jazz Festival and the annual Vancouver Reading Series. But Vancouver is only the starting point. Pop over to Victoria. Surf at Long Beach. Camp in the Okanagan. Explore BC, there are few limits.

University of Northern British Columbia

By Lisa Drysdale

There are mornings when, upon reaching the UNBC campus, you realize that low-lying clouds have effectively erased the city of Prince George lying asleep in the bowl below, and spread out before you is a panoramic vista of wilderness and mountains that foregrounds the isolation and, well, *northerness* that is at once UNBC's best and worst feature.

Inaugurated in 1994 to service the communities of Northern British Columbia, UNBC is a good 10 hours away from the four other BC universities: University of Victoria, Simon Fraser University, Trinity Western University, and University of British Columbia. UNBC provides an essential opportunity to students from northern communities—isolated from the coast by distance and, often, way of life, people young and old embraced the opportunity to get a "higher" education near their home communities.

This said, it should be noted that large portions of UNBC's capital investments came from the area's forestry companies and mills. Popular opinion insists that the delightful view of the pulp mill across the river exists because any trees that obstructed this view were summarily cut down as a reminder of where the real priorities of this mill town lie. Indeed, forestry and related disciplines receive the most funding and the highest profile at this university. The Arts are often overlooked, and there are minimal scholarship opportunities for people pursuing the Humanities. Despite these apparent drawbacks, the humanities at UNBC offer some of the most enthusiastic and varied courses and professors. The classes are small, and the opportunity for one-on-one interaction with the professor is very high.

CAMPUS CULTURE

UNBC attracts a wide variety of people—from those who attend simply because it sits in Prince George and they therefore do not have to travel

Vital Statistics

Address: 3333 University Way, Prince George, B.C., V2N 4Z9

Telephone: (250) 960-5555

Website: www.unbc.ca

Total enrollment: 3,200

Male-female ratio: 47 to 53

Percentage of out-of-province students: 10%

Average entrance grades: 65%

Tuition fees: $2,258 for Canadian students (five courses per semester for two semesters), $5,079 for International students

Residence fees: $1,598 per person per semester

Percentage of students in residence: 17%

Co-op programs: All, but Social Work and Nursing already have practicum components in their curricula.

Financial aid: Scholarships and bursaries from $250–$5,000 per year are available. About 60% of students at UNBC receive financial aid.

Aboriginal students: 190 First Nations students. General First Nations Studies, First Nations Public Administration, Metis Studies, Nisga'a Studies.

Services for students with disabilities: UNBC was designed to be completely wheelchair accessible. Services for Students with Disabilities.

Student services: Athletics and Recreation, Career Development Services, Counselling Centre, Interfaith Chaplaincy, Health and Wellness Centre, Learning Skills Centre, Student Employment Centre.

In a Nut Shell

The university in a phrase: UNBC is a university that pays special attention to the social, environmental, and economic issues of the North.

Best thing about the university: It's brand new and looks like a ski lodge. Also, small class sizes and young faculty.

Worst thing about the university: Location, crappy cafeteria hours, and too much bureaucracy.

Favourite professors: Todd Whitcomb (Chemistry), Hiroe Wood (International Studies), Tracy Summerville (Political Science), Stan Beeler (English), Antonia Mills (First Nations).

Hot spot to study on campus: The agora steps by the Winter Garden.

Quietest spot to study on campus: The library.

Need for car & parking: Yes, please. The buses are awful, and UNBC is quite a walk from downtown. Parking costs about $2.00 per day, $128.50 per semester, $385.20 per year, or $642 per year if you want a plug in (great in theory, but the plug-ins are few and far between). Parking is highly coveted, but both lots are in fairly decent walking distance from the entrances.

Sexually speaking: Somebody somewhere must be having it. The cutest boys are the RRT guys, but there aren't enough to go around (more women than men). Meet for drinks at Sergeant's, but don't expect your love to stay private for long—on a campus this size, inter-student dating doesn't stay secret for long. Try branching out into the community.

Fraternities/sororities: One of each.

Athletic facilities: The Athletic centre is small but ambitious, featuring weights, aerobics, and squash courts. The town itself is big on hockey, with all sorts of recreation leagues and playing-for-fun. A new aquatic centre just opened at the bottom of University Way, about five minutes from campus.

Library facilities: One, with a great acquisitions rate but not enough space. Stuff is already going into storage and is therefore a pain to get to. Take full advantage of the local college library— it's been around since the sixties and has a great collection.

Weather: Cold, mostly. But, surprisingly enough, −20°C in the sunshine is a lot nicer than 3°C in the rain. Get a Mountain Equipment Co-op catalogue and invest in a down jacket—you won't regret it.

Safety on campus: The Commisionaires (on-campus security) are friendly and always willing to walk you to your car. There are direct lines to security liberally sprinkled around the campus, as well as parking-lot alarm centres.

Alumni: 681 graduates and counting. (There were only six alumni before the university opened for full operations in 1994.)

Interesting tidbits: There's 23 km of fibre-optic cable on the campus which measures about 500,000 square feet. The rate of involvement (taking classes, attending events, donating money) with university in the North is now higher than in southern BC. When UNBC first opened the participation rate of high school graduates was about half the provincial average. There are 4,700 windows on campus. There were 120 courses offered in 20 regional centres in 1998–99. UNBC offers the only Northern Studies BA program in Canada.

far from their northern towns, to those who attend from the far sides of the world for the chance to complete a degree at a state-of-the-art university. This makes for an interesting contrast in political ideologies—those who are vehemently pro-forestry and pro-industry to those who are very anti- these very same things. This sparks some interesting debates on bathroom walls, but not much in the way of a true political climate. UNBC students are almost notoriously apathetic when it comes to elections, protests, and petitions—decisions are made with, unfortunately, little student input, then bitterly complained about on the "Flames" bulletin board.

The student government, however, comprises some highly devoted and tenacious individuals and offers great entertainment year-round. It tries to keep the student body informed of the various goings-on, and tries its best to rep- resent UNBC in the wider university community. As well, PIRG, or the Public Information and Reaction Group, which is funded through student fees, calls attention to the left of mainstream political happenings, lobbies for gay and lesbian rights, offers a car-pooling organizational service, and handles co-op organic food orders. They also maintain a great reference library.

ACADEMIC ISSUES
UNBC is a brand new facility, and boasts a young, vibrant, and highly impressive faculty which prides itself on taking a strong interest in the issues and culture of the northern community. The library has a higher percentage of its budget going towards acquisitions than any other university library in Canada.

A Word to the Wise:

1. Go for a hike. Northern BC is beautiful, especially in the fall.

2. Find a winter sport. Getting out of doors in January and February may save your roommates' lives.

3. Befriend your professors. The younger ones are probably as far from home as you are, and are almost always willing to gripe about Prince George over a beer.

4. It's a small campus. If you go to class in your pyjamas smelling of last night's beer, the girl you have a crush on is almost definitely going to see you. On the plus side, it's a small campus. The girl you have a crush on might show up in her pyjamas, and you'll get to see her.

Natural Resources and Forestry are far and away the most popular and highest-profile programs, but First Nations Studies and the new Northern Studies programs are not far behind. The interdisciplinary nature of many programs, like Northern Studies, First Nations Studies, Gender Studies, and Recreation and Resource Technology allows students with non-traditional academic interests to expand and explore many avenues of study.

As stated before, the Forestry, Environmental Studies, and Recreation and Resource Technology programs are touted as being of the highest calibre—and receive the most funding. A new Forestry Lab is under construction, and students in these areas enjoy the opportunity to study such things in a city that is practically run by the forestry companies, and is crying out for tourism development. The hands-on learning opportunities are, therefore, second to none in these disciplines.

As well, though often overlooked, students following the Humanities at UNBC enjoy small class sizes, a great deal of one-on-one interaction with profs and TAs, and the unique position of being part of a flourishing and rapidly developing artistic scene. The English program prides itself on the high level of technological development that has been and is being undertaken by the faculty: The Chair of English specializes in Humanities Computing, and offers such a class. The English faculty members focus on a variety of periods, and have a myriad of research interests. However, recent changes within the faculty, and the fact that many members were hired at the same time, and therefore head off on sabbatical at the same time, have resulted in some confusion over course offerings and availability.

All of the faculties at UNBC, except Nursing and Social Work which contain their own practicums, have the oppor-tunity for co-op placement. Job hunting tends to be highly competitive, especially with the recent downturn in the BC economy. However, tree planting, firefighting, and other forestry-related occupations still offer a large number of students hard work and almost-decent pay over the summer. As well, many of the faculty at UNBC make personal efforts to ensure that their students, particularly grad students, are employed as much of the year as is possible.

REZ LIFE Occupied mostly by first-year students, UNBC's two residence buildings are, like the university itself, only a handful of years old. Set up like miniature apartments, these two buildings offer space for 584 single students: The dwellers of "Rez One" and "Rez Two" share living area, bathroom, and kitchen, as well as their own somewhat minuscule sleeping and studying space, which is furnished with single bed, desk, and chair. There are no residence facilities at UNBC to accommodate families or couples.

The social life is coherent with that of young people on their own for the first time—the parties are loud, and tend to go all night—particularly during the first couple of weeks in September. The drinking age in BC is 19, so in-room parties for the first-year students are fairly common. As well, the residence council and advisors offers floor activities—kind of like big, fun field trips to do activities like laser tag for cheaper group rates. Pub crawls and other events that may involve alcohol, organized by the various campus clubs and social groups, almost always offer free bus transportation from rez into town and back.

This travelling thing is the main drawback to residence at UNBC. Sure there is a short path to the university, but the trek into town involves a good five-kilometre hike if you are transportationally challenged, and Prince George's bus system is notoriously unreliable and inconvenient to use. The last bus leaves UNBC shortly after 9 p.m. Monday to Saturday, there are no buses on Sundays, and a cab ride is going to set you back about $12.

As well, the facilities at the university itself are somewhat limited. The cafeteria maintains hours only as late as 6:30 p.m., while the Winter Garden, UNBC's on-campus pub, has longer hours but somewhat scary offerings for food. The scant sustenance situation may be soon rectified, however: On-campus Starbucks and Tim Hortons are in the works, as are renovations to the decor and menus of the cafeteria and on-campus bistro. The campus corner store offers cheaper pop than the vending machines, and some of the basics for living (toothpaste, Kraft Dinner, and stamps), but, while living in rez, either owning a car or befriending the owner of a car is something of a necessity.

NIGHT LIFE

Prince George offers an exceedingly dry selection of clubs to attend. There is one "rock" club (The Generator) which has live bands each week as well as canned music. This bar is popular with the seventies rock-and-roll crowd, but stands as one of the best venues for live music in town. The Munk, a Top 40-style dance club which was recently decorated in a Gothic style, replete with animated gargoyles and Britney Spears look-alikes, is popular for the 19–24 set. There are also a few country bars, and a small "alternative" club (The Underworld) which plays everything from funky retro to Ricky Martin. The Underworld is packed on Thursdays, which have traditionally been "retro" night, it's also the closest club to Sergeant's. As well, there are some scarier venues which bring knowing looks to the faces of locals, and should probably just be avoided.

The pub scene, however, is great. Forestry towns are drinking towns, and Prince George is no exception. Almost every neighbourhood offers at least one pub and in the downtown there is one on practically every block. The most popular watering hole for students is Sergeant O'Flaherty's—Thursday nights fill up fast with folks from both UNBC and the local community college.

The local rave scene is small, but has devoted organizers and loyal followers. Parties tend to happen about once a month, and are well attended. The advertising is wide-spread, and tickets are always reasonably priced. These parties are really the only way to hear decent house or other electronic music in P.G., outside your own home or vehicle.

ON PRINCE GEORGE

Prince George (or "Pig" as it is affectionately called) is located about nine hours from the nearest metropolis—be it Edmonton, Calgary, or Vancouver. It is nestled in a bowl-like depression at the joining of two major rivers. The scenery can be splendid, but the air quality is not that great.

Temperatures range from 22°C in mid-summer to –35°C in mid-winter. The only way to survive the six months of sub-zero temperatures while retaining a modicum of sanity is to involve yourself in some kind of outdoor pursuit or another—Prince George offers ample opportunity for all kinds of winter entertainment. UNBC is situated at the start of some great hiking/cross-country ski trails, and there is a great system of cross-country trails only 20 minutes out of town. Downhill skiers can head 20, 40, or 120 minutes away from town, depending on what you feel like, and ski passes at the local hills are reasonably priced. Bus service is usually offered on the weekends.

The shopping is less than spectacular, but improving all the time. There are two malls, but downtown is where you'll find the local hemp shop (Zoe's), some quirky gift/decorating shops, a great hair salon (The Violet Lounge), and the best bookstore in town (Books & Company). Coffee shops are becoming more and more prevalent, but very few stay open late enough to enjoy an evening latté after a movie.

Speaking of movies, there are two theatres in town with a total of nine screens. The Moving Pictures film festival rolls through town every year, showing some of the artier Canadian and international fare that the regular theatres disdain, and The College of New Caledonia has a monthly film series that is cheap for students.

There is also some great hiking and sightseeing within a few hours' drive. Barkerville, a completely restored gold-rush-era theme park is worth seeing, but is open only from May to September.

Simon Fraser University

By D. Peter Akman

Standing at the base of Burnaby Mountain, one might never imagine that perched atop is a great university. Wrapped in fog and mist for much of the year, Simon Fraser University stands apart from Burnaby and the rest of Vancouver because it is built on a human-made clearing at the summit of this great mountain.

Founded in 1965, SFU was created as a bold new experiment in education, one that would challenge the brick and ivy look and feel of other North American universities. SFU was built to offer new, cutting-edge teaching methods, create new departments that were not limited to a single discipline, and provide student-teacher ratios that were all but unheard of in any level of higher learning.

Today, Simon Fraser has achieved much of what the founding minds had hoped for. It is at the forefront of liberal arts and science faculties in the country. As well, the Communications department has on staff some of the greatest minds in the Western world and has helped the communications industry make considerable strides.

Along with the Burnaby campus set atop of the mountain, SFU also opened a second campus in 1989 called Harbour Centre. This very different feeling campus seems associated to the Burnaby campus only by name. The long, low, slick concrete malls that many have grown accustomed to have been replaced, in the Harbour Centre version, with the modern comforts of a high-rise building located in the posh financial district of Vancouver. However, these very upscale amenities are not primarily for the average undergraduate student. During the typical semester, only a handful of Communications and Business courses are offered in this modern-day Eden. Most of the use of the Harbour Centre is targeted at businesspeople who want to upgrade their skills or at companies who need a classy environment in which to hold a seminar. Unfortunately, this is not what many believe SFU should be used for. Vast amounts of money were invested in this centre with the belief that it would improve the level of education and continue the ideology set forth by the original SFU. This is not the case. The very leftist radicalism that founded the Burnaby Mountain campus has been discarded and replaced with capitalist ideals at Harbour Centre.

Despite this change towards conservatism, which may be due to the evolving population, more adult students, and a greater multicultural mix, SFU is still very much on the cutting edge of scandal and campus radicalism (keyword: swim team).

CAMPUS CULTURE The SFU Clan varsity program has one of the proudest histories of all Canadian university sports programs. In continuing the need to differentiate themselves from other Canadian schools, SFU became the only Canadian member of the American University Sports Association (NCAA) and also competes in its subdivision (NAIA). As a result, the Clan not only competes against other Canadian schools but also against many American universities. This allows SFU to be the only university in Canada that is able to offer athletic scholarships to its student athletes.

Varsity sports such as wrestling, swimming, basketball, and football have had enormous success since the sixties and have not only won many National Championships but have also placed student-athletes on Olympic, Commonwealth, and National teams. All of these teams have open try-out dates where anyone is able to try grabbing the brass ring.

Along with varsity sports, SFU also offers many other recreational activities and groups, such as underwater hockey, snowboarding, outdoors club, intramural sports, and scuba diving. A student would be wise to participate in these activities in order to maintain sanity during the many weeks of rain as well as to meet others that might be living atop Burnaby Mountain.

Living on top of this mountain and enduring the blowing rain, the humid nights, and the limited contact with the outside world has also provided a heightened awareness of self. SFU is a small, closely knit community that embraces all newcomers as one of its own. Living with fewer than 13,000 other students allows one to feel solitude while at the same time experience a sense of camaraderie, even if it is only to give a quick nod hello on the way to class. In the past SFU made few attempts to ensure the comfort of the students who live far from the city below. However, recently new plans have been

Vital Statistics

Address: Simon Fraser University, Burnaby, B.C., V5A 1S6

Admissions office: (604) 291-3224

Website: www.sfu.ca

Total enrollment: 18,700

Male-female ratio: 44 to 56

Average entrance grades: Arts: 78%; Science: 75%; Commerce: 78%; Engineering: 85%

Tuition fees: $2,517

Residence fees: $929–$1,266 per semester (single and double dormitory rooms); $1,577 per semester (townhouse rooms and graduate student suites); $507–$623 per month (family apartments).

Spaces for students in residence: 1,250 spaces—70% of spaces are given to first-year students. First dibs go to out-of-town BC applicants.

Percentage of out-of-province first-year students: 9%

Financial aid: Scholarships and bursaries awarded to new and continuing students; emergency loans, awards for excellence and service, and athletic scholarships to student athletes.

Co-op programs: All undergraduate programs in the Applied Science, Arts, Business Administration, and Science faculties.

Services for students with disabilities: Centre for students with disabilities.

Aboriginal students: Native Student Centre.

Student services: Chaplaincy, childcare, counselling services, harassment resolution office, health services, international and exchange student services, ombuds office, student employment centre, volunteer resource centre, women's centre.

discussed and changes have been made. Soon Simon Fraser University will be the utopia that was once imagined.

ACADEMIC ISSUES

Unlike many larger universities, such as UBC, SFU has never focused on large law, dentistry, or medicine schools. Instead, the founders of SFU felt that there were other aspects of education, such as interdisciplinary and professional disciplines, that they could focus on. For example, the university's PDP or Professional Development Program is one of the country's most renowned teachers' programs and has produced many of the top educators in the school system today. As well, its Kinesiology school is considered one of the strongest in Canada. SFU also offers interdisciplinary programs in Communications, Gerontology, Criminology, and Management and Systems Science, in which students study computer applications in business.

SFU offers students a broad choice of courses from five faculties (Applied Science, Arts, Business Administration, Education, and Science) and from more than 100 programs. However, first-year students may not be able to immediately take whatever they want. Because of the number of prerequisites needed to move on to second- and third-year courses, many of the first-year courses will be full with second- and third-year students. But take this as a lesson, not as a misfortune. This is the first step in becoming an assertive student who will be able to speak to the professor in an attempt to gain access to these very popular courses. Unfortunately, for those who are unable or unwilling to be assertive, this may mean a longer stay at SFU, and a four-year degree may take five, six, or seven years to complete.

Another aspect of SFU that might help in the quest for the coveted BA or BS. is the fact that SFU is the largest trimester school in English Canada. The choice of courses in the summer is equivalent to that of the other two semesters. As well, this allows those who wish to attend university to begin in any of three semesters: autumn (September), spring (January), or summer (May).

REZ LIFE

Although at this point Simon Fraser University only offers on-campus accommodations to a limited number of students, a new development plan is being considered to expand the numbers in the next 10 or so years. Today, there are only 1,250 places available for 15,000 students. This has been the major reason for SFU's nickname: "The Commuter University."

Residence consists of five buildings: Shell House, Madge Hogarth House, McTaggart-Cowan Hall, Louis Riel House, and Hamilton Hall. Most of the students living in residence are in their first year. Louis Riel House is designed for families. It has 209 small, one- or two-bedroom apartments for couples, students with children, and some single students. Shell House, Madge Hogarth House, and McTaggart-Cowan Hall are small, fur-

In a Nut Shell

The university in a phrase:
Living atop a mountain and getting a solid education at the same time.

Best thing about the university: The view is incredible.

Worst thing about the university: The lack of spaces in residence.

Favourite professors: L. Armstrong (History); N. Blomley (Geography); M. Cohen (Political Science); M. Leier (History); J. Parr (Canadian Studies); G. Teeple (Sociology).

Hot spots to study on campus: Raven's Cafeteria and Bistro; The Highland Pub.

Quietest spots to study on campus: Empty lecture halls.

Need for car and parking availability: A car is nice for surfing and ski trips. Parking is limited, so you might find yourself parking at the bottom of the mountain (don't confuse mountain with hill) and hitchhiking up.

Sexually speaking: There are no lack of places to meet people; on drunken nights at The Highland Pub, through friends, on the bus on the long commute home, by getting involved in clubs.

Fraternities/sororities: There aren't any at SFU.

Athletic facilities: Top-notch. Gym, swimming pool, Olympic weight room, outdoor tennis and basketball courts, squash and racquetball courts.

Library facilities: Two locations: Bennett Library (Burnaby) and Belzberg Library (Harbour Centre). Interlibrary loans can be requested online. Reference desk for help.

Computer facilities: Free access for students to SFU's campus computing network. Computer labs (Academic Computing Services—ACS), with almost 800 computers, located throughout the campus.

Weather: You can surf in the morning, hike in the afternoon, and ski/snowboard at night. Bring some waterproof rain gear.

Safety on campus: Campus Student Patrol provides a Safe Walk escort, and performs scheduled bike, library, and residence patrols on campus.

Alumni: Glen Clarke, BC premier; Bob Molle, wrestler and football player; Terri Nash, filmmaker; John Sawatsky, writer; Lindsay Sparkes, women's curling champion; Sandy Wilson, filmmaker.

---

nished residences with shared washrooms and kitchens. Rooms are all equipped with a mattress, phone jack, desk, and cupboards. Only Madge Hogarth is not a co-ed dorm. This is a single-student dormitory designed for 66 women and contains all of the amenities of the other residences.

The Townhouses are, for the most part, the centre of residence life. These three-story, four-bedroom condominiums are fully furnished and share a common room and full kitchen. Hamilton Hall has 100 studio apartments for graduate students. Again, similar to all of the other residences, it is fully furnished and is only in need of the individual student's personal touch.

A major limitation of these residences is the fact that, unlike many, if not most, other universities, there is no meal plan and all of the restaurants close at five o'clock, and sometimes earlier on weekends. As well, the only place to buy junk food or the necessities has been closed permanently. This leave students on their own to feed themselves and Kraft Dinner won't do!

Another limitation of residence life is the distance to the rest of the world. After the restaurants and school close, the only life around is found 20 minutes, by bus, down the hill at Lougheed Mall. Unfortunately, the highly volatile transit system stops running as early as 10:30 p.m. on some evenings, stranding many film goers at the base of Burnaby Mountain.

This is not to say that rez life isn't great! The close proximity to classes, the two gyms, the squash courts and weight rooms, as well as the parties can keep any lonely soul occupied for hours on end.

The Highland Pub is another way to escape the dreary nights atop Burnaby Mountain. This very sterile and organized pub is placed cozily over the new student services centre, the Maggie Benston Building, and is all the rage on Thursday nights when beverages are somewhat cheaper and all of the student body takes a break from studying and just relaxes. Of course, these luxuries are only meant for those who are legal (i.e., 19 and over). For those who are not, there are many nightly activities and weekend dances in the gym and in the Shell House basement, à la high school.

Other hilltop activities might include a leisurely stroll over to Burnaby Mountain Park for one of the most beautiful sunsets ever seen. As well, hidden in this park is Horizons Restaurant. A great place for fine dining and a romantic night escape. Unfortunately there is no Mr. Noodles on this menu and do be wary of the bill.

NIGHT LIFE

Simon Fraser is primarily a commuter school, so not many students hang out on campus when they don't have classes. During the day, Raven's Cafeteria and Bistro is a between-class hangout for many students. SFU's campus pub The Highland Pub just got a face-lift and has become a favoured watering hole for those students who live in residence (and for those students who *do* stick around after classes). "It's unfortunate that there isn't one typical activity for SFU students except going home," says one student. Since the majority of Simon Fraser students live off campus (due to the shortage of space in residence), most of them are happy to head home after class. SFU's somewhat isolated location in Burnaby offers a limited selection of entertainment options. Off-campus hot spots include The Chameleon Urban Lounge and The Starfish Room, an excellent choice for live entertainment. Another choice hangout is the very hip Subeez Café.

Most Simon Fraser students spend their social lives enjoying their free evenings in downtown Vancouver. Vancouver offers an infinite number of eateries to please your palate—choose from wholesome vegetarian chow to Oriental cuisine from numerous Chinese, Japanese, and Vietnamese restaurants. Students with a hunger for culture will appreciate downtown Vancouver and its broad selection of art and live theatre venues. Join Vancouver's coffee culture and grab a joe at Starbucks Coffee or at other trendy coffee shops.

For students living in the trendy neighbourhood around Commercial Drive in East Vancouver, 35 minutes away from SFU, the night life is lively and energetic. You have your choice of pool halls, coffee houses, and Italian restaurants serving huge portions of delicious pasta for those on a student's budget.

ON BURNABY

For outdoors lovers, the Vancouver suburb of Burnaby offers much to see and do. Simon Fraser University houses an art gallery and the Museum of Archeology and Ethnology for those interested in northwest coast Indian artifacts. Venture off campus and explore the beautiful city of Burnaby. There are many scenic parks that boast impressive views of the mountains, water, and city. You can enjoy many hiking and walking trails, canoeing, windsurfing, and sailing, or lie on the grass, have a picnic and watch the world go by. Check out the "Playground of the Gods" sculpture in Burnaby Mountain Park.

If the great outdoors isn't your scene, then head to Metrotown and shop til you drop at BC's largest shopping centre. Metrotown covers three whole city blocks and has over 500 stores and services, 22 movie theatres, and the Metropolis Entertainment Centre.

Trinity Western University

By Joshua Dunford

Can the words "liberal," "Christian," and "arts" be used in the same sentence? Welcome to Trinity Western University: a different kind of university, Canada's only liberal arts Christian university. Liberal arts is another way to say "balanced education." Trinity is an example of the "true postmodern university."

This university has definitely evolved from its days as a junior college composed of a couple of converted farmhouses in rural Langley, British Columbia, to the present giant, brick student centre with a placid water fountain that sends a pond-water plume skyward—signifying TWU's lofty goals of academia.

Being a Christian university, the Christian faith is integrated into daily life at Trinity Western. Not only are students responsible for attending classes and chapel service on a regular basis, students, faculty, and staff at Trinity Western agree to comply with "Community Standards." They must "refrain from practices that are Biblically condemned" including cheating, stealing, swearing, harassment, premarital sex, adultery, abortion, and homosexual behaviour. Furthermore, students are required to abstain from consuming alcohol, smoking, drugs, and gambling, and they must "maintain modest, inoffensive behaviour in personal relationships." TWU does not allow social dancing on campus and student groups cannot sponsor dance events. TWU does not condone dancing at a club where alcohol is consumed. So does that mean that you can seek worldly pleasures off campus? Absolutely not. Community Standards are more than campus rules because they must be adhered to both on and off campus. Surprising enough, most Trinity Western students are happy to live by these rules. Some students give into temptation (usually around exam time) and sneak off to clubs in Vancouver and Abbotsford to indulge in dancing and God knows what else.

CAMPUS CULTURE The TWU community is diverse and multi-ethnic. Despite its smaller size, Trinity Western contains a wide gamut of student and people types: from "my parents never let me out past 7 p.m.; I've been sheltered in my small town," to "I am 28 and just got back from living in Tibet," to "in about eight weeks English will be my second language." Thankfully this diversity does not come with the usual problem of segregation. One only has to walk through the cafeteria or any other hub of activity to see this. Not that the usual cliques are not present—they do manifest their ugly heads—but they seem to be more common in first- and second-year students. The Lisa who says, "If it doesn't have a name brand on the front, I won't wear it," and the Tony who insists, "Don't talk to me because I am into Gothic speed metal and I won't talk to you unless you are too," don't seem to realize that fragmenting their identity into niche interests just leaves them at a disadvantage for forming important life skills. Well, not until third year anyway. Of course, this is a generalization and is also not limited to the TWU community. One can find this phenomenon anywhere.

TWU offers lots of opportunity to experience different cultures. International student groups frequently hold "lunches" where one can purchase and consume exotic delights from the far reaches of the globe. There is also an opportunity to live in the ESL (English as a Second Language) dormitories. Learn what your Korean roommate eats for a midnight snack at the same time you teach him (or her) the finer points of the best card game in the world: cribbage. From bacterial culture in the depths of the dorm fridge, to the unintelligible drawl of your Texan dorm-mate, to the unfortunate sleeping habits of your roommate, Trinity has an ample selection of culture.

TWU definitely has school spirit. Ah, yes, another "Community Standard": Students are expected to attend university events regularly. Not surprising, the turnout for varsity sports games is high. Trinity Western's men's varsity basketball and men's and women's volleyball teams draw large, enthusiastic crowds who cheer them on adorned in the official school colours of blue and yellow.

TWU offers more than 20 clubs where students can make their contribution to the community and greater society culturally and politically. The pro-life club has one of the largest memberships. You can even join a theatre sports group. Every month, 11:07, a theatre sports extravaganza, entertains students and faculty and guarantees to make you "laugh yourself silly."

Vital Statistics

Address: Trinity Western University, 7600 Glover Road, Langley, B.C., V2Y 1Y1

Admissions office: (604) 888-7511 or 1-888-GO-TO-TWU

Website: www.TWU.ca

Total enrollment: 2,700

Male-female ratio: 42 to 58

Tuition fees: $4,770/semester

Residence fees: $2,740/semester

Percentage of students in residence: 40%

Percentage of international students: 25% (including Americans)

Percentage of out-of-province students: 50%

Financial aid: President's awards: 15 scholarships of $13,000 over four years. General bursaries up to $1,300 and scholarships up to $550 available to students meeting all criteria. Student work and paid leadership positions available. All awards are renewable.

Co-op programs: Business and Communications

Services for students with disabilities: Students with Disabilities Services; wheelchair-accessible buildings.

Student services: Bookstore, career centre, chapel, Counselling and Learning Resource Services, health services, International Students and ESL Student Life Services, orientation program, recreation services, student ministries, writing centre.

ACADEMIC ISSUES

With small class sizes (on average 22 students) and an excellent faculty, TWU is a great place to learn. Dedication seems to be the trend with TWU's professors, because they do not teach at Trinity for a high salary. Profs at Trinity are, for the most part, in love with what they teach, and they also do not shy away from involving themselves with their students' learning experience. From a genetics prof who is at the cutting edge of her field (and has a hard time scaling her "science language" down to our rookie level), to an art teacher who has some of her work in the Vatican, Trinity does not lack skilled and passionate professors. Where else do profs include their home phone number (often accompanied with a "last resort" conditional clause) in the syllabus? But like any school, there are a few professors who make you wonder if their years of research in graduate school lacked what you might call "balance."

Trinity does not have quite the course selection and diversity of a giant university, but relies more on the balanced educational experience that comes with being a liberal arts school. Liberal arts involves taking classes from many other disciplines in addition to the core requirements and electives in your major.

As with any other university, some of the faculties have larger enrollments than others. The major with the largest enrollment at TWU is Business Major. These students are noted for their practical, tidy appearances and "smart-glasses." The Physical Education department is under the impression that they are holding the school together, while smaller niche departments like Physics, History, Geography, Math, Chemistry, and Philosophy consist of extremely dedicated followers who are very proud of their major. Biology is somewhat geared towards future medical studies, but has a solid root in environmental and ecological issues. The Nursing program is a tough professional program, but like many other majors, offers unique overseas opportunities that expand students' minds beyond the glare of the overhead projector. Religious and Biblical study students are acknowledged for reading large volumes, and Education students are the true "keeners" of the school, inhabiting the "silent study" area of the library basement.

One of the greatest assets of the Trinity academic experience is the close interaction with professors combined with the room to involve yourself in as much as you can within your department. From being a lab assistant for first-year Chemistry students, to exhibiting your artwork in the school atrium and library, Trinity offers an open door to exploring your discipline to the fullest.

REZ LIFE

Fire alarms at 3 a.m., brave new adventures, bad eighties posters, and the most interesting living experience of your life is status quo for rez life. Having trouble coming out of your "shell"? Ever wondered if your "interesting habits" are shared by anyone else? Missed out on summer camp all your life? The other half of the university experience can be found within the doors of Douglas, Macmillan, Robson, and Fraser Halls. This is where interpersonal skills are both developed and tested... sort of a practice exam for life. Learn to sleep in adverse conditions, and find

In a Nut Shell

The university in a phrase: A balanced, community-grounded learning and life experience. (You get out what you put in.)

Best thing about the university: The opportunity for personal growth in all areas of life and for involvement in campus life.

The worst thing about the university: Small size of the student population poses some limitations to class and activity diversity. Oh yeah, and tuition is *kinda* expensive.

Favourite professors: P. Hughes (Religious Studies), B. Dodie (Philosophy), E. Stringham (Biology), C. Montgomery (Chemistry).

Most popular bird courses: Recreation Leadership, Marriage and Family, almost any Physical Education class.

Hot spots to study on campus: During the day, the atrium supports many procrastinators, and at night, the place to be is the lower cafeteria (in Douglas Hall).

Quietest spots to study on campus: The highly policed (by over-zealous library staff) "silent study" area. (The library is the best place to fall asleep.)

Need for car and parking availability: You do need a car but only about 38% of students who live in residence have one. Otherwise, the city of Langley is about a 52-minute walk away.

Sexually speaking: The tightly knit community makes dating a somewhat high profile undertaking, but that does not seem to daunt many. Single guys should beware of the many women who seem to be trying to pursue their "Mrs." degree. Remember TWU students must "refrain from practices which are biblically condemned," i.e., premarital sex, adultery, and homosexual behaviour. It's best to keep the details of your personal affairs hush-hush. TWU does not tolerate homosexual behaviour, but some gay and lesbian students quietly attend TWU.

Fraternities/sororities: There aren't any at TWU; however, a lot of rivalry between residences makes life interesting.

Athletic facilities: The gym offers good hours, but lacks space for all activities. The climbing wall is excellent, and the outdoor fields are muddy. A rustic fitness trail winds around campus and is used regularly by a peculiar breed called "joggers."

Library facilities: The Norma B. Alloway Library is surprisingly extensive, and where it lacks in physical volumes, it makes up for with an excellent full-text electronic database of articles and books and access to other online libraries.

Computer facilities: Computer labs with Internet and e-mail access can be found across campus. All students receive e-mail accounts and have access to facilities.

Safety on campus: TWU's campus is well lit and there is an active security presence at all times.

Weather: For those who suffer from Seasonal Affective Disorder (SAD), the greater Vancouver region is a tough place. The weather pattern is usually rain rain rain rain sun rain sun rain sun snow rain. The sunny days of September are quickly replaced by rain and more rain. It's not like a good, heavy rain that lasts for a half-hour before the sun breaks through; it's like a light drizzle that lasts for months. Seriously. Vancouver is still the most beautiful city in Canada, and rain means snow in Whistler (three hours away), but walking to class day after day in drizzle can be somewhat disheartening. Living on the coast allows for mild temperatures year-round, but the dampness causes chill to seep through even the best Gore-Tex you can wrap yourself in.

Alumnus: Deborah Grey, first Reform Party MP in the House of Commons.

out the meaning of life at 2 a.m. in the dorm lounge, all a day-to-day part of residence life.

The starter kit places you in Fraser or Douglas Hall where the cafeteria "cooks" your meals, and your mom calls at least once a week to check up on you. After two years, you can graduate to Robson Hall, which is the second nicest building on campus. You now have to cook your own meals (and budget for food), but your mom still calls at least twice a month. Only then will you be ready for a fourth (or fifth, or sixth...) year in Macmillan Hall. Basically an independent apartment block, Macmillan Hall offers the best of both worlds: the luxury of an off-campus living arrangement and the convenience of still being a five-minute walk to any morning class. You may even warrant (by being an exceptional student or something) one of the two coveted "patio apartments."

The equalizing force of cafeteria food brings together students of every kind, who live under the proverbial roof of residence at Trinity, though it's not quite your mom's home cooking. As much as students complain and gripe because their meal is not quite right, TWU students have it pretty good. Well, unless you plan to eat a lot, then it is rather expen-

A Word to the Wise:

1. Two words: Get involved!

2. Use the resources at hand. Professors are willing to help you, financial aid is ready to support you, and there are about 2,499 other peers who can teach you a thing or two.

3. Live in an on-campus residence to experience the other half of the university experience. Fun gets redefined at 3 a.m.

4. Enjoy the smaller campus. There's no chance you'll get lost.

sive (the debit meal card runs out quite fast if you eat like… uh, someone who eats a lot).

DAY (&NIGHT) LIFE

Nestled in the Fraser Valley of beautiful British Columbia, surrounded by ocean and mountains, TWU offers many opportunities *not* to study. During a single day one could conceivably go to the beach (Pacific Ocean is 23 minutes away), hike a mountain (lots of hikes within 48 minutes), snowboard (five ski hills are within a one-and-a-half-hour drive), get lost in a forest (and ecological reserve behind campus), ride the bus (lots of buses around), or do just about anything else you could dream up. Unless you plan ahead, though, your average un-spontaneous daytime activities are restricted to trips to The Real Canadian Superstore and Starbuck's Coffee. The key to the exciting world of "off-campus" lies in owning a car (or starting a relationship with someone who does).

Like most other university students, as the sun drops below the horizon, TWU students come alive and fan out across the land in search of entertainment, enlightenment, and the eclectic. TWU is located in the small city of Langley, BC. Actually, it's not even in the city limits of Langley. Langley is about 45 minutes east of Vancouver and two and a half hours north of Seattle. Langley is not the most interesting place to spend your Friday night, but it does have its share of fast food, movie theatres, bowling, and coffee shops. If you drive fast for about 31 minutes in the westerly direction, you can arrive in the fantastic city of Vancouver and experience the left-coast culture, music for any taste, professional (sort of) sports teams (NBA, NHL, CFL), theatre, and restaurants where you can get served by monks in sackcloth. Ambient kitschy cafés and live jazz, improv theatre, and street artists, Vancouver has it all. You can even drive 20 minutes to the "sky train" and enjoy the speedy public transit into the heart of the city, which is a cultural experience in itself.

University of Victoria

By Gavin Tong

Once you arrive in Victoria be prepared to forget about the rest of Canada. As one student said, "Victoria is like never-never land: people refuse to grow up and they don't care what's going on outside of their world." This translates to an attitude of self-contentment. People are happy doing their own thing and they really don't care what other schools think. As such, there is little to no inter-university competition, and at the same time there is no rallying call for school spirit.

Six degrees of separation makes UVic an easy place to meet people. The moderate size of UVic is a major plus for those people who shy away from the overpowering concrete jungle that is SFU, or the anonymity that goes with UBC. It's a place where people from small towns and big cities alike can find elements of their hometowns, making the transition to a new urban dwelling much easier and a lot less scary.

The current campus was built in 1963 and has the architecture to prove it. The campus is filled with green space, big trees, mystic vales, ponds, and flower gardens that seem to be in bloom eleven months of the year (the bunnies are a nice touch). Throw in the fact that UVic is a 15-minute walk to a beautiful beach and you will see how the stress and worries of a large workload, a paper due, a botched lab, or a report not researched can be washed away by the serenity of your surroundings. This euphoric natural high contributes to the sloth-like walking speed of the average UVic student. Strolling through campus is the best way to ensure you run into that friend to go hang out by the duck pond for higher contemplation of Nietzsche or go to Bean There for a 50¢ cup of coffee that tastes like it cost 50¢.

Although ethnic diversity at the university is increasing each year, it is still a far cry from a Benetton commercial. As one student noted, "Visually, there seem to be two main groups, white and Asian."

There is definitely a west-coast style that creeps its way into everything from attitude to dress. While the Montrealers dress in all black to march through the bitter winds of winter to their favourite coffee shop, the UVic students tend to dress in a more casual kind of active wear that has been coined "skate, surf, snow."

The campus is truly of medium size: small enough to run into friends without it seeming like some kind of Celestine Prophecy, but large enough that you can still find some anonymity. The best place to run into people is in the SUB or at the fountain in front of McPherson library. Warning: UVic has some of the most persistent and urbanized ducks inhabiting this fountain. They swarm to food like piranhas and they are not too shy to ask for a handout. Should you choose to ignore them do not be shocked if one jumps up on the bench beside you to get a little attention. If you have ever been "goosed" by a friend, just imagine what it's like coming from the real deal....

> "The university aims to teach its students two things—to do something and to be something."
>
> A.L. Burt, historian, "Is Life Worth Living" (1917), quoted by Lewis H. Thomas in *The Renaissance of Canadian History: A Biography of A.L. Burt* (1975).

CAMPUS CULTURE

Everyone agrees that getting involved is the most important thing to do at UVic. If everyone is off doing his or her own thing it is easy to be left behind. So join that kayaking club or surf the waves of Jordan River or sign up with an intramural ball hockey squad. UVic has more than 50 clubs, ranging from political and environmental activism to chess and holistic health. For those who want to get away but must live on a student budget, the outdoors club organizes trips and has equipment for rent. It's one of the best ways to meet people you have common interests with. VIPIRG, Amnesty international, UVic Sustainability Project, and Women of Colour are but a few of the politically and environmentally active groups on campus. The importance of playing a sport cannot be over emphasized. In a city where you can play soccer and ultimate frisbee outside all year round, it is no wonder that UVic intramurals are so popular. Ultimate frisbee is by far the biggest sport, with three different levels of play and over 40 teams. Ultimate players are known for their social skills, and the co-ed factor makes their parties a lot more fun than the rugby boys'. UVic has championships in men's and women's basketball, rowing, soccer,

Vital Statistics

Address: P.O. Box 1700, Victoria, B.C., V8W 2Y2

Admissions office: (250) 721-8121

Website: www.uvic.ca

Total enrollment: 17,500

Male-female ratio: 44 to 56

Average entrance grades: Arts: 73%; Science: 73%; Engineering: 80%

Tuition fees: $2,446

Residence fees: $4,536–$5,960 (room and board).

Spaces for students in residence: 1,200 spaces in co-ed residence with single-sex floors, 376 spaces in cluster housing for senior students, and 181 units in apartments and townhouses for families.

Percentage of out-of-province first-year students: 16%

Financial aid: Bursaries for students in need; work-study funding for on-campus employment opportunities; and repayable emergency loans for students with short-term financial problems.

Co-op programs: Various programmes in Business, Education, Engineering, Fine Arts, Human and Social Development, Humanities, Law Science, and Social Sciences.

Services for students with disabilities: Office for Students with a Disability.

Aboriginal students: Aboriginal liaison.

Student services: Academic advising, chaplain services, career counselling, counselling for study and learning; childcare, health services, international and exchange student services, new students' information centre; ombudsperson, student employment centre, women's centre.

---

ultimate rugby, and many more sports. The facilities and weather make UVic a major competitor in all sports. The Gordon Head gymnasium has one of the best weight rooms for a university in all of Canada. It is roughly the size of two basketball courts side by side, filled with free weights and new exercise equipment. If you're a writer, then you will find that there are a plethora of campus papers to get published in. *The Martlet* is the most popular campus rag and is fairly easy to get published in. *The Ring* is another campus paper but it is more of a propaganda letter put out by the university. There is also *The Emily*, a feminist paper with excellent writers.

ACADEMIC ISSUES

Surrounded by an ocean, UVic is a perfect place to study Marine Biology. "You'll have to pay your dues in the classroom before you can free Willy," says one grad student. "But once you get the chance to be in a boat and see a whale from that close you'll know it was worth it." The Marine Biology program is internationally renowned. Other programs deserving of mention are the Biochemistry/Microbiology, Physics and Astronomy, the Centre for Environmental Health, and the Centre on Ageing. UVic has one of Canada's best Law programs and is the only Law program boasting a co-op. UVic also has a small Creative Writing department filled with award-winning tenured staff and an emerging Business program, which was recently honoured by the Academy of Management, an international group of business executives, managers, and professors, who claimed that UVic was the world's best school when it came to teaching entrepreneurship. The students find the extensive co-op programs to be the most useful academic tool. UVic's co-op program has roughly, 3,000 co-op students spread throughout the different programs, making it the third largest program in Canada.

Perhaps the biggest letdown of UVic is its inability to guarantee students room in the classes they want. "I'm on a waiting list in all of my requisite courses" is the all too common cry of the stressed-out Geography student. Nothing is more frustrating then trying to settle your course load on the first day of classes when you already have a million other things to do. The best tip is to be persistent. Go to the class you want anyway, talk to the teacher make sure they know who you are, and plead, plead, plead. If you can produce tears, you can go far in life. The best thing to do is to register as soon as you can. UVic's registration can be a nightmare using the TREG telephone registration system, but the recent addition of web-based registration should alleviate the pressure on the phone lines. A redial button is key; knowing your course numbers and other options ahead of time is also important. Above all, prepare to be flexible.

Although UVic doesn't require first-year students to follow a set program, not taking the proper prerequisites can really set you back and extend your stay here longer then you may like. But not to worry: If you like it out here you may not want to leave and can join the rest of the fifth-year students who are still in never-never land. Diversity is the spice of life, so if you can, or if you don't have direction, take as many different courses as you can. Your classes will not tend to be much larger than 40 or 50 people, except for the popular courses, which tend to be taught in lecture halls averaging 100 to 200 people. You don't have to declare your major until your third year so you've got room to manoeuvre around, and co-op will let you know what your choice of study may lead to.

REZ LIFE

Applications for residence start in March. Residence housing is scarce so as soon as you're accepted to UVic get your $100 deposit in and apply for rez. There are many different factors that will make or break your ability to get into rez. People with high grades tend to have a better chance of getting in. UVic does not discriminate on where you come from but your gender can be a determining factor on your admittance into residence. At a university where the guy-to-girl ratio is roughly 40 to 60, there is simply less competition for males. Apparently the guys just don't seem to be making those high entrance-level grades anymore. Most first-year students will live in the Lansdowne or Craigdarroch complexes. Lansdowne is the place to go for maniac partying, puke on the stairs, and fire alarms at three in the morning, which are all great ways to meet people. Famous for their floor crawls and eviction notices, Lansdowne treats itself with the least amount of respect and claims to have the most fun doing it. The rooms tend to be small and the music is loud.

The Craigdarroch buildings are supposed to be academic residences. The rooms are larger than at Lansdowne; apparently academic types need more room to study. But this is a good tip: Those that work hard, play hard. And so if you want the best of both worlds—the ability to do work, a slightly larger room, and good times—then sign up for an academic rez like Craigdarroch. All residences are co-ed, so no matter which you pick it won't be as if you've just joined a nunnery. Fun will be had by all.

Those that return to rez in second year will be found in the Gordon Head and McGill residences. Most second-year students looking to live on campus would rather put in a bid at the cluster housing then re-do another year in rez. As one student said, "It was a great time, I met some great people, and I will never, ever, do it again."

NIGHT LIFE

Quite possibly the best thing to happen to Victoria's night life was the $2 drink war. It is now possible to get a $2 beer or rum 'n' coke just about any night of the week. Do expect to line up to partake in these battles, though. Some places have line ups starting as early as 9:30. This can be a double-edged sword: On the one hand, you get into the bar early and have a good chance of securing a table for the night; on the other, you're at the mercy of your own will to keep a good pace of boozing without hurling before 2 a.m. The best and the worst can be seen on a Thursday night at the Blues House, where any drink costs two bucks and every penny pincher can be a big spender. At the end of the night everyone spills out from the bars to congregate like sheep waiting for someone to herd them off to the next party or to the end of the night pizza run at the Brickyard. Casualties of this booze war can be seen the next morning shaking their heads and slowly sipping a cup of coffee over some eggs Benny at John's place or a veggie omelette at the Blue Fox.

For live music, Steamers is the place to go. They always have a loud band playing, good beers on tap, and pool tables in the back if you feel the need to talk to your friends without screaming in their ears. A table-top Galaga game has really boosted their image with all the hard-core eighties generation. A common theme in Victoria is the brew pub. Swan's has been brewing their own beer for 10 years and is the place to go if you want to relax with a few friends and enjoy some good ales. The atmosphere is one of comfort and class without being pretentious. Another favourite for all those people who live on the wrong side of the tracks, in this case the Johnson Street bridge, is Spinnakers brew pub, which also makes its own beer and is situated right on the water in beautiful Esquimalt.

Ravers, funkers, and dancers alike get down to the best DJ's at the Limit and the Jet Lounge. The Limit holds a gay night called "Rumours at the Limit" in honour of Victoria's now defunct gay bar. The G-Spot is a club for lesbians and their friends.

There is also a brand new SUB building, sometimes referred to as the "airport terminal" on account of its bright lights, layout, and sterility. It is also the best place on campus to get a good meal for under five bucks, and it is home to the campus bar and nightclub. Felicita's is the bar to go to after that intramural soccer game or final exam for a round of beers and nachos. Thursday night is again the big night: Felicita's hosts SUB night, where the booze is cheap. The reoccurring theme in Victoria is that cheap booze comes with the price of a long lineup so expect to be waiting at Felicita's door for a while. But do not despair; this is the perfect time to make friends with other pie-eyed people. Smokers beware: Felicita's has a strictly enforced no smoking policy, so it's outside with the butts in rain or shine. If you're feeling a bit saucier, you can don the disco duds and make your way to Vertigo for some retro boogie nights.

In a Nut Shell

The university in a phrase: A perfect balance between academic and active lives.

Best thing about the university: Botanical Gardens, beaches, and big trees.

Worst thing about the university: Not getting the classes you want.

Favourite professors: Prof. Pierce (Immunology), Gerry Poulton (Chemistry) just awarded the Excellence in Teaching award; Jack Hodgins, well-known Canadian novelist (Writing); Lorna Crozier, Governor General's award-winning poet, (Creative Writing); Christopher Garett (Ocean Physics); George Mackie (Biology); Reg Mitchel (Chemistry); Francis Winspear, chair in Public Policy.

Most popular bird courses: Both Psych 100 and Soc 100 are big classes with multiple-choice style exams. If you know how to turn a computer on then Computer Science 100 will be a breeze, the labs consume time but are easily copied from other friends. Pretty much any class that starts with the words "Intro to…" will be very general and geared towards people that don't have a clue.

Hot spot to study on campus: Third floor of the McPherson library, mainly due to the visual distractions, sometimes referred to as the "meat market."

Quietest spot on campus to study: Second floor, northwest corner of the McPherson library, sometimes referred to as the "office." Once the library closes most hardcores head over to the Clearhue building to while away the lonely hours of the night.

Need for car and parking availability: The ability to bike all year long and the fact that your student card doubles as your bus pass really diminishes the need for a car. It is a luxury but not a necessity. Parking is available on campus but is in small supply. If you don't buy a parking permit then you will end up parking so far away from the school that it almost negates the convenience of the car.

Sexually speaking: Getting it on with the people you meet is as common at UVic as at any other university. On a sad note, a report released in 1998 said that as far as the national average goes, residents of BC have less sex than the rest of the country. (Maybe being locked up inside on those cold winter days does have its advantages.)

Fraternities/sororities: They are not tolerated nor are the recognized by the university.

Athletic facilities: The Gordon Head Gym is one of the best in Canada. The workout room is the size of two basketball courts side by side, filled with the latest exercise equipment and free weights. It costs $26 a semester or $44 for two, but it is well worth it. UVic has several gymnasiums, squash courts, tennis courts, pools, and even outdoor beach volleyball courts, all of which are paid for by your student fees, so you might as well use them.

Library facilities: The McPherson library is well stocked and anything you can't find there can be ordered from other libraries, like UBC. One of the most impressive aspects of the McPherson library is its well-stocked music collection. You will not find any Top 40 but its jazz, blues, and classical collections are quite extensive.

Computer facilities: Internet access available. Computer-assisted language learning facility. Fine Arts computer lab and Geographic Information Systems labs.

Weather: There is one obvious reason for the temperate rainforests: The winters are mild, and it rains a lot. The rain here is more of a drizzle that soaks you slowly, unlike Vancouver, where the downpour beats you into the ground. Sunshowers are a common phenomenon and are usually followed by a rainbow, and then more rain. The average winter temperature is 5°C. Students take comfort in knowing that the rainy season starts to dissipate around February (an early spring means early spring fever).

Safety on campus: The Campus Safe Walk program is well used and respected. No matter what time of day or night, you can call Campus Safe Walk and be escorted to your destination by a female and a male security guard. The campus does have some dark areas, such as the wood-chipped trails, but for the most part the university is fairly well lit.

Alumni: Pierre Berton, author; Hon. Robin Blencoe, British Columbia minister of government services; Bob Edwards, BC Supreme Court Justice; Linda Hughes, publisher, *The Edmonton Journal*; W.P. Kinsella, author.

A Word to the Wise:

1. You're not going to go to Vancouver, as much as you think you will.

2. It gets tougher each year; party accordingly.

3. Treat yourself to a good pair of rain pants.

4. See the rest of the island or any of the gulf islands.

5. You're never alone; you will always run into friends, or friends soon to be made.

ON VICTORIA

Victoria is a bit of an enigma as far as cities go. Rarely does it fit into any stereotype or pre-set notion of what a city should be. It is the capital of BC and as such has a strong sense of government control; but at the same time the city has a laissez-faire attitude. This is a city where peaceniks push for civil disobedience while ultraconservatives preach for greater restrictions on everyday life. The downtown is simply beautiful. Flower baskets hang from street poles and garbage is a rare sight on the streets. All of the modern shops are housed in old buildings that have been restored to their original Victorian-style architecture. Tourists dollars are essential to the economy in Victoria and so many shops and areas are targeted towards them. You're not likely to see any UVic students in the Tartan Shop or the Christmas Shop. This is mostly concentrated around the inner harbour, where buskers perform for change with the lights of the Empress Hotel as their backdrop. It's a great place to walk by on a warm night, but you won't find yourself spending any appreciable amount of time there. Away from the inner harbour and more in the heart of downtown is where you find all the coffee shops, nightclubs, bars, and restaurants. They are all close together, so bar hopping can be done without the need for a cab. The biggest problem is getting out of downtown once the clubs close. Most buses stop running around one in the morning, but the night life goes on until two or three. Victoria is not a large city, so most cab rides are fairly inexpensive and many people are fortunate enough to live within walking distance of downtown. Victoria really doesn't have a student ghetto, so students mix into residential neighbourhoods, which are puzzling in themselves. Some houses are grand old character homes indicative of that west-coast beach home. But right next door you'll have the Brady Bunch bungalow that was probably built during Victoria's boom in the seventies. Guess which one you're likely to live in. This is the type of city where making eye contact with strangers is a sign of friendliness and not aggression, where drivers stop to let pedestrians cross the street even if they are the only car on the road. An expression often used to describe Victoria is "home of the newlywed or the nearly dead." Victoria is the retirement capital of Canada, though the university students and retirees rarely interact.

Victoria is easy to escape. Public buses go out to provincial parks such as Goldstream, where you can walk through rainforests, or, if you feel a little more adventurous, climb Mount Finlayson, or re-enact the train scene from *Stand by Me* on the trestle bridge. Buses also go to the ferries to take you to the gulf islands or back to the mainland.

University of Alberta

By Tanya Spencer

"Along with some 400 students and two red brick buildings, we were the University of Alberta," writes R.K. Gordon in *University Beginnings in Alberta*. In the beginning, the U of A campus was not the sprawling 89 hectares it is now. Founded in 1908 by an oil-rich province looking to create a western university to rival Canada's finest, it began with a small faculty led by Henry Marshall Tory and those 400 students and the two red brick buildings. Since then it has grown to almost 30,000 students, more than 90 buildings, and hundreds of faculty members. The University of Alberta celebrated its 90th birthday last year, in somewhat leaner circumstances than it has been used to in the past, due to the decreases in oil income to the province. Although decreased provincial funding has forced cutbacks in programs and increases in tuition, U of A is still a first-rate institution with a tradition of academic and research excellence.

Situated in Old Strathcona, Edmonton, the campus is very classic. With old brick buildings and many trees, it looks very much like a campus you would see in an old college movie. In wintertime, when Physical Plant adorns the trees with strings of miniature white lights and newly fallen snow coats the streets and buildings, it is a truly beautiful place to be.

Old Arts was one of the first buildings built (1912) and is a typical example of "neoclassical brick and stone." By far, the oddest building has to be Biological Sciences, or "bio-sci." Built by a series of contractors who seemed to be unaware of the virtues of communication, it resembles a 15th century castle lego set assembled by a blind man. If you have a class there, go very early on the first day because the building will not make any sense to you the first time you navigate it. There are stories of sinks without drains, offices connected through closets, and new rooms discovered during renovations: Apparently they were blocked in completely and unused for years.

Many first-year courses are held in the theatres of Tory Lecture, or "The Turtle" (look at a campus map, you'll understand the name), which has the claim to fame of not having a single right angle on the outside of the building. The prize for uncomfortable goes to V-wing. Outside it's nice brick, inside it's institution grey with hard, incredibly small seat-desks. Not only are these classrooms impossible to write exams in, they are unbelievably uncomfortable. But unless you take Physics or Engineering, you probably won't have to take a class here. Count your blessings. Rutherford (the Arts library) is the largest library on campus, again with the "old and brick" theme; the upper floors are cozy and quiet, perfect for serious studying. The main floor has lots of windows, and is perfect for people watching when procrastination is the order of the day. Cameron (the Science library) is a bit more modern. It is also noisier and less comfortable. The Butterdome began life as the Universiade Pavilion, but no one calls it that. Designed to celebrate one of the U of A colours (gold), it resembles a very large, very yellow stick of butter. One constantly wonders why they didn't go with forest green, the other official colour.

CAMPUS CULTURE

Most students are from Alberta (Edmonton and rural areas), with about 11% from other parts of Canada and 6% from other countries. Diversity seems to be the motto of Student Groups Services—everything from Banzai Anime to Kung Fu can be found among the 250+ student groups. In first year, when your classes are huge, sometimes the only way to meet someone is to get involved in residence, with a student group, or in sports. Campus rec offers a variety of activities, including kick-boxing and Latin dancing, in addition to the regular aerobics classes. There are also fun intramural sports like inner tube water polo that are very popular.

Fraternity houses (men's and women's) line 87th Avenue. Apart from a few good parties, like the Deke's Bear Country, and a massive concert in the Butterdome in October, they go pretty much unnoticed on campus. They do a lot of good charity work, though, especially with the campus food bank.

The major hangout is definitely the Power Plant, a bar owned and operated by the Students' Union. On Fridays and Saturdays expect a lineup if you're not there by eight or nine. There is also a great little place inside called Dewey's. When the weather is nice and warm, which is not often enough, the large central grassy area, or "quad," is packed with frisbee players and others who crave vitamin D exposure, while

Vital Statistics

Address: University of Alberta, Edmonton, Alberta, T6G 2E8

Admissions office: (403) 492-3113

Website: www.ualberta.ca

Total enrollment: 30,287

Male-female ratio: 46 to 54

Entering grades: 70% minimum, 80% for honours/specialization

Tuition fees: $3,965, more for engineering

Residence fees: Apartment/house: $215–$900; traditional room and board: $3,105–$4,950 for eight months; faculté (room, no board): $1,417–$2,297 for eight months.

Percentage of students living in residence: 12%

Percentage of international students: 6%

Percentage of out-of-province students: 11%

Financial aid: The university provides more than $1.8 million each year in the form of "on-campus" undergraduate awards and scholarships. Of that, approximately $700,000 is awarded to first-entry students through programs.

Co-op programs: Business and Engineering; Science has several Industrial Internships.

Services for students with disabilities: Completely accessible for physically disabled, services for audially or visually impaired students.

Aboriginal students: Native student services.

Student services: Counselling for employment, career, psychological issues, sexual assault victims, appeal help from the ombudservice, chaplains, health services—pretty much anything you can think of.

---

fundraising barbecues line the sidewalk. Whyte Ave., an area near campus that is packed with pubs, cafes, and stores, is also a great place to while away the hours, shopping and snacking and checking out the colourful local culture.

The Bears (men) and Pandas (women) have a strong tradition of athletic excellence. They boast the largest number of Academic All-Canadians. Pandas volleyball has won five consecutive national titles. Last year Bears Hockey and Pandas Basketball were also championship teams. Unfortunately, pep rallies are nonexistent, and while games are well attended, they are not as popular as the athletic department would like them to be. The apathy of the student body also shows up in the dismal voter turnouts for faculty and Students' Union elections.

ACADEMIC ISSUES

The bad news first: Provincial cutbacks have meant amalgamated departments, like Comparative Literature, Religion, and Film/Media Studies. Remember that Sesame Street song "Which of these things is not like the other?" That principle definitely applies here. Plus, tuition has gone up by the maximum 8.9% almost every year, despite much protest by groups like STORM and the Students' Union. Textbooks are also a big dent to the student pocketbook—and expect to wait in line for much of your young life to buy them. Due to the unusual nine-point grading system, it is detrimental to your GPA to transfer from anywhere else. "They don't seem to understand or like the concept of rounding," one disgruntled transfer student commented.

The good stuff far outweighs the bad. The nine-point system translates to your benefit if you transfer to a four-point system mid-degree or apply to grad schools. Despite amalgamations, there are still 200 undergraduate and 170 graduate studies programs offered. Despite funding cuts, the library has the largest number of holdings per student, and is second in overall size for a Canadian research library. The Pharmacy faculty is unparalleled. Medicine, Forestry, and Psychology are extremely strong. The faculties of Nursing and Rehab Med have excellent reputations, as do the faculties of Science and Engineering as a whole. The faculty at U of A have a long list of awards and accomplishments. U of A has the most 3M Teaching Award winners of any Canadian university. Andy Liu, a U of A mathematician, was named Canadian Professor of the Year. Richard Taylor, who was the first Canadian to win the Nobel Prize in Physics, is a professor here. Indeed, there are many brilliant students and teachers.

For the past two years the C.D. Howe Foundation Awards for the top female and male first-year engineers in Canada have gone to U of A students. Pharmacy students have scored overall tops in Canada on the PEBC nine out of the past 10 years.

First-year classes max out at 450 students right now, but new Engineering buildings have lecture theatres of 550+ students. Average courses are about 100 students per class, and if you can't manage to contact your prof, you can almost always get a hold of your TA. Seminars and labs are much smaller (20–30 students) and it's easier to ask questions in them if you're a little shy or overwhelmed. If you need credits for an option, popular classes include Botany 380 (Drug Plants of the World), any course from Film Studies or Classics, Biology 315 (History of Biology), and first-year Psych courses.

A Word to the Wise:

1. Bring winter clothes. Lots of them. Wear them all. You may look like the Michelin man, but at least you will be warm. When it's 30 below zero and the wind is blasting across campus you will be happy that your grandma likes to knit.

2. If you're from out of province or country, live in rez your first year, until you get to know the city. Good, cheap housing is hard to find. Plus, if you don't know anyone in town this is the best way to meet them. Even if you're from Alberta, live in Lister Hall your first year. It's a lot of fun and an experience you won't get another chance to have any other time in your life.

3. If you don't have to, don't park on campus. It's expensive and crazy. Live nearby or take the LRT.

4. Buy your textbooks either before the first day of classes (there are lists in the bookstore or on the net) or two weeks later, otherwise it's insane for line-ups.

5. Don't take Friday morning labs if you like to party. You can't miss a lab, and do you really want that kind of pain?

6. Make at least one friend in each of your classes—if you miss one, then you can borrow notes. Make friends with smart, punctual people who have neat handwriting.

REZ LIFE

For out-of-towners, rez is the easiest place to live, as Edmonton's vacancy rate, especially in the university area, is less than 1%. Look early, we're talking May, and look often if you want a good location. Apply early if you want to live in rez. If you can't get to Alberta to search, can't find anything, want to live on campus, or love activities, programming, and bonding with fellow students, then rez is for you. Seven different residences are owned by the U of A, both traditional and apartment-style.

Lister Hall houses more than 1,200 students, over 50% of them from first year. It is the place to go if you want to meet lots of new people and benefit from tons of programs. It is the largest residence and has a very social atmosphere. However, you can select the noise level you want when you apply, and lots of study space is available, especially during finals. It is a traditional-style residence with a meal plan, and facilities include a computer lab, weight room, and bar/community centre.

Pembina is for students 21 years of age and older. It has a meal plan, nice big rooms, and a great location right next to the quad. If you like to sleep in and want to go to class in your pyjamas, this might be the place for you. A computer lab and piano room are among the amenities offered.

HUB is based on the original concept of a mall surrounded by apartments. HUB is both unique and conveniently located right in the middle of campus. The mall is a popular social/study spot, and facilities include a large community centre and computer lab.

Faculté St. Jean is the French-speaking residence. Fac is quite small, but has a brand new building and a great sense of community. There is a traditional corn-husking party at the beginning of the year. Residents rave about this place, and if you weren't fluent before, you will be soon. You get in trouble for speaking English!

Garneau, which consists of walk-ups and houses close to campus, offers the widest variety of accommodations. The Garneau student association runs a community centre so that students don't miss out on the programs and facilities that characterize residence life.

Michener Park, the couple and family-oriented residence, offers a variety of housing options, like a high rise and row houses. Vanier House is an adults-only building, for those who don't have children but do have a spouse. Michener also runs programs for both kids and grownups.

Newton Place, just purchased this summer, has several different apartment types. A community centre/rec room facility is planned, and programs will be developed this year. Single students, couples, roommates, all kinds of people live here. Since it is right across the street from University Hospital, med and nursing students will really like it.

NIGHT LIFE

The weekend starts on Thursday in Edmonton—the Department of Art History doesn't even teach on Fridays, although everyone else still holds class. Friday morning labs can be a very painful thing, so if you plan on socializing, don't take them. On-campus bars include RATT (Room At The Top) and the aforementioned Power Plant, both run by the SU, and the Ship, in Lister Hall. The Ship is frequented mostly by rez people and is packed on Thursdays for the famous "Ship Night," but the Power Plant and RATT are popular with other students. They are also known for great food, and the Power Plant often has bands.

Nearby Whyte Ave. has a plethora of night spots, including the Iron Horse, Urban Lounge, Squire's, and Rebar. The Iron Horse is popular with an older student crowd and has a lot more mingling and less dancing. Urban Lounge showcases local talent, Squire's is really just for drinking, and Rebar has punk night on Thursday. Almost on campus is Duke's, which is packed Thursday through Saturday with rez folk and those who live close to campus. Really cheap beer and a dubious

In a Nut Shell

The university in a phrase: "It makes sense." It's the motto on all of the signs, and going here really does make sense.

Best thing about the university: The variety of programs, groups, and activities.

Worst thing about the university: The bureaucracy—registration, and red tape, and tuition increases—especially the proposed one to double international fees to $12,000 per year.

Favourite professors: Blackburn (Chemistry), Lewis (Psychology), Laux (Law), Palmer (Anthropology), and any who have won the 3M Teaching Award, like Anne Naeth from Renewable Resources.

Most popular bird course: English 199 (English for Engineers).

Hot spot to study on campus: Cameron reading room.

Quietest spot to study on campus: Health Sciences Library.

Need for car and parking availability: Public transit is okay, the LRT is great, and parking on campus is the root of all evil—always full as well as expensive ($45/month)—but a bus pass is $47/month.

Sexually speaking: Lots of people means lots of options, from one-night pickups to that semipermanent someone. While some close-minded conservatives frown on same-sex relationships, there are support groups like OUTreach and Siderite (in residence). There's also blue jeans day—wear jeans if you support gays, lesbians, and bisexuals—and pretty much everyone wears jeans, whether they knew about it or not!

Fraternities/sororities: They're all called fraternities, even if they're full of women, and not that popular on campus. Rush week is in September.

Athletic facilities: The Butterdome has great facilities but they get busy quickly. Go at non-peak hours. Participate in at least one campus rec intramural or class; they're lots of fun even if you're neither sporty nor coordinated.

Library facilities: Lots of libraries for different subjects, seminars on how to use them, and exchanges with other Alberta institutions. Plus it was the second-largest research library collection in Canada, with the most holdings per student.

Computer facilities: The university provides Internet accounts to students.

Weather: Cold, very cold, lasting more months than it's supposed to. Lots of snow, starting early, accompanied by icy, biting wind. Even if it looks sunny and warm outside, it's probably just sunny and cold. Sometimes in the middle of winter there will be odd spells of warmth—enjoy these, get outside. Love them while they lasts.

Safety on campus: Lots of people means more criminals. However, Campus Security (affectionately known as Campus 5–0) patrols often. There's not enough lighting in several areas; walk to your car or home with a buddy after dark. If you don't know anyone, call Safewalk. A guy and a girl will walk you all over campus, or even take the LRT with you. Women: Highly recommended is the RADS course on self-defence, it's offered many times throughout the year and is well worth the $20.

Alumni: Joe Clark (former PM), Peter Lougheed (former premier), W.O. Mitchell (famous author), Beverley McLachlin (Supreme Court Justice).

---

atmosphere can be found at "the Strat," or Strathcona Hotel.

Downtown is less popular than Whyte, but eighties night at the Rev always draws a big crowd. Señor Frog's is the bar of choice for med students who meet the 21-and-older age requirement. Bourbon Street in West Ed is full of bars, but the "evil mall" (West Edmonton Mall) is not the most popular place in the evenings, at least to anyone who isn't in junior high. Meat-market bars like Club Malibu and Barry T's, both fairly close to campus, are popular with first-year students who haven't yet learned better.

ON EDMONTON

The surrounding neighbourhood of Old Strathcona, around White Ave., abounds with cool boutiques, cozy cafés, and too many bars and pubs to count. In the summer, street festivals like The Fringe are fun cultural relief from academia. Come wintertime, if you are brave enough to venture outside, ice rinks and icy sports abound. Rabbit Hill is the city ski hill. Note that another word for rabbit is bunny and you'll figure out what level of ski hill this is. However, it's not that far to the Rockies, and a zillion ski trips are held by various campus groups all winter long.

The Valley Zoo and the Provincial Museum are typical tourist haunts. Since Edmonton is the capital of Alberta, you can tour the legislature building if you feel so inclined, skate in front of it during winter, or gaze across the river at it if you're on the north edge of campus. West Edmonton Mall is famous for its many shops and indoor waterpark and amusement park. You kind of have to go at least once.

University of Calgary

By Rob South

A little over 30 years old, the University of Calgary is very much the new kid on the block of research universities. Tucked away in the northwest corner of the city, the campus covers a huge portion of land. Viewing the campus is most enjoyable during the summer, as you will find ample green spaces and sun spots. Observers find that while the university is sheltered from the hectic pace of the downtown core, it very much mirrors the city: It started off small, but has always had big plans and is starting to gain the recognition it deserves as a national leader.

The university's humble beginnings were as the Calgary campus of the University of Alberta. In 1967, this campus gained its independence and began the life as the University of Calgary. Funded by the oil boom prior to the national energy program, rapid growth then ensued. This rapid growth has enabled the university to attract a number of top-notch researchers from around the world, as well as to cultivate a number of its own.

The majority of the buildings are 20 to 30 years old, and rather square in nature. It has been a long-term plan of the university's to spruce up the campus by growing ivy on the building walls; unfortunately, it was discovered that the rock used to make the buildings is too acidic and consequently the walls remain bare. This is not to say, however, that the campus is not without its charm.

Situated right beside the popular MacEwan Hall Student Centre is the infamous Rock. Discovered while digging the foundation for the Library Tower, this boulder is now a pivotal part of campus tradition. Students having any opinion to spout or event to announce cover this boulder with the spray-painted words of their choice. Situated near the middle of campus it is hard to miss any new message that the Rock has for the masses.

A few more stylish buildings have popped up in the past decade. The Rosza Centre is western Canada's finest acoustics hall, attracting many top performers to its dignified interior. Scurfield Hall, home to the Faculty of Management, has a lovely skylight roof, giving it incredible natural lighting; additionally, all the rooms are well furnished, as most of the corporate donations have poured into this building. Lastly, there is the Professional Faculties Building, blessed with ergonomic, if not stylish, interiors, a full-sized Tim Hortons, and the handsome Oak Moot courts for the Faculty of Law.

Unfortunately for the rest of the buildings, their interiors could best be described as examples of everything that was wrong with the seventies. Brown is the colour of choice; this is particularly true of the Science Theatres, which remind one of the banned Calvin Klein ads featuring teens backdropped against a run-down basement. Luckily, as with most things at the U of C, improvements are on the way and many interiors are starting to be refurbished.

CAMPUS CULTURE

Last March over 400 students slept in tents to protest tuition increases, so the notion that U of C has no school spirit because it is a commuter school was finally put to rest. Though a large number of students head back home by five o'clock, there is always something to do at the university. The best part about it is that like the rest of the country, most student organizations are cliques, though nobody ever feels bound by their cliques in Calgary, and everyone seems to magically get along. While nobody may agree with your opinion, everybody will respect your right to hold it. There are over 150 student clubs on campus, so leadership opportunities abound.

If student organizations aren't your thing there are two main pastimes on campus: working your body into shape or working it out of shape. On the fitness side, the U of C offers the best athletic facilities in the country, including two indoor running tracks, a covered speed-skating oval, an Olympic-length pool, an indoor climbing wall, weight rooms, several gyms, and countless Olympic athletes—it is inspiring to see Catorina LeMay Doan working out at the same time as you. The late hours and large locker rooms ensure that participants are happy; the huge glass windows and ample couches surrounding most of the facilities ensure casual observers are happy too.

When tired of watching others work their way into the best shape of their lives, students head to Mac Hall. Sitting around and chatting with friends in the massive food court is the most

Vital Statistics

Address: 2500 University Drive NW, Calgary, Alberta, T2N 1N4

Admissions office: (403) 220-6645

Website: www.ucalgary.ca

Total enrollment: 23,843

Male-female ratio: 46 to 54

Percentage of out-of-province first-year students: 10%

Average entrance grades: General Studies: 70%; Engineering: 74%; Kinesiology: 80%; Nursing: 73%; Fine Arts varies by program.

Tuition fees: $3,440

Residence fees: $2,953–$5,078 (room and board); apartments: $1,976–$4,165 (no board plan); family apartments $515–575/month.

Spaces in residence: 1,100 spaces available in single-sex and co-ed settings; 250 spaces for couples/families; 350 spaces reserved for first-year students.

Financial aid: Over 3,000 scholarships and bursaries totalling approximately $4 million each year.

Co-op programs: Various programs in Arts, Science and Commerce, as well as internships in Engineering programs.

Aboriginal students: The Native Centre.

Services for students with disabilities: Disability Resource Centre.

Student services: Academic, career and personal counselling, career services, child care, and residence services.

---

popular activity for U of C students. In the two enclosed courtyards there are a select number of couches available, for which the competition is fierce. Unfortunately, these couches often find themselves occupied by couples too cheap to find a room and too stupid to remember that with the building's mirrored ceilings, everyone can see them make out. When the free entertainment is done, those with cash to blow often head down to the Campus Cove, a large video arcade and pool hall.

With numerous computer labs on campus, electronic entertainment is popular away from Mac Hall too. First-year students are generally particularly enamoured with the habit of rushing from class to forward new e-mails to all their new friends. Consequentially, computer labs have large lineups at class breaks. If you are relying on computer access to get actual work done, head to the library, where they don't tolerate e-mail junkies. Don't, however, head to the reading reserves to get traditional, non-electronic work done, as it is more like a silent meat market than a study hall.

The school year ends with the city's biggest party this side of the Stampede—Bermuda Shorts Day (BSD). Held on the last day of classes, few professors are brave enough to schedule a meaningful lecture. Following a year of hard work, students swarm to the university dressed in their funkiest clothes and start partying and drinking by nine in the morning. The afternoon is filled up with a massive beer garden party and free bands. BSD evenings are spent either at a house party or at one of the innumerable bar parties. Administration is kind enough to give students a few days to recover from their hangovers before final exams start up.

ACADEMIC ISSUES

Every university in the country has been facing a funding crisis this decade and Calgary is no different. What is different about Calgary is

that it took funding cuts much earlier in the decade than many schools out east, and has therefore already adapted to a different mode of operation. For the past several years the whole institution has undergone a process of strategic transformation to move into the university's new style of doing things. The net result is an even greater commitment to research and a planned change in all the undergraduate curricula. When completed, it will be very interesting to see how many of these changes set the university apart from others, and how much was just for show.

Striving to serve the city's business community, many of Calgary's strongest programs have a very professional focus. Engineering, Management, and Law are all darlings of both administration and the downtown business core. That is not to say that the Liberal Arts program has no place at U of C—far from it. There are a wide variety of programs including some Canadian rarities like a full department of Archaeology. Most students have ample opportunity to shop around and decide which discipline or faculty suits them best. The U of C does not operate on a direct-entry basis for most faculties. With the exceptions of Fine Arts, Engineering, Kinesiology, and Nursing, first-year students start off in the Faculty of General Studies. After a year or two students apply to the program of their choice.

Being such a large institution it would be impossible to list all of the programs, nor should you try to sample them all in your first year. Liberal Arts gems include Communications Studies, History, and the small field of Strategic Studies. Psychology is a very popular choice, but the feeling is that the degree is becoming watered down as a result of too many multiple choice exams. Moving toward the hard sciences, the Biology program is decent, with specialization available in Zoology and Ecology. If you are planning to do Bio then Med School, stick around because the Faculty of Medicine is

In a Nut Shell

The university in a phrase: As cheesy as it sounds, the present marketing slogan of "Moving Forward, Building Upward" really suits things.

Best thing about the university: How far spunk, determination, and hard work can take you.

Worst thing about the university: How much of the population goes home at 5 p.m.

Favourite professors: Ron Huebert offers a fascinating overview of the world of Strategic Studies. To quote one student's evaluation of this Poli Sci prof, "If I was to start a new religion, Huebert would be my god!"

On a daily basis, Will Holder's Economics classes generate lots of applause and laughter. This professor's antics have made Economics both understandable and enjoyable to thousands of students; if you have ever taken Economics you will know how hard a feat this is.

Affectionately referred to by students as "Dr. Bob," Robert Sachets is a perennial favourite in the Faculty of Management. Also, if you get on his good side, he may train you to be part of U of C's award-winning business team.

Those looking for a mind-stretching examination of the foundations of Western society swear that Ronald Glasberg's General Studies 500 is better than any acid trip.

Most popular bird courses: Astronomy 205 "Moons for Goons," Geology 209 "Rocks for Jocks," Computer Science 231 "Chips for Dips."

Hot spot to study on campus: MacEwan Student Centre Food Court.

Quietest spot to study on campus: If you don't mind sitting on the carpet, find a corner of an obscure exhibit in the Nickel Arts Museum and relish the silence. Otherwise, any floor above the second in the MacKimmie Library.

Need for car and parking availability: You can get anywhere in the city by bus or C-Train, but it may take you a long time and service does not exist past midnight. So you don't need a car, but you will want to know someone with one, particularly because the city is so spread out. The lists to get a spot in a reserve lot are long unless you are a Scholars' Advantage student.

Sexually speaking: The campus is too big to care who is or is not doing whom. If you're looking to pickup, the Den on a Thursday night is your best bet.

U of C's flagship program and features many of the country's top researchers.

The department of Geomatics is a rarity and is highly recommended. I have never met an engineer who did not like his faculty. Of course, I cannot mention Engineering without mentioning its arch rival, Management. The faculty is strong with lots of business tie-ins; just be careful not to leave with the feeling that money is everything. Besides, if you are looking for good money, Geology can easily set you on the right path, considering the present oil boom. If money is not your concern, you can go to Fine Arts. But a warning: Though the faculty has some excellent profs, it is undergoing major upheaval and has just cut its beloved Jazz studies program. But, the institution is big enough that you are bound to find a program you will like.

REZ LIFE

The university's physical distance from most of the hip parts of the city has made rez kids a tight group. The bonds between rez students are generally formed early on as first-year students are required to stay in the traditional dormitory residences of Rundle and Kananaskis halls. With the number of events and competitions floors organize amongst themselves, it is no surprise students find themselves defining their existence by their floor number e.g., (6R). If you are worried about being afflicted with loneliness at U of C, moving into residence is a sure-fire antidote. Unfortunately, if you are also worried about heartburn, the mandatory meal plan is a great head start to an ulcer.

Meal plan aside, though no one would compare life in residence to a night at the Ritz; the facilities are not comparable to life in the projects, either—which is better than most residences can claim. After first year, students are welcome to apply for apartment-style accommodation. Life in the apartments is quieter and less hectic. The accommodations are generally clean, relatively spacious, and in good working order. It is no surprise they are such a popular lifestyle choice. Applications for apartments are merit based—a high GPA and campus involvement are your best friends here. Fortunately, the university recognized the need for more apartments and added another 400 spaces this year in the newly built Cascade Hall.

NIGHT LIFE

The good news is that Calgary is increasingly becoming a metropolitan city; the bad news is it is doing it one pocket of the city at a time. If you have a car

In a Nut Shell *continued*

Fraternities/sororities: The Greek persuasion lifestyle is virtually unknown to the vast majority of students, but for those who choose to embrace it, they really choose to embrace it. There is a hardcore dedication to philanthropy among the frat pack, with numerous events that lead to competition and dating within the different fraternities/sororities.

Athletic facilities: Simply put, world-class. Olympic-calibre facilities include Calgary's largest racquet centre, Canada's only covered speed skating oval, and western Canada's largest indoor climbing wall.

Library facilities: Excitement is building about the new "Information Commons" set to open in the fall.

With over 160 computer stations, private rooms for group work, and electronic databases galore, getting research done is going to become a lot more enjoyable. Generally, the library is well stocked, with problems occurring in journal subscriptions which were cancelled due to the cutbacks of early nineties.

Computer facilities: Plenty available; check out the Library to get excited.

Weather: Anyone who has lived in the city long enough will tell you if you don't like the weather in Calgary wait five minutes. As a generalization the summers are warm and dry, while the snow-filled winters are made much more bearable by the occasional Chinook—a warm breeze from over the Rockies that can make the temperature rise up to 10°C.

Safety on campus: With ample lighting, six state-of-the-art surveillance cameras, and a 24-hour Safewalk program, U of C is about as safe as they come for a campus this size. That being said, it is located in a big city, so avoid acts of stupidity, such as leaving your books unattended for prolonged periods of time or walking alone to a remote part of campus late at night.

Alumni: Architect of the Java Computer Language, James Gosling; Astronaut Robert Thirst; and more influential Reform Party members than you can shake a stick at.

---

to take you around town, the city offers a diverse selection of bars and scenes for your enjoyment. On-campus night life is mostly defined by the notorious Den, which is in fact two bars. On Tuesday, Wednesday, and Saturday the Den is a nice, quiet, run-down neighbourhood pub, on Thursday and Friday it is a swill-filled, sweaty meat market fuelled by cheap beer and raging hormones. Also on campus are the more demure Max Cafe and the Grad Lounge (the Grad Lounge goes out of its way not to attract undergrads). Max's is more of a restaurant than a bar, but on most weekends it puts on some great cabarets—two years ago Blue Rodeo performed there to an intimate crowd of 600.

When your sense of style dictates that you must move off campus, martini bars are becoming a popular choice. The Criterion is one of the most popular choices with its art-deco interior and surveillance cameras which let you scope out other patrons on TV. The key thing to remember about this scene is that people go to be seen, not to party or talk, so as superficial as it seems, you'll want to make sure you are with your good-looking friends.

The more cerebral choice for the non-dance bar crowd are the pubs. Here you can appreciate your friends for what they think, not what they look like. A good pub will feature both Calgary's best microbrewery beer, Big Rock, as well as a wide variety from overseas on tap. The Ship and Anchor is the most social pub, and the James Joyce is the most refined. Other can't miss prospects include the Rose and Crown, the Kensington Pub, and the Unicorn.

A popular habit amongst Calgarians is to start the night at a pub, then move on to a dance club. The Embassy, the Palace, and the Taz keep the mainstream crowd moving; for something with more of an alternative edge go to the Republik or the Warehouse. If you want a mix of country, dancy pop, silicon, and dirty, middle-aged men, go to Cowboys or Outlaws. Far more than the province's capital, Calgary likes to dance.

If nothing I have mentioned so far sounds appealing, a solution is near: Slum it and catch some great blues at the King

---

A Word to the Wise:

With all the opportunities of such a big school you can have the best time of your life; however, being such a big school you can also feel detached and miserable. So get involved in a student group of some form early on. Those with spunk flourish, so don't be afraid to give U of C all you have. Also, shop around for a major in your first year, but be aware of which programs have what prerequisites.

Edward Hotel, refine your tastes with sinfully sweet jazz at either the Beatniq or Kaos, or give yourself a stomach ache from laughing so hard at Loose Moose Theatre's improvisers. Really, the only group that will be let down by the Calgary scene will be hardcore ravers. Don't get me wrong, raves do occur in the city, but not with the size and frequency that many would like. On a similar note, you will not find many of the dance bars bringing in out-of-town DJs to play until seven in the morning.

ON CALGARY

Calgary is rapidly moving from being the little city that could, to the big city that is. Fuelled by the western pioneer spirit, there is very little this city feels it can't do. Second only to Toronto in terms of corporate head offices, a unique combination of big-business culture, entrepreneurialism and the spirit of volunteerism run the city's agenda. Much more cosmopolitan than naysayers give it credit for, Calgary is an exciting place to live. Perhaps the reputation of being a western hick town comes from "the Greatest Outdoor Show on Earth," the Calgary Stampede; but as much fun as that 10-day party is, once it's over 90% of the people involved stop pretending to be cowboys and just get on with their normal lives. Though sometimes hidden to the casual observer, a sophisticated and diverse number of cultural activities are blossoming in the city.

Like the university, the city is very spread out. Huge suburban committees fill the landscape and new ones appear to pop up everyday. Part of the suburban culture and indicative of the city's wealth is the great exodus to the mountains every weekend, and with the Rockies being so close and so spectacular, who can blame these weekend warriors? During the summer favourite activities include hiking, biking, and rock climbing. In the winter there is skiing, skiing, and skiing. This sense of activity that engulfs Calgarians perhaps explains why it is becoming an ever-increasing challenge to find someone that was actually born in Calgary. Any university student who takes the time to get to know the city soon finds out why moving here is such a popular choice these days.

University of Lethbridge

By Jon Koch

Nestled in the Oldman River Valley, the University of Lethbridge provides a unique aspect to a city that for decades was known only as the home of the High Level Bridge (a mile-long, 400+ ft. high railway trestle built in 1909). Created in 1967, the university found itself sharing a facility with Lethbridge Junior College (now Lethbridge Community College) for two years. The sod turning for the new University of Lethbridge building didn't take place until 1969. Three years later University Hall was completed and opened to the public.

University Hall was designed by world-renowned architect Arthur Erickson, also known for designing the campus at Simon Fraser University. Erickson designed the university to be built into the coulees along the west bank of the Oldman River Valley. At the time, only irrigated farmland was there, so with the construction of the university, the community of West Lethbridge sprang into being. Today West Lethbridge has become a very student-oriented community of 18,000 residents.

There has been some criticism of Erickson's design, most of which revolves around the question of whether or not the university is eventually going to sink into the Oldman River. The other criticism is that the tons and tons of concrete used to construct University Hall have given it a cold, lonely atmosphere. This has led the more creative student bodies to lovingly label University Hall "the box the bridge came in" and "the coffin in the coulee."

By 1999 the University of Lethbridge's campus contained The University Centre for the Arts, the Physical Education Building, Turcotte Hall, the Max Bell Aquatic Centre, the Students' Union Building, and new this year, the announcement of a 250,000-sq.-ft. Library Information Network Centre (LINC). By September 2001 (tentatively) the university will be home to a $37 million library facility. Add to this the Physical Education Annex, Hepler, and Anderson Hall (or "Berm Barn"), and the university is growing at a phenomenal rate. During construction parts of campus can look more like a war zone than an academic oasis.

CAMPUS CULTURE The University of Lethbridge has a small population compared to its older siblings in Calgary and Edmonton. A significant number of students hail from Alberta and the rest of Canada (students from Calgary make up roughly 10% of the student population), and there are also a number of international students. However, students from Lethbridge and southern Alberta make up the majority of the population. It is because of this that some initially find the University of Lethbridge to be a bit "cliquey," as the Lethbridgians generally tend to stick together. Those from outside the city tend to become friends with other out-of-towners. Fear not, however, for it is the general nature of the university that should you make the effort, you can get along with and be friends with just about anyone.

The city of Lethbridge is located in the heart of Alberta's agricultural industry; therefore, its student mix is tempered by a steady influx of rambunctious "ruralties," who always make life interesting on campus. To discover this, you need look no further than the insane popularity of the campus's Almighty House of the Lethbridge Pilsner Club. Created in honour of the one-time Lethbridge-brewed "Pilsner" brand beer, and the now-demolished Fritz Sick Brewery ("The House of Lethbridge"), its ranks swell each year with a disproportionate amount of rural folk looking for a taste of home. Add to this mix a vibrant campus Aggies (Agriculture) Club, and the Rodeo Club with their own unique rural flavour, and you'll get a good idea about campus life.

Lethbridge is also located in the middle of the traditional Blackfoot Confederacy and this is reflected in the existence of the influential Faculty of Native American Studies. In conjunction with this faculty there is the Native American Students Association (NASA), which puts on a yearly Pow Wow and is involved in events promoting awareness of Native issues both on campus and in the community. As well, Lethbridge is in what many call the buckle of Alberta's "Bible Belt" community and with this comes a considerably large Latter Day Saints influence on campus. The Latter Day Saints Students' Association and the Inter Varsity Christian Fellowship are two very

Vital Statistics

Address: 4401 University Drive, Lethbridge, Alberta, T1K 3M4

Admissions office: (403) 320-5700

Website: www.uleth.ca

Total enrollment: 6,000 (approximately)

Male-female ratio: 44 to 56

Ratio of first-year applicants to number accepted: 3 to 2

Percentage of international students: 6%

Percentage of out-of-province students: 12%

Cut-off grade for admission after first round: Arts: 65%; Science: 65%; Commerce: 65%; Engineering: 65%

Tuition fees: Total yearly fees based on six courses per semester times two—$4857.96

Residence fees: Traditional residence (U-Hall)—suite single room $1,039/semester; suite large single room $1,176/semester; hallway single room $1,134/semester; double room $690/semester.

Aperture Park apartments—one bedroom $2,140/semester; two bedroom $1,390/semester; four bedroom $1,300/semester.

Percentage of students in residence: 8%

Co-op programs: Accounting, Advanced Accounting, Agricultural Biotechnology, Agricultural Management, Agricultural Studies, Anthropology, Archaeology, Art, Biochemistry, Biological Sciences, Business Enterprises and Self-Governing Systems of Indian, Inuit, and Metis Peoples, Canadian Studies, Chemistry, Computer Science, Dramatic Arts, Economics, English, Environmental Sciences, Exercise Science, Finance, French, French/German, General Management, General Science, Geography, Geology, German, History, Human Resource Management and Organization, Independent Multi-disciplinary Major, International Management, Kinesiology, Labour Relations, Management Information Systems, Marketing, Mathematics, Music, Native American Studies, Neuroscience, Philosophy, Physics, Political Science, Psychology, Public Administration, Recreation and Leisure Studies, Religious Studies, Sociology, Urban and Regional Studies, Women's Studies

Facilities for students with disabilities: University of Lethbridge is generally wheelchair accessible, with wheelchair ramps, automatic doors, and elevators allowing disabled students to move freely throughout the university.

Student services: Academic, psychological, and employment counselling are all available. As well, a writing centre, housing services, Organization of Residence Students, a health office, a financial aid office, and chaplaincy are also present.

active organizations on campus, putting a less deviant spin on student life through swing lessons, Toast Bars, and Random Acts of Kindness.

Student politics have been a hot sell the last few years, with high voter turnouts and keen interest in the trials and tribulations of the Students' Union. The student newspaper, *The Meliorist*, has remained surprisingly neutral throughout all the mud slinging, but the student radio station, CKUL-FM, is where most of the university's "radical" politics emanate.

ACADEMIC ISSUES

Traditionally the University of Lethbridge has prided itself on its faculties of Education and Management. Students in these faculties make up approximately one-quarter of the total student body. However, in recent years the university has made great strides towards excellence in many other areas, particularly in Neuropsychology. Within the faculty are some of the most respected and accomplished researchers, in particular Bryan Kolb and Ian Whishaw. Kolb received a Canada Council Killam Research Fellowship for his work on stimulating brain cells after injury, and Whishaw was elected a Fellow of the Royal Society of Canada's Academy of Science in 1998–99, and co-authored the premier introductory textbook in Neuropsychology used around the world.

The University of Lethbridge is also an institution that has placed great emphasis on its Drama, Music, and Fine Arts education. This process began in 1967 with the acquisition of the *Moses Sculpture* by Sorel Etog (which, incidentally, is rumoured to have been installed upside down). With this piece the university began the process of acquiring what is now considered to be the finest teaching-based art collection in Canada, worth more than $30 million.

Also, as Lethbridge is the hub of the agricultural industry in southern Alberta, it is only appropriate that the university, in the last three years, has adopted programs in Agricultural Studies and Agricultural Biotechnology. A major aspect of these programs is that the university has entered into articulation agreements with the province's four agricultural colleges. This allows Aggies from across the province who have graduated with a diploma to transfer to Lethbridge and obtain their Bachelor of Arts degree in just two years. The Alberta

In a Nut Shell

The university in a phrase: An environment that excites and ignites learning and where professors and students are colleagues.

Best thing about the university: Its small size.

Worst thing about the university: Its small size.

Favourite professors: Bryan Kolb (Neuroscience), Ron Chambers (Drama), Richard Epp (Drama), Malcolm Greenshields (History), Chris Hosgood (History), Rene Barendregt (Geography), Tom Johnston (Geography), Ron Yoshida (Philosophy), Paul Viminitz (Philosophy), Peter McCormick (Political Science)

Most popular bird courses: Fine Arts 3850, Anthropolgy 1000, Geography 1000, Tennis

Quietest spot on campus to study: The fourth level of the university library—many students don't even know it exists.

Most social spot on campus to study: Sixth-level hallway, University Hall.

Need for car and parking availability: Once-abundant parking has become a hot, pricey commodity. Parking passes will easily run you anywhere from $80–$195 per year. Lethbridge Transit is a cheap and highly recommended means of getting to and from campus if you live more than a short walk away.

Sexually speaking: It would not be fair to call Lethbridge sexually repressed as sex has been known to happen here, but usually issues regarding sexuality are unspoken. If sex is spoken of, the conversation usually revolves around homosexuality and the struggle that many students have in accepting something that many have never encountered.

Fraternities/sororities: Many have tried, none have succeeded.

Weather: Lethbridge is another one of those places where the old adage rings true: "If you don't like the weather, wait five minutes and it will change." It can go from 20° below to above freezing in a matter of hours, though the legendary Chinook winds keep the area relatively mild during the winter. Because of these winds, a lack of snow and ice can be a problem for some. The ground has been known to remain barren for most of the winter. However, contrary to popular belief, the strong winds Lethbridge is known for are infrequent, and usually quite tolerable.

Campus safety: For those students concerned about their safety and well-being on campus, "Safewalk" is once again underway. As well, Campus Security is available 24/7, 365 days a year.

Library facilities: As of right now, many lament the current state of the University Library. What the University does do well is work with other Alberta institutions. The U of L is part of the EUREKA partnership that allows students to access books, journals, and documents from institutions across the province. U of L also has an agreement with Medicine Hat College, allowing students seamless access to both collections. This will all change drastically in 2001, however, when construction on the Library Information Network Centre (LINC) is completed.

Sports facilities: The students at the University of Lethbridge are blessed with having access to many first-class facilities. The Max Bell Aquatic Centre is the only Olympic-size pool in southern Alberta, right on campus. As well, the weight room facility here is second to none, being quite possibly the most popular on-campus attraction for students and the outside community alike.

Alumnus: Alf Bogusky (Director, Vancouver Art Gallery); Wendy Neilsen (opera singer); Douglas Zagorsky (geographer); Terry Royer (President/CEO, Royco Hotels).

Institute of Agrologists has also recognized the degree program as meeting their accreditation standards.

The university is also attempting to stake its reputation in the area of Multimedia and Information Technology. The Bachelor of Fine Arts in Multimedia is a unique program in Canada, and provincial government ACCESS funding also allows advances in the area of Geographical Information Sciences (GIS). There is also a fledgling Graduate Studies program taking root at the university. There are now approximately 200 graduate students, the majority in the Masters of Education program.

REZ LIFE For the first-year student the first few weeks in residence will either leave you jumping for joy or screaming for mommy. For many, the first-year experience begins with initiation to the cavernous accommodations found in the depths of U-Hall residence, or as the locals fondly refer to it, "The Dungeon."

The Dungeon is made up of the bottom four floors of the concrete monolith that is University Hall. Students are assigned one or two to a room, or four to a unit. Life in a four bedroom can be utter bliss, or something markedly less than this. Despite the best efforts of the most capable of RAs, all-night parties have often forced even the most sedate students to become either hardcore debauchers or born again Puritans.

Going right along with the populist herd tactics that dictate university life, all residence students are urged to buy the Food Services Meal Plan. With this plan a healthy diet is about as attainable as an 'A' average during first year. Many students, satisfied with the fact that on an average night they can consume their own weight in beer, find that they finish the year with money still left on their meal plan. This then leads to the phenomenon where those with left-over money on their food cards try to trade food for favours for friends and strangers alike.

Our youth do persevere, however, and many recall with great fondness their years in The Dungeon. Some even choose to spend more years in the bowels of the university. This, of course, is because for approximately the first three months of each semester, the merriment and decadence never end. If this is not for you, you should be looking for accommodation elsewhere.

For those who choose to continue on the rez odyssey, the next step up is to Aperture Park. This consists of four separate buildings: Kainai, Piikani, Siksika, and Tsuut'ina. These are three-story buildings, consisting of both two- and four-person units. These are among the nicest student residence facilities in Canada, with plenty of living space, well-kept rooms, and a large kitchen area. There is often a large waiting list for these residences, and usually doing time in The Dungeon is a prerequisite for moving up to the Aperture. For families on campus, there are townhouses in the Tsuut'ina building. Remember, though: If you wish to live in residence, act early.

The alternative to life in rez comes in the large number of apartment and townhouse complexes all within a 5- to 10- minute walk from the university. There are not too many places that would rate up there with the Waldorf Astoria, but you can usually find close, relatively cheap ($525–$575/month) accommodation well into August. Encouraging news for all you stragglers out there. Parking on campus has become a scarce commodity, and an expensive one at that. The security staff is also very keen on ticketing all who park without a permit. If you are without an automobile, you may wish to invest in a bus pass.

NIGHT LIFE

Stopping short of giving you a definitive judgement on the quality of night life in Lethbridge, I can say one thing: Though entertaining for a while, Lethbridge does not have the same kind of night life as Calgary or Vancouver. Despite being a big draw for small-town folk, American soldiers, and those who are underage in BC and the States, the bars here are much smaller and less varied than those in the bigger centres. Given the small size of the uni-

A Word to the Wise:

1. Try to schedule your classes so that they are either mostly up the hill or at the bottom in U-Hall. With construction on LINC and other projects underway, it will become a logistical nightmare if you don't.

2. Take advantage of Lethbridge's recreational facilities; they are among the best and most abundant in Canada.

3. Take time to see southern Alberta. You will be awed by the area's geographical diversity.

4. The people you see downtown in traditional clothing and black cowboy hats driving crew cabs are not Amish. They are Hutterites, an Anabaptist sect that practice a communal lifestyle at locations all over southern Alberta.

5. Get used to the hundreds of Richardson's Ground Squirrels (or "gophers" as they are known to the locals) that call the U of L campus home. They are everywhere.

versity and the limited number of bars, it's common to see the same faces night after night. If a good time is sought on campus, the only place to go is The Zoo, the campus bar located in the Students' Union Building. Except for Wednesday nights' Geoparty and cheap draft nights on Friday, The Zoo is more of a student and faculty lounge. Along with The Zoo, there is the Duke of Wellington Pub. Located in a strip mall west of the University, "The Duke" is a popular destination on Thursday nights, before, during, or after classes.

On most nights, however, a mass exodus begins. Having suffered various identity crises over the years, Cadillac's Club has opened again, new lights and all. Goose Loonies, which is located in the Lethbridge Hotel, thrives on the youngest of the young, offering cheap booze and even cheaper clientele. Another place is the Nexus Club, located in the basement of the Parkside Inn. The Nexus Club is also in close proximity to Lethbridge Community College, and therefore also draws largely from that crowd. On a different note, one of Lethbridge's newest establishments, the Roadhouse Thirst and Grill has transformed what was once a quasi-geriatric country bar into one of the liveliest nightspots in the city. Half lounge and half dance club, it provides you with both standing and sitting room as you fret over whether to ask that particular guy/girl for the pleasure of their company. Another thing about the Roadhouse is that if all else fails, the Top Hat exotic dance club is right next door. Then there is Ezzies, a big draw for the hard-drinking rural and college crowd. For years this has been the only place to go in town if buckles, boots, and

Wranglers are your game. Here you'll find everything from "goat-ropers" and trailer park cowpokes to your genuine CPRA cowboys, as well as the finest "buckle bunnies" in town, all engaged in a two-steppin' frenzy that only Albertans can do right (no line dancing!). In the category of "unique" there is Club 9-1-1. What was once the city Fire Hall, much capital and effort turned into the most innovative night club in town. The only bar of its kind in Lethbridge, it features several levels, private rooms, and a nice change from the usual.

Lethbridge scores a little higher on the lounge scene. There are many establishments citywide providing sustenance for those wishing to over indulge or kick back in a quieter setting. A number of places such as O'Rileys, Brewsters Brew Pub and Bo' Diddleys offer draft, appies, and NTN Trivia. There is also Fogg n' Suds, whose main drawing card is the 100-plus different beers they offer. Finally, almost every restaurant and hotel in Lethbridge has a lounge of some sort for those looking for something off the beaten track, or try the Cactus Pub and Grill in nearby Picture Butte for a change of pace.

ON LETHBRIDGE

The third-largest city in Alberta is also one of its most beautiful. The Oldman River Valley, which divides the city in two, is home to the largest railway trestle built by the Canadian Pacific Railway in 1909. East and West Lethbridge are connected by Whoop Up Drive, named after Fort Whoop Up, which now sits in Indian Battle Park, once home to American whiskey traders until the NWMP arrived in 1873. Lethbridge is renowned for its vast expanse of green space, Henderson Lake, Nicholas Sheran Park, and an extensive system of walking paths, which are ideal for those wishing to bike, blade, walk, or run. As well, the world famous Chinook winds make Lethbridge one of the more moderate locations in the prairies to spend your winters. There is also a vast array of shopping in Lethbridge, half a dozen major malls, and other big-city amenities which make the city a popular destination for shoppers.

Calgary is a two-hour drive north, with prime skiing in the BC Rockies at Westcastle and Fernie only two hours west. For those who like to hike and mountain climb in the spring and summer, Waterton-Glacier International Peace Park is only an hour and a half southwest, and other attractions, such as Head-Smashed-In Buffalo Jump, Writing on Stone Provincial Park, Fort MacLeod, and the Alberta Temple in Cardston are only an hour's drive away.

To close, the more liberal focus at the university sits in stark contrast to the conservative nature of southern Alberta. One major adjustment for those coming from larger centres is the trend in Lethbridge for businesses (e.g., liquor stores) to close well before midnight. As well, the strong religious nature of many southern Albertans adds a unique element to the community. Do not be alarmed if young men in white dress shirts, black dress pants, and backpacks greet you on the street; they are just Mormons on a mission. Living in Lethbridge is entirely bearable; in fact, it can be downright enjoyable.

The University of Regina

By Cornelia Ratt

Celebrating its 25th anniversary this year, the University of Regina is a "young and dynamic institution." The U of R originated as a residential high school in 1911. Eventually it became a Junior College, and later the second campus of the University of Saskatchewan in Saskatoon. Regina College acquired degree-granting status in 1961, and gained full independence in 1974.

Minoru Yamasaki, designer of New York City's World Trade Center, created U of R's main campus in the 1950s. The campus is located in the Wascana Centre, the largest urban park in North America. Take advantage of these surroundings—there is nothing more soothing than strolling down to the lake after classes! A true gem, by the way, is the old College Avenue campus with its beautiful, ivy-blanketed brick buildings, although only members of the Conservatory of Music have the privilege of studying here. For the rest of us, there is the main campus. Generally, the classrooms are spacious and altogether pretty good. Only the rooms in the Education Building are a trifle depressing, because they don't have windows, which makes for a somewhat claustrophobic feel.

The newest addition to the campus came in 1997, when the $28 million University Centre opened. This building houses the Students' Union, Faculty of Fine Arts, Students' Services, the book shop, and a food court. Some students dislike the Centre and claim it has the atmosphere of a shopping mall, but others appreciate its practicality.

The University of Regina has three federated colleges. Campion College, administered by the Jesuits, became a federated college in 1966. Federation with Luther College became effective in 1971. In 1976, the Saskatchewan Indian Federated College (SIFC) launched its first programs. From less than a dozen students in the beginning, SIFC's enrollment is now over 1,600.

CAMPUS CULTURE

University life involves more than simply taking classes. U of R offers numerous clubs and societies, each of which promise to enrich students' lives. Clubs such as the Campus Recreation Program, the *Carillon* student newspaper, or the Cougar sports teams are just a small sampling of what is available. Moreover, U of R has an active arts community. There are regular theatre productions, film screenings, and visual art displays. The English Department regularly offers literary readings and discussions. The annual SIFC powwow celebrates the university's involvement with Native communities. And then, there is the Lazy Owl, U of R's on-campus bar. The Owl is definitely *the* place on campus to meet people and to drown all worries about the Logic final in a beer (or two, or three…).

Integral to campus life are the end-of-the-semester get-togethers. From the second year on, profs will take their classes to the Owl on the last day of the semester. This is always fun. With some classes, you might have a pretty wild night of excessive alcohol consumption and things that hopefully no one will remember the next day; with others, it might simply be a quiet evening that allows you to socialize and catch up on gossip. Campion's English classes, by the way, are known for the best end-of-term parties on campus!

The student body is diverse, with a higher percentage of aboriginal students than at any other Canadian university. On campus, you might meet students from isolated communities in northern Saskatchewan, international students from Latin America and Japan, or kids who grew up right here in Regina. It is therefore difficult to say what the average student is like. However, U of R students are usually friendly, helpful, and entirely disinterested in politics; the only political issues that gain moderate attention are threatened hikes in tuition fees.

Vital Statistics

Address: 3737 Wascana Pkwy, Suite 100, Regina, Saskatchewan S4S 0A2

Admissions office: (306) 585-4111

Website: www.uregina.ca

Total enrolment: 10,718

Male-female ratio: 40–60

Percentage of out-of-province students: 12%

Percentage of international students: 3%

Average entering grades: Arts: 65; Science: 65%; Engineering: 70%

Tuition fees: $1,532–$1,750 for a full load of five classes

Residence fees: Shared room (two people) $793–$803/semester or $198.25–$208.25/month; single room $1,017–$1,199/semester or $254.25–$307.25/month. Room and board fees range from $755 to $1,040 per semester. Off-campus accommodation ranges from $250–$450/month for a one-bedroom suite to $300–$650/month for a two-bedroom suite to houses at $400/month and up.

Percentage of students in residence: About 5%.

Financial aid: U of R offers entrance scholarships to first-year students, and proficiency scholarships for undergrads with a high grade-point average. (If you receive the latter, your name will be displayed on the University's Honours List for all to see.) Some scholarships are awarded automatically; for others you need to apply—contact the Financial Aid Office for details.

Co-op programs: Administration, Chemistry, Computer Science, Engineering, Mathematics and Statistics, Physics.

Services for students with disabilities: Students who require special services should get in touch with their faculty as early as possible. U of R can accommodate students who have special parking requests, or who need assistance with final exams or lectures. One problem, however, is that not all facilities are wheelchair accessible. So if you have special needs, please check issues such as accessibility asap.

Aboriginal students: The Saskatchewan Indian Federated College will open a new facility on the Regina campus in 2001. Twenty programs ranging from the Cree language to First Nations teacher education. The college provides a quality education based on First Nations culture and traditions.

Student services: Exam registry, tutor registry, first-year services, writing clinic, used bookstore, résumé service, career and psychological counselling. A health clinic with two physicians is right on campus. Students will be covered under the Saskatchewan Health Plan. Travel Cuts (to book flights or full holidays at discount prices).

ACADEMIC ISSUES

U of R's faculties include Administration, Arts, Education, Engineering, Fine Arts, Physical Education Studies, School of Human Justice, School of Journalism and Communication, Science, and Social Work. The federated colleges offer further specialized programs, such as aboriginal languages. If U of R's somewhat isolated location in the middle of the Canadian plains strikes you as lonesome and far-and-away, think again. Taking a degree in Regina might give you an international experience. The faculty is quite cosmopolitan, and the Language Institute offers exchange programs to countries around the world.

What also makes U of R attractive—apart from very low tuition fees—is the small number of students. As an undergraduate, you can be sure to receive maximum attention, because classes are small: first- and second-year level courses average less than 50 students, third- and fourth-year courses have less than 25. This ensures a relaxed atmosphere and allows for intense student-professor interaction.

Moreover, you can gain valuable work experience. Some faculties have co-op programs that allow students to apply their academic knowledge in a real work environment. Moreover, all faculties need student assistants to perform a variety of duties; it's interesting work and will look great on your résumé!

REZ LIFE

U of R offers three different residential lifestyles. College West has single and shared study-bedrooms in suites housing 3 to 11 students. Residence pamphlets usually promise that you'll make lifelong friends there. But then, wasn't Sartre's vision of hell three people locked together in a room? I wonder what he would have thought of 11 students in a suite. No doubt, if your roommates turn up the stereo full blast whenever you wished to study, ate your bagels, and flooded the communal bathroom while showering, residence life would quickly turn sour. So, if this doesn't appeal to you, then you might instead consider Luther College, which offers small rooms for single occupancy, or the Language Institute, which provides both single and shared accommodation in equally small rooms.

In a Nut Shell

Best thing about the university: The people.

Worst thing about the university: No such thing.

Favourite professors: Samira McCarthy (Campion—English); Dr. Chris Murray (English, retired); Dr. Eugene Bertoldi (Campion—Philosophy); Solomon Ratt (SIFC—Cree).

Toughest course: Geology 103.

Hot spots on campus to study: The so-called AdHum (Administration and Humanities building) Pit.

Quietest spot on campus to study: The main library.

Need for car and parking availability: Sure, having a car is nice, especially in the winter. It is no fun hauling home your weekly supply of groceries when it's –45°C. Parking is available at U of R for $54.75 per semester. A car, however, is no necessity. Apart from certain cold spells which make it almost impossible to go outside at all, you'll find that it is easy to get around without a car. The city is small and pretty much everything is in walking distance—and if you don't fancy walking, there's always the bus.

Sexually speaking: It is fairly easy to meet a good selection of members of the opposite sex, but most students try not to get their libido in the way of their studies. U of R is certainly neither a wild party place nor a dating pool. Pink Triangle is a gay and lesbian club on campus.

Fraternities/sororities: There are no fraternities or sororities at U of R.

Athletic facilities: U of R has a fitness centre, gymnasium, swimming pool, sauna, aerobic/dance studio, tennis courts, beach volleyball courts, and outdoor playing fields. Use of any of these facilities is included in the tuition. Moreover, the surrounding Wascana Park has beautiful trails for biking and in-line skating in the summer and cross-country ski trails in the winter.

Library facilities: The libraries on campus hold some 2.4 million items. A user-friendly computer system helps you locate whatever you are looking for. Moreover, the library staff is really, really awesome—friendly, knowledgeable, and resourceful. The people at the reference desk will answer all your questions (don't be shy to ask) and help you to find what you need.

Computer facilities: Computer labs are available for student use for course assignments and projects. The labs are found in the Classroom Building, Education library, and on the fourth floor of the Education Building. The labs are especially busy on Friday nights.

Weather: Weather? Well, we have lots of it here in Saskatchewan. The difference between the hottest month, July, and the coldest, January, is almost 100°C. However, it's really not as bad as it sounds. Southern Saskatchewan has a very dry climate, which makes both summer heat and icy winter weather bearable. Regina in fact is one of the sunniest spots in Canada. The wind, however, is vicious. A windy winter day can make –20°C seem like –50°C. On the other hand, the strong winds ensure that the air quality in Regina is superb.

Safety on campus: The university offers the UR Safer "Walk Along" program. Students can request someone to accompany them to the bus stop, car, etc. Generally speaking, U of R is a very safe place.

Alumni: Ken Mitchell (writer; teaches English here), Guy Vanderhaeghe (writer).

Yet despite these drawbacks, the advantages of rez life surely outweigh the disadvantages. Life on campus is inexpensive, and living close to the university is pretty neat, especially in winter. While your friends who live at the other end of town wait for the bus on cold, dark mornings, you can still sleep because it doesn't take longer than five minutes to get to the lecture theatre!

But if you want to look elsewhere in the city for a habitat, U of R's housing registry can assist you in your search. Since accommodation in Regina is the cheapest in urban Canada, your choice is not limited to suites; you might even consider renting a house to share with other students.

NIGHT LIFE

True: Regina has fewer bars and clubs than Montreal.

False: You can't have any fun here.

Whether you aim to drink yourself senseless as fast as possible or wish to have a nice chat with friends over a beer—you'll surely find the right spot here in town. The Lazy Owl, U of R's on-campus bar, attracts a mixed crowd, from first-year students to profs. Generally, the Owl offers a civilized—though very loud—drinking environment. The Owl hosts concerts throughout the year, which are announced on posters all over the campus; admission is affordable, and the atmosphere is usually great.

The city's most notorious drinking dens are located along Dewdney Avenue. The State attracts the more "alternative" crowd. It offers cheap booze, has low cover charges, and features live bands several nights a week. For those who don't belong to any kind of subculture and who don't have discriminating taste in music, Delbert's is probably the right place. Checkers, a club at the South End of town, is particularly popular with the first-year crowd. The average age here is probably 18, so if you're 25 or older, you'll feel seriously old here. For those who don't fancy clubs and seek a quieter sort of place, there is the Irish Pub. And if your student loan allows for a more sophisticated kind of entertainment, you could also sip a cocktail and smoke a cigar at Danbry's, Regina's most upscale bar. If you can't drink because you're everybody else's taxi service, don't despair. You can have fun without the booze, too—simply go for a late-night coffee at Roca-Jack's, one of the city's in-spots, right in the heart of downtown.

ON REGINA The "Queen City" is an important cultural centre of Canada's Prairie region. Regina is small, but offers a lot for every taste. Stroll through the Wascana Park and feed the geese, or find out about Saskatchewan's history in the Royal Museum. Or, you might want to visit the Mackenzie Art Gallery, which features a major collection of Canadian art. You could also explore the Science Centre, splash into one of the many outdoor pools on a hot day, or browse through the stacks at the Public Library. If you want to take in our cowboy ambiance, you could visit a horse show or the annual rodeo. And if you're more adventurous (or suicidal), try the ejection seat at the Buffalo-Days Fair.

Moreover, Regina has a vibrant performing arts scene: The Globe Theatre offers an interesting range, from Shakespeare to

---

A Word to the Wise:

1. Use the academic programs offered. If you are enrolled in a foreign language class, you can get tutoring, and Campion's English 100 classes have a tutor-mentor program designed to help you with those darn essays. The services are free–so make use of them! Why agonize in solitude over difficult assignments and panic once final exam time comes around when you can get help?

2. Bring warm winter clothes and heed weather warnings. Make listening to the weather report a habit, because being caught unprepared in a blizzard can be dangerous (yes, you really *do* walk in a circle if you can't see).

3. Use the sports facilities; they are great and you pay for them anyway.

4. Never be shy to ask. People here are exceptionally nice and helpful. It's true!!!

---

local playwrights. Did you know that Regina is dubbed the "Hollywood of the Prairies"? There are quite a few film productions here every year. This is very exciting, because sometimes you can see *real* film stars in town—Drew Barrymore, Jennifer Jason Leigh, Keanu Reeves, and Wes Studi were here. If you are lucky, you can be extra in a movie or get some other work on a film set, and maybe you'll even be discovered!

University of Saskatchewan

By Sean Junor

Founded in 1907, the University of Saskatchewan sits on the banks of the South Saskatchewan River. U of S is widely recognized as one of Canada's most beautiful post-secondary institutions with its combination of gothic architecture and Manitoba fieldstone.

The campus covers quite a lot of physical space and is presently experiencing a period of growth. It is now home to Canada's first synchrotron, and this will surely add to the appeal of the campus both domestically and internationally. There are also plans to improve Thorvaslen (the main science building) and rebuild the Kinesiology building. The U of S has many more projects that are awaiting final approval, so "Men at Work" will be a familiar sign on campus.

It's easy to find your way around U of S since the hub of campus is "the Bowl," smack in the centre. The Bowl is home to many events, including all Welcome Week activities and the traditional U of S employee picnic. Every fall, both students and staff gather here to enjoy the sights and sounds of the campus.

The first Arts and Science classes began on September 28, 1909, when 70 students were registered. Over the past 90 years, U of S has grown and changed dramatically. With a student population of over 16,000 students, U of S offers over 58 degrees, diplomas, and certificates in over 100 areas.

St. Thomas More College was established by the Fathers of the Order of St. Basil in 1936 and offers Arts courses, which are also offered through corresponding departments of the College of Arts and Science.

CAMPUS CULTURE

The first phenomenon most people experience when coming onto campus is the wildly inadequate parking supply. The second phenomenon that people notice when entering the campus is the Bowl. The Bowl is a park at the very centre of campus, surrounded by buildings that are circled like wagons to protect it from that nasty marauder, the Real World. Life on campus basically revolves around the Bowl. In the summer, it is a hub of activity, with everything from picnic lunches, sun worshippers, and touch football, to fanatic Frisbee and Rubber Chicken Olympics. During the 40 below winter months, the Bowl is mostly barren and devoid of life. Most students become troglodytes and remain indoors through the use of the tunnels and skywalks that link almost all of the college buildings on campus—something learned from the gophers of Saskatchewan. While some students scurry through the tunnels wearing pyjamas and shorts, even in the winter, there are a few hearty souls who brave the bitter cold to get to class, build snowmen or igloos, or play shinny hockey on the outdoor rink.

Athletics at U of S are second to none and intramural sports are popular on campus, especially hockey. The university is consistently strong in football, men's and women's volleyball, men's hockey, men's and women's track and field, and wrestling. The support that athletics receives is citywide and therefore national events are usually a huge success. In the past year, both the football team and the men's volleyball squad won national championships, an event that instilled even more pride in the Huskies. The Huskies attract great crowds, though attendance for football games can fluctuate with the weather. Huskies clothing and paraphernalia are so popular that it is virtually impossible to go anywhere on campus, or pretty well in the province, and not see someone wearing something. That is the third phenomenon of the U of S campus. For leisure sports, Campus Recreation organizes a host of leagues for students to participate in. There is everything from the very relaxed Super Fun curling, water polo, and soccer leagues to the super intense and competitive curling and hockey leagues. Yes, take note, curling is mentioned twice.

There is a lot of other stuff to do on campus besides sports. None of these activities include (most of the time anyway) cruising the livestock auction for 4-H babes, cow tipping, or throwing things off the bridge.

Aspiring politicians can find their niche in one of the many campus clubs, course unions, college societies, or on the overarching Students' Union, the voice of the undergraduate student body. USSU's five-member student executive provides both advocacy and services to students and puts on a Welcome Week, including a Blue Monday dance, and two separate lec-

Vital Statistics

Address: University of Saskatchewan, Saskatoon, Saskatchewan, S7N 5A2

Admissions office: (306) 966-4343

Website: www.usask.ca

Total enrolment: 16,942

Male-female ratio: 44 to 56

Cut-off grade for admissions: Arts: 65.3%; Science: 65.3%; Commerce: 66%; Engineering: 66.7%

Tuition fees: $3,000

Residence fees: Voyageur Place: $4,000 (double), $4,380 (single); McEown Park: $395/month (one bedroom), $505/month (two bedrooms)

Spaces for students in residence: 1,500 (approx.)

Co-op programs: Agriculture; internships in Computer Science

Financial aid: 1,000 admission scholarships and over 2,300 in-course scholarships each year; Emergency Loans Office.

Facilities for students with disabilities: Office of Services for Students with Disabilities.

Aboriginal students: Aboriginal Students' Centre.

Student services: Employment and career centre, health services, international student advisor's office, on-campus childcare.

---

tures called the Roy Romanow and the Eric Malling. Budding journalists may join *The Sheaf Collective* (not affiliated with the Borg Collective of Star Trek fame in any way). *The Sheaf* is U of S's student newspaper. Almost every week, at least one interesting and controversial letter to the editor appears, usually from some very jaded and disgruntled person. Aside from politics and journalism, there are still tons of ways to become involved, such as volunteering at the Student Help or the Lesbian, Gay, and Bisexual centres.

The appearance of students on campus varies little from building to building. However, the extremes must be noted, since there are those few individuals who seem to fit into their college setting like round pegs in a square hole. In Agriculture, you will often see Herculean belt buckles, cowboy boots, and Wranglers. Next door in Engineering, however, it is not unheard of to witness pocket protectors (very rare, bonus points for spotting these) and holstered calculators. Incidentally, in mid-September, there is usually a lively rivalry between the Aggies (Agricultural students) and the Engineers. Across campus in Commerce, Tommy Hilfiger dominates the scene, while in Arts and Sciences there is a mixed bag of tricks. For the most part, though, the attitudes and dress you will find on campus are very relaxed and casual.

New students should consider going to the U of S Orientation, a fun and informative program that makes the transition from high school to university relatively painless. Orientation offers a variety of small-group activities led by upper-year students in the same college or major as you, barbecues, an information fair, a dance, and other fun-packed events over the course of two days.

If you do not attend Orientation, meeting people can be challenging. It really depends on what program you are enrolled in, on what classes you are taking, and if you are willing to go out of your way to meet new faces. Students in the professional colleges, such as Agriculture, Commerce, Engineering, Pharmacy and Nutrition, and Kinesiology enjoy a close-knit atmosphere with smaller classes and more social activities.

ACADEMIC ISSUES

The University of Saskatchewan has a large array of direct entry and non-direct entry programs. There are 13 colleges including Agriculture, Arts and Sciences, Commerce, Dentistry, Education, Engineering, Kinesiology, Law, Medicine, Nursing, Physical Therapy, Pharmacy and Nutrition, and Veterinary Medicine. What this means to you boys and girls is a diversified program base, giving U of S students a strong and rich environment to learn and grow within. Class sizes in first-year courses can get up to 350 students, or be as focused as four students in some of the upper-year seminar courses.

One of the aspects that you will find at U of S is that it is focused on providing to the people of the province of Saskatchewan, which means that you gain a lot of tools here no matter what your background and will end up being among some of the best. Many of the programs are very well received by the private sector both nationally and internationally. What can be bad about this is that some teachers can focus too narrowly on research or certain aspects of teaching, forgetting that it is

In a Nut Shell

The university in a phrase: U of S is a institution rich in character.

Best thing about the university: The geographical location and the sports teams.

Worst thing about the university: Parking availability on and off campus.

Favourite professors: Every year the Students' Union awards 10 Teaching Excellence Awards. Recent winners include Paul Bidwell (English) and David Smith (Political Science).

Most popular courses: Engineering and Agriculture.

Quietest spots to study on campus: Murry Library.

Hot spots to study on campus: Commerce Reading Room and the Bowl.

Need for car and parking availability: There is very limited parking on campus and even less available off. Make other arrangements.

Sexually speaking: The U of S has a vibrant dating scene. This is because close to 90% of the students come from smaller centres in Saskatchewan and now, for the first time, they are exposed to options. Combine this with the friendly attitudes of the students and you have a dating jackpot.

Fraternities/sororities: The province of Saskatchewan is not elitist at all. As a result, the fraternity/sorority aspect of university has never caught fire. However, there are close groups in Engineering, Commerce, and Agriculture.

Athletic facilities: Two swimming pools, three squash courts, a racquetball court, a tennis courtyard, a curling rink, a hockey rink, four gyms, three weight rooms, one fitness testing lab, and 12 sports fields. The U of S needs a new hockey and curling arena to replace the ancient Rutherford Arena. Also, the football stadium could use some renovations.

Library facilities: One main library and seven branch libraries; overall, facilities are okay, but the recent move to cut journals and periodicals are hurting the learning environment.

Computer facilities: Inadequate for the number of students on campus. There is one computer for every 25 students and this is unacceptable for a major university.

Weather: The weather in Saskatoon is generally dry and sunny. Summer daytime temperatures range from 20ºC to 35ºC (68ºF to 95ºF). Evenings are cool, requiring a light sweater or jacket. Winter temperatures vary from 5ºC to –30ºC (40 degrees F to –22ºF). Average annual rainfall of 245 mm ensures lush gardens, parks, and golf courses. In winter, snowfall is sufficient to encourage many winter sports.

Safety on campus: The campus is really safe and that is a direct result of a first-rate Security Services division on campus.

Alumni: John Diefenbaker, Sylvia Fedoruk, Ray Hnatyshyn, Guy Vanderhaeghe.

not all about reputations and "weeding," it's also about giving students access to tools that will help them critique and challenge the world around them.

Students have lots of representation in committees and boards dealing with student discipline and grievances. Make sure to always check with your professor, the department head, your Students' Union, and the Office of Registrar, because the university binds students upon registration to all policies within the registration calendar and those of your college (fun, hey!). Ignorance isn't an excuse to these people…know what they expect of you!

REZ LIFE

One of the best decisions that a student can make when first enrolling at U of S is applying to live in the on-campus residence, known as Voyageur Place. Space is available for roughly 300 men and 270 women. Seager Wheeler Hall, the university residence located off campus, holds 305 students, but those spaces are very hard to come by. There are no reserved rooms for first-year students, so it is basically first come, first serve. The best bet to find a place is in Voyageur Place, where nearly half of the residents are in first year.

Voyageur Place is a great place to live in if you're from out of town. Rez fees cover the following: a room (a single if you're lucky, double otherwise), three meals a day during the week, two meals a day on weekends and holidays, laundry service for bed sheets, the association fee, and the opportunity to walk to over half of the college buildings without ever having to go outside. There are many different facilities offered within rez, including a coin-operated laundry, a weight room, a game room with pool tables and a foosball table, a gymnasium, study lounges, kitchenettes, and big-screen TV lounges.

The Voyageur Place Residents' Association (VPRA) represents all students living in Voyageur Place and organizes an average of two social functions a month. That's 16 days of guaranteed nonstop fun. VPRA also provides a forum by which complaints may be made about the exquisite dining facilities, security issues, and the like. The association holds a seat on University Students' Council, thereby representing rezzies' concerns to the whole university. VPRA also runs several sports and recreation leagues, the most notable of which is the Rez Floor Hockey League, which contains some of the most exciting and violent sporting action to be found in western Canada.

It is often said that the best place to meet people is in rez, where you can meet other students in similar situations. For many rezzies, this is their first time away from home, and therefore, they are also getting used to the idea of life on their own. Because of this, you would have the opportunity to grow and learn with others like you. It is also good to get to know people who are in the same courses in order to get help with tests or (God forbid!) homework assignments. In fact, you will meet so many people that it will be very difficult to walk across the campus of 17,000 students without knowing anyone.

If you ask anyone who lived there, they would tell you that the best choice they made in coming to U of S was to live in rez.

NIGHT LIFE

Saskatoon has plenty to do during the night hours, contrary to popular belief. Students can generally be found in many bars around the city. On Sunday and Monday, Champs on 8th Street is extremely busy. On Mondays, Fridays, and Saturdays, the Sutherland is packed. The Broadway district has plenty of good watering holes, which are busy on the weekends, including: Amigo's, Lydia's, Hose and Hydrant, and the Wash and Slosh. On Fridays, Louis', on campus, is the place to be and you better come early because it lines up in a hurry. Louis' also has more live shows in a school year than any other campus bar in Canada.

If the bar is not your scene, then maybe a slower pace is in order. The Black Duck and Maguires Pub are fine places to meet friends and share stories and a pint of ale. If you're looking for more elbow room, there are many trendy coffee shops around both Broadway and the Downtown districts.

Saskatoon is home to major Canadian junior hockey, as well as excellent junior football. The Saskatchewan Roughriders are just a short two-and-a-half-hour drive away in Regina and boast the best fans in the world.

There is no shortage of movie theatres in Saskatoon, as students can choose between the over 25 different screens, and yes, there still is a drive-in.

ON SASKATOON

Saskatoon is one of Canada's hidden gems. Canadians often are quick to say that all the city has is snow, but that is simply not true. On any given week the city is alive with activity.

Saskatoon enjoys more hours of sunshine than any other major Canadian city! Cycle, jog, or enjoy a casual stroll through beautifully landscaped parks and natural areas of the Meewasin Valley Trail, along the South Saskatchewan River. For those who love to play, the city offers many golf courses, swimming pools, and tennis courts. Spectators can enjoy hockey, thoroughbred racing, and stock car and drag racing. Also, Saskatoon is the only Canadian stop for the PROP Formula One Powerboat Races!

Saskatoon is a four-season destination with much to offer visitors. History comes alive at many exceptional museums, including the Western Development Museum and its popular main street—Boomtown 1910. At Wanuskewin Heritage Park you can experience 6,000 years of the history of the Northern Plains Indian people. Cruise or paddle down the river, enjoy Saskatoon berry desserts, and view Saskatchewan wildlife up close! Strap on your skis, dust off your snowshoes, lace up your skates, or for the more daring—try snowboarding!

A cultural oasis, Saskatoon boasts several professional and amateur theatre groups, a symphony, and numerous art galleries. Many festivals and special events are celebrated annually, from Winterfest in February, to the ethnic celebrations of Folkfest. The renowned SaskTel Saskatchewan Jazz Festival, the innovative Shakespeare on the Saskatchewan Festival, the mind-boggling Saskatoon International Fringe Festival, and the popular Ex, Saskatchewan's Summer Festival, all guarantee good times!

Saskatoon, in the heart of a province known for its agricultural bounty, offers a wide variety of dining choices, from gourmet to family, from hearty to exotic. Shopping will be an exciting and rewarding experience with friendly, courteous staff welcoming visitors in an assortment of shopping malls, specialty stores, boutiques, and gift shops.

Brandon University

By Jill Wilson

Founded in 1899 with roots as a small Baptist college, Brandon University celebrates its centennial anniversary. BU has much to celebrate—it boasts a nationally and internationally renowned Music program and has pioneered innovative programs in the fields of Native Studies and Education. Brandon also attracts students because of its small, intimate class sizes and personal attention from professors.

Although Brandon has the smallest student population of Manitoba's three universities, its physical campus is larger than the University of Winnipeg and prettier than the University of Manitoba. BU's campus is a blending of both heritage and modern buildings. BU's Original Building (1900) and Clark Hall (1906) were completely renovated in 1996. The campus is compact and you can get across the campus easily (although the harsh winters tend to freeze your limbs are you scurry from class to class, so most buildings are connected by underground tunnels). The jokes made about University of Winnipeg being a "big high school" are not made about BU, even though it has fewer students and less prestige. Brandon's campus feels more like a traditional university, one where you can enjoy the grounds and sense that the institution has a history. But there's a price to pay for the "real university" atmosphere. Brandon is the coldest university town in Canada. On some February mornings, thoughts of literally freezing to death on the way to class cross people's minds.

For those coming from rural communities in Manitoba and southeastern Saskatchewan, however, BU is not only appealing, it's often a preferred option. "There are a lot of people from rural areas at BU," explains one student, "because it's less of a culture shock to come here than it is to go to Winnipeg."

Brandon definitely has a rural focus. BU's president Dr. Dennis Anderson emphasizes, "BU's mandate is the rural, northern, remote, aboriginal sectors of the province. We have a mandate to make available quality educational services that are demanded by people in those geographical areas and from those racial groups."

CAMPUS CULTURE

The Knowles-Douglas Student Union Building (SUB) is the hub of activity at BU. This cathedral-like, sunlit building houses the campus bookstore, the arcade, the hair salon, and SUDS (Student Union Drinking Spot). To occupy yourself between classes the SUB is the place to be and be seen.

If you're worried about fitting in, it is impossible to describe the typical Brandon student. There is a relaxed and casual attitude among students and you'll see many students sporting Mountain Equipment Co-op gear—you'll need to pack on layers since Brandon is Canada's coldest university town. Seventies retro garb is another stylish look.

Brandon offers many opportunities to participate in campus life. Be the first to know what goes on on campus—write for *The Quill* student newspaper. Be a superstar and volunteer for BUSR, the campus radio station, or run for office in BUSU (Brandon University Students' Union). Be a sport—try out for a Bobcats varsity team. Beat the freshman fifteen—get involved in campus recreation. You can join everything from badminton and beach volleyball to floor and ice hockey. Campus Rec also organizes other recreational outings, including camping, canoeing, hiking, and skiing. Join a club, like one of the more popular ones, SUDS Mug Club (you can just imagine what that's all about).

Vital Statistics

Address: 270-18th St., Brandon, Manitoba, R7A 6A9

Admissions office: (204) 727-9784

Website: www.brandonu.ca

Total enrollment: 2,625

Male-female ratio: 37 to 63

Average entrance grades: Arts: 60%; Science: 60%

Tuition fees: Arts, Business Administration, Education: $2,972.34; First Nations and Aboriginal Counselling, General Studies: $2,972.34–$3,213.84; Music, Science: $3,213.84.

Residence fees: $1,785–$2,803 (room only); $2,160 (board); off-campus housing: $300–$525 per month.

Number of spaces in residence: 800

Percentage of international students: 2%

Percentage of out-of-province first-year students: 7%

Financial aid: Entrance scholarships valued from $200–$1,500 and bursaries from $200–$500, given to students entering the faculties of Arts, Science, Education, Music and General Studies. About 15% of first-year students receive financial awards.

Co-op programs: Geology

Services for students with disabilities: The Services for Students with Disabilities program provides support for students with learning, emotional, and physical disabilities.

Aboriginal students: Native Student Services; Services for First Nations and Aboriginal students; Elders Program ensures that the educational experience will be a successful and pleasant one for BU's First Nations and Aboriginal students and their families.

Student services: Academic, career, and personal counselling services, childcare centre, international students organization, learning skills centre, mature student services, peer support centre, tutorial services, writing centre.

Orientation Week is a great introduction to university life at BU, where you can do one if not all of the following: Get drunk, party, wake up and not be able to figure out exactly how you got there, or where you are, or who you were…, learn to function on the least possible sleep, get drunk, make five very very close friends whom you might see again, but probably not recognize when you're sober, get drunk, puke, party…well, you get the picture.

In September, don't miss Shinerama, the best campus party and annual fundraiser for cystic fibrosis research. After BU students help raise money for CF, a huge social gathering is held that usually draws more than 1,000 people. "Everyone goes to Shinerama," says one student, "You have such a great time and everything's a blur the next day."

ACADEMIC ISSUES

Brandon is most famous for its Music program, which was the first of its kind in Manitoba. It is among the most prestigious music programs in Canada and has garnered much respect internationally. BU offers a Bachelor of Arts program in Music Arts, and a Bachelor of Music program with options in general and applied music, school music, and performance and literature. There is a Master's program in performance and literature and music education.

BU has a long-standing commitment to the Native population of Manitoba. Twenty-five percent of BU's students are of Native backgrounds. "We had one of the first Native Studies departments in Canada," President Anderson boasts. The Native Studies department offers a new Bachelor of First Nations and Aboriginal Counselling program and Canada's first comprehensive program of its kind, the Elders Program, which includes spiritual and traditional counselling and performance of relevant ceremonies. The department also publishes the *Canadian Journal of Native Studies*, which is circulated internationally.

> **A Word to the Wise:**
>
> Register early; there's no guarantee that you'll get the courses you want, even the ones you need to graduate.

Brandon also offers a wide array of programs including Business Administration, Computer Science, Psychology, and Sociology. Other academic highlights include a program in Ichthyology (a.k.a. fish biology) and the School of Health Sciences' Psychiatry and Nursing degree programs.

Brandon may not have the academic reputation of U of T or McGill, but, as the Dean of Arts points out, "It has a lot of small classes, and we've always fought to maintain them." The median size of a first-year course is 37 people. Professors at Brandon know their students by face and name, and consequently know when you're ditching classes. Students have excellent relationships with BU's professors and many students can even attest to going for a drink with their profs after class. In the tradition of Oxford University in England,

In a Nut Shell

The university in a phrase: For those who find the University of Manitoba big and impersonal and the University of Winnipeg too radical, BU is a great place to get a solid education.

Best thing about the university: Small classes and personal attention from profs.

Worst thing about the university: Its conservative nature.

Most popular bird courses: Behaviour Modification (a.k.a. "B-Mod"): An easy A, a guaranteed B.

Hot spots to study on campus: The SUB (Knowles-Douglas Student Union Building).

Quietest spots to study on campus: The library.

Need for car and parking availability: Most students either walk or drive to school. A car is not necessary, but it's great to have. Good luck finding parking—it is a big problem on campus.

Sexually speaking: The romance situation at BU is bleak. "There are a lot of locals here," says one student. "People have known each other here for years, which tends to take the bloom off the rose."

Fraternities/sororities: A fra-rori-what?

Athletic facilities: Currently three teams known as the Bobcats: women's basketball, men's basketball, and men's ice hockey. There are also a number of different intramural sports to choose from.

Library facilities: John E. Robbins Library has over one million volumes. Online assistance can answer general reference questions such as "What is the population of Timbuktu?" The BU library is also a full depository of Manitoba Government Documents. Library study carrels wired for notebook computers.

Computer facilities: Students receive a personalized account, have unlimited Internet access, and access to over 160 PCs in computer labs across campus.

Weather: You'll learn about the brrr necessities. You haven't experienced winter (a.k.a. hell) until you've lived in Brandon. Because BU is set in the vast, open prairies, it's quite flat, so the wind chill is unbelievable.

Safety on campus: Student-run Safewalk Program escorts you around campus and off campus into the surrounding neighbourhoods.

Alumni: Douglas Campbell, former premier of Manitoba; Trent Frayne, columnist and sportswriter for *Maclean's*; Dr. Robert Howland, former chairman Atomic Energy Commission of Canada; Jim Lewthwaite, news editor, *Brandon Sun*; Dr. Doug Peters, former chief economist and senior vice-president of Toronto-Dominion Bank.

students are assigned a professor at the start of the school year who acts as their personal academic advisor.

REZ LIFE Residence at BU is assigned on a first-come first-served basis, so apply early. If you're coming from outside Brandon and you're in first year, then don't sweat because rez is guaranteed for you.

There are three possibilities for residence life at BU: McMaster Hall, a co-ed high rise; Flora Cowan Hall, for women; and Darrach Hall, for men. McMaster Hall is the largest residence and has 400 spaces in double and single rooms. One bonus about living in Mac Hall is that the washrooms are semiprivate, which means you share a washroom only with the room next door. McMaster Hall boasts a music practice room, a TV lounge, and a games room. If you're worried about fighting over the remote and reliving

life at home with your siblings, all rooms in McMaster Hall are wired with cable TV and high-speed cable Internet connections.

Flora Cowan Hall is a traditional women-only residence and has 210 spaces in single and double rooms. Flora Cowan features comfy and cozy lounges (one has a fireplace), multipurpose rooms, and a kitchenette. Flora Cowan Hall is known to be the most spirited for its many social and recreational events. "Flora Cowan is the best residence to live in, because it's a nice building and the women are really motivated to get involved in residence life."

Darrach Hall, a traditional men-only rez, houses 190 men in single and double rooms. Darrach Hall has free cable outlets, a weight room, and boasts the best TV lounge, complete with sports and movie channels.

Brandon's residence propaganda asks the question, "Why live anywhere else?" "Because it's too damn expen-

"A" for Academic Fraud

In 1972, an "associate professor" of the department of psychology played with the minds of BU faculty, staff and students. Martin Bohn, who taught classes during the 1971–72 school year, was exposed as being a taxicab driver by vocation. He fled the university, was later arrested, and pleaded guilty to 13 counts of fraud.

sive," is the answer given by many students. A single room in McMaster including a meal plan can run you about $620 a month, compared to the $300 to $500 a month you would spend living off campus.

Of course, living in rez is an incredible opportunity to make friends and meet new people. Another undeniable perk of living in rez is that you can wake up 6 minutes before class starts and make it to class on time. To minimize winter's bite, the three residences are connected to the dining hall via glass-enclosed tunnels, and the dining halls are in turn connected to the Student Union Building.

NIGHT LIFE

Brandon is not a cosmopolitan centre, but students don't seem to mind. Brandon has a lot of bars and going out is not as expensive as in Winnipeg. On campus, domestic brew at The SUDS bar/lounge flows cheaply. Don't miss the $1.95-a-mug deals. SUDS also offers different theme nights—Karaoke one night and Movie Night another. It also provides a venue for local talent to show their stuff—if you have a band, it's almost impossible to get booked at one of the off-campus bars, who favour out-of-town acts. Tone it down a notch and enjoy Coffee House Nights at SUDS for poetry readings and great music. Check out The Elephant Room Java Jive and have a stompin' time.

Off campus, popular drinking holes include the Winter Palace bar and The Double Decker Tavern. If you're starving for something other than the bar and pub scene, wine and dine at Over the Moon or The Princess Café greasy spoon. If you're looking for something quieter, catch a movie at the new Capital Theatre four-plex movie theatre.

ON BRANDON

Brandon, a.k.a. the Wheat City, has a population of 40,000 and is "Friendly Manitoba's" second-largest city. It is located two and a half hours away from Winnipeg. Brandon is a huge small town and boasts small-town warmth and hospitality. You can relax and enjoy the numerous parks around the city, or picnic on the banks of the Assiniboine River, which winds through the valley.

There is plenty to do here, from art galleries, museums, and theatres to cinemas, nightclubs, and bars. Throughout the year, the city offers festivals and events to keep you busy. Major attractions include the Brandon Jazz Festival and The Royal Manitoba Winter Fair, and movie buffs can enjoy the Brandon Film Festival.

Don't miss the International Pickle Festival. You'll have to see it to believe it.

University of Manitoba

By Monique Trottier

The first week of classes at the University of Manitoba is by far the most dynamic and energetic time of the year. The main Fort Garry campus, located on 274 hectares in south Winnipeg, on the inside of a loop in the Red River, is buzzing with more than 21,000 undergraduates attending barbecues, beer bashes, and, of course, classes. U of M's programs in Dentistry and Medicine are concentrated at the Bannatyne Campus in central Winnipeg, but most of the university's 78 degree, diploma, and certificate programs are based in the Fort Garry campus. Any tour of the university grounds will verify that U of M certainly is a city within the city.

As classes progress and the weather gets cooler, a peculiar phenomenon takes place: The number of students seen walking around campus dwindles. Have students discovered that they are not cut out for the rigours of university life and dropped out? No, they have simply taken to the tunnels. U of M has an underground tunnel system that would make even the most winter-ready prairie dog jealous. During the winter months (and autumn months, depending on Mother Nature's wrath), this cozy, subterranean warren serves as a passageway between buildings, allowing students and faculty to avoid the bracing cold of the Manitoban winter. Unfortunately, it takes far longer to traverse the campus by taking the tunnels than by taking the direct route above ground.

By relying mostly on the tunnels to get from place to place around the campus, people fail to take in the beauty of the campus. U of M, established in 1877, is western Canada's oldest university. Two of the original campus buildings still standing are the Administration Building and Tache Hall, both built in Georgian style in 1912. Another building of interest is the Wallace Building, erected in 1986, home to the Department of Geological Sciences. It has a post-modern design, where the structural and mechanical systems that are exposed are painted in a variety of bright Lego colours. Inside is a small museum and display, which includes seismographic devices that record and display earthquake data from around the world.

CAMPUS CULTURE

More than 85% of the student population are enrolled in undergraduate studies, and most are residents of Manitoba. Students from Winnipeg tend to hang out with long-time friends from high school, whereas the students from outside of Winnipeg tend to live in residence and make close-knit friendships within residence. The rest of the students are from Ontario, typically northern Ontario, or are international students.

U of M is characteristically a day campus. Despite night classes offered, by nine in the evening the campus is deserted, except during exam time, when students jam-pack the libraries and study carrels. The result is an overall apathetic student body, with a fundamental lack of support for the Bisons, the university's sports teams. The Bisons' intercollegiate competition includes football, volleyball, basketball, hockey, gymnastics, swimming, and other major sports. The Bisons have exceptionally good women's basketball and men's and women's volleyball teams. These games usually have a good turnout. Manitoba played host to Summer Pan-Am Games and as a result many of U of M's athletic facilities have been renovated and upgraded, including the Frank Kennedy Physical Education Centre, the Max Bell Centre, University Stadium, and the Pan-Am Gymnasium.

On campus, The Club pool hall is a choice hangout for students. The Club is open early in the mornings, perfect for cram sessions and adding final touches to a paper due that same morning, and late in the evening for pool, snooker, and video games. The faculty lounges are also popular meeting places and the chosen locale for many concerts, beer bashes, and barbecues throughout the year. The Black Hole Theatre produces a number of plays during the regular session.

Vital Statistics

Address: University of Manitoba, Winnipeg, Manitoba

Admissions office: (204) 474-8808

Website: www.umanitoba.ca

Total enrollment: 21,083

Male-female ratio: 46 to 54

Percentage of international students: 3%

Percentage of out-of-province students: 11.7%

Cut-off grade for admissions: Arts: 63%; Science: 63%; Engineering: 73%

Tuition fees: Arts: $2,893; Science: $3,212

Co-op programs: Computer Science, Ecology, Environmental Science.

Financial aid: 1,000 admission scholarships and over 2,300 in-course scholarships each year.

Facilities for students with disabilities: Disability Services.

Aboriginal students: Aboriginal Student Centre, Aboriginal Focus Programs, Aboriginal Business Education Program.

Student services: Academic, career, and personal counselling, chaplains, health services, housing services, on-campus child care.

For students coming from cozy stamp-size high schools, U of M can seem daunting. You can easily get lost in the shuffle and no one cares what you look like. U of M students are generally laid-back and relaxed. No one cares if you live or die on campus, so naturally, students wear whatever they want.

A Word to the Wise:

1. Student life at U of M is hardly ever portrayed as glamorous. The cold winter temperatures, the prairies, the lack of school spirit, and the vastness of the campus almost encourage students to be cynical about Winnipeg and their university. But university life, no matter what campus you are on, is what you make of it. There are plenty of things to do and see at U of M, and in Winnipeg; you just have to get out there and do them.

2. Registration can be a nightmare. If you take too long to punch in the codes, the system hangs up on you. It is a good idea to work with a partner when registering for the first time. This way, if the course you have selected is full or unavailable, one person can punch in the next set of codes while the other searches through the registration guide for another section. One advantage of this system is that Monday morning and Friday afternoon classes can be avoided, ensuring every weekend is a long weekend.

As for clubs and societies, the university's fraternities and sororities do not have a strong presence on campus. Popular organizations tend to be the sports clubs and the student councils, as well as the colleges. Membership to one of the colleges encourages student involvement in the college's student council and participation in college-sponsored events. Sign up for sports clubs like wall climbing, scuba diving, and kayaking.

Each faculty generally has some form of student government, as do the residences. The main council is UMSU, the U of M Student Union. The council is elected annually in the spring and there are a number of student representative positions available for first-year students. Get a jump-start on your university career and address the issue of school spirit (or lack thereof). Make a difference and join Amnesty International or Anti-Racist Action. UMFM 101.5, U of M's campus radio station now broadcasts throughout Winnipeg, which will hopefully boost morale and school spirit.

ACADEMIC ISSUES The size of the university, in terms of student population and physical layout, has often been the source of alienation for a number of students. At first, newcomers to U of M may find the campus huge and intimidating. Scrap the old advice about picturing a crowd in their underwear so that they seem less intimidating. To make the transition from high school to university easier to swallow, U of M prescribes a course called Introduction to University. Introduction to University is exactly that—a course that focuses on essentials to survive and succeed in university, including study habits and note-taking techniques.

U of M also offers University 1, a compulsory first-year program for all students entering directly from high school. University 1 is an attempt to address the concerns of students making the transition from high school to university. In University 1 students register for credit courses from a variety of faculties and schools, and participate in a series of orientation and advising experiences to support their academic studies. Its aim is to ensure that students have the necessary interests, aptitudes, and abilities that are needed to be admitted into year two in their chosen faculty. The program does not affect the time or money it takes to complete a university degree.

Situated in the heart of Canadian agriculture, U of M offers agriculture-related programs such as Agribusiness, Agroecology, and Crop and Livestock Management. U of M also offers programs in Architecture, Arts, Dentistry, Education, Engineering, Human Ecology, Law, Management, Medicine, Nursing, Pharmacy, Physical Education and Recreation Studies, Science, Social Work, and the schools of Art, Dental Hygiene, Medical Rehabilitation, and Music.

First-year courses are typically large, with over 250 people per session for courses such as Psychology, Biology, and even English. The key to registering in smaller classes is to look for the class location in the registration guide. Courses offered in the colleges often have smaller class sizes.

REZ LIFE

The residences at the U of M provide 950 lucky students with the opportunity to live on campus. By far, the best thing about living in residence it that the residence acts as a small community. The residents often share classes together, create their own study groups, and participate in a number of extracurricular activities, such as car rallies, inter-mural sports, boat cruises, parties, and field trips. Although living in residence often means minimal privacy and noise disturbances, there is a heightened sense of university spirit and community among residence students.

There are five residences on the Fort Garry campus, Speechly and Tache residences, University College, St. Andrew's College, and St. John's College. Each residence has its own unique characteristics. Speechly and Tache fall under the same administration but retain their own character. Tache Hall is the oldest and largest residence, with a warm and friendly ambiance complete with oak trim and open fireplaces. Mary Speechly Hall houses 245 residents in a 10-story contemporary high rise, with the main and 10th floors serving as lounges. Many rooms have a great view of the Red River to the south.

UC, opened in 1964, provides lecture and office space for the Faculty of Arts. Stargazers may be interested to know that UC houses the university planetarium. The college residence is located in the seven-story wing. Each floor serves as a smaller

"My only other memory of Winnipeg is the sensation of having felt for a moment what life in the arctic regions must be like."

Lefcadis Hearn, American writer, "A Winter Journey to Japan," Nov. 1890, *Harper's.*

community within the larger residence community. Floor parties and inter-floor sports competitions are often the best ways to meet people in UC. Students who are "allergic to cleaning" may be interested to know that weekly maid service with linen is available in UC. UC also has unique floors, such as Scholars' Floor, Seniors' Floor, and Outdoor Adventure Floor. Speechly/Tache and UC have had a healthy rivalry for many years, and during the first week of classes there are a number of sports events and tug-of-war contests between the two residences.

The smaller colleges, St. John's College and St. Andrew's College, offer students a quieter environment, but the same sense of a close-knit community. St. Andrew's College is the first Ukrainian-language college opened by the Orthodox Church in North America. It is home to a large Ukrainian cultural and religious library. St. Andrew's is located on the far west corner of the campus and is characteristically a quiet residence. St. John's College, one of the founding colleges of the university, includes a chapel and residence as well as teaching and administrative areas.

NIGHT LIFE

Night life on campus includes sports events, Wise Guys Bar and Grill, and socials. A "social" is a Manitoban word meaning a party held to raise money for the organization sponsoring the event. The most popular socials tend to be the homecoming social, the Halloween social, and the Management socials. For rez students seeking evening entertainment off campus, car pools tend to be the most reliable form of transportation because the bus routes onto campus are infrequent after midnight.

There are definitely plenty of places to go and people to see off campus. Popular watering holes include Scandals, Die Maschine, and the Palladium dance clubs. Check out the Pembina Hotel bar, St. Charles Hotel, and Shooters pool hall, where you can test those smooth pickup lines. Wise Guys Bar and Grill, The King's Head, the Riverside Roxy, and Ice Works also guarantee a good time.

O'Reilly and O'Toole's Irish pubs and the Round Table, an Irish steakhouse and lounge all guarantee a good time. If the idea of green beer leaves you feeling a little, well, green, you can always indulge on dessert and sip an Irish cream coffee in a trendy café or coffee house near campus. A little farther from campus, there are a number of country-music bars for line-dancing lovers. Film buffs can catch a movie at The Silver City

In a Nut Shell

The university in a phrase: The University of Manitoba is as large and diverse as its student population.

Best thing about the university: The campus socials, the lounges, and the recreational facilities.

Worst thing about the university: The parking. Parking passes are released on a first-come, first-serve basis, and the good spots are quickly filled.

Favourite professors: John Rempel and David Arnason (English), George Toles (Theatre), Peter St. John (Political Science), Robert Altemeyer (Psychology).

Most popular bird courses: Geology (a.k.a. "Rocks for Jocks") and Computer Usage (a.k.a. "Computer Useless").

Quietest spots to study on campus: The third floor of the Elizabeth Dafoe Library, the Sciences & Technology Library, and the Sony Study Centre in the Management building.

Hot spots to study on campus: The Arts lounge and carrels, the Science lounge, and the second floor of the Elizabeth Dafoe Library.

Need for car and parking availability: Accessibility to campus is limited so a car is almost a necessity. Parking passes are available but good spots are limited. Many people end up parking in U-Lot, the second-farthest lot from campus. Loony Lot is even farther and in the winter, the wind blows across the soccer fields and parking lots, making for a frigid walk to class.

Sexually speaking: The women are far more attractive than the men. But during the winter months everyone is concealed in heavy winter clothing anyway. Regardless of unflattering attire, the weekly edition of the student paper, the *Manitoban*, has an entire page devoted to personal ads. GLASS (Gay Lesbian and Bisexual Association of Students and Staff) is located in University Centre. GLASS has a small reference library, free safe-sex supplies, and information and support for students and staff.

Fraternities/sororities: They do not have a huge presence on campus. Frat parties are heavily promoted on the student bulletin boards, usually with coloured-paper photocopies that use Calvin Klein models for images.

Athletic facilities: New facilities, makeovers and facelifts, and resurfaced tennis courts resulting from the 1999 Summer Pan-Am Games.

Library facilities: There are 12 university libraries, two located on the Bannatyne campus. The larger libraries include Elizabeth Dafoe Library and the Sciences & Technology Library. Self-serve photocopiers are located in the libraries—but buy a copy card because only a few machines take coins.

Computer facilities: IBM and Mac computer labs are scattered across campus. Each student has e-mail access and space allocated on the server for a web page. Printing and student computer advisors are available.

Weather: Winnipeg weather varies, not only from day to day but from hour to hour, especially during spring and fall. Rainy mornings may be sweltering by noon and lightly snowing in the evening. In winter, students learn about the brrrr essentials and how to brave the cold. Keep warm by piling on layers of wool sweaters. You'll need them. Also, make sure your car is plugged in. The campus security office provides booster service during the winter. Summers are beautiful and warm, but beware of mosquitoes, "the seasonal provincial birds." Stock up on insect repellent.

Safety on campus: Security Services, Safewalk, and blue light phones around campus to contact security office.

Alumni: Izzy Asper; Manitoba premier Gary Filmon; Assembly of First Nations Grand Chiefs Phil Fontaine; Marshall McLuhan, communications guru; Heather Robertson, author; Ed Schreyer, former governor general.

Frosh week: Frosh week is a barbecue and beer extravaganza. Each morning different faculties sponsor a pancake breakfast. Afternoons are devoted to barbecues and beer bashes. The key is to watch for the B**R posters, listen for the music and scope out the promotional tents offering free souvenirs, drinks, and condoms.

multiplex movie theatre located in St. Vital mall or at Cinema City, a discount theatre with an admission price of $2.50. Two-for-one coupons are often available in the student newspaper, the *Manitoban*, and Tuesday nights are half-price.

During the summer, festivals are the main events and in the winter months bars, socials, and movies are the favoured forms of entertainment. For those brave souls who dare to venture into the bitter cold, there is also tobogganing and skating at a number of parks in Winnipeg.

ON WINNIPEG Winnipeg has 650,000 of the warmest and friendliest people ever. There is a blending and co-existence of more than 43 different cultural groups who call

Winnipeg home. There is an abundance of restaurants that serve up traditional and exotic food, from roti to couscous, from bannock to dim sum. Winnipeg also boasts more than 130 days of annual festivals and celebrations. Oktoberfest, a German festival with polka bands, beer swilling, and sausage sizzling, attracts students by the bus load. On its student night, city buses are chartered to provide transportation to and from campus, and students from Winnipeg's universities and colleges party together into the wee hours of the morning.

If it's culture you crave, take a peek at the numerous theatres, museums, and galleries across the city. For those on a tight budget, student admission prices and half-price days are regular features at a number of cultural events. For less than $20, students can see The Royal Winnipeg Ballet and the Winnipeg Symphony Orchestra perform on dress rehearsal nights. For sports enthusiasts, the CFL Winnipeg Blue Bombers football team, and the Goldeyes, the Northern League baseball team, provide excellent entertainment.

Winnipeg is blessed with 2,300 hours of sunshine annually and guarantees a white Christmas. You may be interested to know that Winnipeg is the Slurpee capital of the world. On average, 4,500 Slurpees are sold per 7-11 store each month in Canada, but in Winnipeg, 6,800 Slurpees are slurped on average.

Winnipegers are proud of international achievements. For example, Valour Road, formerly called Pine Street, in the west end of Winnipeg, was named in honour of three young soldiers living on the street who each earned the Victoria Cross for bravery.

Did you know that there is a connection between Winnie-the-Pooh and *Winni*peg? Winnie-the-Pooh was inspired by a Canadian World War I regimental mascot called Winnipeg, and a bronze statue at the Assiniboine Park Zoo celebrates the connection. Another cartoon favourite, Bugs Bunny, was designed and christened by Winnipeg's Charles Thorason. And speaking of looney toons, in addition to producing over 30 million loonies annually, Winnipeg's Royal Canadian Mint produces coins for up to 40 different countries.

University of Winnipeg

By Chen Chekki

The U of W story began nearly 130 years ago as a log building named Manitoba College. Sixty years later, in 1938, it transformed into United College. The province of Manitoba later granted it university status, chartering it as The University of Winnipeg on July 1, 1967. Most current and former students now acknowledge it as one of Canada's pristine medium-sized undergraduate universities that's highly reputed for the accessibility and attention instructors give to their students.

Upon approach to the front of the south campus, a sense of royalty is felt upon first glimpse of stately Wesley Hall—a.k.a. castle building—which literally looks like a castle. At 105 years old, it is rumoured to be haunted by supernatural entities, though this has never been confirmed by CSIS. In summer, precision-flowered landscaping lines the walkways and manicured greens out front, complimented by a huge, 25 ton astroid-sized rock. This is one of the few universities that boasts a traditional September rock-climbing competition — the Great Rock Climb.

If you're one of the unfortunate souls to have arrived by car, may your hunt for a parking spot begin. There is no student-designated parking, because in the urban jungle core of downtown Winnipeg parking space is at a premium. Parking is a breeze during off-peak hours or when classes are not in session, but when school's on—good luck. Here, mastery of parallel parking is a survival skill. Even if you get a spot, you have to run outside to repark when your time expires every one or two hours. Regardless of where you catch a spot, make sure you strictly adhere to time limits and park properly. Around here, battle-ready parking ticketers will track your car like an enemy submarine. You will alleviate major stress by taking one of the 12 reliable bus routes leading to U of W, biking, or walking.

North of the castle building are a bunch of blander-looking buildings melded into one big building making up most of the university. Walking in from the south entrance, you'll be in the five-storied Centennial Hall. Security personnel are seen lounging in a bunker-like enclave, followed by students and staff using the single campus ATM, as well as small pockets of students, staff, and potential loiterers just standing around. The InfoBooth is a short distance away, where the infamous "know it alls" on campus are seen, capable of answering any question, ranging from a prof's phone number to the facts of life. The recently remodelled bookstore is just a few more footsteps down the hall, where September lineups are known to stretch out the store entrance almost as far as the eye can see. The new Quickstart Textbook Reservation System, which pre-orders texts for first-year students, is designed to reduce such lineups. As far as getting around is concerned, the choice is yours—whether you transport yourself up to the classroom-filled floors of Centennial via elevator, stairs, or the vastly preferred escalator route.

To the east of Centennial lies Riddell Hall's cafeteria, where the lunch specials are tempting, luring students and profs to power up side by side.

Below Riddell is the new three-level Bulman Student Centre. It houses the Students' Association, student paper, and other critical student groups. The centre also hosts three free phones. It's a place where students come to play pool, visit the arcade, study, and take the almighty student nap on one of a few sofas, futons, or cushy chairs. For the germaphobic type, here are the newest and generally cleanest public washrooms to be found on campus.

On the Northern edge of campus is Lockhart Hall, consisting mostly of stark, dimly lit halls leading to classrooms. For those who still wish to puff their way to their graves, it also has the only smoking area on campus.

Vital Statistics

Address: 515 Portage Ave., Winnipeg, Manitoba, R3B 2E9

Telephone number: (204) 786-7811

Website: www.uwinnipeg.ca

Total enrolment: 6,000

Male-female ratio: 39 to 61

Percentage of international students: 4% (approx.)

Average entering grades: Early Admission: 70% average on best three university entrance courses, including at least one of university entrance English or Mathematics. Conditional Status: 50-59.99% average on best three university entrance courses, including at least one of university entrance English or Mathematics. Requires participation in first-year support program. Not eligible for early consideration.

Tuition fees (domestic): Arts and Education: $3100 [30 credit hours] Science: $3600 [30 credit hours] Visa Student: Arts and Education: $5500 Science: $6300

Residence fees: No residences. Private accommodations are between $300 and $500 per month throughout Winnipeg and footsteps away from the U of W. Students' Association operates a housing registry.

Co-op programs: Biology, Chemistry, Environmental Studies.

Financial aid: Over $500,000 in entrance and undergraduate scholarships plus $70,000 in bursaries.

Services for students with disabilities: The Office for Students with Special Needs arranges tailored assistance based on individual need. The university offers wheelchair accessible buildings and ramps, mobility assistance, transcription/typing assistance, note takers, provision of educational materials in alternate formats, etc.

Student services: Student Health Plan; Students' Association; Housing and Parking Registry; Interfaith Centre; Exams Registry; Food Bank; free phones and printing at Bulman Centre; *Arts and Science Review* journal; Peer Support Services; Petrified Sole Used Book Store; *Uniter* [student newspaper]; Student Employment Centre; LGBT Centre; Photo Club; Women's Centre; EcoMAFIA; UWSA Handbook; arcades/pool, etc.

The most intense studying occurs in upper levels of the library, where the strong, silent type can retreat in private carrels and enjoy ample sunlight in many areas and munch on snuck-in food.

Another top study location is the fifth floor of Centennial, which has an open, sunny feel, as well as Bulman, where you'll find sleep-addicted students glued to the best cushy seats on campus.

CAMPUS CULTURE

U of W has a diverse student body, although the Asian economic flu has decreased the number of international students coming from that region. Students here will have no problem meeting people of all different ethnicities, colours, and religions. In fact, there are 13 ethnic and religious associations on campus, plus over 26 other student groups, including special interest, entertainment, and academic. The added social flavour of these groups attracts more attention than student politics, which most find as interesting as an overly ripe banana. Voter turnouts are consistently low, and most students are like deer caught in the headlights to scandals rocking the Students' Association.

The mood at U of W is generally cheery, which is common amongst Winnipegers in a province where the licence-plate logo reads "Friendly Manitoba." When the mercury hits −35° Celsius you can still go almost anywhere and be greeted by a

A Word to the Wise:

1. Dress warmly in winter or risk losing valuable body parts, or whole body, to frostbite.

2. Take advantage of free printing and phones down in Bulman.

3. Stay alert of drunk panhandlers near the university and don't give, or else you'll just attract more of them.

4. Keeping valuables in lockers is risky—locker break-ins have been a problem here.

5. Mind all parking rules and time limits because parking ticketers slither everywhere, viewing your car as their primary source of income.

6. You can save a bundle by chasing down used text ads placed on crammed bulletin boards all over campus. If you place an ad on them, monitor it constantly or else yours will quickly wind up buried by at least five others.

In a Nut Shell

The university in a phrase: A cosy, intimate place to learn and socialize.

Best thing about the university: Accessibility and attention given by profs to students, and friendly atmosphere.

Worst thing about the university: Drunks and panhandlers lurking near the university, and parking.

Favourite professors: D.A. Chekki (Sociology); A. Turner (English); W. Carlyle (Geography); D. Topper (History); Tomchuk (Physics); Kerr (Physics); L. Carrothers (Political Science); E. Allen (Psychology); Zhao (Statistics).

Most popular bird courses: History of Science 29.2900/6; Astronomy 38.1701/6.

Hot spot to study on campus: Mezzanine of Bulman Student Centre.

Quietest spot to study on campus: The fifth floor of the library is super-quiet, followed by the fifth floor of Centennial, and during off-peak hours, the Bulman Student Centre.

Need for car and parking availability: Don't drive if you don't have to. If you're a full-time student—parking is a nightmare, unless you are willing to pay for it. But searching for it is stressful, especially when you're trying to make those early morning classes. Parking meters and "free zones" allow only one to two hours before you have to run out to repark or risk at least a $15 fine. This is difficult to do when you are trapped in classes all day. Walking, biking, or transit will save you BIG stress, money, and time.

Sexually speaking: Whether you're hetero, lesbian, gay, or bi, you should have no trouble finding a soul mate on this campus. Students from all walks of life manage to find that special someone, so there's no reason why you can't, unless you choose not to.

Fraternities/sororities: What's a fraternity? Sorori-what?

Athletic facilities: Duckworth Centre was built to transform out-of-shape students into in-shape ones. So whether you choose to jog, lift weights, or play sports, the facility is first class and like SNL's Hanz and Franz used to say it is always ready to "pump you up!"

Library facilities: The library uses the intuitive computerized search system known as Mercury, and students can also access U of Brandon, U of Manitoba, and the public library system. Reference staff are super-friendly beings who never leave a question unanswered. On the downside, callous feet develop standing in line to use one of the few working copiers when classes are in full swing. Your day is brightened by sunlight that shines in all the right places, making for a comfortable, quiet study and research environment.

Weather: You learn the harsh meaning of the term "Winterpeg" when snow and ice hit the city hard for about five bone-chilling months. But Winnipeggers are known to take more pride in their winters than summers. Not to scare anyone, but daytime temps once bottomed out at –41ºC in February of '96. The instructions are simple: Dress like an Eskimo for most of November through March.

Safety on campus: The university offers a mobile security patrol that also gives student escorts to home or vehicle within certain boundaries. Emergency phones and video surveillance have proliferated throughout campus.

Alumni: Fred Penner; former Winnipeg mayors Bill Norrie and Susan Thompson; Lloyd Axworthy (Minister of Foreign Affairs); Margaret Lawrence; Brad Roberts (Crash Test Dummies); Michael Phelps (CEO of West Coast Energy); William Ross (Canadian ambassador to Columbia).

smile (or at least a friendly person). Even the drunks and panhandlers nearby the university are considered relatively harmless and easygoing. U of W is one very happy place.

The university is sandwiched between CBC Radio/Television and the Greyhound-Greygoose bus depot, so familiar news reporters are often seen roaming around campus with their cameras, and buses are constantly coming in and out. Take a short stroll down the sidewalk and discover all the amenities of a big city—Winnipeg's third-largest shopping mall, department stores, and countless restaurants. It is also right across from one of Winnipeg's busiest thoroughfares, making it all seem like there's more action outside the university than inside.

Liberal-mindedness oozes out of this place like lava from a volcano. The president of the Students' Association committed to a centrefold spread in his underwear for the student paper, using portions of the library for the photo shoot! Beaming through citywide airwaves is the campus radio station CKUW, broadcasting mainly alternative talk and music shows, such as Testoster-Tone, Dreamweapon, and The Sex Files. The Lesbian, Gay, and Bisexual Centre, which also distributes free safe-sex supplies, is well supported and accepted by the student body. The U of W serves as a place where you are more respected for being unique rather than similar.

ACADEMIC ISSUES

Programs at this university have been evolving at a steady pace over the past few years. The U of W was Manitoba's first university to offer telecourses (live broadcast classroom lectures) through television, enabling TV dinner couch potatoes to channel-surf between their lecture and their favourite soap. The university often acts as a feed school to professional programs such as Medicine and Dentistry, with many graduates receiving acceptances into grad schools and professional programs all over Canada. Popular co-op programs and joint programs with Red River College include Applied Biology, Chemistry, Environmental Studies, and Communications. There is also a new dual-degree program in Engineering with the University of Minnesota's Institute of Technology.

Students can now complete their entire Education degree here rather than do their final year at the University of Manitoba, as was formerly the case. The university recently purchased a nearby building for $4.7 million to free up space for the Department of Theatre and Drama and for Communications courses. There will also be a $1.5 million expansion of the Duckworth Centre Athletic Facility, scheduled to be completed by August 2000.

Science courses are known to have first-rate lab demonstrators, with plenty of attention given to individual students—a U of W hallmark. A few lucky students have been known to wind up in first-year Chemistry labs with as little as five students! Intro Psych, Bio, and Astronomy are generally huge, and one or two oversubscribed "bird" courses, like History of Science, sometimes force overflow students to park their butts on the floor for the first week until room switches are made.

Course emphasis here is primarily undergraduate (five graduate degrees are offered), very liberal, and interdisciplinary.

STUDENT FACILITIES/SERVICES

The quality of facilities and services provided to U of W students is pleasing. Newly introduced in 1998 was the comprehensive Student Health Plan, in which full-time students are automatically enrolled and part-timers are given the option. Notable coverage includes 80% of prescription drug costs up to $2,500 per year, and 70% of vision expenses (including an eye exam) up to $100 every two years. This by itself exceeds Manitoba Health coverage and is seen as one of the best perks from attending this university. Student Health Services furthers this by offering a Wellness program, medical referrals, blood pressure screening, and other health-related services.

The Student Employment Centre posts many jobs that aren't found in HRDC search engines or newspapers. It also hosts the annual Job Fair so students can learn about a variety of careers in the public and private sector.

U of W does not have student residences, but private accommodations in downtown Winnipeg are plentiful and reasonably priced, considering every amenity you need is right nearby. The Students' Association provides a free housing-registry service.

The Office for Students with Special Needs accommodates registration assistance, class materials in alternate formats, note takers, and many other services tailored for each student. The university is accessible to persons with physical challenges. Proving its accessibility, a visually impaired student recently graduated at the very top of the convocating class.

A food bank operated in partnership with Winnipeg Harvest serves to supply staples to students and alumni.

Students fearful of the price of new texts can go to the Petrified Sole Used Book Store. Prices are okay, but students have to buy early to get the text they want due to fast sellouts. Better bargains can be had through private ads on bulletin boards everywhere.

Say "Cheese"! The Photo Club is open to student membership for a small fee, and is complete with darkroom, processing, and printmaking equipment.

The student newspaper, *The Uniter*, begs for student contributions. It is not the exclusive club most people think it is. Paper staff are generally a lively, energetic, approachable bunch who always welcome visitors to the office to write, learn, and goof around a bit.

Student counsellors and Peer Advisors are nonjudgemental listeners who provide advice on all pressing personal issues, and have special expertise on Native concerns.

Whether you turn into a real-world go-getter after graduation, or an overeducated bum, The Alumni Association awaits you. For a $10 fee, your membership entitles you to continued library privileges, and discounts from the on-campus computer store and the Duckworth Athletic Centre.

NIGHT LIFE

Campus socials where "alcohol" is the key word rarely turn out to be huge. There are no on-campus pubs, so most weekend partying occurs off campus. Winnipeg is a sprawling town where night life gets clustered into various bars throughout the city. Some popular places for students to go—and let's face it, screw the homework and get wasted—are Die Maschine, Mirrors Pub-Club, U4IA, and Zaxx on Jefferson. There are plenty of others, but that will depend on the kind and age of peers you're with, and the type of music you like. There's a place for almost everyone here. You just have to search it out.

ON WINNIPEG

As the geographic centre of North America and home to about 650,000 people, Winnipeg (Winterpeg) is not the snooze-fest or icebox people think it is. With 2,300 annual hours of sunlight it might as well be known as Sunpeg. Snow melts away in April and for about five months, gorgeous summers pump so much dry heat, it would impress even a Floridian. This city could be thought of as a recreational urban jungle with over 850 parks and the largest number of elm trees and urban deer (over 600) than any other North American city. People breath easy in Winnipeg's clean air, rendering smog alerts nonexistent and a clear view of the breathtaking Northern Lights. It is one of only three Canadian cities that guarantee a white Christmas, and hosted Canada's largest-ever sporting event—the Pan-Am Games—in the summer of '99. Must-see places are The Forks, where you can shop, dine, and traverse the riverwalk…when it's not overflowing. The Art Gallery is itself art, looking like a concrete slice of triangular Swiss cheese. It displays the largest Inuit art collection on the continent. See the Royal Canadian Mint pump out some of the 30 million loonies it produces annually, an Imax movie at Portage Place, a horse race at the Assiniboia Downs, or explore the indoor 1.2-mile downtown walkway system with over 900 businesses. You may choose to dine in one of over a thousand quality restaurants in the city or go for a McDonald's Big Mac^{TM}. Winnipeg is only an hour's drive from the US border, and there was a time when Manitobans could do their groceries for a better deal in tiny Grand Forks. But Canada's limp loonie has reversed the traffic flow. Winnipeg's ethnically diverse population (largest number of Aboriginals of any Canadian city and largest Francophone population outside Quebec), plus over 43 other ethnic groups across Manitoba and an ample selection of nightclubs, make Winnipeg a happening, snowman-hugging party town. Dig it?

Brock University

By Travis Mason

A little big school or a big little school, however you put it, Brock University is situated in St. Catharines, Ontario, atop the tree- and trail-filled natural wonder known as the Niagara Escarpment. No matter which view of Brock you take, the juxtaposition is meant to suggest that whatever one's academic, social, or personal needs or desires might be, Brock is able to deliver. There is a sense, however, that anything cited as one of Brock's many strengths can also, and with some validity, be considered one of its weaknesses.

Founded in 1964 (and still not a single loss in CIAU football!) Brock became a sort of concrete castle of undergraduate academia looming above the city of shift-working lunch-bucketeers below. Although the city and Brock are neatly segregated geographically, they do tend to exist in a more or less symbiotic manner. Brock's annual economic impact upon the Niagara region (of which St. Catharines is the largest city) is $190 million. Let us assume the obvious, that this is a positive impact. In return, the city of St. Catharines provides ample resources for the university's co-ops and new Experience*Plus!* and MedExperience*Plus!* "careers-oriented work experience program[s]." The programs' new slogan "Your Career Starts Here!" has some within the Brock community quietly concerned about the future direction the university plans to take.

St. Catharines' population and position is mainly a result of the impact industry has had on it over the years. It has come to be known as a factory town, home to such companies as General Motors, Hayes-Dana, and Thompson Products. Because of its location in the Niagara region, however, the industry presence is not necessarily a bad thing for the university crowd. Niagara and its surrounding area provide enough cultural fodder for those who have both the interest and the finances. If you have some money and a means of transportation, you can do almost anything, from taking in dinner theatre in Port Dalhousie to downing shooters at a downtown bar. If your means are limited (as is almost inevitable for most university students) then so are your choices. There are still a lot of choices, though, so do not be discouraged; be imaginative. And be aware that there are several opportunities to take advantage of your student status to receive discounts on anything from a Whopper Combo to tickets to the Shaw Festival in Niagara-on-the-Lake.

In an attempt to add to—and in the process help define—the region's dedication to local art and culture, the campus, both indoors and out, includes a veritable exhibition of quite possibly some of the ugliest sculptures you might ever see. The most famous (infamous?) of these is the large, hollow (both literally *and* figuratively) horizontal rocket/phallic whatever, the "She-Wolf." The art is not all bad, of course, not by a long shot. There is a new addition this year just outside Decew Residence that seems interesting, not to mention slightly more aesthetically pleasing.

CAMPUS CULTURE

Despite the myth that Brock is a university inhabited mostly by locals (dispelled by the fact that local high school students want to get the hell out of this town, as high school students anywhere are wont to do), 65% of first-year students are from outside the Niagara region. This includes international and out-of-province students. There are many clubs and organizations that reflect the diversity of the student population. During Orientation Week tables are set up in a common area outside the Alumni building to give new students an opportunity to see what is available and encourage participation. These clubs are student-run and those behind the tables are generally very approachable. Students can also become involved in the Brock community in a number of other ways, both directly and indirectly, depending on one's preferences. If you are interested in journalism or politics, the *Brock Press* is always searching for willing writers and editors; if that seems a little too committed for your taste, write a letter to the editor or send a short "unclassified" to that hot girl/guy in your math class whose mere presence is responsible for your failing grade on the last quiz. Brock Radio is finally up and running (CFBU FM 103.7) and reflects as much as anything on campus the cultural diversity and desire for real alternative radio programming. Brock's literary arts journal, *The Harpweaver*, a faculty/student collaboration, is entering its sixth year of publication and is looking stronger than ever, with excellent local and international lit-

Vital Statistics

Address: 500 Glenridge Ave., St. Catharines, Ontario, L2S 3A1

Admissions office: (905) 688-5550 ext. 3434

Website: www.brocku.ca

Total enrollment: 10,453

Male-female ratio: 43 to 57

Percentage of out-of-province first-year students: 0.5%

Average entering grades: Humanities/Social Science: 70%; Math and Science: 70–80%; Physical Education: 70%; Co-op: 80%

Tuition fees: $814.60/credit; includes all ancillary costs.

Residence fees: Single: $2,720; double: $2,445; Village Residence: $2,980; plus meals plans.

Percentage of students in residence: 14%

Financial aid: OSAP; various entrance scholarships and bursaries. Student employment, especially with the new Experience*Plus!,* whose website is expected to post 2,000 jobs by December 1999.

Co-op programs: Accounting, Business Administration

Services for students with disabilities: Special Needs offers academic accommodations for special-needs students and provides technical support. Wheelchair-accessible buildings.

Aboriginal students: Brock Native Students' Association; Native Student Advisor

Student services: Counsellors and therapists for personal counselling; academic advising; Career Services; Child Care, Computer Based Training; Health Services; Sexual Harassment Office; Student Development; International Services.

erature, visual arts, and book reviews. Of the many conferences that take place on campus throughout the year, one of the most widely recognized is the "Two Days of Canada Conference," a multidisciplinary event with talks given by an international array of respected scholars concerned with all things Canadian.

If arts and politics aren't your favourite ways of getting involved in extra curricular activities, don't worry. Brock's sports and recreation facilities are among the best in the country. St. Catharines itself has been recognized as the sports capital of Canada (okay, it's also been recognized by Johnny Carson as the doughnut capital, so draw your own conclusions). In 1999, for example, St. Catharines played host to the World Rowing Championships, with Brock's residences acting as Athlete's Village. There is a seemingly endless supply of intramural sports and activities that range from co-ed water polo, basketball, and floor hockey to fencing, yoga, and aerobics. State-of-the-art rowing and swimming facilities, as well as the addition of Harrison Hall, the new Student Health Services and Athletic Therapy Clinic building, have all helped to establish Brock's credibility as a university that can contribute to athletics both locally and internationally.

What is lacking at Brock is the opportunity for greater interaction between students who live on campus and those who don't. There is an ongoing project that is meant to solve this problem by offering the opportunity for off-campus students to participate in any residence activities of which they might otherwise be left unaware, called, appropriately enough, Brock's Off-Campus Society. This may help to spread the award-winning school spirit displayed in residences—one that the rest of the school for the most part doesn't yet know exists.

ACADEMIC ISSUES The seminar system is an informal yet remarkably rigorous way of escaping the clutches of big, boring lectures filled with note taking and the drone of a professor's voice. As a required component of their credit, small groups (about 20) of students meet for one hour per week to discuss lecture material. In disciplines outside the Humanities, labs and tutorials are the seminar's equivalent. Considered by most to be Brock's greatest asset, the real learning occurs in the seminar room. Sometimes the conversations that start in the seminar become on-going conversations with professors and fellow students. In addition to the seminars, there is a (fairly well-observed) open-door policy regarding professors' offices. And, with the advent of e-mail (most profs provide addresses willingly, even invitingly), the free and open exchange of ideas is able to flourish healthily at Brock. There are those who would rather see the university move away from what they consider to be a time-consuming (read expensive) method of interaction, however. Imagine how much money would be saved if all students from the different seminars were placed into one large lecture hall.

Academically, then, the atmosphere at Brock seems precariously balanced, thanks to a planning report which insists on the need for mighty changes. The ultimate goal (to be realized over a five-year period) is to become "a competitive, comprehensive university" focusing on "a broad range of graduate and professional programs." There is to be "a greater emphasis on career development programs that prepare students for the world of work"—remember that slogan! There is going to be, of course, a commitment to Brock's greatest strength (seminars), but how long of a commitment remains

In a Nut Shell

The university in a phrase: Take away the 'B' and Brock University becomes Rock University!

Best thing about the university: Seminar system.

Worst thing abut the university: Possibility of too much change; potential loss of seminars.

Favourite professors: I. Brindle (Chemistry); Z. Marini (Child and Youth Studies); C. Merriam (Classics); M. Rose (English); B. Crick (English); K. Dyer (English); G. Nathan (Philosophy); J. Sorenson (Sociology); J. Black (Physics).

Most popular bird courses: Introduction to Astronomy 1F00; Introduction to Writing 1P80.

Hot spot to study on campus: Isaac's

Quietest spot on campus to study: The library is the quietest with the Pond Inlet a close second.

Need for car and parking availability: Public transit is pretty good in St. Catharines. There are always buses going in and out of Brock. There is enough paid parking for the number of cars, but free parking tends to fill up rather quickly. It isn't paved, but if it was, it wouldn't be free. Semester or year-long passes can be purchased, or you can pay each time you park.

Sexually speaking: No wild orgies, but no apathy, either. People are interested but mostly in a playful, short-term kind of way. The LGB (Lesbian, Gay, and Bisexual) Club.

Fraternities/sororities: What's a fraternity?

Athletic facilities: World-class; enough said.

Library facilities: The library is located in the Arthur Schmonn Tower, floors 2–10. The computer system is improved and easy to use, which is a good thing if you need to find something that Brock does not have—a likely scenario. Not that there are no useful resources, but chances are bigger, richer libraries have what you are looking for. The photocopy debit card is a great idea, but watch out for lineups and machines that are out of order. The Student Union (BUSU) has its own copiers, with a separate debit card—it wouldn't hurt to have access to both.

Computer facilities: Seven computer labs—four PC and three Macintosh—for word processing, spreadsheets, statistical analysis and web browsing. Internet access and e-mail accounts for students. Labs are open every day and most evenings. Senior student advisors supervise labs. Most rez rooms are fully wired for access to the Net.

Weather: Warm weather from May to November. Bundle up for the cold winters.

Safety on campus: Brock has instituted the Foot Patrol to escort students to their cars or residences at night. The campus is well lit and there are many emergency posts with direct phone lines to Campus Police.

Alumni: Dennis Hull (former NHL all-star, broadcaster); Kevin McMahon (award-winning Toronto filmmaker); Father Sean O'Sullivan (youngest member of Parliament before entering the priesthood); Rick "the Temp" Campanelli (MuchMusic VJ).

---

to be seen. The key word throughout the report's administrative rhetoric is "innovation," striving to reinvent and improve all existing programs to coincide with the development and perfection of new ones. This leads to the question of graduate studies at Brock. On the surface graduate studies are seen as a good thing—prestigious, etc.—but one must consider what this has the potential to do to Brock's identity. Brock is primarily an undergraduate institution with only a few graduate degrees offered. This is seen as a strength, along with the seminar system, that is feared may be "innovated" out of existence. There is the possibility that with increases in enrollment, and the planned commitment to more graduate programs, professors' attention would shift from undergrad students to graduate students.

The concerns lie mostly within the Humanities, unnerving considering the Humanities represent 19% of total undergraduate course enrollment, second-highest behind the Social Sciences. However, since the numbers are not growing exponentially within the other disciplines, administration cannot justify leaving the Humanities out of their long-term plan. There is actually talk of co-op programs for English and Philosophy. Brock currently offers co-op education programs in Sports Management, Business Administration, and Accounting, all areas where co-op benefits students in a practical sense. There is concern about maintaining a credible intellectual climate in the departments. (This is surely as necessary as a department that creates its own climate, namely the new "prestigious" Cool Climate Oenology and Viticulture Institute, in which students study the science of growing grapes and wine making.)

Brock has an impressive full-time faculty and boasts an impressive research commitment. The high calibre of professors at Brock also makes the open-door concept of learning that much more rewarding for students. Despite the changes, Brock is maintaining its penchant for a student-focused atmosphere.

REZ LIFE

Brock residence is among the finest in Canadian university living. There are four residences to choose from, and all are relatively affordable and new. If you respond on time and your OAC average is 75% or more, Brock guarantees you a place in residence; the same applies to international and out-of-province students (minus the grade-average restriction). Queenston is the off-campus residence located downtown, and considered the party rez. It is the oldest and most traditional of the residences, with a shared bathroom on every floor. Two of the on-campus residences, Decew and New Residence, are similar in structure. Decew has the option of double rooms with a balcony for each; two rooms per bathroom is a distinct advantage over Queenston. The recently added Village Residence is a system of townhouses with four single rooms per house, and each house includes a kitchen, lounge, and even central vacuuming. All residences have air conditioning and are fully wired to accommodate all computing needs. As for meal plans, Decew and New Residence have options which allow a certain number of meals per week in a common dining hall. The other two are not associated with the dining hall but residents are able to purchase (as are all students) a declining-balance meal card that can be used throughout the campus.

NIGHT LIFE

St. Catharines is no Toronto, granted, but there is enough of a party atmosphere to satisfy most anyone who cares to party. Aside from the campus bar, Isaac's, which poses as a pub and holds Pub Night every Thursday, students can go to Brock Night at Font 54 (Wed.), Big Buck's (Fri.), Arizona's (Sat.), and Lakeside (Sun.). While Big Buck's is the only downtown club mentioned, it is joined by non-dance bars such as Millennium, Pow-Wow, and Sweeney Todd's, with the others mentioned found scattered throughout the area. The city's largest mall, the Pen Centre, houses the London Arms, a British-style restaurant/pub that is good for a pint after seeing a movie at the new SilverCity Theatre. Need to pull an all-nighter and feed the munchies? Perkins is the place for 24-hour service, friendly staff, and a bottomless cup-o-joe. Need to feed that urge to gamble? Check out Casino Niagara in The Falls after taking a walk to see one of the seven wonders of the natural world. Just don't lose next year's tuition and the keys to your parents' car betting at the craps table.

A Word to the Wise:

1. Take advantage of any discounts you can get with your student card. Check out the Brock Box Office on a regular basis to see what's going on.

2. Watch out for crazy drivers in and around the university. People speed along the roads like there are no pedestrians at all and rarely stop at the cross-walks. Minor accidents shall soon have a monopoly on the "Crime Report" section in the *Press*.

3. If you live off campus chances are you'll need to go uphill to get to class and downhill to get home. On Brock hill, obey the signs and *don't* pass cyclists on the way down. Watch out for deer (trust me); and during the winter make sure you have a car that can handle non-plowed slush-covered 40 degree angles (trust me on this one, too).

4. Take advantage of the sports facilities; play some intramurals.

5. Beware of the Taco Bell smell in Thistle Corridor.

ON ST. CATHARINES

A mostly urban city that happens to be situated within a fair distance of anything fun, it is growing into one of the most heavily populated retirement communities. If movies and the bars are not enough, and the Pen Centre and Fairview Mall become boring, plan a trip to Toronto, an hour drive from St. Catharines. Niagara-on-the-Lake is a nice day trip, even if you can't afford tickets to the Shaw Festival; take a picnic and walk along the Parkway or take a look at the quaint little shops along Main Street. Buffalo is just to the south if you want to see a hockey game (keep your eyes peeled around campus for frequently organized bus trips).

If Canadian history is your gig, the region offers an abundance of places and stories to explore: the War of 1812, the battle of Queenston Heights, a terminus of the underground railway, and viewing ships moving through the Welland Canal. There is also the St. Catharines Museum.

Carleton University

By Ryan Ward

As World War Two waged on overseas, a group of scholars, part of the Ottawa Association for the Advancement of Learning, came up with the idea to offer part-time education opportunities to men and women who had relocated to Ottawa. Carleton College opened its doors on September 21, 1942, with President Henry Marshall Tory at its helm, in what is now Glebe Collegiate on First Avenue in Ottawa. An interesting feature about this university is that it was the first university to be founded by neither the church nor the state. By 1946, the college was already administering degrees in journalism and public administration, though it did not have the authority to award degrees. In 1952, Carleton was awarded provincial legislation to give out degrees and the school that started with 600 students began to grow. Construction began four years later and created what is known today as Carleton University along the banks of the Rideau River.

Carleton's architecture is very unique. Many of the buildings have a modern feel to them, while others, well, you could say they've been there for a long time. The largest structure on campus is Dunton Tower, towering over the city with a 22-floor view. Its modern look overshadows the original buildings that make up the academic quad: Tory Building (named after Carleton's first president), Paterson Hall, and the MacOdrum Library, the first three buildings to be built at Carleton. Since that time, the campus has branched out with the modern Mackenzie Building and Minto Centre, home to the faculty of Engineering, and the Architecture building next door.

Carleton Athletics has an olympic-size swimming pool and a reconstructed fitness centre with quite a bit of equipment to work out on. As you move along University Avenue from the Athletics complex, there is the bastion of business enterprise, the Carleton Technology and Training Centre. Inside is the prescription shop, health services, a computer and Internet shop, dental centre, eye glasses shop, Treats, and many other businesses to suit your needs.

The Administration Building, or Robertson Hall as it is now known, looks on an eyesore of a parking garage (although it is good to go star-gazing on the 16th floor at night), and the Rideau Rapids. Robertson Hall houses the heads of the university including the president, vice-presidents, as well as Alumni Services, senate and board-of-governor representatives, Department of University Safety, the Awards Office, Graphics Services, and University Communications. Its semi-modern structure is much more pleasing from the inside, and Alumni Park, where summer convocation ceremonies are held, is just out back. On the farthest part of campus, the Loeb Building sits with all its rustic charm. From the outside it looks like any other old building, but inside you enter the labyrinth of halls linking the four towers that make up the building. If you have any classes here in first year (for Arts students, there is a pretty good chance you will), leave really early and learn your way around the building, and bring pebbles along so you can find your way back.

The best part of Carleton is its use of green space and the accompanying lot of furry creatures you'll see around campus. This is a place where groundhogs, squirrels, and other animals regularly appear on your walks to and from class. The next best part of Carleton has to be below the surface, in the university's tunnels. You can get to any part of campus through the tunnels. Watch out for reckless tunnel cart drivers, though, because they tend to crank their golf-mobiles through at alarming rates. On those cold Ottawa winters, these tunnels, although very musty, will be your best friends, and if you are really bored, take a look at the tunnel paintings, especially throughout residence. Finally, if you enjoy just hanging out, the University Centre (Unicentre) is the best place to go on campus. Come visit Rooster's Coffeehouse and have a mocha or a beer (after 11 a.m., of course), and play a game, or 20, of euchre. Rooster's is a place that is destined to suck you in, and if you are a regular there, it becomes the place "where everybody knows your name."

CAMPUS CULTURE

Carleton University prides itself on its large number of out-of-province and out-of-country students. Everywhere you turn, there is another different type of culture performing different rituals, selling baked goods, or putting on displays throughout the school. With a large population of international students, it really feels like a multicultural university.

Vital Statistics

Address: 1125 Colonel By Drive, Ottawa, Ontario, K1S 5B6

Admissiona office: (613) 520-7400

Website: www.carleton.ca

Total enrollment: 15,801

Male-female ratio: 54 to 46

Percentage of international students: 4.3%

Percentage of out-of-province first-year students: 19%

Average entering grades: Arts: 67% (Humanities), 80% (Journalism); Science: 70%; Commerce: 70%; Engineering: 79% (overall average)

Tuition fees: $3,822

Residence fees: Double rooms range from $5,261–$5,625 depending on the meal plan; single rooms range from $5,931–$6,295 depending on the meal plan.

Percentage of students in residence: 10%

Co-op programs: Architectural Studies, Aerospace Engineering, Applied Physics, Biochemistry, Biology, Business, Chemistry, Civil Engineering, Communications Engineering, Computer Science, Computer Systems Engineering, Earth Sciences, Electrical Engineering, Engineering Physics, Environmental Engineering, Industrial Design, Mathematics and Statistics, Mechanical Engineering, and Software Engineering.

Financial aid: 10 Chancellor's scholarships valued at $5,000 per year for four years, for the top 10 students entering university; scholarships for everyone with an 80% entrance level or better, valued between $500 for 80–84% and $3,500 for at least 90%. Anyone from the national capital can receive an additional $500 for an 80% or more. OSAP is available. In addition, students can apply for bursaries from the Awards Office at Carleton.

Services for students with disabilities: The Paul Menton Centre is the place to go for academic accommodation, with Attendant Services in residence to help students with their daily needs. The Carleton Disability Awareness Centre is also on campus to work with students with disabilities and to provide a place to be social.

Aboriginal students: 1.5% of the university is of Aboriginal ancestry.

Student services: There are many services for students, the most important of which are a full-time Ombudsperson, Career Services, and Health and Counselling Services. The Students' Association offers various services, including a food bank, and a fax machine. There are different service centres for various interests.

Aside from Carleton's multicultural pride, there is much more to be proud of, including the amount of activities available to participate in. There are over 100 clubs and societies to suit everyone's needs, including the Cannabis Club, Ravens 'R' Us, Political Issues Club, Dorchester Debating Union, and the Friends of Zeus. There are all sorts of clubs, including drinking clubs, political groups, and religious clubs. These clubs run various activities, from boat cruises to paint ball to guest speakers. As well, the academic societies represent practically every department. Among the most active are the Engineering Society, Law Society, and Political Science Society.

The university can be apathetic, especially around election time—14% is about the average voter turnout for a general election. Getting involved in the political process or in other areas of the school are good for those résumé-driven students who want to make the best of the university environment. Carleton has eight service centres, more than any other university in Canada—the Woman's Centre, Bill Ellis Centre for Mature and Part-Time Students, International Students' Centre, Carleton Disability Awareness Centre, Volunteer Centre, Gay, Lesbian, Bisexual, and Transgendered Centre, Carleton Foot Patrol, and Photo Centre. You will hear about these centres during Frosh Week, particularly the Carleton Foot Patrol. There are about 250 volunteers every year and you get to walk around in co-ed pairs with a walkie talkie and a flash light, or you can drive the tunnel cart.

If you are a sporty individual, Carleton Athletics is the place for you. Whether swimming in the Olympic-size swimming pool or working out in the weight room, there is a lot to do. You can also participate in any of the recreational leagues and play some volleyball, basketball, or soccer. If you think you are good enough, Carleton also has 17 varsity teams to try out for. Football is now gone from Carleton, but a golf team has been added to go along with the competitive soccer, basketball, nordic skiing, swimming, waterpolo, and field hockey teams. Carleton has had various athletes go on to play for the Canadian national basketball and football teams over the past few years.

The Carleton University Students' Association is also a large part of the Carleton culture because it operates most of the activities for students, including all the clubs and societies, service centres, and a handful of other activities. If politics is your thing, every February Carleton has a general election to fill council and executive positions. The president and finance

In a Nut Shell

The university in a phrase: Carleton is a place for everyone, specializing in high-tech, specialized fields, or just general arts and offering a wide range of activities for students, with a kick-butt social scene for all to take part in.

Best thing about the university: The number of activities to get involved in!

Worst thing about the university: Apathy among most students around election time and toward some of our sports teams.

Favourite professors: Paul Attallah (Mass Communications), Roger Bird (Journalism), Paul Azzi (History), Pauline Rankin (Canadian Studies), Conrad Winn (Political Science), Michael Runtz (Biology), Franz Szabo (History).

Most popular bird courses: Natural History (61.192), Computer Science for Social Science Students (95.101).

Hot spot on campus to study: Rooster's Coffeehouse

Quietest spot on campus to study: The library or Loeb Lounge

Need for car and parking availability: Ottawa has a good bus system, although it is nice to have a car to get around, especially if you want to stay out past 1:30 a.m. There are eight parking lots, including the Parking Garage, with room for about 3,000 vehicles in total. Prices are $295.20 for the Parking Garage, Lot 6 (residence), and Lot 5 (Athletics). There are also pay parking lots including: Lot 1 (Library), Lot 2 (Unicentre), Lot 5 (Athletics), and the Parking Garage.

They cost $1.15 per half hour to a maximum of $10. Lot 6 (residence) has a $5 flat rate for the day but there are no exit privileges.

Sexually speaking: Whatever your pleasure, Carleton is the place to come for sex. Residence is a favourite hangout for those active folk, and finding condoms is not a problem. Condoms are available at Health Services, the GLBT Centre, and from all Res Fellows on each floor in residence.

Fraternities/sororities: The attitude toward fraternities has been quite positive at Carleton. The Students' Association has given them access to all venues and allows them to wear their letters, sell goods, and recruit during the year without hassle. Most people have no problems with them because they do a lot of good for the community by raising money for different charities and having various events on and off campus.

Athletic facilities: Besides the Olympic-size swimming pool, our fitness room has just been expanded to give more room for people to work out and lift weights. A climbing gym has been added to replace the squash courts, and Carleton has three fields to play sports besides the main field for varsity athletes. The gym is in need of an enlargement but it will be some time before changes are made.

Library facilities: There are five floors of books of all kinds. Although the library does not have books on some subjects, you can also access the University of Ottawa library, the National Library, or the National Archives. Ottawa has lots of facilities

to get books on every subject.

Computer facilities: Carleton has over 3,058 computers in 74 labs throughout the campus. Some computers are only available for graduate students, but most are available for all to use. For residence students, there are labs available in St. Pat's building and Lanark residence. Each lab is equipped for laser printing with a printer card. Printing costs 10c per page.

Weather: In the summer, the temperature can get pretty hot, even exceeding 30°C. The fall can be kind of cold once October comes round, in the 12–18°C mark. The coldest time is the winter, when the average temperature is usually about –15°C, although it can drop to as low as –40°C. In the spring, the temperature starts to go up to the 10–16°C mark.

Safety on campus: Carleton prides itself on its campus safety, with the Department of University Safety watching over campus 24 hours a day, in conjunction with their community protection program and their security officers. In addition, there is the Carleton Foot Patrol's Walk-Safe program. In the last few years, incidents on campus have dropped significantly with only a few cases of stolen goods, exposures, and other types of incidents.

Alumni: Among the best of Carleton's alumni are media mogul Conrad Black, Jane Gilbert (formerly of Global Television), Ottawa Mayor Jim Watson, journalist Peter Worthington, actor/comedian Dan Aykroyd, and Federal Industry Minister John Manley.

commissioner, as well as council, are elected positions, and there are hiring boards for the remaining executive positions. The vice-president and director positions tend to change names regularly, but the jobs remain the same: handling internal and academic matters of Carleton, lobbying, and running the service centres.

ACADEMIC ISSUES

With so many different universities across Ontario and Canada, Carleton University tries to distinguish itself from other universities. In the early 1990s, its idea was to have high continuation but low admissions standards so people could always go to university no matter what—this attitude coined the phrase "Last Chance U." Since 1996, Carleton has experienced a metamorphic transformation, raising its academic entrance average, phasing out low enrollment language courses combining similar programs, and basically pushing to become a high-tech, innovative, and business-oriented university.

Carleton has made providing scholarships a priority, investing millions of dollars into scholarships available to those who have attained at least an 80% average. It has also moved toward providing more co-operative education programs so graduates can have a better chance of finding a job right out of university. Students can participate in every level of academic politics at Carleton, including the New University Government, who attend and can vote on faculty and departmental boards, and the University Senate. Each year there are elections for both. This gives the chance to vote on various academic issues that will affect you and other students, including program changes, scholarships, new academic bodies, and new programs. Between 1994 and 1998, the university's enrollment dropped from about 20,000 students to present levels, but this year universities across Ontario received the highest level of applications and acceptances by students for next year. This year too, the average entrance grade for general Arts courses at the university is on the verge of clearing the 80% plateau.

REZ LIFE

Carleton has five undergraduate residences and one graduate residence. The best of the bunch is the newest residence, Stormont-Dundas house, which is less than a decade old. It has the lovely decor of Ikea beds and dressers, with spacious areas to store as much as you can inside. If you did not get into Stormont-Dundas, the other residences will suit you well. Russell and Grenville are now non-smoking, as

are all the other buildings in residence, so if you must smoke, enjoy standing outside in the cold during those −40°C winters. This is the first year Grenville became non-smoking. Russell changed a few years back. The size of the Grenville rooms is much more pleasing than some residence rooms in Glengarry, but we'll get to Glengarry later.

Lanark is quite similar to Russell and Grenville, with its rustic 1960s look, but the added bonus of Lanark is that there is a computer lab in the lobby that is open 24 hours. This makes it easy to stagger out of your room (if you do not have Internet access there) and finish an essay due the next morning. If you want a small, intimate floor, the first floor of Lanark is the smallest floor in residence with about 30 residents. On the second, third, and fourth floors, there is an open area with a couch to sit and watch people walk around outside along Library Road, or you can go to the television lounge and watch a little TV.

This takes us to Glengarry or so-called Glencatraz. Picture this: 11 floors, with about 60 people to every floor, constant fire alarms (important fact: the elevators are not to be used during alarms), and windows that don't open. If one person gets sick (which always happens in residence), the germs travel through the entire residence. And anyone who wants to live in residence in first-year, better expect to take on a roommate. I would suggest getting to know your roommate at the beginning so you can see if this person is someone you can spend the rest of your year with. If not, switch roommates as soon as possible with another person on the floor. This is the best way to make the most of your residence experience. If this doesn't seem like the ideal living situation, try to get yourself a suite. They at least are equipped with a shower and two bathrooms, in most cases, and you won't have to share the communal bathroom with everyone else on the floor. There are usually five suites per floor, just watch out for the room you get. Some rooms are very large, others are nicknamed "The Coffin."

Finally, for those graduate students wanting a place to live

A Word to the Wise:

Get involved. Don't just sit back and do your work, or you will burn out in no time. Carleton has the resources to give you the chance to get ahead in your career. You just have to give the university a chance to work for you and you will go far.

on campus, Renfrew is the place to live. It looks as much like the older buildings, Lanark, Russell, and Grenville, but the rooms are nice and spacious. There is not very much to them except for a wooden bed, a dresser and a bathroom that you share with your neighbour. Renfrew offers convenience and a lot of people to talk to, but it is expensive.

In first year, it is a good idea to live in residence. If you like visitors, simply leave your door open and you will be sure to have some within five minutes. Get to know the people on your floor and go out and do things; there are bound to be lots of people who want to do things all the time, making it easy to organize a sporting event or movie night or whatever. Remember, it is going to be a long year, especially if you've never experienced university before, and residence life can make it really enjoyable. There are lots of activities, planned by the Rideau River Residence Association, including pub nights, scotch and cigar nights, writing for the *Resin* (the longest serving residence newspaper in Canada), tunnel painting, and Res Week. If you can afford it, residence is definitely worth it, but in future years it is nice to live off campus. There is a lot of housing available all around Carleton University, including student ghettos at the end of the Canal and in Ottawa South and the Glebe, all of which are walking distance from the university.

NIGHT LIFE

Ottawa is a great place to be if you want to go out and have a good time. And with Hull, Quebec, right next door, it is easy to hop across and visit one of la belle province's many excellent party establishments, where the drinking age is just 18 (as opposed to the minimum drinking age of 19 in Ontario). Back in Ottawa, you can check out the world-famous Byward Market and enjoy some of the many great watering holes that have been around for decades. Among the best bars of Ottawa are: The Great Canadian Cabin, Minglewood's, Stoney Monday's, On Tap, RJ's Boom Boom Saloon, and some new establishments, like The Factory. You might note that many of the bars that are around right now may not be around in the next few years, but don't worry—something else will surely be there to take its place. The best nights of the week are at the end of the week; save Wednesday nights for Carleton's world-famous "Wednesday

nights at Oliver's." If you like karaoke, Mondays and Wednesdays are great to find karaoke throughout the city and at Carleton as well. The Bree's Inn, Carleton's residence bar, has its big nights on Tuesdays, with a DJ and some great music. The bar has been redone to look great, and it is a good place to talk to lots of people from residence. Be sure to say "hi" to Johnny Teuscher—when he dies, his ghost will haunt this bar. Carleton has four on-campus bars to choose from: the Bree's in residence, Rooster's, Oliver's, and Mike's Place in the Unicentre. Mike's Place is the graduate bar, while Rooster's and Oliver's are operated by the Students' Association.

ON OTTAWA

Where else can you find the Parliament Buildings, the world-famous Byward Market, four universities (the University of Ottawa, St. Paul's University, the Université de Quebec à Hull, and Carleton University), two colleges (Algonquin College and La Cité Collegiale), the border of Hull, Quebec, all packed into one little town? This place has so much to do, including playing paint ball, participating in a game of Laser Tag, shopping at a variety of malls, visiting lots of touristy places, like the Museum of Civilization, the Mint, and the Canadian War Museum, and lots more. Also, one day every year is devoted to the biggest party in Canada—Canada Day. On Canada Day the streets of downtown Ottawa are closed off from cars and hundreds of thousands of people gather for a massive bash in the downtown core, with concerts going on everywhere. It is an incredible experience whether you are a tourist or you live there year-round. Ottawa is also a great place to participate in a variety of different sports leagues. There is hockey, basketball, volleyball, soccer, baseball, and ultimate leagues that operate throughout the year, or you can stroll, roller blade, bicycle, or jog along the canal. There is so much to do in the city, and with a thriving population of party-goers who come out virtually every night of the week, it's also great as a university town. Ottawa is becoming the high-tech capital of Canada with Nortel, Corel Corporation, and many other high-tech firms operating in the city. If you look closely you may even see government ministers jogging along the Rideau Canal in the morning.

University of Guelph

By James Kirkpatrick

"Moo U"—this is the term not so affectionately given to the University of Guelph. Although the history of the university is steeped in livestock, Guelph has developed into one of Canada's most popular and accomplished comprehensive universities. Guelph provides most of your typical university programs, but it also includes some rare species, like the Bachelor of Landscape Architecture program. The university is situated in the convenient community of Guelph, convenient in that you can get to any one of eight neighbouring universities, by car, in about an hour and a half. That is, if you ever find a reason to leave this beautiful campus.

There's a reason why cows and sheep can be found on the University of Guelph campus, and that is because vehicular traffic has been pushed to the outside to allow for the unfettered movement of humans and other creatures. Although the university school year doesn't let you appreciate the campus in all its summer blossoming splendour, there is still enough character to keep you happy.

It appears the university was doing quite well financially during the period of "brutalist" architecture (a descriptive architectural style), erecting large concrete buildings across the campus; these monoliths, however, are just one ingredient of Guelph's campus. With its base as an agricultural and horticultural school, the campus has a warm country feel to it, with its barns, greenhouses, wide variety of trees, and ever-present historic buildings. The Kodak moment on campus is sitting on Johnston Green with Johnston Hall in the background while you milk a cow.

For research and recreational purposes the campus has an Arboretum to the east, and a "Dairy Bush" (where you can find both animals and married people) to the west, and for no reason, at least for the poor students, there is a golf course to the north. However, all the shopping, bars, restaurants, and concrete you could want are a mere 5-minute bus ride or 20-minute walk away.

Once the blustery southern Ontario winter weather comes, students spend little time appreciating the graces of the campus and more time running from building to building, wishing they could get themselves into the infamous, and off-limits, tunnel system underneath the campus (they're not that interesting…oops, I mean, who knows what they look like or if they even exist?).

Expect to see as wide a variety of people on campus as you do animals in the barns. Although Toronto ships a lot of big-city kids down the 401 to Guelph, the diversity of programs and the mysterious quality of Guelph make it the gathering spot for all sorts of people.

CAMPUS CULTURE

The students at the University of Guelph are, let's say, active. From running the premier out of the city during a protest to milking cows in the University Centre, there is no shortage of things to do in and around campus. The only thing that isn't diverse about the campus is the fact that six or seven out of every ten people you see will be women. Not bad for those seeking the female persuasion.

Walking the halls of the University Centre (UC, not UC Centre), you will come across a gaggle of clubs and groups to get involved with. The campus radio station (CFRU), the politically correct *Ontarion* student newspaper, and the just political *The Peak* student newspaper make up the core of the student media, and share the second floor of the UC with the other student groups. If you're looking for a friend, though, or anyone else for that matter, they are more likely on the first floor drinking coffee, in the newly expanded Centre 6.

Despite a general lack of interest from the majority of the student body, Guelph occasionally does quite well in sports. On the men's side, the football and hockey teams have been successful lately, and on the women's side, hockey, and especially rugby, have been perennial winners for the school. Most students at Guelph seem unaware of Guelph's athletic achievements, but it's nice to know, if ever you were asked, that Guelph represents itself well in sports.

Although there is always a lot to do at Guelph, the most likely things you will end up doing are falling asleep in the library, or running into someone you know on campus for the thousandth time that day.

Vital Statistics

Address: University of Guelph, 50 Stone Rd. E., Suite 158, Guelph, Ontario, N1G 2W1

Admissions office: (519) 824-4120

Website: www.uoguelph.ca

Total enrollment: 13,835

Male-female ratio: 39 to 61

Average entrance grades: Arts: 65%; Science: 83%; Commerce: 70%; Engineering: 78%

Tuition fees: $4,140

Residence fees: Single accommodation: $2,712–$3,286/two semesters (room); $,2130–$3,110/two semesters (board); $4,842–$6,396/two semesters (room and board).

Percentage of students in residence: 38%

Percentage of international students: 4%

Percentage of out-of-province first-year students: 2%

Financial aid: over 1,000 undergraduate scholarships, including 13 President's and Dick Brown Scholarships, valued at $20,000 each; OSAP.

Co-op programs: Agriculture, Applied Human Sciences, Biological Science, Commerce, Engineering, Environmental Sciences, Physical Sciences, Social Sciences.

Services for students with disabilities: Facilities for physically disabled, deaf, hard of hearing, and visually disabled are available.

Aboriginal students: Student organizations, run by students.

Student services: If you can't find what you need on your own, the Central Students' Association or your Residence Assistant can point you in the right direction for psychological, financial, academic, or employment counselling. Child care and health care are on campus, as well as cultural services and an ombudsman.

ACADEMIC ISSUES

Guelph's growing reputation has started to attract students for reasons other than the non-traditional degree programs. The mix of programs and students helps create the rich mixture of students and programs at the university. Programs such as landscape architecture, environmental science, food science, hotel and food administration, and horticultural science are just a sampling of the interesting degree choices available at Guelph, on top of the normal assortment of sciences, arts and humanities.

The Ontario Veterinary College (OVC), Ontario Agricultural College (OAC), and MacDonald institute were the forming bodies of the modern University of Guelph. The OVC and OAC in particular continue to play a big role in the university, with half the people at Guelph trying to get into one of these colleges. Looking at the donation board for the university and seeing a who's who of Canadian food producers, it's easy to see what sort of research keeps the university going. However, the university has realized the value of a wide range of programs, and has seen a dramatic increase in the amount of applications in recent years. Guelph is starting to lose its reputation as a hidden gem, as more and more people are finding out about it, and is consequently raising the standard to get in.

Guelph is one of the most comprehensive universities in Canada, and possibly one of the most highly competitive programs to get into is the Veterinary Sciences program. Getting into med school is a breeze compared to the chore of getting into Vet Sci. Co-op programs have steadily increased at the university as well, but make sure you've done your homework: entering averages are ranking higher every year.

Once you get into Guelph, there are certain courses that have warning labels attached, but for the most part, the toughest test is getting in. After first-year class sizes dwindle to small class rooms, or if you are in a specialized program, you can expect to get to know 20 or 30 people in your program pretty well; you will be sharing all of your classes with them. The small size of Guelph does create one drawback, which is that the classes you need are often only offered once or twice a year. So, if class times conflict, you might find yourself having to take a required first-year course in fourth year.

REZ LIFE

Guelph offers a wide range of residence experiences. First-year students are guaranteed a spot in residence, but this promise, coupled with an increase in admissions, creates some interesting room assignments. The residences and food services at the university also have a good reputation; this combination entices a large group of people to return to residence for a second year. This mixture of first-year and upper-year students adds to the diverse character of the residences.

Named for geographic location, the residence system is made up of the South, East, and North residences. In a quick summary, you could say that in South you get to know a few people really well, and in North you get to know a lot of people not so well.

The South residence is one building. As the story goes, this concrete maze was designed by a prison architect in order to deter social revolution by students. Thus, there are no large gathering spaces and the layout of the building is generally confusing and annoying. The building is broken down into three sections, Maritime, Prairie, and Mountain, though this breakdown does not make the building any simpler in finding one's way. South does have its perks, namely two cafeterias, so one can go for weeks without stepping outside, except for classes, of course. The arrangement of rooms also allows for small groups of people to get to know one another well. Clusters of four to six rooms are popular for returning students trying to create their own community. The ominous look and feel of the building often scare people, especially in the first weeks, but most are happy to call the monster "home" after a short time.

East residence is also one building, with a range of apartments that can accommodate from four to twelve residents. This place is generally for returning students who try to get an apartment with friends. It is a transition living space for people not quite ready for off-campus life.

The North residences are made up of a cluster of buildings. Lennox/Addington is a pair of buildings that exist in symbiosis. The two buildings create a sort of enigma of Guelph residence. There is no defining role for the residence. An assortment of all years live there and have a lot of fun doing so. Lambton is the all-first-year residence, the wild card of the

---

A Word to the Wise:

1. Don't buy textbooks; you'll end up with a collection of $100 books on statistics and chemistry. Professors will put a class copy at the reserve desk in the library, and if they don't, ask them and they will. Failing this, buy them used.

2. At the end of first year when you and your friends think it would be a good idea to go back into residence together for one more year before going off campus–don't. Most regret it after the first month of their second year.

3. Beer in the bottle is not allowed in University of Guelph residences, so get used to hard liquor, wine, or cheap American beer, which is about all you can buy in a can.

4. Don't tell people that you are going to be a vet until you get into the Vet school. Save yourself the humiliation and the self-loathing that comes with verbosity.

5. Because Guelph is semestered, you must keep on top of things. September may seem like a bowl of cherries, but remember, things pile up fast and before you realize that your hangover has passed, those papers will surely amass.

bunch, and also the loudest, raunchiest, most obnoxious, and most fun of all the residences. No one here has learned to take school seriously yet, and therefore it is fun for a few months, until you realize you have exams. Johnston Hall is the historic jewel of the campus and the upper floors house a rowdy bunch of students. Because it is also home of the OAC offices, a lot of "Aggies" (Agricultural students) tend to get housed here, and on Wednesday nights you better be in the mood for country music and drinking, or find somewhere else to be. Mills Hall and MacDonald Hall are the men's and women's residences, respectively, although with the low number of male students at Guelph and changing social attitudes the male residence is about to become a thing of the past. Both of these are cozy places and have a relationship with one another, tied to old school traditions. International House, Maids Hall, and Arts House provide alternative housing for special interests, and are quite popular though often forgot about.

Single rooms can be found everywhere but in Lambton, but the odds of getting one are scarce, especially if you are a first-year student. You also have to have a meal plan in all the residences except East, and you will be thankful for it, with the great selection of eateries all over campus. Guelph's food selection will have your friends visiting from other universities when they realize why they are deteriorating and you are glowing with a nourished smile.

NIGHT LIFE Although there are constantly organized bus trips to other nearby cities, there is a nice range of night life in Guelph to keep you within the city limits. For the country music lover, there is the weekly "Aggie Pub," a tradition at Guelph, and fun for all, if you decide to go. Line up for tickets early, or you'll be riding the mechanical bull elsewhere. The Ranch on the outskirts of town is also sure to please the boots of any country boy/girl.

Pubs are plentiful in Guelph for the people in their "Carlsberg Years." Shakespeare Arms, The Penny Whistle Pub, Sherlock Holmes, and The Woolwich Arms all can provide the dark beer, and even darker atmosphere, you want.

If you want to drink without the Irish theme, the Green Room in the multitalented Bookshelf can serve you a nice cocktail in a soothing environment. If you're unsure what to do, the Bookshelf is probably the best place to try and decide. Apart from the bar, there is a restaurant, café, bookstore, and cinema, all under one roof.

Also qualifying under the drinking-without-a-theme category would be Jimmy Jazz, Squirrel Tooth Alice's, and The Albion. Guelph can be seen in a nut shell in The Albion, and most people will become a regular there without realizing why or how. The drinks aren't that cheap, and the atmosphere is unfinished at best, but there is something there that keeps you

In a Nut Shell

The university in a phrase: In first year you go home every chance you can get; by fourth year, you go home for a few days at Christmas. In essence, Guelph grows on you.

Best thing about the university: At Guelph you quickly begin to feel like the head of the class. With so many friendly people crammed into a small space, even if you only have two friends you're likely to run into them twice a day on campus. With the constant friendly greetings from friends and acquaintances, a bad mood is hard to come by, except for the misanthrope in you.

Worst thing about the university: The university is, let's say, a little confusing at best with its billing. You may find yourself getting a bill, or a cheque for that matter, in the mail with no explanation for it. If it's a bill, check with administration who can tell you what mysterious hidden fee it is for. If it is a cheque, spend it right away. Also, be sure to investigate fees that you can opt out of, and do it early 'cause there are deadlines for opting out of fees for dental plans and bus passes.

Favourite professors: Matt teaches Music and Popular Culture, and with two large classes each semester, he has probably taught half

the student body. Matt rides the Greyhound in two nights a week to deliver the same lecture both times, with equal and amazing enthusiasm. He loves Rock 'n' Roll, and he has the hair to prove it. Jeff Mitscherling teaches a variety of Philosophy classes with his specialty being Plato. Plato becomes infinitely more interesting when heard about from a guy with bare feet and track pants.

Most popular bird courses: Music and Popular Culture, also known as Rock 'n' Roll 101. This course covers music of the past 100 years and its effect on society, which means you figure out how African tribal music from the early 20th century influenced Led Zeppelin. Introduction to Geomorphology, when taken without the lab, is passable by any standards. Known as "Rocks for Jocks," it fits in nicely as that elective requirement for the student who doesn't really want to learn anything in their elective.

Hot spot to study on campus: First floor in the library, anywhere outside, and the University Centre are sure bets for students who don't actually want to study.

Quietest spot to study on campus: If you're looking to get work done, shut the door to your room, or

go to a residence study room, where you are about as likely to run into a fellow student as you are your mom and dad.

Need for car and parking availability: If you live off campus your house is probably closer than the parking lots. Guelph is a relatively small community, geographically speaking, and the bus will take you quickly between the three hubs of the city (mall, university, and downtown). Besides, your student card doubles as a bus pass and that is included in your student fees.

Sexually speaking: Guelph is not going to be the set for the next Porky's movie; however, with a strong female contingent on campus, most guys find themselves with a lot more friends who are girls than guys, and therefore more opportunities for love. Girls should reconsider holding onto that high school sweetheart, as the pickings are few and the competition fierce. Same-sex love is not shunned at Guelph. All one has to do is attend a meeting of Guelph Gay, Lesbian, Bisexual Equality or OUTLINE (gay, lesbian, bisexual, transgender) student groups, to find their niche.

Fraternities/sororities: There isn't really much of an attitude at all; if there is one, it is negative. Guelph

coming back for more. Jimmy Jazz is also indescribable in its charm, but you will most likely end up there if the Albion is full.

There are a trio of dance clubs for the person who doesn't want to dance to bass throbbing beats or repetitive ting-tangs. Tending to play all things spawned by the grunge and goth movements, the Trasheteria, Van Gogh's Ear, and the Underground offer you an earful of really, really, really loud music. They also have specialty nights if you're looking for a place that plays house, or where DJs spin records. Van Gogh's has three floors, each with its own mood and loudness, so you are free to pick and choose.

The granddaddy of them all is The Palace. Every city has one of these ridiculous dens of debauchery. If you want laser lights,

tight clothes, and plenty of the latest dance music, you should plan to become a regular at The Palace. You won't find many people who haven't been here at least once, and depending on your definition of cool, it's the place to be, or the place to mock. Regardless, it is packed every night, so if you need the reassurance of a full house to have a good time, come here and come early.

The two on-campus bars also see a lot of action, especially since they are about a five-minute walk from any residence. The Brass Taps, which is known as "The Keg," the name it had before it fought it out with the steakhouse, is the more popular of the two by far. Lineups are a common occurrence here, as early as 8 p.m., and once inside if you don't run into someone you know, you must be new in town. You can also

In a Nut Shell continued

seems to have one fraternity and one sorority, but odds aren't good you'll run into someone who is in one. The university won't allow their presence on campus, according to the charter.

Athletic facilities: The Twin Pad Arena is fairly new, and well used. The Stadium is minimal and the Athletic Centre has three gyms, a pool, weight room, and "circuit" room. Plans were recently snubbed to dome over the soccer field and make it artificial turf for full-year training, but the fight is still on.

Library facilities: The library is oldish, but newly carpeted, and storing everything under one roof is definitely a plus. There is the specialized OVC library, mostly for Vet students, but the general student won't need to go there. The Guelph library has also recently amalgamated its catalogue in an on-line search engine with Wilfrid Laurier and University of Waterloo. Material from their libraries can be requested through computers at the

University of Guelph and will generally reach you in a couple of days.

Computer facilities: If you just need to check your e-mail, surf the web, or do word processing, it can be done with ease on campus, in the library or in one of the scattered computer labs. Expect a lineup, especially in the library computer pool, and especially in the evening. You can also print from these computers. If your needs are more advanced, say, computer graphics or drafting, you'd be best to invest in your own computer, since the university can't keep up with the demand. The university provides you with a free e-mail account with an ancient-looking but effective interface, and you can access the Internet from off campus for free if you're willing to dial a hundred times, or you can pay a small fee to get an immediate and quicker connection.

Weather: From September until December the weather is generally nice to slightly not nice. However, from

January to April it is cold, windy, and snowy, with March and April being dominated by repeating patterns of melting and freezing, making it a very slushy experience.

Safety on campus: Campus Police patrol the campus at all hours, and there is a dispatcher at beacon call to send the police out to any problem. An ever-growing number of "blue poles" around the campus have a direct line to the campus police station. Safe-walkers are available to a late hour to walk you between buildings on campus, and a reasonable distance off campus. Residence Assistants and Residence Managers are on duty in and around the residences all night long. The Raithby House Drop-In Centre is also open late for counselling.

Alumni: Roberta Bondar (astronaut), John Kenneth Galbraith (economist), Jane Siberry (musician), Jane Urquhart (author)

---

catch live music here Mondays through Wednesdays. The popularity of the Bullring, the other on-campus bar, is similar to that of a high-risk stock. People rarely know when the place is going to be open and when it is, it doesn't always fill the attendee with joy. It usually gets clients by way of overflow from The Keg. One night you might be lined up to get into The Keg, and next, you might find yourself at the Bullring.

Two other bars that may or may not have ever been entered by a student are Wally's and The Diplomat. If you feel like Christopher Columbus you can try one of these places.

For a night out without alcohol, Guelph doesn't offer much in the way of cafés; the only successful downtown café burned down a couple of years ago. Live music is scarce and can generally be found scattered at a variety of the aforementioned bars. Movies come by way of the Cineplex at the mall, the Bookshelf, and the 3-Star, which would be just as easy to get to by plane, and once you get there, you'll wish you hadn't.

ON GUELPH

Guelph's size is enough to afford most of the creature comforts. However, if you are used to

Toronto, or anything other than Sears for shopping, you'd better hop on a bus to Toronto, because the pickings are slim beyond the basics. Downtown is filled mostly with bars, restaurants, and stores that sell things that you really don't need.

The Speed River winds its way through Guelph, providing a series of parks along the way. Guelph also has a rich assortment of mountain bike trails. Nearby, Elora Gorge provides tubing excitement, and there are plenty of spots to camp and hike in the near vicinity.

Many of the diverse programs that the university offers are also specialties of the community and allow many students to stay on and live in Guelph. The rich agricultural and veterinarian traditions that are part of the university are also part of the city and the surrounding countryside. Guelph is in the range of commuter cities for Toronto, and lots of people are starting to realize the value of this community. Guelph has fought long and hard trying to keep its heritage, and keep developments such as big box stores out. Guelph has retained its beauty amidst the development of southern Ontario, so get there while you can, and stay on to keep it the way it is.

Lakehead University

By Brent Evans, Luigi Aloia, and Greg Severight

Situated on Lake Superior in Thunder Bay, Ontario, Lakehead University is the epitome of the northern Ontario experience. Surrounded by wilderness and adorned with a man-made lake, Lakehead University is truly a University of the North, and is distinctive in the Ontario university system as such.

Originally founded as the Lakehead Technical Institute in 1946, classes commenced in 1948 in rented quarters in downtown Port Arthur. The first university courses were added to the curriculum in 1948. The Lakehead College of Arts, Science, and Technologies was established in 1956 and proclaimed in 1957. Second-year Arts and Science Courses were added in 1962, and the college was granted under the original act "university powers" to establish facilities and to confer university degrees. The first degrees in Arts and Sciences were granted in May 1965. The Lakehead University Act of 1965 was given royal assent in June 1965 and came into force July 1, 1965—Lakehead University was continued under this new charter.

Many changes have occurred since those rented facilities in 1948. The original college site comprised 32 hectares. Today, the campus stretches across 140 hectares, with 54 buildings and 40 hectares of landscaped and well-maintained greenery. It is truly one of Canada's most beautiful campuses.

CAMPUS CULTURE

Your alarm rings and wakes you for your 8:30 a.m. class; you hit the snooze button three times. Suddenly you realize you have five minutes to get there. Worry not, you will make it on time. Lakehead is a small campus and no one cares what you look like, so you can go to class with bed-head and stink like a rodent and no one will think twice about it. After all, Lakehead is probably the most unfashionable and worst-dressed school in Canada (besides, when it's 25 below outside, who cares where your Gap khakis are). That's right; Lakehead is not renowned for wearing designer clothes. Instead pyjama bottoms, T-shirts, fleece sweaters, and winter jackets are all the rage at LU—the keyword here, ladies and gentlemen, is: f-l-a-n-n-e-l....

Okay, now on to our next word (and it's a biggie, kids): i-s-o-l-a-t-i-o-n. That's right. You will come to a full understanding of this word at Lakehead as the closest major Canadian cities are Winnipeg (eight hours away) and Sault St. Marie (also eight hours away). So everything you need will be right here in Thunder Bay, whether you like it or not. Most students fly to school. Yes, that's right, they fly. Thunder Bay is in Ontario, but is a gruelling 15-hour drive from Toronto—to say the least, a long haul (do the math: 15 x hourly consumption of Tim Hortons (h), when (h) = coffee + donuts (c + d), with a mixed variable of tobacco (t)...and the answer...p, that's puke. Thanks, but I'll book a flight. Approximately 86% of the university's enrollment comes from out of town and most of these students are from southern Ontario. So if you are a long way from home, don't worry, you are not alone.

It is true that Thunder Bay is far north and with this come some preconceptions that must be addressed. Contrary to popular belief there are running water, electricity, real houses, and current movies, and, we don't take dog sleds to class...we use snow shoes (kidding). This said, we are still known as the school of the Great White North for a good reason. In fact, one day two years ago, Thunder Bay was recognized as the coldest place on the planet; this included both the North and South Poles. Yes, six months of the year Lakehead University is covered by snow and ice, but Lakehead students don't mind. In fact, the philosophy here is whatever doesn't kill you, makes

> The classrooms vary a lot here. Some rooms are big enough to hold more than 500 students, while others cannot hold 20. There are also a lot of interesting rooms around campus. We have a Star Trek room, a Snake Pit (or two, depending on who you talk to), and The Bombshelter. If you have classes on the fourth floor of the Centennial building, leave early; you will get lost (it was designed by LU engineers). If you have any classes in the School of Nursing lecture theatre, look at the ceiling, there are two playing cards stuck there (a jack and something else).

Vital Statistics

Address: Lakehead University, 955 Oliver Road, Thunder Bay, Ontario, P7B 5E1

Admissions office: (807) 343-8110

Website: www.lakeheadu.ca

Total enrollment: 6,787

Male-female ratio: 49 to 51

Percentage of first year applicants accepted: 63%

Percentage of international students: 2%

Percentage of out-of-province students: 4.5%

Cut-off grade for admissions: Arts: 65%; Science: 65%; Commerce: 67%; Engineering: 67%

Tuition fees: $3,914

Residence fees: $4,882–$5,147 (meals included); no meals in townhouse: $3,716

Percentage of students in residence: 63%

Co-op programs: Computer Science, Economics, Forestry, Mathematics, Physics, and Commerce.

Financial aid: Scholarships are automatically offered to all entering full-time students with first-class standing on six OACs or equivalent at the time of offer of admission. Additional scholarships/awards and bursaries are available by application, with 25% of entering high school students receiving scholarships. Over $1 million in entrance scholarships, in addition to in-course scholarships, awards, bursaries, and transfer awards, are available.

you stronger. Students must find a way to keep warm and they do this by the most conventional means available: lots of beer and, well, let's just say lots of close contact.

When students aren't "making friends" and consuming alcohol, they are out supporting the Lakehead Thunder Wolves. Fridays and Saturdays are dedicated to the big games and the crowds pack the "Thunder Dome" to cheer on the basketball and volleyball teams. The Dome has a long-standing reputation as being one of the loudest and rowdiest facilities in the league. Visiting teams are quite often forced to bring in fan-heckling units to subdue the untameable crowds—a grand lesson in the practice of futility. Sporting events are not to be missed at LU and often manifest into some of the biggest bashes of the school year.

If sports are not your thing, then worry not. Lakehead accommodates the athletically unin- clined as well. There are hundreds of different clubs and societies to choose from, from journal- ism to chess, social activism to outdoor action; Lakehead is your pusher-man of extracurricular activities. It is here where the benefits of a small, isolated campus come shin- ing through. Students are forced to create their own worlds and as a result there is no lack of choice. If there is a particu- lar club or society that a student feels was overlooked, he or she has the ability to simply create it. Lakehead is big on these aspects and is willing to throw the money around; all you have to do is ask.

All in all, Lakehead students are warm and friendly, active and aware of their university, go to class, love the Thunder Wolves, love their beer and have no clue as to what is going on in the world outside of Thunder Bay.

ACADEMIC ISSUES

Lakehead is not world-renowned for its high academic standards—a reputation that it is trying to shed by raising its standards and getting rid of the hobos and vagrants that sleep in the lecture theatres. Believe it or not, Engineering is one of Lakehead's biggest and best programs. The first thing that may come to mind when you think of Lakehead is probably not Engineering, but it may be soon. It has recently acquired one of North America's 500 fastest computers and new government funding for the Engineering program. The faculty is growing rapidly and continues to draw a wide variety of students from across Canada and worldwide. Engineers still think that they rule the world, and the rest of us let them go around in their befuddled hazes. One component of LU's Engineering program that is unique in Canada is the college trans- fer program. Every summer the campus is overrun with students who have completed stud- ies in a college Engineering program. After a long sum- mer session at Lakehead, these college graduates are welcomed into the third year of LU's Engineering degree.

Aside from Engineering, Lakehead offers disciplines in all the major faculties, such as Business Administration, Science, Education, and Arts. The Faculty of Education offers a one-year Education degrees for graduates, as well as a Concurrent Undergraduate Education program. If you loved colouring and gym in grade school, Education is for you. Forestry is well situated at Lakehead, as Thunder Bay is lush in that department. It is, after all, Thunder Bay—a city known for its lumbering efforts. Foresters spend the first two weeks of September in the bush of northwestern Ontario, and each year some never come out. For those who are not quite ready to venture out into the bush, or into anything in particular, there is always that post-secondary god-send we call Arts. At Lakehead, like everywhere, there is a wide assortment of programs to choose from in the faculty of lost souls, such as History, Philosophy, and English. Lakehead also offers professional degrees such as Kinesiology, Nursing, and, of course, the famous Outdoor Recreation program, which is regarded as the best the country has to offer (and no, it's not the only one). Despite the fact that the administration has been slow to cope with the growth of the program, it remains very popular, and "rec'ers" are one of the most easily identifiable groups on campus with their flannel pants, Gore-Tex coats, Mountain Equipment Co-op packs, and patchouli-smelling hair.

Lakehead's position in northwestern Ontario makes it ideal to meet the needs of the large Native community in the area and is perhaps the best-facilitated post-secondary institution for Aboriginal students. Offered is the Indigenous Learning program, the Native Language Instructor's Program, and the Native Teacher Education program. In addition to this list, Lakehead has recently introduced the Native Nurses Program and the Native Access Program for Engineering.

Another benefit of a small university is that there are generally smaller class sizes and greater dialogue between students and professors. Lakehead is no different than other institutions, and but it is proud of its ability to provide an intimate and personal learning environment. This is a benefit that cannot be overlooked when considering a university. It is often the case that students in smaller, less reputable schools get a better education than those of the bigger institutions. Lakehead, because of its size, provides this possibility.

REZ LIFE Set in the rugged beauty of northwestern Ontario, Lakehead University residence hugs the wooded banks of the McIntyre River. If you are looking to meet a ton of people and have a great time doing it, residence is the place for you. The residences are a community to themselves and have a unique neighbourly feel. Recall one of your LU keywords: isolation. It is not easy to escape from the campus, and so students are left to amuse themselves around res-

idence and on campus. For this reason the residences are always rockin' and teeming with things to do (hey, no one leaves, so the party never ends). Since leaving the campus is such a task, the weekends are fruitful and eventful with lots of rez sports, BBQs, frosh fests, air bands, concerts, Santa Claus parades, and other crazy events. Isolation does wonders for the partying arts, and no matter how wacky or zany your idea is, chances are its been done at Lakehead, and if not, how about this weekend? Anything goes in these abodes.

Residence consists of six buildings and can accommodate 1,139 students. Bartley Residence is a three-story dormitory configuration of 10 connected houses and is co-ed, with male and female students in alternate rooms. It is the place to be if you are the social butterfly who can't get enough action. Prettie Residence is the place to be if you are the quiet, reserved type. It is also co-ed, with male and female students in alternate rooms. Phase I, II, and III are townhouses which consist of four-bedroom units and are occupied by upper-year students. Halliday Hall, better known as the "Avila," is by far the nicest residence. The first floor has been designated male and the second floor as female. It was originally a convent for nuns; then the building was donated to the university. It has its own cafeteria, gym, and

Speaking of classes, try not to take 8:30s! They may not sound bad on paper, but if you can possibly avoid them, do. There is nothing worse than studying until four or five in the morning and then having to wake up at 8:00 (or 8:15, or 8:23) for a class that you really don't want to go to. Stay away from night classes, too, at least in first year. Three hours was a long time to sit through Saving Private Ryan, and that was a damn good movie. Imagine spending three hours listening to your professor talk about introductory Psychology, or something else just as riveting. It's tough. The ideal class schedule would be classes between 10:30 and 4:30, Monday to Thursday (believe me, after your first Thursday night here, you'll wish you had Fridays off).

In a Nut Shell

The university in a phrase: Relaxed, comfortable, and teeming with that genuine Canadian warmth.

Best thing about the university: The city and location.

Worst thing about the university: The city and location.

Favourite professors: Kim Federson (English), Allan Gilbert (Chemical Engineering), Ken Deacon (Biology).

Popular bird courses: Geography 1100; Family Law: Political Studies 2315.

Quietest spot on campus to study: The landing by the Upper Lecture Theatre.

Most social spot on campus to study: The Outpost.

Need for a car and parking availability: A car in Thunder Bay is a bonus. Make sure you get a car with a block heater as in the winter your engine might freeze. Parking is available on campus for less than $100 a year and that includes an outlet for you to plug your car in for those cold winters.

Sexually speaking: It is easy to find that special someone. I would describe Lakehead as a pick-and-choose type of university. There is something for everyone; you just have to decide what you are looking for.

Library facilities: Lets just say that it's getting better.

Athletic facilities: Generally speaking, they aren't bad but are standard. Don't go looking for the exceptional. The wilderness is your sporting facility.

Weather: It is almost always sunny in Thunder Bay. This makes the summers awesome and the winters cold. The good thing is you almost never have to wear a rain coat.

Campus safety: This is an extremely safe campus. You are more likely see a bear while you walk on campus than you are to get mugged, etc.

Alumni: Arnold Park (CEO of McCain); Goyce Kakegamic (Native artist).

church. It is a little out of the way, but the rooms are worth the extra trek. The building only contains 77 rooms, so reserve your place early.

All residence students (except those in townhouses) are on an all-you-can-eat meal plan, so eat up. The only problem is that the experience becomes a little repetitive. The food itself is what you can expect from any cafeteria and does the job. However, you should leave meals a little early in order to avoid the Disneyland lineups that are sure to be found snaking from the bathrooms. The all-you-can-eat meal plan means you'll never be hungry, but we all know that quantity is never suggestive of quality. It is never glamorous eating, but at the end there are no dishes to clean and there was no labour expended in its creation, so who's complaining? In a nut shell, the whole experience is like being three years old again. You come in, your food is placed in front of you, you have no idea what the hell it is except that it is hot, you stick your face in it and eat as much as you can, and after you're done, it's off to the crapper for relief, and then it's bed time. Come to think of it, that is the whole undergraduate experience, in a nut shell.

NIGHT LIFE

So, here's the situation: You are a first-year student looking for a good time. Well, you are in the right town. Let's start with one of Thunder Bay's most exciting night spots, Coyotes, where, for three bucks and proper ID you can party with the big bad boys and take home a small piece of the Wild West (bad draft and gas in the morning).

After you find yourself properly fuelled for fun (usually about six rye-and-gingers), hit the dance floor to dance your night away with some 35-year-old townies.

If you're looking for cheap drinks, cheesy rip-off cover bands, and biker chicks who are old enough to be your grandmother, then the Inntowner is your place! After a few drinks, and a spin or two on the dance floor, sit back and listen to the sick sounds of some drunken big-haired woman banging on the high notes of "Crazy Train" by Ozzy Osborne. Make sure you only go on a Friday or Sunday because you won't want to see the place sober, especially when drinks are full price.

If you're feeling a little lonesome and want to test some of those smooth lines you've acquired from your latest manual, than it's off to Armani's you'll go. Cut some rug and get jiggy with it, sauce up, and try your luck. You get the picture.

By far the best and most popular establishment is the Outpost, which is located on campus and is the largest on-campus pub in Canada. Thursday night is Pub Night, which means 700 students gettin' loose and bustin' a groove while another 500 students wait in line to get into the madness. The Outpost also features live music and has showcased such bands as Big Sugar, Wide Mouth Mason, Tea Party, I Mother Earth, and Run DMC.

ON THUNDER BAY

Thunder Bay is Ontario's 10th largest city and is the world's largest grain-handling port.

A Word to the Wise:

1. Get involved with as much as you can. There is more to university life than grades.

2. Check out the Sleeping Giant; you will not be disappointed.

3. Try to live in residence for your first year, that way you will get to know the city as well as meet some people you may want to live with later.

4. Get last year's tests.

5. See you at the Outpost on Thursday nights.

6. There is no shred of evidence that life should be taken seriously. So have fun.

Now, that is something to be proud of. Known as the "gateway to the west," it is a necessary stop on the unforgiving route across Canada, after which there is nothing for a very long, long, long time.

It is an interesting city that has a small identity crisis. To the outside world it is known as Thunder Bay, but locals still separate the amalgamated towns of Port Arthur and Fort William (it doesn't help that the streets have different names in each part of the city). The university itself is located smack dab in the middle of the two cities, affectionately called "the inter-city." This area of the city is growing fast. With new businesses, such as Applebees, Wal-Mart, Future Shop, Chapters, Danier Leather, and other crappy stores, Thunder Bay is quickly following suit in the suburbanization of small town Canada.

Let's be honest, there is not a whole lot to see in Thunder Bay, except the town itself. It is northern, which leaves a little grit in your teeth. The winters are fierce, the summers are moderate, and you are miles from any major urban centres. The combination results in character, and boy does it ever have that. Most tend to think that the middle of nowhere is a curse, but the truth of the matter is quite the contrary: It is a gift. A 15-minute walk outside the city will take you to some of the most beautiful and unspoiled wilderness in Ontario. It is an outdoorsman's paradise in its pristine state. With hundreds of parks and outdoor activities it is difficult to get bored. Weigh the options; spend an afternoon climbing the "chimney" of the Sleeping Giant or go shopping at the Gap; take a canoe trip on lakes untouched by man or sit in traffic. "I'll take Thunder Bay for 200, Alex."

Laurentian University

By Tannys Laughren

Looooooo loo koo koo koo koo koo koooooooo... Loooooooo loo koo koo koo koo koooooooo... No, this is not a misprint. Do not be mistaken. If you would kindly remove yourself from the present and reflect on a certain SCTV skit from the eighties featuring two beer-drinking Canucks in work-boots and toques, you will recall their anthem of the North. Yes, that's right, Bob and Doug McKenzie. You remember those two hosers who did their best to put Canada on the map? Well, this is the image that many have when they think of Laurentian: toques, beer, parkas, and plaid (all of which should be placed on the shopping list if you plan on attending Laurentian). Not to say that Laurentian is a school of hicks or sheltered personalities, but the Northern spirit is very much alive at Laurentian. Urban dwellers can stop reading and turn to McGill because if the wilderness is not your thing, then Laurentian cannot accommodate the spirit of your being. However, if you have that Group of Seven sentiment for the North, than Laurentian will quickly become home sweet home.

Nestled between two lakes and surrounded by forest, Laurentian's campus is easily one of the most beautiful in Canada. It is a school of the North and for the North, catering to regional sentiment rather than attempting to lure in students from across the country. But that's only because it doesn't need to. In many ways the university is a microcosm of the Canadian experience, complete with chilly winters, rustic outdoorsy attitudes, bilingualism, and a vibrant Aboriginal contingent. It's the stuff of Pierre Berton and A.Y. Jackson rolled into a little pocket 10 km outside of Sudbury, Ontario. Oh yes, upon arrival, you will want to bellow out Bob and Doug's anthem of the North.

In contrast to the rustic surroundings of Laurentian are the oxymoronic buildings of the campus. As if in complete defi-ance of the imperfections of nature, the buildings are strangely modern. In many ways the campus resembles a small-scale architect's model, where geometric cones and rectangles are glued together and placed on AstroTurf greens. Even stranger is that the architecture somehow works and blends itself in with its rustic wilderness. One needs to look no further than the Health Sciences building or the Desmarias building. It's not to say that Laurentian is not without its eyesores. The Parker building is about as bad as they come. Let us just say that yellowy-orange is only aesthetically pleasing in the fall and is a colour combination that only nature can get away with. Remember, it is the contrast that make the other buildings work. Weak duplications of nature's fall hues are a safe-guarded secret that only the Great Mother knows (lessons well learned from the fashion of the seventies).

Laurentian has been "hun-gover" by its reputation as a noto-riously wild party centre. There is no question that Laurentian students "get jiggy with it," but its students are adamant about Laurentian's acad-emic side. One English student remarks: "Don't think for a minute that the students here don't know how to party—that's one thing they do well, but not to the extent that many would have you believe." Contrary to the popular opinions of the past, Laurentian does have students who are very serious about their studies. Competition to get into programs and stay there has insured this, and by those later years many students have hung up their beer cans in favour of burning the midnight oil. On the other hand, everything is relative and what may seem like a raging party to a softy from the South is the norm of the North. Loooooooo loo koo koo koo koo koo koooooo...Bienvenue à Laurentian.

Vital Statistics

Address: 935 Ramsey Lake Road, Sudbury, Ontario, P3E 2C6

Admissions office: (705) 675-1151

Website: www.laurentian.ca

Total enrollment: 4,289

Male-female ratio: 43 to 57

Cut off grade for admissions after first round: Arts: 72%; Science: 77%; Commerce: 73%; Engineering: 73%

Percentage of international students: 1%

Percentage of out-of-province students: 2%

Tuition fees: $3,765

Residence fees: $2,290–$2,725 (without meals); $3,390–$4,741 (with meals).

Percentage of students in residence: 28%

CAMPUS CULTURE

Laurentian is a regional university and as such tends to take on the flavour of the Sudbury area. The university is officially bilingual but there are actually three separate cultures represented—English, French, and First Nations. The university student population is overwhelmingly English, but the French and First Nations population is strong and vocal. A larger percentage of students are from the Sudbury region, but the students who venture to the Great White North from the Sunny South are always an extremely strong presence and have provided the student union with most of its executives. However, one thing remains constant: Laurentian students love to drink. It has been rumoured for several years that Laurentian was featured on Letterman's top 10 list of hard-drinking North American campuses. One thing is certain: next to water, Molson Canadian is the most abundant liquid found on campus. Students, as of recent, have become increasingly more active around campus. The student union elections usually garner a 25% to 30% turnout, and this past year 500 on- and off-campus students virtually shut down the university for a day (sure, there were hot dogs and bevies but people were genuinely concerned...honest!).

Laurentian has many different clubs and programs for people to join, including the juggling club, clubs for all three major political parties, and a very strong intramural program with water polo, badminton, and hockey (go figure). Laurentian's athletics are strong, with nationally ranked women's and men basketball teams (Go Vees!), and, of course, hockey flourishes at this northern Ontario university. Overall, the average Laurentian student is pretty aloof about academic issues, but is usually quickly indoctrinated into the small-town approach of saying hello, helping you boost your car's dead battery; and reading the newspaper (*Lambda*), though they will not admit that. They will usually be found at the Pub on Thursday night getting served by Woody and his staff.

ACADEMIC ISSUES

Laurentian has the dubious distinction of having more classes available per student then any other university of its size. There is ongoing discussion about increasing the efficiency and streamlining the offerings, but the suggestion always gets mired in the administrative process (the SGA is still missing a couple of executives who are rumoured to still be attending a senate meeting). The university offers several very strong professional programs: Sports Administration (SPAD); Commerce, Mining Engineering (you do field work at the Big Nickel—just kidding); Physical Education (PHED); and Nursing are all strong in the undergraduate area, with Human Development, Business Administration, and Humanities topping the Master's programs. Several professors at Laurentian are top-level researchers involved in some pretty strange stuff (just check out Unsolved Mysteries and see Dr. Persinger talk about his UFO theories). The General Arts and Sciences programs at Laurentian offer a wide range of courses, led by knowledgeable and, get this, approachable faculty (a rarity in the undergraduate experience). Class sizes are very small, and in almost all cases you will call your prof by his or her first name and be given their home phone number in case of emergencies ("umm...hello Professor Persinger...umm... about that paper, well...you see last night I was abducted by aliens and well...I need an extension"). You can be sure that by the end of your stint at Laurentian you will have had at least one beer with all of them.

REZ LIFE

Laurentian in many ways is residence. It is one of the few universities where the students choose to stay in residence for most, if not all, of their post-secondary education. This is because of the convenience of living on campus and the spirit of the students that stay there. Whether you are at LU to party or you are serious about school, you will find

In a Nut Shell

The university in a phrase: What else can be said: "The North Rocks!"

Best thing about the university: Intoxicatingly communal.

Worst thing about the university: Exhaustingly bureaucratic.

Favourite professors: J. Mount (Commerce), R. Dyck (Political Science), F. Mallory (Biology), O. Mercedi (Native Studies), D. Pearson (Environmental Studies).

Most popular bird courses: Physics 1801, Contemporary Science, (walking to class is about all you will learn about the study of movement).

Quietest spot on campus to study: Third floor of the library.

Most social spot on campus to study: Student Street Study Lounge.

Need for car and parking availability: A car in Sudbury is not a necessity. Parking on campus is available, but the plug-in spots are harder to come by and you will need them in January! Most students are forced to park in the Parking Pit (it used to be a swamp and still sort of is),

and a word to the wise: Bring a compass. Those missing executives not at senate are rumoured to be parked in the Pit.

Sexually speaking: The Pub is usually a place where you can find companionship for the evening, but LU is a small place, and people are sure to be talking the next day! Students seem to be pretty level-headed about relationship matters and many settle down after first or second year.

Attitudes towards fraternities: Frats do not exist at Laurentian, although several of the unofficial off-campus residences resemble Animal House at its best.

Weather: We are below the tree line, and it actually becomes very green here in the spring and summer. We receive an average amount of sun, rain, etc., but we do see a lot of the white stuff in the winter. It does get very cold here in January and February, but for the most part it is a dry cold as opposed to a bone chilling damp. Either way you'll freeze your little heinie off…looooo loo koo koo koo koo koo koooooo…

Campus safety: LU is a safe

campus, but it is very sprawling. We have a very active Walkhome program that just purchased a bright yellow van to ferry students around. The Walkhome team offers students a drive home all through the year, seven days a week. Next year security/safety cameras will be installed, further increasing campus safety.

Library: The library at LU is well maintained and has a very good acquisition-to-student ratio. However, it is also facing budgetary restraints and the hours of operation are not as accessible as they once were.

Athletic facility: LU has an Olympic-size pool and good gym facilities. The Student Association just issued a levy from each student to ensure that the weight and cardio room is well stocked. Students pay a hefty athletic fee, so take full advantage of the services and facilities.

Alumnus: Olympic swimming gold-medal winner Alex Baumann; former Ontario deputy minister of Northern Development and Mines Donald Obonsawin; Senator Marie Paule Poulin.

that residence can accommodate both. There are six residences on campus, three of which have religious affiliations. There is also a mature student residence that is designed as an apartment complex, complete with bathroom, kitchen, and living room. The remaining two residences, Single Students Residence (SSR) and University College Residence (UC) are the main residences on campus. Each are joined to form a single complex; however, they differ completely in structure and personality.

SSR is an apartment-style complex where four to six students live together in a single unit. Each unit has a kitchen, TV room, two bathrooms, and storage. First-year students live with a roommate and upper-year students get singles. It is a unique lifestyle because it allows for independent living with lots of support from roommates, if you should so desire. It also allows you to cook for yourself and save a little money, instead

of depending on the meal plan. One major downfall of this rez is cleaning. Members of each apartment are responsible for keeping the rez tidy, so if you get a group of lazy roommates, things will get messy fast. SSR has a mixture of student types—some love to party and some don't. The great thing is both can be happening on a floor simultaneously, without one disturbing the other, because of the structure and size of the building.

UC is a dormitory-style residence. Each floor houses 24 students in a combination of single and double rooms with a complete common kitchen and living room. The floors are co-ed; however, the bathrooms are not. This means that students may have to travel up or down a floor to shower if the bathroom on their floor does not correspond to their sex. UC has a copious amount of spirit due to the communal living style, hence the unity of the floors. As well, UC has upheld much of its traditions even with increased pressure to become

A Word to the Wise:

1. There are a thousand and one uses for milk crates. If you can obtain some from home, grab them in multiples of five. You can use them as bookshelves, cupboards, whatever you want.

2. Hit up the Salvation Army or Value Village for some crazy clothes. Many social events in rez require disco getup. Those thrift stores are also great places to get furniture (the uglier the better).

3. Learn to love beer in a can—each bottle found in rez means a $10 fine—a case would be one expensive night of drinking.

4. Toughen up—it is cold out there in winter, but not too cold to wear a jacket to the Pub. Most people make the dash outdoors in sub-zero weather to save a loonie at the coatcheck. It looks silly but it saves.

5. Feed the fox on campus. He has lived here longer than most of us and has forgotten how to hunt. Failing this, feed one of the skinny students who blew all his OSAP coin on canned beer and Du Maurier Regs

NIGHT LIFE

Thursday night is Pub Night and the rest of the week is based around that. There is only one bar on campus, called the Pub Downunder. It is a popular hangout for students, especially for those living in residence. The Pub has introduced a patio that should enhance the atmosphere.

The rest of Sudbury on the other hand has no shortage of places to go at night. Like any other university town, each off-campus establishment markets its own night to capitalize on the social scene. LU is somewhat off the beaten path; therefore, in order to get around, you need a designated driver, or a cab. Sudbury public transit is unreliable at night, but don't worry, you can pack yourself and about a dozen of your closest friends into the cabs with a good tip. Most cabs will get you anywhere for a $10 flat rate, which is helpful, because Sudbury is quite spread out. Sudbury is a little behind the times when it comes to variation within the bar scene; however, it is catching up. In the last while, smaller, more tailored establishments are popping up, allowing students to pick and choose their favourite hot spots. If you are out, Mingles, Ralph's Sports Bar, or Cactus Pete's should top the itinerary. If you just want to hang out with some friends, then Peddlers Pub, L'il Havanas, Grumblers, or Notre-Dame Bowl offer a more laid-back environment. If you do not like the bar scene, you are out of luck unless you play bingo. A Sudbury Saturday Night isn't far off Stompin' Tom's perception.

ON SUDBURY

Sudbury is a very diversified community, quite different from the mining town of 20 years ago. It is located on the Canadian Shield and offers a multitude of trees, lakes, and, of course, rocks. Sudbury has aggressively pursued diversification in areas other than mining, and is striving to become a leader in tourism, education, business, and government. Sudbury's best natural resource, however, is the people. The residents of Sudbury are culturally and politically diverse and are world renowned for their hospitality and sense of community spirit. Sudbury is a major centre of the North and offers world-class medical facilities for half a million people of northern Ontario. Visitors and temporary residents to Sudbury should not miss the opportunity to Go Underground at the Big Nickel, or visit Science North. The city is also becoming well known for its arts festivals, such as the Fringe Nord, Northern Lights Music Festival, and the Cinefest Film Festival. Take advantage of the natural beauty of the North and visit one of the many beaches or parks in the Sudbury area.

more tame. Partying and studying are balanced in this building, based on the academic calendar. For instance, September is a madhouse, but it tapers down as midterms approach. Most students are courteous to others' needs, and will find acceptable places to party when someone on the floor needs quiet. In the event that a student is having a difficult time coping, whether it be academically, personally, or socially, there is a great deal of support for them in residence. During Frosh Week (and yes, we still refer to first years as frosh), there is almost a one to two leader-to-frosh ratio. This gives the new students a guiding hand through the first while. As well, each floor has a Residence Assistant who is trained to deal with a variety of situations. In the event that the RA is unable to help, he or she will refer the student to the appropriate service on campus. The RA ensures that living in residence is enjoyable and livable for all. RAs also delegates social positions on the floor and helps program fun events for the residents. They organize such things as formals, scum crawls, sporting events, etc. The bottom line is, no matter what your problem or passion is, someone in residence can accommodate you. LU rez is a rockin' place to live. There is always something fun going on and there are always people around to hang out with. The more involved you get, the better your stay will be.

McMaster University

By Katy Sternbergh

It is quite likely that every McMaster University student has encountered the following scenario at some point in his or her university career:

The question, "And where do you go to school?" is suddenly posed by a family member, an old friend, or even a co-worker at a summer job.

Said student looks up, smiles, and replies, "McMaster."

Poser of question pauses, frowns (or maybe even gives a faint choke), and mutters in a much lower voice than before, "Isn't that in ... Hamilton?"

Student sighs, rolls eyes, and proceeds with caution. "Yes."

Poser of question suddenly stammers. Poser of question is trying desperately to mask the fact that images of steel workers, polluted factories, and a hacking, green-faced populace dance through the poser of question's head. Poser of question suddenly gets uncomfortable, even steps back a pace or two. Poser of question laughs a bit louder than expected in an attempt to remain casual. "Oh. I've, uh, driven by Hamilton before. I pass it on the QEW on the way to Niagara Falls. There are, er, lots of factories there, no?"

Said student is prepared for this reaction. In fact, said student used to have this very same reaction before actually moving to Hamilton. Said student remains dead pan. "Yes, it's the armpit of Ontario."

Poser of question is relieved, and laughs again. "Well, it's only four years."

McMaster University is indeed situated in Hamilton (a.k.a. Steeltown, The Hammer, and yes, The Armpit of Ontario) and has been there ever since 1930. Named after wealthy senator William McMaster (1811–1887), McMaster was first established as a Baptist university in 1887. Originally, the building was located in downtown Toronto, situated just north of the University of Toronto in a collegiate, gothic-style building on Bloor Street West (which now houses the Royal Conservatory of Music). By the 1920s, McMaster was already ranked as one of the four principal institutions of higher learning in Ontario (along with Queen's, Western, and the University of Toronto), but with only a few hundred students, McMaster soon began to feel overshadowed by U of T, its large academic neighbour.

The search for a new location began, and in the late 20s, Hamilton's Board of Parks Management won the bid for the school with an offer of $100,000 and an impressive 103-acre site, which included Cootes Paradise, a large ravine area and bird sanctuary that houses some extremely rare plant species due to the unusual climate and wind current (thanks to the nearby Niagara escarpment).

So here we are, nearly 80 years later, still overshadowed by three larger Ontario universities, and still fending off misconceptions that we all have to wear gas masks. That being said, why would anyone want to attend this institution?

I, for one, ended up choosing McMaster because of its name. When it came down to it, I really didn't have much information to go on when comparing universities (an ignorance you, the reader, are luckily trying to avoid). So in the end, I decided I really wanted to have my degree say "McMaster," simply because I thought it sounded regal and commanding. Needless to say, and despite my original aversion to the city's steely nature, I'm glad I chose the school, for it has much to offer and much to love.

CAMPUS CULTURE McMaster witnessed a mini-revolution in school spirit last year when the McMaster Students Union (MSU) resurrected its old spirit group, the Mac Maroons. An incredible 600 students joined the group, as well as an organization of cheerleaders who show up at pretty much every campus event wearing maroon overalls and roller blades. A lot of us find them corny and loud, and have reservations about their bizarre knighting ceremonies, but they have managed to make a significant difference in terms of enthusiasm and school pride (not to mention the fact that some lucky garment company is making a fortune off those overalls). Joining the Maroons is a great way to make friends, especially for upper-year students who find they're nostalgic for residence life.

With approximately 12,000 full-time undergraduates, and a location only 45 minutes from Toronto in the heart of Southern Ontario, Mac's campus offers an impressive cultural mosaic. The largest cultural groups at Mac are most likely the

Vital Statistics

Address: Hamilton, Ontario, L8S 4L8

Admissions office: (905) 525-9140

Website: www.mcmaster.ca

Total enrollment: 16,411

Male-female ratio: 44 to 56

Average entrance grades: Arts: 75%; Science: 80%; Commerce: 80%; Engineering: 82%

Tuition fees: $3,903

Residence fees: $2,860 plus $2,425 for the meal plan

Percentage of students in residence: 24%

Percentage of out-of-province first-year students: 2%

Financial aid: Entrance scholarships include 12 McMaster Scholars Program scholarships, 15 four-year scholarships, 190 one-year scholarships, and 120 merit awards; bursaries and OSAP are also available.

Co-op programs: Biochemistry, Biology and Pharmacology, Chemistry, Environmental Science, and Medical and Health Physics

Services for students with disabilities: Centre for Student Development provides advice to applicants with disabilities; Special Needs Association.

Aboriginal students: First Nations Student Association.

Student services: Career Planning and Employment Centre; Health Services; Centre for Student Development provides counselling, writing clinic, and ESL classes.

Indian Students' Association, the Muslim Students' Association and the Chinese Students' Association. The Society of Off-Campus Students is also a thriving social club, as is the McMaster chapter of Ontario People's Interest Research Group. Another popular club is the McMaster Celtic Society; are any of its members actually Irish? Most students join this club because it's sponsored by Guinness.

The queer community at Mac is definitely nothing to scoff at, either. Last year, the MSU created the Gay, Lesbian, Bisexual, and Transgendered Centre, an officially recognized and amply funded student service. The centre hosted its first-ever GLBT formal, and offers excellent and discreet counselling services for students. In fact, this year's MSU president is openly gay, and was so during the entirety of his campaign.

Despite the fact that McMaster does not have any journalism or media-related programs, the university is home to an award-winning campus radio station, CFMU, and an award-winning student newspaper, *The Silhouette*, one of only two broadsheet campus papers in the country.

Since Mac has gained quite a reputation for both its hospital and its innovative medical and science research facilities, it tends to attract a more than average amount of undergraduates in the Science and Engineering programs. Not only are the professors top notch (even though most undergraduates say they don't have a chance of even getting close to them until they're in graduate studies), but the university tends to favour these programs when budget time comes around. That being said, the vast majority of Mac's undergraduate population still remains to be the lost and listless liberal arts majors, divided up between the Humanities program and the Social Sciences program. And, as is the typical climate with most of the nation's universities, this artsy majority continuously feels underfunded and underappreciated as they watch valuable

courses face extinction due to lack of funding.

There is, however, a silver lining to this atmosphere of oppression. The underdog status of the cynical arts community tends to breed quite a lot of creative output, and while it can be difficult to find (making it all the more interesting), there is a small yet thriving population of actors, writers and visual artists.

McMaster is certainly not a hotbed of political activity, but for a mid-sized university, it's not doing too badly. You could call McMaster students the "strong and silent" types. For instance, a year ago, the students union voted to nix its membership with the Canadian Federation of Students, mostly because they found the group to be irrational, knee-jerk activists filled with hot air. They chose instead to join the Ontario University Students Alliance, a more subdued and professional group who prefer to negotiate with members of the provincial ministry in their offices, as opposed to picketing on their lawns. This move seems somehow indicative of Mac's general attitude; political moderacy with a rational, down-to-business attitude. As a Mac student, be ready to trade in your Birkenstocks for a pair of no-nonsense loafers.

ACADEMIC ISSUES

As already mentioned, McMaster is definitely best known for its innovative researchers in the fields of medicine and science (more specifically, Biology and Chemistry). Several of McMaster's professors have won national and international awards, the most notably being Bertram Brockhouse, who won the Nobel Peace Prize in Physics in 1994. Funds for these programs, however, are concentrated in upper years and graduate studies, so there's nothing terribly spectacular about the first-year science courses.

For those students interested in environmental sciences, McMaster makes great use of the surrounding wetlands and forests located in nearby Cootes Paradise. And because the campus is nestled on the edge of the beautiful and unique Niagara Escarpment , while it is also situated next to one of the country's most polluted cities, there is no end to fascinating studies of species growth and plant life.

Where McMaster leads in its Sciences programs, it severely lacks in its Engineering program. There is no formal co-operative education program, and Mac has never been able to establish an adequate reputation in the field—a vital requirement for the job-obsessed Engineering student. I should add, however, that several research chairs have recently been established by private corporations such as Stelco and 3M in the Department of Engineering, so they're not doing too badly.

For the liberal arts student, Mac has chosen quite an interesting way of dividing up the disciplines. Rather than offering an arts program, McMaster has the Humanities program (with departments like Philosophy, English, History, Drama, etc.) and the Social Sciences program (with departments like Political Sciences, Sociology, Religious Studies, Psychology, Social Work, Kinesiology, etc.). This kind of division within the faculties is one reason that some students have chosen to come to McMaster. The first-year student is now able to avoid taking many of the annoying general interest prerequisite arts courses forced on students by other universities.

REZ LIFE One of the first things you learn when you go to Mac is the fact that one of its nicknames happens to be "Suitcase U." It is imagined that the moniker stems from the fact that a large number of the university's undergraduate students commute from the nearby cities within the Golden Horseshoe area, and a large number of the approximately 3,400 students living in residence tend to pack up for the weekend and head home. However, for those of us who did live in residence, the experience was a terrific one and it's a highly recommended way of integrating yourself into the university social scene for your first year.

The residences are divided into two quads—the North Quad and the West Quad. The North Quad is home to the "regular" residences, building after indistinguishable building nestled on the North end (surprise, surprise) of Mac's campus. The buildings, five in all, are all pretty much the same size, are all co-ed, and are all filled with rowdy youngsters who party a lot and wear their pyjamas to class. Each rez does, however, have its own slight difference. First, there's Woodstock Hall, which is grungy and tall but tends to breed great-looking hippies and is known to throw wicked hall parties. There's McKay Hall, which has lofts on the top floor, and direct indoor access to the Commons cafeteria, so in the winter you don't have to go outside or even get dressed before trudging there for breakfast. There's Brandon Hall, which is the biggest and tallest of the buildings, and is situated right on the edge of Cootes Paradise, so if you're lucky enough to get a room on the west side of the building, you've got yourself one hell of a view. There's also Whidden Hall, which is renowned for its vandalism, excessive partying, and general craziness. Finally, there's Hedden Hall. Hedden is the newest residence of the lot (built in 1994) and by far the cleanest and nicest of all of the buildings. It is also situated on the edge of Cootes, and residents have been known to see fawns grazing outside their windows in the early hours of the mornings. However, Hedden residents are also required to have a certain high school grade average in order to be admitted, so they tend to be snotty and self-important among the rez community. Nobody else seems to like them, but hey, it's a small price to pay for their luxury digs.

The West Quad residences are a little more cultured than the North Quad, which tends to earn them much ridicule during Frosh Week. All of them also have absolutely amazing views of Cootes Paradise, since they're all situated in a semi-circle around the edge of the ravine. First, there's Matthew Hall, which is home to both the Quiet House and the International House. High school students wanting to live in either "lifestyle residence" have to write feel-good, "why I want to live there" type essays in order to be admitted (which usually weeds out the vast majority of the competition). The Quiet House is, well, pretty self-explanatory, and in the International House, Canadian students get paired up with international roommates (that sounds very cool, and I for one certainly wish I had written that stupid essay way back when). Then there's Moulton Hall and Wallingford Hall, the two all-female residences. Wallingford is one of the original campus residences from the 1930s, so it's absolutely gorgeous. However, there's a rather strict policy about male visitors, and did I mention it's an all-female residence? Moulton is the larger and newer of the

THE BRAIN

math skill

writing skill
(improves with coffee)

ideas
(dumb & good)

Music

party central
(always wants to take over the rest of the brain)

sexuality
(yeah! it's pretty low brain activity)

In a Nut Shell

The university in a phrase: Not too big, not too small. It's an attitude-free environment, ideal for finding your own identity.

Best things about the university: Cootes Paradise, innovative degree programs, inexpensive living.

Worst things about the university: Steeltown reputation, favouritism with Science and Health Science programs.

Favourite professors: M. Vorobej (Arts & Science), B. Bryniak (Business), L. Parisi (Health Sciences), W. Hanley (French), M. Gibala (Kinesiology), M. Lovric (Math), W. R. Datars (Physics), S. Sammon (Social Work), G. MacQueen (Religious Studies), B. Baetz (Engineering), Dick Day (Psychology), Don Woods (Engineering)

Hot spot on campus to study: Togo Salmon Cafeteria

Quietest spot on campus to study: The Dell (it's outside, so only during warm weather); Health Sciences Library, second floor; lounge in University Hall.

Need for car and parking availability: There's no need for a car within the city of Hamilton, but a large portion of the Mac population commutes from nearby Stoney Creek, the Mountain, or Burlington. Year-long parking passes range from $104–$160, and there are regular shuttle buses from the outer lots to campus.

Sexually speaking: Mac is a pretty laid-back university, but the social scene is hopping. The university is big enough to offer a large variety of choices for friends and mates, but small enough to make it very easy to meet new people. Gay, Lesbian, Bisexual, and Transgendered Centre (GLBT) provides on-campus support and regular social activities.

Fraternities/sororities: They are not officially recognized at the university, and despite their whining, it doesn't look like they will be anytime soon. However, if it's your thing, both sororities and fraternities do some good charity work, and also do some heavy-duty recruiting at the beginning of the year.

Athletic facilities: Gyms, dance studio, 50-metre swimming pool, racquetball court, squash courts, Fitness Centre, Sports Medicine Clinic, men's and women's sauna, outdoor playing fields, tennis courts.

Library facilities: Mac's library has Bertrand Russell's Nobel Peace Prize.

Computer facilities: Computers available around campus. E-mail accounts for Mac students.

Weather: The climate is slightly more moderate than neighbouring Toronto, and the winters are relatively decent. January and February can get pretty cold, but it's not like the Prairies or anything. The good thing about a moderate climate is the fact that the school gets wimpy if and when there's a storm. For instance, last year, during a major snow storm, the university officially closed for two days. You'd never get that in Saskatchewan.

Safety on campus: Student Walk Home Attendant Team (SWHAT) made up of one female and one male, provides a safe escort around campus.

Alumni: Mac was a veritable nest of comedy back in the seventies, with comedian alumni like Martin Short, Dave Thomas, and film producer/director Ivan Reitman (yes, that's right, and while most Canadian universities claim one of their residences was the inspiration for Animal House, we have proof!). Other alumni include astronaut Roberta Bondar, Lincoln Alexander, master of magic Doug Henning, economist Harold Innis, and Ontario Liberal Party Leader Dalton McGuinty.

two, and has the highest rate of returning students of any of the residences. It also has a quite a reputation when it comes to throwing great parties. And then we have Edwards Hall, which is actually located much closer to the centre of the campus, and was, until this September, the university's all-male residence. Housing Services has recently decided to make the building co-ed, which is too bad. Not only do I feel sorry for any women who now have to use their disgusting bathrooms, but the residence had a great reputation for spirit and chivalry on campus. Sure, they were rowdy, but it's the oldest residence on campus, and its presence and boot camp antics will surely be missed. Finally, there's the Bates Residence (more commonly known as the Bates Motel), the apartment-style housing located on the northwest tip of campus. This residence is reserved for upper-year students, and the majority of the apartments contain four bedrooms. It's quiet, cheap, and conveniently located, and the main living areas in each flat are quite large. The catch, however, is the fact that each bedroom is absurdly small—barely large enough to contain a single bed and desk. Oh well, at least they can run home to use the bathroom between classes.

Between the two quads, all of the residences are located in close proximity to one another, which makes for a lot of fun, if not a lot of peace and quiet. The noise is most felt during Frosh Week and Homecoming Weekend, but the spirit and camaraderie which abounds among the residences is a sight to behold. Rez life is definitely not for anyone, but it's a great way to make good friends immediately while we wait for our true friends to eventually find us.

NIGHT LIFE

In first year, the term "night life" pretty much means one thing: finding a place to get really, really drunk. As such, and for those with drinking on their mind, Hamilton is a more than adequate city for those adventurous types looking for ways to amuse themselves after dark. In fact, residents of Hamilton like to drink—a lot. While the city is certainly not a bustling metropolis, it has an unusually large number of bars per capita, and offers a wide variety of watering holes. Since Hamilton has a reputation for being gritty and downtrodden, a smaller, dirtier, darker, and more depressed urban neighbour of Toronto, this lends to its need to assert a kind of rebelliousness through drinking. That being said, the majority of Hamilton's plethora of bars are kind of seedy and would no doubt fail a thorough health code check, but a select few are quite good fun.

For most students who live on campus, or in the surrounding student ghetto in Westdale, there are ample choices. First of all, Mac has three on-campus bars: The Downstairs John, The Rathskeller, and The Phoenix. The John is the largest of the three, with a club-like atmosphere, an impressive band lineup, and long lines after 11 p.m. The most popular nights for The John are Thursdays and Saturdays, and the majority of its patrons are first- and second-year students, making it a veritable meat market of tube tops and muscle tees. The Rat is a bit more relaxed, and offers a more pub-like atmosphere with cozy wooden booths and a billiards room. The hot night at the Rat is Friday, and since the bar is nestled among the university residences, the vast majority of its patrons are first-year rez types who've stumbled drunkenly over for last call. Finally, there's The Phoenix, a pub owned and operated by the Grad Students' Association. It's a nice place to get drunk in the afternoon (as many profs and TAs will tell you), and it has a big-screen television and a large and private patio. So, if you're interested in sharing a pitcher with friends while watching the WWF, this is a great and cheap place to do it. However, the atmosphere is not really conducive to getting silly and sloppy drunk into the wee hours of the night. Since The Phoenix is located on the floor directly above The John, lots of people will wander here from there. The best offerings by way of live music tends to come either from La Luna, a smoky roadhouse tavern which also happens to have the city's best falafel sandwiches, or The Hudson, a trendy martini lounge with really hot bartenders and beautiful pool tables downstairs.

If you're drawn to the hypnotic, thumping bass of the dance club, there are several options downtown. To name only

A Word to the Wise:

1. Get to know and use the services available to you as a student, especially the Career Planning and Employment Centre and the Centre for Student Development.

2. Discover Hamilton. Also, bring a bike with you to Mac, and take time out of your studying schedule to commune with the nature that is Cootes. There's more to life than studying, and the time spent exploring will pay off in the long run.

3. Always go to tutorials, even if they're on Friday mornings. It may seem like a waste of time, but the more you participate in interactive group learning, the more your TA will like you and the better your marks will be. You may even discover that you're learning stuff.

4. Take advantage of the drop and add period at the beginning of each semester. If a class doesn't initially appeal to you, it's better to switch into another course that's more interesting, rather than let it drag on. Drop and add is convenient and free of charge, and your chances of doing well in a class improve dramatically if you actually like the course.

5. Always keep abreast of required courses. Too many fourth-year students find out too late that they didn't take the required credits for a certain degree, only to discover a particular course is not offered during that specific year. Besides, you'll want to take your easier electives in later years, when the workload is harder.

6. Everyone's grades drop in their first year. Don't panic, but don't use it as an excuse, either.

7. University is first and foremost about learning about oneself, not about career preparation. It is perfectly normal for university students not to have a clue what they want to do with the rest of their lives, so don't panic if you change your mind on a weekly basis.

a few, there's The Syndicate, the most fashion-conscious and pretentious of the lot; The Border, a cheesy bar with a Western motif, beefy bouncers, and plenty of hicks; and Fever, a gothic, rowdy dance pit for those who fancy the alternative scene.

If, however, you just like to sit with friends in a more relaxed, pub-like atmosphere, then Hess Village is a definite must-see. Hess is essentially one downtown street lined on both sides with outdoor patios. This is a great place to go before the nights get too cold, and by far the most popular attraction in the city. In the summer months, Hess is always hosting some kind of outdoor music festival, where the street gets closed of to traffic and a giant beer tent fills the street. It's extremely crowded, and very expensive, but it makes a great place for people watching. However, once the patios are closed for the winter, Hess is little more than one tiny, expensive bar after another. Hamilton's pièce de resistance is definitely Sláinte (pronounced "slawn-chay"), an authentic Irish pub which claims to have imported every single thing in the bar (except for the outside walls) directly from Ireland. It's a veritable drinking wonderland, with intricate woodwork, lots of cozy rooms, and loud group singing.

ON HAMILTON

The fourth-largest city in Ontario, the total population of the city of Hamilton is over 360,000. As any Hamilton resident will tell you, the city is divided into four very distinct regions: West Hamilton, Downtown, East Hamilton, and the Mountain. Each area has its own unique flavour.

West Hamilton: The university campus is situated on the edge of West Hamilton, and the neighbourhood has an interesting demographic. Half of the residents are impoverished students in search of culture and mirth, and the other half are wealthy professionals in search of a quiet, cultured environment in which to raise their posh little kids. The result is a lot of cafés and health food stores, and lots of parks, too. As I mentioned before, McMaster houses a giant wildlife sanctuary called Cootes Paradise, part of a total of 7,000 acres of conservation areas in Hamilton. It's a hiker's and mountain biker's dream, complete with winding paths through thick forests and along large ponds. It's truly a great treasure, and an idyllic escape from the stresses of academia. In fact, one of the amazing things about

> "Hamilton is Canada's best-kept cultural secret. Locked in its lunch bucket are: Canada's most beautiful cultural centre, art gallery, unique philharmonic orchestra, theatre companies, gastronomic delights, the finest botanical gardens, and Steel City's most special resource—its proud and ambitious people."
>
> Boris Brott, conductor of the Hamilton Symphony, a remark made October 2nd, 1979.

Mac is the fact that, besides being so close to a city the size of Hamilton, a mere 10-minute bike ride either to the north or to west will land you in farm land or at such southern Ontario treasures like Webster's Falls or the Bruce Trail.

Downtown: Okay, the city core is a bit dumpy, and there are probably two vacant store fronts for every non vacant one, but there is a definite coolness to this Steel City. There are plenty of movie theatres and restaurants, and the city is large enough to provide a thriving arts community, and often attracts big-name bands. There seems to be an underdog feel to Hamilton, always trying to assert its urbane qualities in the shadow of its larger neighbour, Toronto. As a result, the downtown core has an edge to it, an attitude of gritty hipness. Hamilton also has a very reliable bus service, and full-time Mac undergraduates have an unlimited bus pass during the academic year (covered by a supplementary fee within tuition). If, however, the urbanite finds the city to be a bit lacking, Hamilton happens to be conveniently located only 45 minutes from Toronto, so you can reap the benefits of Toronto's night life without having to live there.

East Hamilton: This is the part of Hamilton most people drive by on their way to Niagara Falls. It's home to all of the steel factories, and the housing situation is depressing. It's essentially a Mike Harris nightmare of urban decay, and while it's interesting to visit, most Mac students keep away from this end of town.

The Mountain: The name is terribly misleading, for there's no mountain to be found, but nevertheless this is the name of the suburban sprawl which looks down on the city of Hamilton from atop the Niagara Escarpment. There are some nice malls up there, but it's pretty much a wasteland of gas stations and grocery stores.

Nipissing University

By Ed Garinger

Nestled in a 295-hectare campus that features walking trails, cross-country skiing trails, and waterfalls, Nipissing University makes its home in the picturesque community of North Bay. To the geographically challenged, the idea of the university being located in "North" Bay means that NipU is in the middle of nowhere, somewhere far, far up North. Another misleading impression is that NipU is a school in the North, for the North. These assumptions are simply not true. Nipissing attracts many students from southern Ontario and isn't as far as you think, it's a little over a three-hour drive north from Toronto.

Being a school in North Bay does not mean that students and faculty get around campus on snowshoes or skis and bundle up in parkas; that's only in the winter. (Just kidding!) It's not surprising that Nipissing, being a small university, fosters a close-knit atmosphere where everybody knows everybody, though everybody does not necessarily know everybody else's business. To escape from the sometimes claustrophobic atmosphere, students can take advantage of the great outdoors that surround them. Physically active students can be at one with nature by cross-country skiing or playing hockey on a man-made pond.

NipU is not a hot bed of political activity and does not exude diversity like other universities, but by the same token, students at NipU cannot be lumped together. Sure, you'll find granola eaters and tree huggers here, but contrary to a city slicker's belief, NipU is not a school full of country bumpkins and hicks.

Nipissing University remains mired in relative anonymity, despite the fact that it graduates over 500 students a year from one of the most revered Bachelor of Education programs in all of Canada, and despite the fact that it has been providing a university education since 1967.

Prior to receiving its charter on December 10, 1992, Nipissing was an affiliated college of Laurentian University. Nipissing University opened in 1967 with seven professors and 49 students. In 1972, it moved from its original location in downtown North Bay to its current site at the Education Centre.

Since receiving its charter, Nipissing has grown by leaps and bounds, offering degrees and diplomas in over 35 streams in the Faculty of Arts and Science as well as the Faculty of Education. The university expanded its faculty to 77 full-time in 1998–99, 63% with tenure and 75% with PhDs, while opening a satellite campus in Muskoka.

Nipissing University's students have garnered international acclaim, winning prestigious national and international awards for their academic and social efforts. Nipissing has global partnerships in places such as St. Lucia, Nepal, Barbados, Zimbabwe, Florida, and Tennessee, consequently attracting students from as far away as Zimbabwe, Australia, Germany, Mexico, South Africa, and other places.

Nipissing takes pride in its individuality, promoting its size, location, and history. As a university with predominantly undergraduate programming and roots in teacher education, it emphasizes its differences from other institutions, using them as selling points for attracting new students.

CAMPUS CULTURE

Despite the diversities within the student body that make it next to impossible to describe the typical Nipissing student, an overwhelming commonality is found in participation and a genuine concern for the school's success in the community, both academically and socially. Like any other post-secondary institution, Nipissing has its problems with student apathy, but at NipU, apathy means a more than 50% participation rate. With Frosh Week, Winter Classic, the many clubs, intramurals, and varsity athletics rounding out the spectrum of student activity, there is something of interest for literally every student to get involved in.

The student clubs run the gamut of student interests, and are overseen by the Nipissing University Student Union (NUSU). A sample of these clubs includes NEAT (Nipissing Environmental Action Team), BACCHUS (Boosting Alcohol Consciousness Concerning the Health of University and College Students), *The Hibou* (official student newspaper), The Sign Language Club, NCCF (Christian Fellowship), The Word Society, The Biology Society, NUBS (NU Business Society), The Ski Club, NUDE (NU Drama Entourage), The French Club, and The Philosophy Society. Everyone is free to join any club they wish, and new clubs can be formed at the start of the academic year, with monetary and resource support, provided they meet the criteria set out in the NUSU constitution.

Vital Statistics

Address: Nipissing University, 100 College Drive, North Bay, Ontario, P1B 8L7

Admissions office: (705) 474-3461 ext. 4515

Website: www.unipissing.ca

Total enrollment: 1,856

Male-to-female ratio: 1:2

Percentage of international students: 1%

Percentage of out-of-province students: 2%

Average entrance grades: Arts

and Science: 67%–75%

Tuition fees: $3,781.00

Residence fees: $3,385 (without meal plan)

Percentage of students in residence (approx.): 28%

Co-op programs: None

Financial aid: Scholarships and honour awards include President's Scholarships valued at $12,000, Carl Sanders Scholarships from $500–$2,000, 150 Tuition Assistance Awards $1,000, government loans.

Facilities for students with disabilities: Special Needs Services

Aboriginal students: Aboriginal Services, Aboriginal Teacher Certification Program, Native Classroom Assistant Program, Native Special Education Assistant Program.

Student services: Academic advising, personal development counselling, job placement services, peer tutor program, health services, math drop-in centre, student residence office, writing skills program.

Nipissing University's varsity sports teams are called The Lakers and they compete in the OCAA and OUA. Men's and women's teams compete in volleyball, soccer, curling, cross-country running, and nordic skiing. On-campus fitness facilities include weight and cardio rooms with a 21,000-square-foot Athletics Facility with gym, squash courts, and fitness centre currently under construction.

ACADEMIC ISSUES

Nipissing University places an emphasis on teaching. NipU is best known for its highly competitive teaching programs offered through its Faculty of Education. The Orientation to Teaching Program prepares students for the Bachelor of Education program. Nipissing also boasts a unique Native Classroom Assistance Program. Business Administration, Environmental Science, and Psychology are also popular majors among students.

Class sizes vary from five students in upper-year honours courses to 150 students in first-year introductory courses. One of Nipissing University's main selling points as well as something they take great pride in is the interaction that is possible between faculty and student body, due to the low student-to-instructor ratio. Unlike many other larger universities, interaction with professors is considered essential to academic success, and is subsequently well provided. The only drawback to all of the academic benefits of this one-on-one professor-student interaction is the detriment to the occasional (or habitual) slacker. If you skip lectures, the instructor not only notices, but takes note.

Doing a research paper? Plan ahead. If you are planning on doing any sort of research for a paper or a project, especially one where there will be competition for the same resources, get to the library first. Even if you do get there first, it is more than likely that you won't find what you're looking for. Nipissing's library holdings are…how do you say…less than desirable. Fortunately, for those students who crave relevant research materials, the library does have a good borrowing relationship with other institutions. It does, unfortunately, take a while to locate the material, and then get it into the student's hands. So, as previously mentioned, plan ahead.

REZ LIFE

One of the most attractive characteristics for first-year students is Nipissing's two residences. The "new" residence, called Founder's House, is located a picturesque 15-minute walk, or 5-minute bus ride, away from campus. It is apartment style with four individual rooms to a unit, along with two full baths and a furnished kitchen. It is a Nipissing-only residence in which all first-year students are guaranteed a spot. Founder's House has quiet rooms in which to study, a games room, and a television lounge on each of its five floors. With a paid residence fee at Founder's House, each student receives a bus pass for North Bay's wonderful transit system, good for the duration of the fall/winter term.

The "old" residence is townhouse style and contains six individual bedrooms and one and a half baths. This residence is right on campus and is shared with Canadore College. Its rules are less rigid, and it's a little bit cheaper, but there are less amenities than at Founder's House. However, the biggest bonus is being able to roll out of bed for those 8:30 classes and not worry about changing out of your pyjamas. A short

In a Nut Shell

The university in a phrase: Small classes, big minds.

Best thing about the university: Faculty of Education, small class sizes, professors know your name.

Worst thing about the university: Inadequate library, professors know your name.

Favourite professors: Prof. Ron Klingspon, Assistant Professor, English Studies; Dr. Donna Jowett, Assistant Professor, Philosophy and Women's Studies; Dr. Robert Surtees, Professor, History.

Most popular bird courses: First-year Computers.

Hot spots to study on campus: The Wall campus pub, the cafeteria.

Quietest spot to study on campus: The library, where else?

Need for car and parking availability: No real need for car, parking available, relatively expensive.

Sexually speaking: Thin walls in residence.

Fraternities/sororities: There aren't any at NipU.

Athletic facilities: Brand new athletic complex to be completed by summer 2000.

Library facilities: Sub-par.

Computer facilities: Adequate. Computer "HandsOn" Workshop.

Weather: Bitter cold in the winter and hot in the summer.

Safety on campus: Security and Campus Walk program escorts you anywhere on campus.

Alumni: 17,000 and counting (including Mike Harris, Richard Todd).

two-minute walk, and you're ready to catch those final Zs in the back row of your introductory Psychology lecture.

Both residences have ample parking and laundry facilities, and both are located right on the bus route, making it easy to get to the mall, the grocery store, and the bars.

There are plenty of social aspects to rez life, with rez-oriented events planned for its residents. These events can range anywhere from barbecues to speakeasys, and, more often than not, are pretty lame. The biggest socially beneficial happenings on rez are self-planned, spur of the moment get-togethers that usually involve a keg, some eighties tunes, boys, and girls.

NIGHT LIFE

Most regions across the country will try to lay claim to the best and biggest partyers. Northern Ontario, and specifically North Bay, is no exception. There is no lack of watering holes, clubs, or coffee houses to choose from. The problem is differentiating them from one another. The only choice you really have is the amount of smoke in the air, and what age group you'd like to hang out with. Luckily these two characteristics are in direct correlation.

With good reason, the most popular student hangout is the campus pub, The Wall. The Wall is one of the biggest campus pubs in the province, and houses some big-time concerts including the likes of The Tea Party, 54-40, Big Sugar, The Matthew Good Band, I Mother Earth, and Hayden. It is open during the day with a full roadhouse menu, and lays claim to Tuesday nights with wings and pitcher deals and Yuk Yuk's comedians. The Wall also owns Friday nights with the best prices in North Bay, a wicked DJ, and a huge dance floor with lights, prompting the bar to be at capacity with a lineup every Friday.

Other popular bars are located on Main Street in the downtown area. The Moose has a great rooftop patio during the warmer months, and has the best wings in town—free with cover on Wednesday nights. Wylder's Music Hall is the place to catch live music just about every night of the week, having played host to musical acts of every genre in the country, but beware the age and air-quality factors. The best part of the downtown scene, though, is the myriad of food joints ready and able to quench that drunken hunger. Old reliables like Subway, Pizza Pizza, 2-for-1, and hot dog vendors are all present, but the favourite among students is The Leaning Tower of Pita.

ON NORTH BAY

What is there to say about North Bay? Located on Lake Nipissing, North Bay is a community of close to 60,000 people and serves as a commercial centre for one-quarter of a million people. As such, everything you could ever need is available. Unfortunately, needs and wants are different things. Those coming from a major urban centre such as Toronto might be bored with the trees, fresh air, and slower pace in lieu of disdain and gridlock. Having said this, North Bay is a university and college town and therefore does have almost anything one could ask for, including theatres, plays, clubs, sporting venues, and events. It's only an hour away from Sudbury, four hours from Ottawa, and three hours from Toronto, so it's easy to go somewhere big for a little excitement on the weekend.

As with most towns in the North, it does get cold in the winter months, but it gets equally as hot in the summer months. The transit system isn't bad and the town is safe, with plenty of things to do. And, if you can't find something to do, there's always your homework.

University of Ottawa

By Sarah Mayes

Situated in the downtown core of our nation's capital, the University of Ottawa is one of a handful of bilingual universities in Ontario. This defining characteristic lends a distinct feeling of diversity to the campus, and the bilingual nature is reflected by the capital city itself. When walking to class, it is not unusual to hear conversations in a number of languages, nor to hear people switch from French to English mid-sentence. This may seem weird if your education in French ended after grade nine, but you can survive at Ottawa quite well even if you have no idea what the past tense for *parler* is. Everything (and I mean everything!) at the U of O is conducted in both official languages and the administration prides itself on being fully bilingual. In recent years, the university has quietly let go of a language requirement that demanded every student pass a proficiency test in his or her second language. Nobody seems to have noticed.

The campus itself is quite architecturally distinctive. The only building that looks at all traditionally academic is Tabaret Hall. That is probably why the administration plasters pictures of Tabaret all over its university propaganda. Once you head into the centre of campus you are either confronted with featureless grey buildings or someone's misguided attempt at controversial architecture. Morisset Library looks like there ought to be police interrogations going on inside. In contrast, the bright colours and modern looks of Brooks Residence make it seem like a gingerbread house in the middle of a concrete forest. If you want to look back fondly at the ivy-draped halls of your alma mater, don't come to Ottawa.

CAMPUS CULTURE

There is a sharp divide between the two main groups of students on campus. The Anglophone and Francophone populations are like two neighbours who acknowledge the other's existence but aren't about to invite them over for a barbecue. There are two official student papers, for example, *The Fulcrum* and *La Rotonde*. The respective editorial staff seem to be blissfully unaware of each other and often feature the same cover story in different languages, with different spins. Many French social events, such as the popular Improv games, go virtually unnoticed by Anglophone students. Surprisingly, there is little political tension on campus, at least not of the separatist variety. Canadians around the country who despair at the idea of French and English existing in harmony should venture down to the Agora one day around noon.

If you are searching for your own special niche at U of O, you won't have to look very hard. Special interest groups abound and take themselves very seriously. The Unicentre, which is the core of student social activity, often houses displays from such diverse groups as the Canadian Lebanese Student Association or the Ottawa Christian Fellowship. Walking through the Unicentre at lunch you can sample international cuisine and get an earful of Marxist rhetoric all at the same time. If you really want to go unnoticed, however, try student politics. Ottawa U students are nothing if not apathetic and despite efforts every year to recruit student voters, the number of students that come out and actually vote is abysmal. Even tuition increases can't seem to mobilize students. Despite the fact that almost every student you talk to is concerned about rising tuition fees, a rally organized last year had a turnout of about six students who spent much of their time yelling at their peers that it was their fault tuition was going up. You can find a student community at Ottawa, but as a body it is more concerned about what you are doing Friday nights or when that big paper is due than something as trivial as politics.

ACADEMIC ISSUES

Stuck geographically between two of the biggest academic powerhouses in Canada, McGill and Queen's, many Ottawa students suffer from a feeling of intellectual inferiority. The truth of the matter is that Ottawa has a solid academic reputation and has built up many programs to levels unparalleled throughout the rest of Canada. The Criminology program, for example, is an excellent speciality and a big draw for many students. Ottawa's proximity to Parliament Hill also allows Political Science students practical experience they wouldn't be able to get elsewhere. The School of Rehabilitation Sciences is a recent addition that is emerging as a strong faculty. Professional

Vital Statistics

Address: 550 Cumberland Street, P.O. Box 450, Station A, Ottawa, Ontario, K1N 6N5

Admissions office: (613) 562-5700

Website: www.uottawa.ca

Total enrolment: 22,695

Male-female ratio: 42 to 58

Average entrance grades: Arts: 70%; Science: 70%; Commerce: 70%; Engineering: 70–75%

Tuition fees: Most faculties: $3,334; Engineering: $3,659

Residence fees: $2,301 (shared room); $2,678 (single room); meal plan: $1,625–$2,250)

Spaces in residence: 2,100 (approximately)

Percentage of out-of-province first-year students: 16%

Financial aid: Scholarships are available to all students entering the university with an average above 80%. These scholarships are renewable provided you maintain an average of 90% or higher. Full-time students who are entering and are receiving OSAP can get a $500 bursary. There are numerous other bursaries and scholarships available through the Financial Aid Office.

Co-op programs: Arts: Environmental Science, Geography, History, Mathematics Concentration in Geography, Linguistics, Economics, Translation; Science: Chemistry, Mathematics-Science; Social Sciences: Leisure Studies, Political Science; Engineering: Chemical, Civil, Computer, Electrical, Mechanical, Computer Science.

Services for students with disabilities: Centre for Special Services.

Aboriginal students: Aboriginal Resource Centre, employment and education program, Law education equity program.

Student services: Academic and career counselling service, campus ministry, career and employment centre, computing services (free e-mail accounts), health centre, housing service, international students' office, peer helping centre, study skills workshop, tutoring, women's resource centre, writing centre.

---

schools are also quite notable. A unique feature of the university's Law school is that it offers students the opportunity to study both Canadian law systems, the French droit civil and the British common law system. Not wanting to be the last to jump on the bandwagon, Ottawa has also begun to build its roster of co-op programs. The advantage of doing co-op at Ottawa is that often you don't have to leave the city to complete your work term since computer companies, government office, and museums abound here and are all ideal work placements for students.

Class sizes at the U of O are generally quite manageable. The professor-student ratio at the undergraduate level is one to eight and the largest lecture theatres only hold several hundred students, and are usually used only for first-year survey courses. Once you get to upper-level lectures you can have classes as small as a dozen people, especially in seminar settings. TAs and professors are usually friendly and accessible. If you want to stand out, don't bring them an apple, just show up during office hours.

Given the bilingual nature of the university, students are invited and often encouraged to take courses in their second language. You can even take a course in French and write your exams and papers in English. Students entering Ottawa should take careful note of the requirements of their specific program. Many degrees are offered in both languages for three years but the final year must be taken in either French or English. Many Sociology students, for example, get burned

when they decide to upgrade to an Honours degree only to discover that their fourth-year courses are only offered in French. Then they grumble all the way to Carleton to complete their degree. First-year students should also try to register as early as possible, as returning students often register at the beginning of April to avoid the fall rush. Although there are places reserved in first-year classes, prospective frosh who wait until July to register may find themselves facing a limited choice, especially if they were aiming for upper-year classes; nobody wants to take advanced Calculus as an elective. The amount of hassle at registration and the quality of academic services you receive often depend on which program you are in. Students in general programs often face large lines when attempting to resolve academic problems through a faculty. Honours students are usually invited to deal directly with their department, which means that there is a good chance your academic counsellor will learn your name. There are some advantages to sticking around for that extra year.

Despite the somewhat friendly rivalry that exists socially between Carleton and Ottawa, the two schools have taken steps to ensure that their students get to experience the best of each of these institutions. Credits are frequently transferable between the two universities and a shuttle bus runs throughout the day, ferrying students from campus to campus. The U of O has also recently formed a partnership with IBM. The prime recipient of IBM's largesse will likely be the new School of Information Technology and Engineering (SITE), but the

In a Nut Shell

The university in a phrase: You go where?

Best thing about the university: Location and diversity of the student population.

Worst thing about the university: The frequently disorganized administration.

Most popular bird courses: Witchcraft and Occult Traditions, Introduction to Leisure Studies, Human Sexual Behaviour.

Hot spots to study on campus: The Nox, Le Solstice French café.

Quietest spots to study on campus: Any of the private study rooms in Morriset.

Need for car and parking availability: If you live anywhere close to campus you don't really need a car as grocery stores, malls, etc., are all within a 15-minute walk. There is a great bus system in Ottawa and many students that live in outlying areas take that route. Parking around the university is scarce and quite expensive. Parking violations are strictly enforced.

Sexually speaking: Students at the U of O are generally quite open sexually. If you want some action the best time to get hooked up is in the fall before the parkas come out and everyone becomes unrecognizable. Because of the high concentration of students living together, residence is another quick way to get lucky. Rainbow Friends provides support for the gay and lesbian community.

Fraternities/sororities: Fraternities and sororities exist at U of O and are a heavy presence during Frosh Week and in January when they are trying to recruit. Other than that they pretty much keep to themselves and don't make waves, beyond the odd charity event in the Unicentre.

Athletic facilities: Sports complex—three gyms, 50-metre pool, 10-metre diving tower, aerobics, dance studio, climbing wall, skating rink, playing fields, squash and racquetball courts. The gym, housed in Montpetit Hall, has cheap membership and houses fairly up-to-date equipment. Prepare to wait in line for machines, however, as the workout rooms are frequently packed. A huge new Sports Complex is being planned for September 2000.

Library facilities: Three main libraries: Morisset (Arts, Social Science, Science and Engineering), Law, and Health Sciences. The university often gets slammed for lack of library resources but in reality houses not only a good English collection but also a large French collection. Students are invited to use the Carleton Library as well as the public system and the National Library.

Computer facilities: Over 15 computer labs with over 1,500 workstations.

Weather: September and October are usually great weatherwise, but you can pretty much rule out the rest of the year. Between the ice, the snow, and the frigid temperatures, winter in Ottawa is not for the faint of heart. At the end of winter and just in time for exams is slush season, when the entire city turns into one big lake of freezing cold, dirty water. If you're daring enough to brave the cold, don't miss out on Winterlude and skating on the Rideau Canal.

Safety on campus: Volunteer foot patrol. Protection Services is quite visible around campus even if their emergency posts with blue flashing lights seem more silly than effective. Protection patrols the campus on foot and in cars and is quick to respond to any situation. The student-run Foot Patrol WalkHome program expands with every year and is a valuable resource for students with night classes who live off campus.

Alumni: Hon. Robert de Cotret; Mary-Lou Finlay, CBC journalist; Maureen McTeer, lawyer; Alex Trebek, host of *Jeopardy!*; Roch Voisine, singer.

administration predicts that all the students will feel the benefits of this partnership (this remains to be seen). This appears to be part of the administration's attempt to capitalize on the university's proximity to the computer firms of nearby Kanata, a region sometimes known as the Silicon Valley of the North.

REZ LIFE

The three main residences at the University of Ottawa, Thompson, Marchand, and Stanton, rise over campus like three frosh-filled behemoths. Each of these residences are high-rise towers housing about 500 students each, which makes fire drills memorable. Thompson is the largest residence, with 20 floors crammed full of students who get by on Kraft Dinner and a prayer. The advantage to living in this rez is that it is connected to the main body of the university through above-ground tunnels. Thompson residents are the ones that show up to class in their pyjamas in the middle of January because they've only just rolled out of bed 20 minutes ago. Thompson is also the only residence that is entirely smoke-free. Somewhere along the way this Goliath acquired the reputation of being a party residence, a claim that is not always entirely unjustified. This is probably due to the fact that it houses the largest number of students and in past years had the most relaxed quiet hours. Now every residence has floors that are designated with specific quiet hours.

The two other residences, Stanton and Marchand, are connected to one another and on the canal side of the campus. Marchand provides some single-sex floors and has a greater number of single rooms. It is therefore considered something of a drag and is often favoured by returning students who want to remain in residence but aren't necessarily interested in the type of active lifestyle to be found in Stanton or Thompson. Students entering Marchand should be warned that the rules there are strictly enforced. If you think that life at Marchand is going to adapt to you, think again. Stanton, like Thompson, is co-ed, with varied quiet hours. The Francophone residence, LeBlanc, is somewhat smaller and houses about 150 students and has a female-only wing. Residents tend to keep to themselves. Upper-level students have the option of moving into Brooks Residence after their first year of study. This residence is set up in apartment-style units and is a stepping stone between residence and the scary world of off-campus housing. Brooks has fewer residence advisors but quiet hours after 11 are still enforced. Apartments are available in two-, three-, and four-bedroom units. The two- and three-bedroom units are scarce, however, and students should be warned that if they do not apply in a group of four there is a strong possibility that they will end up living with strangers. First-year residence is guaranteed for Franco-Ontarians, scholarship students, exchange students, and persons with disabilities and special medical needs. In the past couple of years, as enrollment has gone up, more and more first-year students have found themselves trying to find off-campus housing in the middle of August. Rumours are flying that a new residence is in the works, but they may have to build it on Parliament Hill given the lack of space on campus.

NIGHT LIFE

Despite what Toronto or Montreal aficionados will tell you, for a city of its size and somewhat staid reputation, Ottawa has a lively night life. This could probably be accounted for by the fact that it is a tourist attraction in the summer and houses students from two universities and one college during the rest of the year. The more common opinion, however, is that it is too damn cold in the winter to do much else. First-year students will be introduced to the Byward Market during Frosh Week and will probably not get sick of the dozen bars there until their third year. The Market is a 10-minute walk from campus and offers just about anything you are looking for. Desperate singles craving pulsing dance beats and scantily clad members of both sexes need venture no farther than The Factory or RJ's Boom Boom Saloon, both aptly named. If jeans and a T-shirt are more your idea of bar apparel, The Cabin and Stoney's both play a greater variety of music (Nine Inch Nails, Lauryn Hill, and Kenny Rogers all on the same night) and provide a more casual atmosphere. There are many small pubs located in the Market which thrive on Irish beer and cheap wings. Perhaps the most popular student hangout of this sort is Minglewoods, which suffers from a confused identity—pub by day, bar by night. Those who need a bit more of a rush should head to Atomic, arguably the most cutting edge club in Ottawa. Atomic offers a rave environment, is open after hours and plays some of the most innovative music to be heard in the capital region. It's not for everyone but it is the only place where you can party till dawn and then head to Nickels for breakfast. Once students have exhausted the pleasures of the Market they can venture down to Elgin Street, generally serving a somewhat older crowd. For live music, the best venues are Zaphods, which showcases a wide variety of local talent, and Barrymore's, which books locals but also brings in bigger names that aren't quite big enough for the massive Corel Centre. There is also a thriving bar scene for those students with alternative lifestyles. These bars are some-

A Word to the Wise:

1. Buy a good pair of boots. They will be your most valuable possession in January.

2. If you get a chance, stay in Ottawa during the summer months. Job opportunities are fairly plentiful and you will get to experience the perks of the city without slush, snow, or ice. Off-campus housing is also cheap as many students sublet.

3. If at all possible, avoid the meal plan.

4. Make sure you take advantage of all the cultural opportunities that Ottawa has to offer, not just those that can be found in the Market and are best enjoyed with a bottle of beer in your hand.

5. Live in residence and experience Frosh Week. Both are excellent ways to meet friends and have access to the city around you.

what harder to find but the Lookout is one situated close to the Market.

On campus, the night life consists of the Nox on Thursday nights. For some reason, Nox staff couldn't pay people to hang out there on a Saturday and yet students regularly line up on Thursday nights and pack the place. As bars go, the Nox isn't bad, if somewhat dark, and seems to undergo renovations every other year to make it more appealing to a very fickle clientele. Other staples of the campus scene are the Royal Oak and Fathers and Sons. Fathers and Sons is located just off campus and is affectionately known as "F and S." Despite a somewhat tasteless menu, it is packed no matter when you go by, from their famous two dollars and change breakfast special till drunken hockey players stagger out in the wee hours of the morning. The Oak is one of a chain in Ottawa and offers the student beer connoisseur a nice, relaxed atmosphere and a large selection on tap.

ON OTTAWA

There are many advantages to being situated in a city that is meant to be the glittering centre-piece of a country. Within the downtown core and a short walk from campus are housed many prominent museums and cultural hot spots. The National Arts Centre, for example, is right over the canal and offers student discounts on some performances. The National Library provides not only literary gatherings but is a valuable source of research materials. For excitement of a less cultural variety students can head to the Rideau Centre, which is about a block away from campus and is perfect for that midafternoon craving for the Gap. Of course, one must not forget the Rideau Canal, one of the city's most popular attractions. In the winter, the canal turns into a huge skating rink, complete with beavertail stands (a local treat that is something like funnel cake; recently the chain has gone national). The canal runs alongside the campus and is open for several months of skating, beginning with the popular festival Winterlude. Students living farther down the canal have been known to skate to school, and the canal is also a great way to spend a snowy Saturday afternoon. Even in warmer months the nature walks that run parallel to the canal and throughout the city make for a nice place to walk, bike, or rollerblade. The tulip festival in the spring and the Jazz festival in the summer are also big tourist draws, though many students aren't around then to appreciate them.

The fact that the university is located so close to downtown means that students get the advantages of living in a city and can still feel like part of a community. It is not unusual to run into familiar faces on Rideau Street or to find yourself shopping next to a professor in the local grocery store. The neighbourhood of Sandy Hill, which surrounds the university, has a large student population and is a colourful place to live. Like in any city, the downtown area of Ottawa is not always a safe place. In recent years there have been problems in the Market late at night and several incidents of violence in the Rideau Centre. In general the people downtown are friendly and accommodating, especially if you listen to their tales of alien abduction.

Queen's University

By Leigh Anne Baker

Queen's is a midsize university with a strong sense of community and school spirit and an excellent academic reputation. It also offers the kind of party lifestyle that would cause its Church of Scotland founders to get down on their knees and start praying for our souls—not that anything illegal (well, maybe illegal by Kingston's stringently enforced by-laws) is going down. Queen's students are into working hard and playing harder, whether that involves massive keg parties or holding mock debates in the House of Commons (Queen's Model Parliament pulls weight). It's probably not what the founders had in mind, though, when the school was first opened in 1842 to train clerics and others. Queen's lost the last of its denominational control in 1912, but thank God it didn't lose its spirit—school spirit, that is.

The campus today is covered in the school's tri-colours (the official Queen's colours of red, blue, and gold) and students sporting ugly Queen's jackets and other school paraphernalia. Just watching the students walk by the old limestone buildings on campus is enough to fulfill all your ivy league fantasies. The buildings are beautiful and the campus is very green, with three large playing fields, a park, and trees lining the main drag, University Avenue. The main campus is situated on the waterfront of Lake Ontario, in one of the oldest and prettiest parts of Kingston. The entire campus can be walked top to bottom in 15 minutes and is right near downtown Kingston.

The student village, formerly known as the ghetto, lies on the north side of campus and is one of the best things about the campus. Although there is a problem with the standard of housing and landlords, living in a neighbourhood full of students is worth it (if you don't think so, you could always move a few blocks farther away from campus where the housing is cheaper and nicer). It's total socialite heaven. There is always something happening, whether it's parties, lounging on the porch, playing ball in the street, dropping by to visit friends on the way home, or just hanging out and watching the world go by.

CAMPUS CULTURE

Most students chose Queen's either for its size, academic reputation, or the smaller town life. While not as diverse as a big-city school, Queen's attracts students from a variety of backgrounds and is enriched by a number of cultural groups, societies, and clubs. The typical Queen's student is straight out of high school, top of their class, involved in sports and activities, and filled with Queen's spirit. Many would-be students are turned off by Queen's private school, upper-middle-class reputation and the perception of snobbery that goes along with it. In reality, status at Queen's is determined by your intelligence and personality, not by where you shop or what neighbourhood you're from.

Extracurriculars are huge; many people participate in activities because they're genuinely interested, all do it to pad their résumé (this is actually a good idea because it will make a huge difference in fourth year, when you and everyone else have the same academic qualifications). Most students are super busy and they like it that way. Student government (Alma Mater Society or AMS) is very popular; it's the largest and only entirely student-run student government in Canada. With over 1,000 volunteer positions and more than 300 paid positions, you too can keep your hot little overachieving hands busy by volunteering for a committee. There are commissions for handling all the important issues and related activities, covering everything from academic affairs to social issues. Then there are the student-run services, such as Walkhome, the UBS-Exchange used bookstore, Studio Q (our very own TV station), and the pubs. On top of all that, you could

Vital Statistics

Address: 99 University Avenue, Kingston, Ontario, K7L 3N6

Admissions office: (613) 533-2000

Website: www.queensu.ca

Total enrollment: 16,849

Male-female ratio: 47 to 53

Percentage of international students: 3%

Percentage of out-of-province students: 15%

Average entrance grades: Arts: 79%; Science: 85%; Commerce: 90%; Engineering: 85%.

Tuition fees: Domestic students—Arts and Science: $4,529. 54; Commerce: $4,617.04; Engineering: $5,738.04. International is a hell of a lot more.

Residence fees: Single: $6,640; double: $6400; economy double: $5,125; triple: $5,800.

Number of spaces in residence: 85% of first-year students live in rez and after that everyone moves out to the village.

Financial aid: Queen's University Entrance awards range from $110 to $12,000; in-course scholarships from $100 to $6,000; bursaries from $200 to $2,000; loans from $200 to $2,500; a needs-based work-study program, a summer work experience program, and emergency funding are available. There are also government aid, Queen's loans (90 day and long term), and financial counselling.

Co-op programs: Biochemistry; Concurrent Education and Rehabilitation Therapy; Engineering.

Services for students with disabilities: Technical aids/assistive devices; accommodations for exams, tests, and assignments; classroom accommodation; special needs staff to work with other departments to resolve accessibility concerns; workshops.

Aboriginal students: Four Directions Aboriginal Student Centre provides support for the Queen's University Aboriginal community.

Student services: Academic, financial, employment, and psychological counselling; Career Centre; Health Services; Writing Centre; Apartment and Housing Service; child care; multiple resource centres for Aboriginal students; human rights; women; lesbian, gay and bisexual issues; sexual health.

always make your faculty proud by whipping up some fab stuff for their committees and executives. There are also over 200 clubs and associations, covering everything from the arts, to media, to politics, to volunteer for and get involved with. The inter-university sports teams, the Golden Gaels, are popular. There are 39 men's and women's teams, covering 23 sports. If you are not looking to get that sweaty that often, there are always the intramurals, as well as the instructional and recreational sports clubs, to practice everything from aikido to white-water paddling.

ACADEMIC ISSUES

The first mark back from Queen's is usually pretty damaging to the old ego. For students with the highest average entrance grades (86.8%) of any university in Canada, it's not so fun to find out you're not the smartest in the class anymore. Then again, it is pretty cool to be around so many smart kids because it adds so much to the general discussion and sense of competition. Queen's offers undergrad programs in Engineering (Applied Science), Arts and Science (including Life Science), Commerce, Concurrent Education, Nursing, Physical and Health Education, Fine Arts, and Music. Queen's also offers international experience in the form of third-year exchange programs with over 50 universities all over the world. The school owns Herstmonceux Castle in East Sussex, England, thanks to alumni Alfred Bader, which offers an excellent field and class study program for first- and third-year students.

All of the programs and faculties at Queen's have excellent reputations, although in the faculty of Arts and Science, Political Science and History are especially well known. The top two primo undergraduate faculties are Commerce and Engineering. Commerce is hard to get into and hard to get kicked out of. If you pass all your classes and keep your average above 65% (although everyone does a hell of a lot better than that), you are guaranteed an Honours degree at the end of four years. The program is extremely job-oriented; the "Commies" have their own career centre and recruitment opportunities in fourth year. Queen's Commerce is one of only a few prestigious business programs in Canada that recruiters come to visit. Recruiters also focus on the Engineering program, and Queen's has the highest percentage of women students of all Canadian engineering programs. Engineers are famous for working hard and partying harder, painting themselves purple, pulling huge pranks on campus, and for their legendary grease pole climb during Frosh Week.

The Arts and Science programs are very competitive. Be aware that many programs weed out struggling students. However, if you are up to the challenge, this ensures that only the students that really want to succeed, do. In the end this maintains the high-quality standards of the Arts and Science programs. The deciding factor of who's in and who's out tends not to be brains so much as time management skills and motivation, so don't get scared and wuss out before you even start.

REZ LIFE

Residence is all about embracing new-found freedom and showing off your ability to live away from mom and dad—hence the weekly rituals of staying up all night for no reason and partying till you pass out. First-year social life revolves around the residences, where many people meet their core group of friends and future housemates. Rez is a great way to get used to university life and is highly recommended. They feed you (except dinners on Sundays) and they have laundry in the building (first years have no idea how lucky they are). Dons and floor seniors are there if help, information, or comfort is needed; however, if it isn't, they will let you be as long as you don't cause major problems (i.e., throwing up in the hallway, burning things, breaking stuff). Everyone accepted into first year gets guaranteed residence, as long as they send in their form and pay their deposit on time. Single, double, economy double (small doubles with bunk beds or loft beds), or triple rooms are available. When you apply for rez you state your top choices of buildings, type of room, lifestyle preferences (early bird vs. night owl stuff), and the school will attempt to match you. Whether you get what you want is questionable, but problems can usually be solved quickly.

Victoria Hall is the newest and largest residence. This co-ed rez is located between the two cafs on Main Campus and is known as party central. The rooms vary in size, from small singles, to doubles, to triples, to big doubles which might be used as triples temporarily until they can find room (i.e., someone in rez moves out) to place extra bodies. The big bonus is the private bathroom shared between every couple of rooms.

There are four residences bordering Leonard field. Gordon-Brockington is a great rez. It's attached to Leonard caf, is co-ed, and has big rooms. Across the field is Morris. Morris is co-ed with standard rooms, although some have excellent views of the lake. All male Leonard Hall is at the top of the field and on top of the caf. It is one of the last bastions of maleness at Queen's, with all the smells and rituals that go along with it. While most men don't choose to live there, they all seem to enjoy it. Next door is all-female McNeill. The all-female rezes have a two visitors per resident rule. Also, the resident must escort visiting men in and out of the building, although it doesn't matter when or how long they stay (as long as you haven't built yourself a little love shack and invited him to stay permanently, of course). The two people rule may or may not be a big deal, depending on how much you like to entertain in your rez room. There are always other places to hang out.

Adelaide, Ban Righ, and Chown girls have got it made for convenience. These all female residences are the closest to the school buildings, and they live over (or right beside) the newest caf. They have nice single and double rooms that are relatively large. The only drawback is that they are subject to the two visitors and male accompaniment rules.

Waldron Tower is the furthest rez from the centre of campus (five minutes from Ban Righ caf) and the walk is windy in the winter. However, if having your own sink, huge closets, and a single room is your thing, you will be a happy little clam. The bathrooms are co-ed and so are the showers. However, there are individual change stalls attached to each individual shower stall, so it's not as bad/fun as it sounds.

Jean Royce Hall is on West Campus. It is a very long and boring fifteen minute walk from Main Campus. Meal plans are optional, but you'll want one because meal times are the biggest social events of the day. Its main claim to fame is the best caf food at Queen's and the fact that from some of the upper-floor rooms, you can see into the inmates' yard of the prison across the street. Don't worry about the prison, though; it's maximum security, so no one ever gets out.

NIGHT LIFE

Kingston's night life is all about drinking and dancing and doing it big style. If you're used to going to a wide range of clubs and bars catering to different tastes and crowds, you may find Kingston a little limited, but what is missing in selection is made up for in sheer debauchery and fun. On campus there are the student-run Alfie's Pub, QP, and Clark Hall Pub. Alfie's is one of the best bars in Kingston and a favourite upper-year haunt. It's the perfect place for dancing (with a stage for busting mad moves) and hanging out, and the crawl home is short. The QP is upstairs, where you can sit on a couch, watch the big screen TV, listen to music, and entertain yourself with testing the long list of fab and fun cocktails. Clark Hall Pub, run by the engineers, is most famous for Ritual, when the pub opens at noon on Fridays for some heavy drinking lasting all afternoon, or until you pass out in the corner.

Off campus the main bar area is at the intersection of Division and Princess, conveniently located at the northeastern corner of the village. A.J.'s Hangar is very popular with the first years for getting messy, picking up, and fighting for a turn on the speaker. Stages plays good music for a night out dancing, and offers trashy bar games and a chance to fraternize with the "townies." The Trash is an excellent bar, spinning great alternative tunes for a packed dance floor busy getting down and dirty. The Brass has one of the cheapest pitchers in town and is a great place to hang out, get drunk, and tell stories. The Cocamo, down by the water, is famous for cheap drinks and the loudest music in town (your ears will ring all the next day).

In a Nut Shell

The university in a phrase: Queen's is a small university with a strong sense of community and school spirit and an excellent academic reputation.

Best thing about the university: The work hard, play hard balance.

Worst thing about the university: The lack of diversity.

Favourite professors: Lee Sabrigar (Psychology); Jim Lee (Geological Sciences); Douglas Stewart (Art History); Peter Aston (Microbiology and Immunology); Bill Cannon (Business).

Most popular bird courses: Classics 203—Myth and Religion; Physics 010—Physicists in the Nuclear Age; Spanish 010—Beginning Spanish I.

Quietest spot to study on campus: The Fireside Lounge, the basement of Douglas.

Hot spot to study on campus: Stauffer's first floor.

Need for car and parking availability: Everything is so close that it's not really needed, although it is nice to drive to the cheap grocery store, laundromat, and liquor store when in upper year. If you do bring a car, students living in residence can't get parking passes for the lots on campus. You can rent a driveway close by for about $20 to $30 a month. You could leave your car on the road, except that come December 1st, you will get ticketed every single night until April.

Sexually speaking: Queen's is a fairly small school and it's easy to meet people. You can always find someone who knows the person you're interested in, and they can hook you up with introductions and info. The problem is that everyone else can find out about you in the same way, so while there is a fair bit available, do be selective, or people will call you names.

Fraternities/sororities: There aren't any at Queen's.

Athletic facilities: The Physical Education Centre (PEC) was renovated in 1997. There are machines, free weights, a pool, squash courts, aerobics, skating rink, and an indoor track. Outdoor tennis courts and fields are well kept. There are recreational sports clubs, intramurals, instructional sports, competitive clubs, and inter-university athletics, basically covering every sport under the sun. Everyone gets a "free" membership; it's included in the fees. The best thing about the gym is that, for a fee, there is a gym uniform service. It includes a very small towel and a clean uniform; the great part is that when you're done you give it all back and they wash it, and you don't have to worry about digging that stray, smelly sock out of your bag.

Library facilities: There are seven libraries, with over 6.6 million library items and 2.09 million volumes. What this means is that there are mega holdings per student. Stauffer Library, for the Humanities and Social Sciences, opened in 1995 and is beautiful, with tons of seats and windows, Internet hookup, and group study rooms. Douglas Library, for Engineering and Sciences, was renovated in 1997, and also has Internet hookup and very nice reading and study areas.

Computer facilities: There are computer labs around campus and most have Internet access and offer IT support. You usually have to wait for over half an hour to check your e-mail at labs that are open to all Queen's students.

Weather: Kingston is beautiful in the spring and summer. Then in the fall it starts raining. Then in the winter it snows. All year around there is a lot of wind, and unfortunately it has a bad bite.

Safety on campus: Unfortunately a neighbourhood full of students, with every other house being full of young women, attracts the odd weirdo. That said, Queen's has an excellent Walkhome service running every night. Campus security does 24-hour patrols and there is a Blue Light system. Over the entire campus, although not in the student village, there is a blue light in view. If you push the button, you are connected to Security and they can come immediately.

Alumni: Authors Robertson Davies and Michael Ondaatje; Gord Downie from the Tragically Hip; John Crosbie, former Conservative Minister of Finance.

The Shot is the only proper way to finish off the night. It's usually pretty quiet till twelve, when the hordes of thirsty students arrive all at once. It's the kind of place that people swear they need a break from—it's usually packed so tight you can hardly get from one end to the other and you have to wait forever for a drink in the lineup—and yet everyone comes back for more. Finally, no night is complete without a stop at Za Master for a pita, slice, or poutine. This drunken pig-out ritual is the real reason for the "freshman fifteen."

If getting messy or yelling over music isn't your thing, Kingston has fabulous pubs, cafés, and restaurants. The Toucan, Brew Pub, and Tir Nan Og are all cool and cozy, and serve great pub grub. Kingston also has a wide selection of reasonably priced restaurants, including an assortment of ethnic

A Word to the Wise:

1. Go and see your prof if you have a problem or don't understand something. It may seem like you are one of an anonymous bunch in class, but if you go and talk to your profs during office hours, they will bend over backwards to help you out. Honest. Except, of course, if you are lying to them to get an extension, or are having problems because you haven't done your work. Then they are not as nice.

2. Bring waterproof gear, including a bag. Also, make sure you have solid, waterproof shoes/boots with a good tread because the sidewalks in the village aren't cleared in the winter (it's the tenants' responsibility and apparently nobody owns a shovel), and you'll be hurdling snow banks, for sure.

3. First year does matter, when you're trying to graduate in a program of choice or get into grad school.

4. Live in rez first year, even if you've taken time off and even if your friends have a house and you could live with them. You'll meet so many more people and won't get stuck with absorbing your friends' friends. Same goes for Frosh Week, it just has to be done.

5. Don't buy your books the first week of school because you will wait in a monster lineup. Go the week before to the campus bookstore or UBS-Exchange used bookstore (also on campus); and they will have book lists for each class (check what section you're in first). Or, wait till the week after and see if you can find used books from an upper year through signs on the wall or word of mouth.

6. Lock your rez room when you are not in it or when sleeping. Do not leave your things unattended for even a few minutes. Even though this may make you feel like a distrustful, paranoid freak, things do go missing, and it will save you so much grief and heartache.

foods. The Grizzly Grill, Mekong, Curry Village, and Wooden Heads are among the best. There are also a number of restaurants that cater to students, offering huge portions and cheap prices. Stooley's is highly recommended, as long as you have lots of time; service is notoriously slow.

The student village is always happening, although certain times of the year merit extra-hard partying. Frosh Week, whether you're frosh or not, is a blast. The next big bender is Kill McGill and Homecoming, when you show off your school spirit and coveralls (the baggy mechanic outfits you got in Frosh Week) and cheer your painted face off at the football game during the day. Then at night you hit up the massive keggers and packed bars, sing the Oil Thigh (the school song that involves a cancan-like leg swing) with old, drunk alumni and basically party like a rock star all night long. After that comes Hallowe'en, when everyone searches for funny and original, yet hot and sexy, costumes. Welcome Back Week after Christmas break is yet again another week of far too much fun. Next is Reading Week, although not much reading gets done. Then everyone hunkers down and hits the books 'til the final blowout, the last day of exams.

ON KINGSTON

The most interesting and happening part of Kingston is the area around the school. The waterfront and downtown are 10 minutes away and have an assortment of excellent stores, restaurants, and coffee houses. The area is kicking in the warm weather, with tons of patio culture. A farmer's market, with gorgeous and cheap veggies, is on three times a week. There is a small but active arts community, as well as the frequent exhibitions of the Queen's students' artistic endeavours. The town is rich in history and full of huge, old limestone buildings. It was even the capital of Canada between 1841 and 1843, and has the historic plaques to prove it. Kingston is a booming tourist area in the summer, when the downtown teems with people. The rest of the year it is most popular on sunny days and weekends.

Kingston is centrally located between Toronto, Ottawa, and Montreal, making weekend cultural/party getaways easy, as it is only approximately two and a half hours to each of the cities. The cheap Tricolour buses leave the school on Fridays and return Sundays ($18 to Ottawa, $23 to Toronto, $25 to Montreal, all including tax). There are also train and bus stations, plus a small airport. Beg or borrow a ride to hike in Frontenac Park, ski in Quebec or the States, or party like a mofo in Montreal or Toronto. The great thing about Kingston is that one can experience life in a relatively small town and still have easy access to three of Canada's most interesting and happening cities and the beautiful Ontario cottage country. However, it's so easy to get sucked into Queen's life that some out-of-province students never see more of Ontario than Kingston and the Toronto airport. With some of the most beautiful countryside in Canada within a day's drive, these people are missing out by not exploring a little further.

Royal Military College

By Barrett Lincoln Bingley

Kingston has been a military centre since 1673, when Count Frontenac built Fort Frontenac at the mouth of the Cataraqui River. The RMC campus is situated on Point Frederick, a small peninsula just to the east of the downtown core of Kingston, and just opposite the site of Frontenac's original fort. This scenic location, at the junction of Lake Ontario and the St. Lawrence River, is one of great historical importance. It has been occupied as an active military site since 1789, and during the War of 1812 it served as the major naval station in Upper Canada. Ships of the Royal Navy, built at the Point Frederick dockyard, helped preserve Canada from American occupation. By 1871 the majority of British regulars had been recalled to their home country and the Canadian Parliament saw an urgent need for a school to train officers for the Canadian Forces. Accordingly, in early 1874, the government of Sir Alexander Mackenzie (prime minister between 1873–74) took steps to establish a military college. After feverish construction on the Fort Frederick Peninsula the college opened June 1, 1876, to its first class of eighteen, known as the "Old Eighteen."

Today's campus still has the original buildings used in 1876 (some far before that), but has expanded to cover the entire peninsula. RMC can be divided into three areas architecturally: military-oriented buildings, academic-oriented buildings, and sports-oriented buildings. The majority of the buildings in the first category are at the end of the peninsula, located around the Parade Square and Inner Field. The Parade Square itself is as important as any building; indeed it is considered sacred ground by the cadets. It is where drill is learned, "corrections" are carried out, and the awe-inspiring Ex-Cadet and Graduation Parades are performed. The Inner Field is the first sports pitch built on the grounds and is still used today for rugby matches and inter-Squadron contests. Lining the entire right of the Inner Field are the residences. Constructed of limestone and built in an old, castle style of architecture, they are an impressive site. Across the field the Senior Staff Mess provides a nice contrast with its classy, unassuming style. Beside it, the Stone Frigate, an old Royal Navy Warehouse and the first residence constructed at the college, sits in its own little world. At the tip of the peninsula is the restored site of Fort Frederick, now a free area where cadets can let their hair down a bit. Completing this rough circle are Currie and Mackenzie buildings, which are built in grand old British style and face the Parade Square. The Sawyer and Girouard buildings best exemplify the academic buildings. Quite modern, they were built in the seventies and utilize a starker, minimalist style. Situated behind Mackenzie, they are not at all typical RMC buildings but give a sense of progress to the campus. Sawyer, used by the Faculty of Science and Engineering, is by far the hardest building to get around in. Any Artsman who is forced into the engineer's domain for whatever reason often becomes hopelessly lost after turning more than two corners.

Hidden out of the way, the sports buildings are across the highway, reached via an overpass that can get very slippery in the winter. The hockey arena is small and a bit rundown but serves the needs of RMC's small population. The Sir Archibald Macdonell Athletic Centre is a monstrous, ugly concrete building that nevertheless houses a top-notch athletics program. Numerous sports fields are available, all with a great view of Navy Bay and Lake Ontario.

Placed throughout the green, rolling grounds of RMC are various military monuments, including the standard artillery pieces. Of note are the tanks from WWII and the Korean War, the restored CF86 Sabre aircraft, and the bronze cadet statue affectionately known as "Brucie." There are also a number of war memorials, all of which are humbling in the sacrifice and honour that they represent. Chief among these memorials is the Memorial Arch, constructed June 25, 1923, to honour the ex-cadets who have died in Canada's wars. It is an immense limestone construction that is dear to every cadet. A cadet will only pass through it twice, once on being accepted to the college and once upon graduation.

Overall the campus is beautiful, from its views, to its restored building, to its monuments set amongst the plentiful trees.

CAMPUS CULTURE

Royal Military College is unlike any other university in Canada for two reasons. The first being that it is a military college and therefore one will find things on that curriculum and in everyday life that

Vital Statistics

Address: P.O. Box 17000, Stn Forces, Kingston, Ontario, K7K 7B4

Admissions office: (613) 541-6000

Website: www.rmc.ca

Total enrollment: 920 officer cadets, 1200 total students

Male/female ratio: 3 to 1

Ratio of first-year applicants accepted: A two-tiered selection process is in place. Perhaps one in four competitive applicants get selected in the final round.

Cut-off grade for admission after first round: Not used. Admission is based on combination of academic and military potential. Most successful applicants have marks over 80%.

Tuition fees: $1,524. Regular Officer Training Plan Cadets (the majority) have tuition waived. Reserve Entry Training Plan Cadets pay tuition, rations, and quarters.

Residence fees: Rations are around $217 per month. Quarters are about $83 per month. This comes directly out of our salary. There are also many miscellaneous college expenses, such as mess dues, tracksuits, and the like.

Facilities for students with disabilities: No students at RMC have disabilities.

Student services: Computer services, trainers, nutritionists, physiotherapists, padres, councillors, and a large number of military support services.

would never be found in a civilian university. The second is the size of college; only about 930 officer cadets attend RMC. The number of students goes up to around 1,200 if the graduate students are included. This small size provides a sense of a close-knit community and makes it possible to do things that are logistically impossible at larger universities. The ultimate goal of any cadet who enters RMC is to become a competent, well-rounded officer in the Canadian Forces. This goal and its implications resonate throughout life at RMC. To aid every cadet in this goal, life at RMC has been divided into four pillars, each of which must be mastered for graduation to occur. The pillars are academics, military, physical fitness, and bilingualism.

The academics pillar is structured to be much the same as civilian universities, with RMC granting degrees in Arts, Engineering, and Science. One major difference is the core curriculum, meaning that all officers graduating from RMC will have some courses in common. Consequently, Engineers and Science people must take some Arts elective courses, including mandatory History and psychology courses. On the flip side, Artsmen will take the dreaded Calculus course, a general Science course, as well as various Engineering and Science electives. Another major difference is that attendance at all classes is mandatory. "Corrections" will result if a cadet is found skipping for no good reason. Corrections can really hurt on Monday mornings. Also, while attending class everyone wears the same uniform, although not the same one all year round (there are about nine different uniforms, with two or three variations each), but everyone will wear the dress of the day. While at first glance this might look stifling, it actually provides a sense that you belong to a community, and a sense that everyone in uniform will do their best to help you if you need it. Also, included in the curriculum are courses not seen anywhere else, such as drill and compulsory physical

training. These help to keep up the military pillar when it seems all one can think about are the upcoming finals and that History term paper due on Friday.

The military pillar of RMC is what really sets it apart from other universities. It is the reason some students would never go anywhere else, and the reason some people are afraid to even apply. It is difficult to encapsulate all that is the military pillar of RMC in a few words; the scope of it is enormous as it influences each and everything you do at the college. Just to get into RMC a candidate has to first complete the Basic Officer Training Course in St. Jean, Quebec. This eight-week course is a sort of "Welcome to the Military—you are at the bottom of the pile," introduction, where one learns the basics of life, such as how to polish boots, make beds, and do 13-km forced marches. After this intro the new candidate is shipped off to Kingston. The recruit now commences on an experience that some have called the toughest period of their lives, and others have called the most invigorating time of their lives, and that no cadet will ever forget. It is called Recruit Term and it is hell. During this time you are not yet considered a member of the college and are not permitted to speak to any senior cadets. This six-week period starts in late August and finishes on the spectacular Ex-Cadet Weekend, the first weekend in October. You only go to school for the last four weeks and it is the first time in many people's lives that school seems like a blessing from God. During Recruit Term a cadet is assigned to a "flight" of about 25 cadets, which is then attached to one of the 10 squadrons in the college. There are cadets of every year in each squadron and the senior cadets take control of the recruits. During Recruit Term every second of your life is controlled for you. It is an indoctrination into the college during which the new recruit learns the enormous amount of knowledge one must have just to survive at RMC. By the end of

RecTerm, as it is popularly known, a cadet knows how to survive inspections by high-ranking cadets, how to make a bed in under two minutes, how to change complete military uniforms in less time than it takes to brush your teeth, and how to do drill for hours at a time. Not all of Recruit Term is feverish work; the weekends are marked with some fun events. The Recruit Tabloids is the first of these, a competition by all of the recruit flights in various sporting events. The whole school comes out to cheer on the recruits, with points being counted towards the Commandant's Cup, which is a trophy given to the top squadron of cadets at the end of the year. There is also a drill competition, which, if your flight does well, makes the countless hours spent practicing on the parade square in the blazing sun all worthwhile. The College Regatta is the first event where the recruits are close to really being a part of their squadron. It is a relaxed day comprised of boat and canoe races in Navy Bay. The entire college competes in this one. The last and most memorable event of Recruit Term is the Obstacle Course, a two-hour exercise in teamwork, mud, and misery. Every recruit in every flight goes through this historic course that can only be accomplished through an enormous amount of teamwork. The crowd for this event is enormous as the whole college, parents, friends, and the general public all come to watch. It is something that has to be experienced to be believed. After that is the Ex-Cadet Parade, where a recruit becomes a first year and real life at the college begins.

After making it through RMC's six-week version of Frosh Week, cadets are still entrenched in the military pillar of RMC. All cadets have morning inspections, although not every morning, with the frequency of them decreasing the more senior a cadet is. Uniforms must be kept up to standard and military footwear polished. First-year cadets must wear their uniforms into town whenever they leave campus. All other years can wear civilian clothes. The longer a cadet has been at the college the more privileges he or she accumulates. Fourth-year cadets are generally left to their own devices to accomplish whatever duties they have. Besides the freedoms, seniority means greater responsibilities, as many of the duties of the college are handled by cadets who must demonstrate that they are up to the challenge.

The military side of the college is also responsible for weekend activities. Some weekends are leave weekends and cadets are free to do what they want. Others are duty weekends that are allotted to military training. Sometimes the training is general, such as leadership seminars, and sometimes it is branch specific, meaning you get different training depending on whether you are in the Army, Air Force, or Navy. There are military competitions that involve using leadership skills as well as proving you are physically up to the challenge of being an officer. One team specifically for this purpose is the Sandhurst Team, which goes to an international military-skills competition at the United States Military Academy (our little school usually kicks the Americans' butts, too!).

One other notable aspect of the military pillar is the parades that RMC puts on. The cadets practice for weeks for the two big ones, the Ex-Cadet and the Grad Parades. Being on parade, in front of thousands of people, is an amazingly proud feeling that cannot be matched anywhere else.

The third pillar is physical training. All cadets must pass tests taken three times a year, which gauge their fitness. Staying in shape for these tests is not exceptionally hard because time is scheduled for sports and other activities, and during these times sports are given priority over everything else. All cadets must participate in either an intramural or a varsity sport, which take place after school and on weekends. Between the two virtually every sport is offered at RMC, despite its small size. Hockey and rugby are two of the most widely played and supported sports. Besides the team play, two hours of physical training is fit into the academic schedule, and first years often have morning training sessions. Also, whenever cadets are in tracksuit, they must be running. You can get in serious trouble if you are caught walking. Cadets are very much encouraged to work out, run, etc., on their own time. All of this leads up to a Cadet Wing (that's what the cadets are collectively referred to as) that is extremely fit.

The fourth pillar is bilingualism. Every cadet must be bilingual before he or she graduates. RMC is totally bilingual, offering virtually all courses in both English and French. All cadets take classes in their second language until they are bilingual; once this is achieved, those classes become spares, something very much sought after by the engineers. RMC also has the language of the week, whereby the first 15 days of the month all business is conducted in French and the next two weeks in English.

The trick for each cadet is to balance each of these pillars so as to become proficient in each of them, not be overwhelmed, and still have personal time to develop as an individual. All pillars must be passed in order to graduate.

There are many things about RMC that do not fit into

In a Nut Shell

The university in a phrase: The university with a difference.

Best thing about the university: The close-knit community.

Worst thing about the university: Uptight senior cadets.

Favourite professors: L.Robinson (English); Dr. Dunnett (Economics); Dr. Luciuk (Geography); Dr. Yawie (CompSci); Capt. White (CivEng); Dr. Weir (ChemEng).

Quietest spot on campus to study: At night, definitely the cafeteria underneath Yeo Hall. On the weekends Fort Frederick is a great place to study if the weather is nice.

Most social spot of campus to study: The Snake Pit or your room.

Need for car and parking availability: A car in Kingston is great to have if you live near enough to drive home on leave weekends; otherwise, it is not a necessity as the city is fairly compact. Parking is very limited as the only place to park is Constantine Parking Lot. This lot is also over a kilometre from the residences.

Sexually speaking: While cadets are allowed to date, no sleepovers are allowed at the college. Either date a Queen's girl with her own room or be prepared to shell out for a hotel.

Weather: During school there are two nice months of weather—the first and the last. Otherwise, it is raining or absolutely freezing.

Eating facilities: Cadets eat at the Yeo Hall Mess all year round. While the fare can get a bit monotonous after four years, the food is good. Healthy choices and vegetarian meals are always available.

Computers: There are separate computer labs for the Engineers and Artsmen. The labs are often full at peak times but are open well into the evening for those who must check their e-mail and don't have their own computer.

Library facilities: The Massey Library for the Arts side of the school is small but has a limited selection on a number of topics. It makes up for this by having an unsurpassed collection in such topics as military history, war memorabilia, and strategy.

Athletic facilities: The SAM Centre and the other sports buildings are currently undergoing massive renovations to make them the best facilities in the Forces. Already a world-class weight room exists. There will be a new pool, ice surface, and covered trackhouse added to the already impressive SAM.

Alumni: Air Marshall (Ret'd) Billy Bishop, General (Ret'd) deChastelain, Air Commodore Leonard Birchall, Senator Molson (CEO of Molson Corp.), Col. Chris Hatfield (NASA astronaut). More generals, colonels, and CEO's than you can shake a stick at.

the four pillars. This is because they are more specialized interests. There are a huge variety of clubs at RMC, traditional ones such as the precision drill team and the Army club, as well as totally non-military ones like the debating club, drama club, and outdoors club. While everyone at RMC must roughly fit the officer cadet mould, there is so much individuality within the Cadet Wing that once someone has gotten to know the cadets they could never accuse them of being carbon copies.

The other thing that cannot go unmentioned about the RMC culture is the fondness of the Cadet Wing for enormous parties. There is no sex or drinking in the residences, so instead of little room parties huge Wing-wide bashes are held. There are about nine really big parties each year, about half of which take place in the new cadet drinking mess. The two biggest parties to note are the Bav, loosely related to Oktoberfest, and the Christmas Ball. The Bav takes place around Hallowe'en and consists of all the cadets partying their brains out with music courtesy of the DJ Club. Unbelievable amounts of beer are downed by all present at this event. The Christmas Ball is a gala event. Cadets attend in their highest order of dress,

their scarlet tunics. Everything is ultra-classy. Cadets, once clearing the reception line, are free to mingle with some generals and colonels or engage in some ballroom dancing with their dates. From the champagne to the display by the highland dance team, the night is unforgettable.

RMC is composed of many different aspects and many different types of people. A cadet's life is usually full to bursting. Sometimes the only thing that lets one keep it all together is the fact that everyone at RMC supports each other. With such a small school you eventually get to know everybody. Knowing everyone also means that rumours fly faster than light. Of course, the level of safety on campus at RMC is also unsurpassed. The best thing about everyone living together and sharing hardships and good times is that by the time you graduate you will have solid, lifelong friends.

ACADEMIC ISSUES

Although it started out as solely an Engineering college, RMC has come to offer degrees in the Arts as well as the Sciences. As the second-oldest Engineering college in Canada, RMC has always offered a top-notch education in Engineering and continues to do so today. The engineering program is uniformly hard, regardless of the branch one specializes in. Any free time or spares an engineer at a civilian university may have is taken up by the mandatory Arts courses and by the military aspects of RMC. Also, having a mix of military and civilian professors allows the cadets the chance to see the world of Engineering from all sides. A boast on the back of the RMC's engineer's T-shirts is that they have 100% job placement. This is actually true, however funny it may sound. This is due, of course, to the obligatory military service after graduation.

The Science faculty is relatively small and offers a limited number of degrees so that they may have greater depth in the courses they do offer. One program that benefits greatly from the small size is the Computer Sciences program. Because of the small number of students, they have excellent access to the extensive resources available to them.

The Arts faculty offers a small, concise number of degrees. There are no courses offered in Biology, Sociology, Anthropology, or a number of other social sciences. Additionally, no courses are offered in the Fine Arts. There are courses available in Psychology, quite a varied selection actually, and while it can be taken as a minor there is no degree offered in it. What the faculty does offer is English, French, History, Politics and Economics, Business Administration, and Military and Strategic Studies. The English and French departments cover all the time periods of their respective literatures in quite a number of ways but do not offer many courses which drill down on one particular topic within a period. History, like at any university, has some bland professors and some fantastic ones. Courses have more of a military bent and the faculty benefits from being on a campus that makes the history of war and human conflict a very real issue in the minds of the students. The faculty often hosts national History symposiums, which the cadets are encouraged to attend. Not much is offered in way of women's history or social history. The Business Administration program is one of the tougher Arts degrees. The workload can get very strenuous and it is a tough program to switch out of, unlike the others, which can be fairly interchangeable. The Politics and Economics program is very good, due to the fact that it has some of the most energetic, interesting teachers in the school. It is a composite degree in which courses in Geography can also be taken. Many graduates of this program are sought after by top Canadian firms, which try to get grads to forsake the military for an existence with less mud and danger. The Military and Strategic Studies degree is only offered at RMC and is a combination of history and politics. Often seen as a degree only for those who intend to stay in the military for life, it offers courses with a decidedly military content, focusing on

global and regional politics and conflicts. Some very passionate professors within this faculty are interested in helping cadets become better officers through knowledge not easily gained elsewhere.

While RMC does its best to offer a plethora of courses for its small size, the Principal and Commandant realize that RMC does not offer everything. Therefore, cadets are allowed to take some courses at Queen's University should they wish to augment their degree.

The student-teacher ratio at RMC is excellent. The largest classes are the first-year History and Economics courses, numbering at close to 100 students. From there the numbers drop drastically. Average class size for first year is around 30 students, with the average getting lower the more advanced the course. By fourth year, average class size is down to less than 20 students; often the classes have less than 10 students. This provides a great chance for student-teacher interaction and the teachers get to know every student in their class.

RMC does offer graduate degrees for both full-time and part-time students. Full-time graduate studies are available in Arts, Sciences, and Engineering.

REZ LIFE At RMC 95% of all officer cadets live on campus, the exception being the few married cadets who have families and reside in married quarters at CFB Kingston. Cadets live together, in the same squadron, for four years. You get to know your neighbours really well. Roommates are a standard thing for first years and are assigned. If you are having trouble with your second language, chances are you will end up with someone who speaks the opposite language. By the time second year rolls around you may have your own room, may get to choose a roommate, or still be assigned one. Most third and fourth years get their own rooms, but not always if the squadron is a large one.

There are four buildings that house the 10 squadrons. The Stone Frigate houses One Squadron. This is the only squadron that is situated across the Parade Square, away from the rest of the blocks. The Frigate is one of the oldest buildings on campus, but the rooms themselves have been upgraded and are certainly liveable. The Frigateers, as they like to call themselves, fancy themselves in their own little world over there and have many traditions not found elsewhere in the college. All of the other residences are on the opposite side of the parade square and are connected by a series of covered walkways known as the 401. Two, Three, and Four Squadrons all live in Fort LaSalle, with one squadron occupying each floor. LaSalle was built in 1912 but was gutted and redone in 1995. It is by far the nicest residence, with carpeted rooms and other amenities not found elsewhere. There are enough rooms that any second-year

A Word to the Wise:

1. To survive Recruit Term, join a varsity team and go to church. Both of these activities allow you to escape for a few precious minutes. If you attend the Bible Study at the Commandant's house and are offered cookies, accept. The Commandant's wife is rumoured to make the best cookies in the Forces.

2. Bring civilian clothes. Although you won't wear them much at first, you will eventually get the chance.

3. Get a Queen's girlfriend or have relatives close by. You will need a haven to get away from the madness sometimes.

4. Get involved and volunteer. Make your mistakes now when they don't really matter and no one's life is at stake.

5. Come in the best physical shape of your life.

6. Make friends with the UTPNCMs. They are people who have been in the military for a while and now attend RMC. They can be counted on to help you out.

7. Work on your bilingualism every chance you get.

8. Go to RMC for the right reasons; remember, you are there to become an officer.

cadet that lives there gets his or her own room, and even the odd first-year cadet will as well. The only negative thing about LaSalle is that the closets are too small to fit all the uniforms, let alone any civilian clothes one might want to hang up. Fort Haldimand is where Five, Six, and Seven Squadrons live. It is one of the most beat-up residences, but aesthetic improvements have recently been done to make it liveable. However, certain larger problems persist. The hot water will not be fixed until the building is gutted and redone. A nice perk was the replacement of all the old washers and dryers with brand new ones, meaning laundry is no longer a week-long chore. With a ping-pong table, microwave, TV, VCR, and plush chairs, the nicest lounge in the school is Seven Squadron's in the basement of Haldimand. The last residence is Fort Champlain, the home of Eight, Nine, and Ten Squadrons as well as the Cadet Wing Headquarters. This is the building most in need of repair and is also the building farthest away from the school and sports buildings. With Cadet Wing Headquarters located here the first-year cadets must always be on their toes to ensure they do not miss greeting a senior cadet occupying a high position in the school.

The conditions of all the dorms except for LaSalle will soon be changing as a new dorm is currently under construction. Once this one is finished, each old residence will be gutted and refitted to bring it up to the standard of the new dorm. This process will take several years, but RMC will have all new dorms as of 2005.

There are some fairly strict rules in place regarding the blocks, the most notable being that no drinking or sex is allowed in the rooms. Violation of this can result in serious consequences. Also, because high-ranking officers in the Canadian Forces, including generals, frequently want to see our residences, they must be kept clean at all times and the rooms are subject to random inspections. Computers are allowed in first year but only after Recruit Term, and don't bother bringing your stereo until second year because you won't be allowed to keep it. First-year rooms can be pretty stark because, as with everything at the college, seniority brings the perks and fourth-year cadets have their rooms decked out better than many bachelor pads in the civilian world. You can have a phone in your room but it's a real hassle to get the line changed when everyone changes rooms at Christmas. The residences at RMC will never see the kind of huge parties one finds at civilian universities, but the blocks are very sociable places. With everyone so close together it is easy to find a study partner or get all your friends together for a night out on the town.

NIGHT LIFE

Kingston is not a huge party town, but with RMC, Queen's, and St. Laurence College all situated close to the city centre there is no shortage of quality pubs and clubs.

Most cadets will start a night of drinking up in the cadet drinking mess, the Snake Pit. This is a great place for first years as it is about the only place they can go without being in uniform. Free pool and cheap drinks make it a great jumping-off point. From there it is easy to walk or take a short cab ride to any of the bars in town.

The best pubs in town are the Tir Nan Og and the Wellington. Both Irish pubs, they frequently offer live music and have the best selection of beer in the city. The atmosphere is friendly and energetic. The Kingston Brew Pub offers good food and quite a few microbrews to be found nowhere else. For an older crowd the Brass and Grizzly's are the best bets. They offer the chance to talk, watch the game, and just generally chill. For a quieter, English-style pub try Toucan's. This bar serves what are possibly the best nachos ever. Last is the Queen's Pub, which RMC students may go to if a Queen's student accompanies them. It has very nice décor, but is not recommended for first years as they will have to go in uniform and may get hassled. Four clubs exist in Kingston, with Thursday being the hot night to go out. Three of these clubs,

Kokomo's, A.J.'s Hangar, and Stages are standard dance clubs, playing Top 40 stuff and serving ultra-cheap beer. If you are going out to get smashed and hit on some Queen's students, these are the places to go. The last, the Trasheteria, is an alternative club not often frequented by cadets.

Something should be mentioned about restaurants, since bringing one's Christmas Ball date to a top restaurant for supper before the Ball is pretty much de rigeur. Chez Piggy's is a very nice spot with excellent cuisine for somewhat reasonable prices. Same for Casa Dominico. The most upscale restaurant, with the prices to prove it, is Clark's On King. It is expensive but exquisite.

ON KINGSTON

Kingston is a city that has always had close ties to the military. CFB Kingston is right up the road from the college and many times cadets will be on that base getting kit, training, or doing administrative chores. The base also has a golf course cadets are free to use. Closer to RMC is Fort Henry, a historic site that is open for tours. Cadets will get to know the hills of Fort Henry very well during Recruit Term as they run up them time after time. The hills also make for some great sledding during the winter months. The four Martello towers constructed for the defence of Kingston in the 1840s can be seen in various spots around the city.

Kingston Penitentiary is a gigantic structure housing some of Canada's more infamous inmates. After four years of living in Fort Champlain some senior cadets feel they are actually in the pen.

Queen's University is within easy jogging distance and provides a nice change of scenery. The library there is also open to RMC students, and any Artsmen wanting to write a decent paper on any non-military subject will end up doing his or her research there.

Downtown Kingston is not very big but offers some interesting shops and is fairly safe at night. The Kingston Locks are the most scenic area of the city and offer a chance for some good fishing.

Ryerson Polytechnic University

By Christine Ibarra

It's hard to concentrate on school when fun and excitement lie just around the corner. Students exercise self-control most of the time, but for students who give into the temptation, paradise lies a mere block away. It's very easy to blow OSAP money and your whole summer's worth of savings in a one-stop shopping spree at the Eaton Centre. Neon lights pulsate and hypnotize you into entering various mega music stores, where you can stock up on tunes to accompany study sessions. Ryerson Polytechnic University is located on 20 acres in the heart of the hustle and bustle of downtown Toronto, right beside the Eaton Centre. The campus lacks the ivy and limestone feel of traditional universities. Its buildings are close together so there are no long treks to get to class. These buildings are a mixture of old and new, the newest being the appearance of the shiny $25-million Rogers Communications Centre. This is Canada's pre-eminent centre of digital culture, housing Ryerson's schools of Applied Computer Science and Image Arts, Journalism, and Radio and Television Arts.

At a convocation ceremony, Lorne Michaels, creator and executive producer of *Saturday Night Live,* was dead serious when he motivated Ryerson graduates by saying: "You're young, you're Canadian, you've got a degree. You can do anything. Get clear, and take your shot." Michaels, the graduates he addressed, and the present students at Ryerson already know that an education from Ryerson is their ticket to secure employment after graduation in an insecure world.

In June 1993, Ryerson was granted university status and since then, Ryerson Polytechnic University has been trying to shake the "Rye High" high school image. Ryerson's motto—*Mente et Artificio,* with mind and hand—alludes to the fact that Ryerson focuses on a hands-on approach through applied learning and professional programs.

It's hard to build a reputation in a mega-city with two other universities and their long-standing international repu-

tations and years of traditions. Ryerson is constantly upgrading, researching using innovative ideas, and developing new graduate programs.

CAMPUS CULTURE Ryerson's student body encompasses many facets of Canadian culture. More than 30% of Ryerson students are members of visible minorities. On campus, there are many cultural groups that reflect the cultural and ethnic components of the student body, such as Ryerson's Chinese Students' Association, Filipino-Canadian Association, Muslim Students' Association and Indian Students' Association.

Rye students are also wide ranging in age and maturity. Close to half of Ryerson students come fresh out of high school. The rest of the student population is made up of mature students who have real-life and work experience, graduates from other universities, and students transferring from other universities. This mixture of people, students of all ages and from diverse backgrounds and situations, results in an environment full of individuality and diversity.

Ryerson focuses on more than just young people starting their degrees. Students at Ryerson gain practical knowledge for the real world. Unfortunately, many Ryerson students are faced with real-world problems. Many students are married and supporting themselves and their families. Many students finance their way through school by working part-time; some even work full-time. Balancing school, work, and family leaves little, if any, time to participate in extra-curricular activities.

Students with time to spare can join various intramural teams, such as basketball, ice hockey, inner-tube water polo, soccer, and volleyball. Exercise your body at the Recreation and Athletics Centre (RAC) and register in martial arts and dance classes, or join the scuba or fencing clubs. Express yourself and write for *The Ryersonian,* Ryerson's weekly paper. RyeSAC Games Room is a choice hangout where you can

Vital Statistics

Address: 350 Victoria St., Toronto, Ontario, M5B 2K3

Admissions office: (416) 979-5036

Website: www.ryerson.ca

Total enrollment: 20,854

Male-female ratio: 48 to 52

Percentage of out-of-province first-year students: 4%

Average entrance grades: Arts: 68%; Science: 68%; Commerce: 69%; Engineering: 68%; Journalism: 80%

Tuition fees: $3,285–$3,535 (plus $374 incidental fees)

Residence fees: Pitman Hall $6,586–$7,202 (including meal plan); ILLC $7,702–$7,902 (including meal plan); O'Keefe House $2,861 (no meal plan).

Percentage of students in residence: 4%

Co-op programs: Administration and Information Management, Applied Chemistry and Biology, Chemical Engineering (mandatory co-op program), Electrical Engineering, Journalism.

Financial aid: Entry-level scholarships ranging from $500 to the full value of university tuition. In-program scholarships between $100 and $3,000 based not only on academic achievements, but also on accomplishments in field placements, performance, design, and production work. Scholarships and Awards by special category: student athletes, international students, Aboriginal students, students with a disability. OSAP, general bursaries, emergency loans are also available to eligible students.

Facilities for students with disabilities: Access Centre provides fully equipped exam/study rooms, a lounge, a self-directed learning unit, a fully accessible kitchen and washroom, and appropriately designed chairs and rest facilities for persons with disabilities.

Aboriginal students: Aboriginal Student Services; Aboriginal Student Circle.

Student services: Career Centre, Centre for Student Development and Counselling Equity, Harassment, and Safety Services, Health Centre, Housing International Services for Students, Mathematics Centre, Student Services Information, Student Peer Support, Writing Centre.

---

play foosball, air hockey, or video arcade games that will seriously test your hand-eye co-ordination. The Second Cup coffee house at the south end of campus is always packed with students getting their caffeine fix.

It is impossible to describe the average Rye student. Fashion students change their style as often as they change their underwear and sport the latest trends in funky and ultra-cool clothes. Business students dress for success and will even wear suits to class. Other students focus less on fashion and wear baggy cargo pants, tear-away pants, vests, and brand-name running shoes for the often long commute home. Oh, and don't be surprised when you see blue hair, body-pierced and tattooed students who make heads turn. This is another common aspect to fashion at Ryerson.

ACADEMIC ISSUES

Ryerson graduates get jobs and get ahead. According to a survey of the class of 1996, more than 97% of Ryerson graduates had jobs within two years after graduation; 98% of grads in Business, 98.8% in Nursing, 99.1% in Engineering, and 100% in Radio and Television Arts, Applied Computer Science, and Applied Chemistry and Biology all reported being employed within two years of completing their program. "The statistics show that Ryerson prepares students for careers," says Dr. Claude Lajeunesse, President of Ryerson. "Our history of relevance and responsiveness, and our focus on meeting the needs of employers and students are reflected in the incredibly high employment rates for Ryerson alumni."

Years ago, high school students wouldn't even consider Ryerson among the contenders for a post-secondary education. Today, soon-to-be university students and graduate students alike are dying to get into Ryerson.

Ryerson boasts programs in Aerospace Engineering, Fashion, Hospitality and Tourism Management, Image Arts, and Nursing. Ryerson offers Canada's first degree program in Midwifery and the only undergraduate degree program in Graphic Communications Management in Canada. Ryerson's programs in Journalism and Radio and Television Arts offer excellent breeding ground for careers in Canadian media, and are a great way to get a head start in a city that has four daily newspapers and a host of other media options to choose from.

Business students learn about the inner workings of the business world and leave Ryerson well equipped for the rigours of fast-paced working environments.

Programs are very structured and offer few options. You should have your mind set on what career path you are going to follow and stick with it.

It's difficult to mix and mingle with students in different

programs. It is easy to make friends within your program considering you take back to back classes with them, and depending on what program you're in, you can spend up to eight hours of the day together.

FROSH WEEK

Ryerson refers to New Student Week as Ryetonium. Ryerson wants to make new students feel at home and leave them with a great first impression. The Ryetonium Universe kicks off orientation with exciting icebreaker activities, including tours of Toronto, scavenger hunts, barbecues, pub outings, academic survival sessions, information seminars, and lots of free goodies. One of the first things that new students learn right away is that you don't have to fly south to the Caribbean to party on an island. One of the highlights of Ryetonium is the Island Picnic and the annual parade.

REZ LIFE

Landing a space in Ryerson rez is easy— if you're coming straight out of high school and live outside the Toronto area, especially if you're from a rural area with no big-city experience. A whopping 80% of Ryerson students are permanent residents of Toronto and its outlying suburbs. The Ryerson population is primarily made up of commuter students who live with their families, either their parents or their children.

If you live in rez, you'll walk away from Rye with a completely different experience than commuter students will have. Living in rez at Ryerson is a far cry from *Animal House*, but you can count on lots of parties, pub crawls, and a great social environment for making friends.

Ryerson offers three residence lifestyles to choose from. Behind door #1 is the historic O'Keefe House, which accommodates 33 students in double and triple rooms and offers a large shared kitchen, lounge, television, and laundry facilities.

Behind door #2 is the International Living/Learning Centre (ILLC). The ILLC used to be a hotel and has been transformed into an 11-storey residence with 252 spaces. Not only do you get an extra-large single room, but each room comes with an en-suite bathroom, a twin, double, or queen-size bed, desk, dresser, and even cable TV. Some rooms also have a pull-out couch for those unexpected guests. As a resident of the ILLC, you must purchase a meal plan. As part of a living/learning lab, students from the School of Hospitality and Tourism Management operate the ILLC.

Lastly, behind door #3 is Pitman Hall. This 14-storey co-ed residence offers space for 555 students in much-coveted furnished private rooms. Pitman provides several areas for students to meet other students and rendezvous for a study session or romantic encounter. Some rooms are equipped with a

kitchen, so you can prepare your own meals. Students without cooking facilities have to buy a meal plan.

If you can't stomach the idea of eating cafeteria food or eating your latest creation, then taste the world and dine at any of the numerous restaurants specializing in authentic Chinese, Japanese, Indian, and Thai cuisine. Chow down at the fast-food chains that serve up tasty eats, from a mean burger and fries to tacos and nachos. You can purchase a meal for under $5, but remember every meal adds up, both in dollars and in inches.

If you're considering living off campus, The Ryerson Housing Registry helps you in your search and lists a variety of accommodations along with rates, addresses, and telephone numbers. Shared accommodation costs about $400 per person, whereas private apartments, depending on how many rooms, can run you dry. Bachelor/one-, two-, and three-bedroom apartments can run anywhere from $500–$900, $900–$1,300, and $1,200+ respectively. Make sure to find out if the rental price includes utilities. If not, expect to add 10% to your rent. Finding affordable accommodation in Toronto can be mind-boggling. It's hard to find a half-decent place in Toronto at a reasonable rate, but they're out there. Start pounding the pavement early and you may be one of the lucky ones.

NIGHT LIFE

Toronto is a great city for night owls and insomniacs. The club scene in Toronto is definitely happening and you can choose from many venues. The entertainment district around Adelaide and Richmond streets has a distinctly electric atmosphere and a broad selection of clubs and lounges to please any preference.

Dance to loud ear-deafening thumps of bass at Limelight the Niteclub, the Joker, and Whiskey Saigon, which all play top hits and mainstream music. Get to Whiskey early or you'll find yourself waiting in a block-long lineup. Hit the Phoenix Concert Theatre and get jiggy with it.

Test your smooth lines at Vinnie's, where big kids can play video games under the influence. Satisfy the post-club munchies at Mr. Pong's Chinese Food parked outside and waiting for you in a mobile truck. Within staggering distance to campus, you'll find The Big Slice to satisfy the late-night pizza craving.

On the way home to the 'burbs via the Don Valley Parkway, commuter students make a pit-stop at George's BBQ on Dundas Street for barbecue chicken and fries.

For more elbow room and a laid-back atmosphere, sip a coffee and e-mail friends while you LOL at a trendy Internet café.

On campus, Oakman Houses' The Ram in the Rye pub is "rammed" with students looking for house specials and Heine

In a Nut Shell

The university in a phrase: A quality, hands-on education that prepares you for the real world.

Best thing about the university: Hands-on approach to learning.

Worst thing about the university: Lack of student involvement, broken-down escalators.

Favourite professors: Notable faculty include CBC broadcaster Stuart McLean, who teaches journalism, and Yew-Thong Leong, one of the architects who designed Toronto's SkyDome.

Most popular bird courses: Ryerson's programs offer little choice because they are so structured.

Hot spots to study on campus: Basement of Jorgenson Hall; on the rocks by Lake Devo; the RAC.

Quietest spot to study on campus: In the confines of the library. The higher you go up, the quieter it gets.

Need for car and parking availability: Finding parking in downtown Toronto is a hellish experience. Depending on what street you park on (assuming, of course, that you actually find parking), meters can cost $1 or $2 per hour! Ryerson is right on the subway line. You can easily hop on a train or streetcar to take you where you have to go.

Sexually speaking: 80% of students are commuters—they either live with their parents or are married. RyePRIDE serves members of the campus gay community.

Attitudes to fraternities: Indifference. The few who join fraternities belong to U of T-based ones.

Athletic facilities: The Recreation and Athletics Centre (RAC) includes a large, supervised fitness centre with machines and free weights, six gyms, six international squash courts, three studios, a golf cage, a traverse climbing wall, an indoor running track, a 25-yard pool, saunas, and several change rooms.

Library facilities: Needs improvement. When all else fails, seek and you shall find what you're looking for—at the Metro Toronto Reference Library or at U of T.

Computer facilities: The Academic Computing Information Centre operates six teaching labs and two drop-in centres equipped with more than 1,300 microcomputers, UNIX workstations and graphic terminals. Available applications range from word processing, web publishing, and e-mail, to specialized research and engineering applications such as CAD/CAM, to finite element analysis, statistics, GIS, and image-processing software.

Weather: Picture-perfect autumn; cold in the winter, but minimum snow falls in downtown Toronto; amazing summers.

Safety on campus: Walk and Watch safety escort program. A security company patrols the campus. The front desks at the ILLC and Pitman Hall residences are staffed 24 hours a day.

Alumni: Lida Baday; Brian Bailey; Jim Bullock; Wendy Mesley; Valerie Pringle; Bill Reid; Issy Sharp; Alison Smith; Tyler Stewart; Margo Timmins.

of the Austin Powers kind and the classic Heineken on draft. The Ram is also the only smoker-friendly place at Ryerson.

ON TORONTO

The biggest challenge of living in Toronto is deciding what to do. It's impossible to take advantage of the infinite number of things that happen. There aren't enough hours in the day (or night) to check out all the concerts, exhibits, festivals, plays, and tourist attractions. Before you suffer from brain drain, venture a little bit further from campus and explore some highlights of the city.

Sports nuts can root for the two-time World Champions the Toronto Blue Jays and the CFL's Toronto Argonauts at the SkyDome. Cheer on the NBA Toronto Raptors and the Toronto Maple Leafs at the newly erected Air Canada Centre.

On a clear day, ride an elevator up the CN Tower and take in the spectacular view of the city and the Toronto Islands. Walk across the glass floor and try not to quiver as you look down the 1,815-foot tower. On your way down, challenge yourself and walk down the tower's 2,570 steps—if you're in tip-top shape, it shouldn't take you more than 20 minutes.

Studying and living in Toronto is about the excitement of big-city life in a multicultural urban centre. Toronto has a vibrant cultural scene with a cornucopia of culture spilling out, and relations between ethnic and cultural communities are generally congenial.

University of Toronto

By Christine Ibarra

Founded in 1827, the University of Toronto is Canada's largest university, with more than 53,000 students—enough people to fill the SkyDome. U of T enjoys a long-standing international reputation of academic excellence in teaching, research, and learning and offers an exceptionally rich curriculum as well as the widest range of programs among Canadian universities. It's easy, however, to feel isolated and awed simply by the size of campus and the sheer number of students. Students who feel overwhelmed and intimidated can easily find the campus to be impersonal and unfriendly. On the other hand, thousands of students quickly adjust without too much difficulty to living the big-city life at U of T's St. George campus.

U of T is *sooo* huge, it cannot possibility be described adequately in just a few pages. It is divided into seven colleges: Innis, New, St. Michael's, Trinity, University, Victoria, and Woodsworth, all on the downtown St. George campus, and two suburban campuses: U of T at Mississauga (Erindale College) and U of T at Scarborough. Each college has its own unique character. Trinity students are commonly known as elitist and Innis students are known to do just about anything for a free meal, including attending presentations on nutrition, money management, or sex in exchange for free pizza and pop. Each college also offers other unique features to maintain its identity, such as various social traditions, religious affiliations, residences, and even architecture.

U of T's eclectic buildings attract tourists and Hollywood movie producers alike to take advantage of its picturesque campus. University College is built in the Romanesque style. St. Michael's College, enclosed by grand wrought-iron fences, boasts older buildings from the time of the French Basilian Fathers. At the heart of the campus is a collection of Victorian houses, once the private homes of prominent Canadians. A medieval castle gracefully adorns Victoria College. Rumour has it that there are more ivy-covered buildings there than at Oxford or Cambridge. These historic landmarks, as well as the more modern buildings, add personality and character to the campus, and are also clever ways to distract students from their desperate treks across campus from one class to the next.

It's very near to impossible to walk up St. George Street, the main street that runs through the campus, without being tempted by the aroma of food wafting from the series of chip trucks parked along the side. In them you'll find everything from hot dogs to delicious, though salty, Chinese food.

During the winter the campuses truly become winter wonderlands. Students can always be seen frolicking in the snow or setting up residence vs. residence snowball fights. One student from the Scarborough campus even smuggled food trays from the cafeteria and "tray-boganned" down the snow-covered hills of the campus grounds. The cafeteria staff is believed to have been blissfully unaware.

CAMPUS CULTURE

Some students can be seen wearing "Uni-diversity" T-shirts that reflect the variety within the student body, faculty, course offerings, and programs. Diversity at U of T means a rich mix of students from a variety of cultural and ethnic backgrounds. U of T garb can range from Birkenstocks and wool socks to U of T paraphernalia to business attire to the latest in downtown fashion. Anything goes.

U of T is a big-city university whose students are primarily made up of commuters (a.k.a. day-hops). After class, thousands of day students make a mad dash to get off campus, leaving ample opportunity for those students who want to get more involved in campus life to do so. U of T offers a large variety of student clubs and associations. There is the Chinese

Vital Statistics

Address: St. George Campus, Awards and Admissions, 315 Bloor Street West, Toronto, Ontario, M5S 1A3

Admissions office: (416) 978-2190

Website: www.utoronto.ca

E-mail: ask@adm.utoronto.ca

U of T at Mississauga: 3359 Mississauga Road North, Mississauga, Ontario, L5L 1C6

Admissions office: (905) 828-5399

Website: www.erin.utoronto.ca

U of T at Scarborough: 1265 Military Trail, Scarborough, Ontario, M1C 1A4

Admissions office: (416) 287-7529

Website: www.scar.utoronto.ca

E-mail: askadm@scar.utoronto.ca

Total enrollment: 52,691

Male-female ratio: 45 to 55

Average entrance grades: Arts: 74%–78%; Science: 74%–84%; Commerce: 73%–77%; Engineering: 80%–89%

Tuition fees: Arts & Science: $3,835; Architecture: $4,136; Engineering: $4,550

Residence fees: $6,150 (double room with meal plan); $5,000–$6,000 (single room without meal plan)

Percentage of students in residence: 9%

Percentage of out-of-province first-year students: 3%

Percentage of international students: 4%

Financial aid: 1,000 admission scholarships and over 2,300 in-course scholarships each year; U of T now guarantees that no student with admission requirements will be denied entrance because of financial need; bursaries and UTAPS also available.

Co-op programs: Arts Management, Computer Science, Environmental Science, International Development Studies, Management and Economics, and Early Teacher Project at Scarborough; Art and Art History, and Theatre and Drama Studies at UTM; Professional Year Experience.

Services for students with disabilities: Special services to persons with disabilities and/or health considerations.

Aboriginal students: First Nations House, home of the Office of Aboriginal Student Services and Programs.

Student services: Academic, career, and personal counselling, career centre, chaplaincy, health services, housing services, international student centre, legal services, on-campus child care, ombudsperson, race relations, sexual harassment office, student government, women's centre. Health and Dental Plan administered by the Students' Administrative Council for full-time undergrads.

Students' Association, Korean-Canadian University of Toronto Students' Association, and LGBT OUT (Lesbians, Gays, Bisexuals, Transgendered of U of T) to name a few. There are lots of extra-curricular activities to participate in, from boxercise to fencing, and for the truly adventurous and "nature-oriented," there are even nude swimming and buff volleyball. The "socially conscious" can join OPIRG (Ontario Public Interest Research Group), a group that acts as a fearless watchdog on the administration and "advocates all causes." Aspiring journalists can write for *The Varsity*, U of T's largest student newspaper, or for various college newspapers, such as *The Strand*, *The Mike*, *The Woody*, or the *Innis Herald*. Students interested in politics may be interested to know that the Students' Administrative Council president makes in excess of $18,000. Not a bad way to finance your post-secondary education, hmm?

The Varsity Blues is a fitting name for U of T's varsity football team since the turnout for most games is virtually non-existent. It is also representative of U of T's omnipresent issue of school spirit (or lack thereof) and student apathy.

> "Canadians should... start counting their blessings, beginning with Toronto, which is a modern miracle—a city that has become better as it has become bigger."
>
> George Will, syndicated columnist, *Washington Post*.

Actually, the average turnout for a football game is roughly 5,000 people, including the fans (mostly high-spirited alumni), the Lady Godiva Memorial Band, and the faculty. But with a stadium built to seat 21,000 people, a mere 5,000 onlookers is like a drop in the bucket. However, Varsity Stadium's problems may soon come to an end since there are plans to tear down the stadium to build a smaller one and a food complex.

Sadly, many U of T students fail to take full advantage of the top-notch athletic facilities at their disposal. U of T has a fantastic varsity sports program and churns out Olympic-calibre athletes in a variety of sports, from field hockey, and soccer to synchronized swimming. The intramural program is equally impressive, with men's, women's and co-ed teams playing against each other in inner-tube water polo, touch football, hockey, basketball, and volleyball. The Varsity Blues Athletic Banquet is one of the most successful annual cross-campus events, with members from every athletic team in attendance.

If you do one thing at U of T, go to Orientation Week.

In a Nut Shell

University catch phrase: Great Minds for a Great Future.

Best thing about the university: Incredible location and library resources.

Worst thing about the university: Big class sizes.

Favourite professors: S. Campbell (History); M. Danesi (Semiotics); D. Foot (Economics); C.K. Govind (Neuroscience); R. Iton (Political Science); A. Itwaru (Caribbean Studies); A. Lam (Mathematics); G. Rezai-Rashti (Women's Studies); Marty Wall (Psychology).

Most popular bird courses: There aren't any.

Quietest spots to study on campus: A corner of Robarts Library; Emmanuel College Library.

Most social spots to study on campus: Sigmund Samuel Library, foyer of Joseph L. Rotman Centre for Management; Laidlaw Library.

Need for car and parking availability: Parking is limited and very expensive. Cars parked at expired meters are ticketed (and some towed). A car is not necessary. In addition to good old-fashioned walking, biking and roller-blading are popular modes of transportation. The Toronto transit system is clean, safe, and inexpensive, making getting around a breeze.

Sexually speaking: Easy to find a partner in rez; more difficult for commuter students to engage in romantic encounters, LGBT OUT (Lesbian, Gay, Bisexual, Transgendered, Queer), Freedom Alliance for Lesbians, Gays, Bisexuals & Friends, and gay-positive student groups.

Fraternities/sororities: Neutral attitude

Athletic facilities: Two modern athletic facilities offering basketball courts, drop-in fitness classes, running tracks, squash courts, swimming pools, tennis courts, weight rooms.

Library facilities: Second largest library collection in North America, with over 50 libraries and 8 million volumes.

Computer facilities: Leading-edge computer technology and labs. E-mail and Internet access available to all U of T students.

Weather: Warm summers, cool winters with the occasional snowstorm; otherwise, minimal snow falls.

Safety on campus: WALKsafer, a service providing student accompaniment to destinations around campus after dark. A team of two patrollers (one female, one male) will meet you anywhere on or around campus within five to ten minutes. Pre-booking is available and it's free.

Alumni: Former prime ministers William Lyon MacKenzie King and Lester B. Pearson; writers Margaret Atwood and Stephen Leacock; Dr. Norman H. Bethune; actors Raymond Massey and Donald Sutherland; film directors Norman Jewison and David Cronenberg.

This is a great opportunity to make friends and to get to know people. Each college invests a lot of time and money into making your first taste of U of T an enjoyable and memorable one. Unlike other universities that have cut Frosh Week down to a couple of days, at U of T Frosh Week is a five day (and night) all-inclusive trip to frosh craziness. Frosh Week is packed with fun and exciting events such as boat cruises, "theme" (wacky hat and ugly shirt) dances, and water-balloon fights. Students take to the streets of Toronto on a street-closing Frosh Parade. Don't be surprised to see your picture in the Toronto papers the next day. Multinational corporations take advantage of this huge turnout and give out freebies of mugs, agendas, CDs, condoms, and endless samples of over-the-counter medication (Tylenol, Advil, and Claritin). Commuter students need not despair; most colleges can pair you up with a student living in residence and you can bunk with them for the week so you don't miss out on all the fun.

If you don't attend Orientation Week, meeting people can be a challenge. It all depends on what program you're in, what courses you're taking, and whether or not you're will-ing to make the effort to start a conversation. Students in professional faculties such as Engineering, Pharmacy, and Architecture enjoy a close-knit atmosphere with smaller and more intimate classes, whereas students in Life Sciences and Commerce faculties often feel like they're just a number in the crowd.

ACADEMIC ISSUES

From an academic standpoint, U of T is without a doubt the best teaching and research institution in Canada. The first electronic heart pacemaker was developed here and the infant cereal "Pablum" was created here.

Introductory courses tend to be packed to capacity with hundreds of students flocking into tiny lecture halls. Multiple-choice (or multiple-guess) methods of testing are commonly used, due to the enormous class sizes, but more likely as a means of "weeding" students out of the course.

Class sizes can vary anywhere from 1,600 students (BIO150Y) to a mere five students (Finnish Studies). Most first-year classes are packed to the max and unless you get to class early, you usually end up sitting on the cold, butt-numbing steps in between the aisles (totally against Fire Marshall regulations). But regardless of class size, don't expect to coast blissfully through your courses at U of T. After a couple of weeks of class many first-year students enrolled in, say, Human Biology, quickly find themselves wondering whatever possessed them to also enroll in Calculus, Biology, Chemistry, Physics, and Psychology all in one year. These classes combined entail over 15 hours of lectures and tutorials per week, not to mention over 9 hours of laboratory work.

So many decisions I feel like a Picasso!

As at many large universities, it is difficult for first-year students to interact with their professors. In fact, it is quite possible for a student to go a whole year without talking to a single person on campus. The cries of despair from those first-year students drowning in over-populated classes have not, however, gone unheard. U of T now offers seminar courses to first-year students with an intimate class setting limited to 20 students, taught by a tenured professor. There are more than 70 seminar courses from which to choose. Plus, you can breathe a sigh of relief knowing that none of these courses have a final exam.

There are over 50 libraries available on campus and lots of study space, but even so, finding a place to study during exam time can be extremely difficult.

REZ LIFE

U of T offers two very different kinds of university life to its students—there is residence life and commuter life. If you can afford it, live in residence (at least for your first year). Living on campus has its perks: You can sleep in and wake up 10 minutes before class, form study groups, and meet upper-year students with old notes and exams. And, even if you're from inside or just outside the Greater Toronto Area, no worries. There's space for you. Residence is guaranteed for all first-year students. All you have to do is check off the box on your U of T admission application indicating your interest in residence accommodation. If you get that thick envelope in the mail before July 1st, you've landed yourself a spot in residence.

The majority of residences are "traditional style," where students have a private or shared room. All other facilities, including dining rooms, games rooms, lounges, study rooms,

and bathrooms are shared. There are two apartment-style accommodations: Innis and Rowell-Jackman Hall. Scarborough and Mississauga offer apartment- and townhouse-style residences.

A meal plan is usually included in residence fees. But if the idea of "university food" doesn't sit well in your stomach, don't worry because U of T is located smack dab in the middle of trendy cafés, vegetarian restaurants, and ethnic (Chinese, Italian, Japanese, Indian) restaurants galore, enough to satisfy any kind of craving.

Once rez students do finally decide to venture into the world of off-campus housing, they will be bombarded with the inevitable stress of finding a decent, rodent-free place to live that is close to campus, isn't completely run down, and not astronomically priced. The vacancy rate in Toronto is very low, so make sure you start your house hunt early.

NIGHT LIFE

Where do U of T students party? On campus, the HangaR, a popular commuter hangout by day, is transformed into a club at night (it even offers free Latin dance lessons on some nights). The HangaR also features live bands and other surprises on "Wednesday Night Live." Surrounding the campus, there are various pubs and bars to start off the night, where one drink turns into two, and two turns into three o'clock in the morning. Check out the James Joyce, the Ferret & Firkin, Sneaky Dee's, the Pawnbroker's Daughter, The Madison ("The Maddy"), and O'Grady's, a new Irish-style pub. The Brunswick House, nicknamed "The Brunny," was established in 1876, and is one of Toronto's oldest beer houses. It continues to lure students, year after year, with its picnic tables and kegs of beer (rumoured to be recycled). Be prepared to go home with "Brunny grime" all over you—a film of cigarette ash, dirt, and beer that will not come off. Einstein's serves up pitchers of beer for under $10 and platters of huge, mouth-watering chicken wings. You can inhale the biggest slice of pizza you've ever seen at Papa Ceo

---

Room service anyone? U of T promises a space in residence to all first-year students. This year, the university guaranteed a room to more students than it could accommodate. Two hundred (un)lucky students were not assigned a room in a traditional residence on campus. Instead U of T booked two floors in the plush digs of the Primrose Hotel. U of T is also paying for the students' TTC (public transit) fare.

A Word to the Wise:

1. Get your hands on the legendary ASSU Anti-calendar. It contains evaluations of courses and instructors by students, as well as feedback and ratings of the difficulty of the course and workload.

2. T-card: never leave home without it. It is both a student ID and library card. It is also a "smart card" that can be used like a debit card to pay for photocopies in campus libraries and junk food from vending machines. You must have a valid T-card to write final exams, vote in student elections, and use athletic facilities.

3. Get involved! To succeed at U of T and enjoy your university years here, you should join at least one student club or organization. You will meet other students who share some of your interests, and once you get involved, you'll find you can't stop– it's like an addiction.

4. Make some extra cash by taking part in a study offered by the Department of Psychology or School of Management. Masters and PhD students are always looking for guinea pigs to complete their theses.

5. When all is said and done, and before you march proudly across the campus green to Convocation Hall, remember to show your GRADitude. Make your mark through the Graduating Class Gift Campaign with a class gift that can be as cool as purchasing comfier couches or redoing a pub for future students.

at a price that even Scrooge would approve, then hop into a cab for a quick ride to Toronto's entertainment district, where mainstream dance clubs such as the Joker and Whiskey Saigon pull in huge crowds every weekend. Just around the corner is the Montreal-inspired Peel Pub—get there early to avoid the lineup. Further south, off Lake Ontario, the Docks and the Guvernment let you experience, first-hand, exactly what it feels like to be a sardine.

ON TORONTO

Toronto is Canada's largest city, and one of the most culturally and ethnically diverse in the world. One great thing about Toronto is that you never run out of things to do. Mega movie complexes, live theatre, film festivals, music, dance, sporting events, restaurants, cafés—you name it, Toronto's got it. Visit the CN Tower and SkyDome, home to the Jays and the Argos. Check out the Air Canada Centre, hunting ground of the Raptors and ice territory of the Leafs. Shop till you drop on Yonge Street or Queen Street or, if you have money to burn, shop in posh Yorkville. Challenge your friends (and enemies) to a game of paint ball or laser tag. Slip into a mega-bookstore and enjoy a good book and a specialty coffee. Wander through the Art Gallery of Ontario and the Royal Ontario Museum. Multiculturalism is widely celebrated in Toronto through a series of annual festivals and events such as Caravan, Caribana, and the Dragonboat Races, as well as in different districts around town where cultural traditions are dominant: China Town, Little Italy, Greek Town on the Danforth, to mention but a few. Torontonians are widely accepting of people of different races, creeds, and sexual orientations. Toronto offers all of the benefits of a cosmopolitan city, but it also has big-city issues such as the homeless, panhandlers, and squeegee kids.

University of Toronto at Scarborough

By Christine Ibarra

"If somebody would give me about two dozen very old elm trees and about fifty acres of wooded ground and lawn—not too near anywhere and not too far from anywhere—I think I could set up a College that would put all the big universities in the shade."

—Stephen Leacock

The University of Toronto at Scarborough is exactly that. Nestled in the extreme east of the suburbs of Toronto on 300 acres of beautiful parkland, and established in 1964, Scarborough College is made up of one huge grey concrete building surrounded by student housing residences, wooded areas, and greenery. Scarborough College is located 33 km east of the downtown campus, which translates into a 35-minute car ride away or just over an hour's commute by public transit.

Scarborough is a self-sufficient college: It boasts a gym and recreation centre, outdoor sports fields, a library, a bookstore, a small theatre, a campus radio station (CSCR), two cafeterias, Mr. Sub, Pizza Pizza, a donut/coffee shop, vending machines, and best of all, a campus pub, The Attic. There is ample parking (although the outer parking lots are far away from the campus buildings) and 114 townhouses with space for 520 students in two villages. Student services at Scarborough include centres for academic and career counselling, child care, financial aid, and health and wellness, as well as special services for persons with a disability. Scarborough even has a "Pink Room," where students can usually study in peace and quiet.

There are lots of opportunities for students to get involved. Students can write for the student newspaper *The Underground*, or join numerous clubs and societies, such as the Association of Biology and Chemistry Students, Scarborough Campus Chinese Club, Indian Students' Association, Muslim Students' Association, West Indian Student Connection, and Students' Administrative Council (SAC) to name but a few.

There are many preconceptions about Scarborough and why students choose it over the downtown St. George campus. Probably the most fundamental reason is that it is a smaller campus, and like most smaller campuses, Scarborough is a close-knit community. But here, close-knit means a high-school-like atmosphere made up of a mere 5,100 students. In fact, there is a great deal of truth to the claim that Scarborough is just one big high school, complete with cliques and "in" places to hang out or study (e.g., the Meeting Place, Bladen Library).

Students at Scarborough usually get a bad rap and don't get much credit for having gotten accepted into Scarborough. Granted, some programs do have a lower admission requirement than the main downtown campus, but competition is stiff and it is actually more difficult to get into Scarborough's much sought after programs than most people think. Among these popular programs are the co-op programs in Arts Management, Computer Science, Environmental Science, International Development Studies, Management, and Economics. Scarborough also boasts unique programs such as Neuroscience, the Early Teacher Project in Physical Sciences, and the Education of Teachers of French Program; the last two ultimately lead to admission into the Faculty of Education at U of T. Contrary to the popular belief that most students who attend Scarborough do so because they live in the area and find Scarborough closer to home, the fact is many students make the trek to the 'burbs for Scarborough's unique and innovative programs.

Classes are relatively small compared to classes on the St. George campus, so an added plus of the Scarborough campus is that professors get to know you by name, and consequently also know when you're skipping class. By far, however, the best thing about Scarborough is that you still get a degree from the University of Toronto without getting lost in the shuffle of 53,000 other students.

University of Toronto at Mississauga (Erindale College)

By Christine Ibarra

UTM can be found tucked away on 224 acres, 33 km west of the St. George campus, on the tranquil banks of the Credit River. UTM is a community on its own: Erindale has a radio station, *The Medium II* student newspaper, a bookstore, a career centre, health services, apartment- and townhouse-style student residences, a theatre, and an art gallery with contemporary art and an impressive Canadian art collection. In addition to The Blind Duck pub, there is also a Panzerotto Pizza, Wing Machine, Tim Hortons, and Mr. Sub. There are numerous clubs to join, such as the Forensic Society, Vietnamese Erindale Students' Association, Muslim Students' Association, and Polish Club at Mississauga, as well as athletic and recreation programs. UTM also boasts a new Student Centre, a state-of-the-art student services facility—getting involved at Erindale will be that much easier since student services are all in one building.

With a student population of 6,200 students, UTM makes up the largest Arts and Science Faculty at U of T. Like the main downtown campus, Erindale attracts some of the brightest and best students in Canada. Contrary to the popular belief that students attend UTM because they didn't get into the St. George campus, many students choose UTM as their first choice. UTM offers unique programs including Exceptionality in Human Learning, Professional Writing, and for the not-so-squeamish, Forensic Anthropology. UTM also offers two co-op programs in conjunction with Sheridan College, one in Art and Art History, and the other in Theatre and Drama Studies. UTM offers the traditional Bachelor of Arts, Science, and Commerce degrees, and a new Master's in Professional Accounting degree. UTM provides students with access to the best of U of T (professors, extensive library resources, and athletics and recreation programs) without the worst (huge class sizes and isolation). No matter which U of T campus you choose to attend, you will still get an impressive degree from the University of Toronto.

Trent University

By Michele Murphy

Welcome to the tree-hugging, granola-munching, tofu-slurping, slogan-spewing, Birkenstock-wearing, dread-lock-sporting, politically correct capital of Ontario, or as some prefer to call it, Trent University.

Sometimes it seems as though all the stigmas and stereotypes attached to Trent have become a self-fulfilling prophecy. Trent definitely thrives on individuality and activism, but not on exclusivity. Don't fret if you are not inclined to respond to all the calls to protest and hell-raising; as long as you leave your hang-ups and judgements at the door and open your mind to a different kind of environment, Trent could be just what you've looking for.

Located in Peterborough, Ontario, Trent is one of the province's youngest universities, opening its doors for the first time in 1964. Trent is also, by design, one of Ontario's smallest institutions of higher learning, with 3,700 full-time undergrads and 1,200 part-timers. These differences are only the beginning of what sets Trent apart from other universities. If you seek the perpetual frat party, likened to those depicted in dozens of popular Hollywood films, then read no further. Trent is not for you. Trent is a different kind of place and it offers a different kind of experience, one that will effectively dispel all the preconceived notions you may have.

There are three campuses at Trent. Two (Peter Robinson and Traill) are located downtown. The largest campus (Symons) is located on the northern edge of the city, along the banks of the Otonabee River. According to the British traditions upon which Trent was founded, the university functions on what is called "The College System." There are five residential colleges at Trent. Each student, whether they choose to live in residence or not, is affiliated with one of them. Though conceived with ancient ideals, Trent has left the past behind to forge a unique culture that is all its own.

Despite its size, Trent has become David to the larger universities' Goliath in many areas. Trent has remained unbeaten in football since 1964. The fact that Trent has never had a football team does nothing to quell the enthusiasm for this accomplishment. Trent's rowing team is unsurpassed in spirit and strength, and come October, arrogance can be readily added to this team's list of attributes. Every year around this time is "Head of the Trent," a huge rowing regatta that brings schools from all over to compete in Trent's waters. The event takes place on Symons campus and all the rowers like to believe that the onlookers are there to stare in awe at their technique. Truth be told, most come for the beer. Whatever your priorities, don't miss this event. It's a huge party and tons of fun. Everyone you know (and want to know) will be there, congregated on the steps of Biko Library.

A note on Biko: The pamphlets will tell you that the main library is actually called Bata. The Bata company had operations in South Africa during apartheid. Many students protested the name of the building without success. As a form of revolt, the library was renamed Biko by students and student newspapers. Stephen Biko was a famous anti-apartheid activist. Now, how many other schools do you know of with that kind of conviction? That's the beauty of Trent students, they've always got a plan to stick it to the man—and a slogan to match.

CAMPUS CULTURE

There is no such thing as the quintessential Trent student. The student body is a mosaic of backgrounds and cultures. At Trent you will find Peter-Patch locals and international students, Toronto natives and small-towners from North Bay. In general, Trent students are laid-back, relaxed individuals who readily embrace diversity.

There are strong support systems in place within the Trent community for feminism, queer activism, environmentalism, Native culture, and all other issues under the sun. Trent students tend to be extremely passionate and vocal about these issues, which makes for an environment that is rooted in tolerance and acceptance. Beyond all the fanfare and slogans of protest lies a group of awesome people who generally wish to cultivate a safe space for everyone. Racism, sexism, homophobia, and other forms of discrimination are about the only things that are met with outright hostility in this community.

The College System has a huge influence on identity at Trent. Students tend to define themselves not according to program of study, but by their college affiliation. On paper, your college affiliation functions as an administrative foundation. In reality, the stigma attached to your college of choice will haunt you, mould you, and basically define you for the entire time you are at Trent.

Each of the five residential colleges has its own culture, and each exists as its own subcommunity within the larger Trent environment. Picking your college affiliation is an important decision, one that may seem difficult without prior knowledge of the system. To help you make a more informed decision, take the short personality quiz in the box on the right.

ACADEMIC ISSUES

Course content at Trent is excellent, although selection is slim (such is the curse of the small university). Due in no small part to this setback, Trent has become renowned for "inter-disciplinary" education. Bet you never heard that one before. This means that you can major in anything you want. Literally. You can choose to major in one of the departments, you can choose two departments and complete a joint major, or, in the true spirit of Trent, you can complain that structured departments stifle your creativity, and opt instead to create your own major. This is accomplished by soliciting the help of a faculty member and mixing courses from all different departments. This individual-based form of learning is only one of Trent's many pioneering efforts.

Trent also believes in the core importance of small classes and tutorial instruction. You will enroll in classes where you are one of eight students. Trent professors mark your papers themselves. You will know your professors by their first names, and you may even have their home phone numbers. You will go for a beer with your prof after class and wax philosophical about the universe and the meaning of life. Some profs are known to reschedule exams so that students can make it to the bar in time for a Leafs game. In short, re-think your notion of the "stuffy academic" before you enter a Trent classroom.

If you are having trouble finding resources or developing an angle for a particular essay, e-mail one of your

---

PICK THE MOST ACCURATE DESCRIPTION OF YOURSELF:

A) The Compulsive Joiner. You have endless supplies of school spirit. You have aspirations to become involved in every club, group, and event at the university. Your scrunchie always matches your plaid flannel pants.

B) The Jock. Getting drunk is your recreational activity of choice. For you, recreation time is any time. You would join a fraternity if Trent had one. You think keg parties are cool.

C) No label quite defines you. This is because you have no attributes which stand out. You are generally laid back and apathetic. You have no interest in academic success.

D) The Freak. You have a minimum of three body piercings and/or tattoos. You are apathetic about school spirit, but relentlessly outspoken about everything else. Birkenstocks are your footwear of choice.

IF YOU CHOSE "A" – You belong at Lady Eaton with all the other keeners.

IF YOU CHOSE "B" – You belong at either Otonabee or Champlain. They're both pretty much the same.

IF YOU CHOSE "C" – You belong at Traill. You have a bright future of rustication appeals ahead.

IF YOU CHOSE "D" – You belong at PRC. Everyone else just wishes they did.

---

friend's professors. Busy as they are, Trent profs are always willing to discuss your project and help you out. Trent is truly an academic community, and its structure encourages interactions that could not occur in a huge institution where students are merely numbers. The downside? The professors know your name and your face, so when you cut class, they know that, too.

You won't find Engineering or Medicine at Trent. You will, however, find Business Administration, Comparative Development, and even Cultural Studies, a department which explores theatre, art, music, film, and the media. If you choose to major in Cultural Studies, you will, no doubt, be ridiculed on a regular basis by those who believe that the program is not "practical." This is jealousy in disguise. Anybody who comes to university for a "practical" education is squandering large sums of money and would be better off at college. If you hope to major in the Natural Sciences, you'd be better off at another

Vital Statistics

Address: P.O. Box 4800, Station Main, Peterborough, Ontario, K9J 7B8

Admissions office: (705) 748-1332

Website: www.trentu.ca

Total enrollment: 4,900

Male-female ratio: 35 to 65

Percentage of out-of province students: 5%

Average entering grades: Arts: 66%; Science: 66%; Commerce: 70%

Tuition fees: $4,231.12

Residence fees: $4,950–$5,250

(double room with mandatory meal plan); $5,346–$5,646 (single rooms with mandatory meal plan)

Financial aid: Scholarships are automatically granted to students with an overall average of 80% or more; general bursaries available to undergraduates by application in September and January.

Co-op programs: None.

Services for students with disabilities: The Special Needs Office provides support to students who are differently abled. Those with

mobility impairments beware: There are lots of stairs on campus, and not nearly enough ramps and elevators.

Aboriginal students: The Native Studies Department offers a two-year diploma designed for students of aboriginal ancestry, as well as a two-year diploma in Native Management and Economic Development. Native Studies and Trent University Native Association.

Student services: Trent Central Student Association, personal and academic counselling, Academic Skills Workshops.

school. Rumour has it that your kind exist here, but these tall tales were concocted solely for comic relief. If you can't write a paper, you won't last long at Trent.

Peterborough and The Kawarthas boast a tightly knit First Nations community. Much of this is reflected in Trent's Native Studies Program. You haven't lived until you've seen one of your housemates stay up all night, strung out on caffeine, trying to memorize enough Ojibway to pass the exam.

Women's Studies is also a popular choice, a program which has only recently been offered as a full major. These classes are generally made up of 99% women, and 1% Sensitive New Age Guy. This is unfortunate, since in these courses, students are exposed to fantastic perspectives and theories which are often not given the exposure or attention they merit in other courses.

If you're one of those tree-hugger hippie types, there's no better place to get an Environmental Science/Studies degree than at Trent. They don't call it "The Natural Choice" for nothing. Since most of Symons campus is preserved as a nature area, your research will be tangible and meaningful in ways which textbooks are unable to accomplish.

A component to many Trent programs is the option to study abroad for a year, paying Trent tuition. This is an opportunity to explore an entirely different culture and environment, and gain university credit while you're doing it. My advice: Conquer your fears, get on the plane, and GO. You'll never have another chance like this again.

REZ LIFE

Rez is a bit like summer camp. You live in a tiny room surrounded by dozens of other people, many of whom will become friends for life. Dwelling in close quarters

has its difficulties, but your housemates will inevitably become like family, and by the end of your first year, you'll wonder how you ever got along without them. Residence is the perfect place to carve out a niche in this crazy university playground, and it's a must for first year.

The big rez question at Trent is downtown versus Symons, and there's no easy solution to this dilemma. Downtown advantages include accessibility to bars, stores, and community facilities. On Symons you're steps away from classes, computer facilities, and Biko Library. It's up to you to evaluate your priorities and choose the rez location that's best for you.

One of your first rez experiences at Trent will be Frosh Week, except at Trent it's not called Frosh Week, it's called Intro-Week, and there's no booze allowed. Before you scrap Trent as an option because of this fact, consider this: The no-alcohol policy is imposed for university-sponsored events only. At night, you are free to roam the city in search of a watering hole. As well, there is something to be said for meeting people for the first time while sober, as opposed to inebriated beyond all recognition. While sober, you are less likely to make a complete and utter fool of yourself in the first week of school, and that's if you bother getting involved in the lame Intro-Week activities. They consist of scavenger hunts, water fights, barbecues, and such. If you're the Lady Eaton type, you'll be up and ready to go at 7 a.m. If you're the PR type, you'll throw things at anyone who foolishly attempts to wake you up at such a ridiculous hour.

The lowdown on rez is this: Yes, the food sucks, and no, you will not have any privacy. You *will* have a kick-ass time, you *will* meet kick-ass people, and you *will* feel like you're a part of the community, and that's what makes rez worth it, no matter which one you choose.

In a Nut Shell

The university in a phrase: Everyone affiliated with Trent University will find a reason to be offended by this write-up.

Best thing about the university: The people.

Worst thing about the university: Red tape and back-asswards administration.

Favourite professors: C.V. Boundas (Philosophy), John Wadland (Canadian Studies), Ian Storey (Classics), Suzie Young (Cultural Studies), David Sheinen (History), David Poole (Math), Deborah Berrill (Con-Ed), Veronica Hollinger (Cultural Studies).

Most popular bird courses: Cultural Studies 100, Oral Narrative; Computer Studies 101.

Hot spot to study on campus: Biko Library steps.

Quietest spot to study on campus: Top floor of Biko Library.

Need for car and parking availability: Everything is within walking distance, and the Trent Express runs pretty frequently. Unless you want to chauffeur your friends everywhere, and pay a ridiculous amount of money to park on Symons, leave your wheels at your parents' house.

Sexually speaking: Sex is all we ever talk about! Be prepared for open communication and broadening your horizons.

Fraternities/sororities: There aren't any at Trent.

Athletic facilities: Pitiful work-out room, 25-m pool, rowing facilities (of course), full-size lighted playing field, sauna, tennis and squash courts, and a gymnasium.

Library facilities: One at PRC and one at Traill (these are hardly worth mentioning), and Biko on Symons which isn't too bad.

Weather: Fall is *stunning*, winter is long and cold, summer is beautiful.

Safety on campus: Trent Walk Home Program; Emergency First Response Team; Security Department regularly patrols campus buildings, parking lots, and pathways; emergency outdoor telephones around campus.

Alumni: Grand Chief of the Grand Council of the Crees, Matthew Coon Come; Olympic gold medallist in rowing Rob Marland; founder of Doctors Without Borders James Orbinski; actress Nancy Sakovich (*PSI Factor*).

NIGHT LIFE

Peterborough bars are great because each one has its own character and purpose. The bars are also really close together, so if your mood changes, it's easy to bar-hop. First year tends to be a blurred sequence of "Piggy-Trash" Wednesday nights. The Pig's Ear is a Peterborough institution. The decor is a charming cafeteria motif, with bright lights and wood panelling. There is a jukebox, a pool table, and with the right group of people, a great time. The beer is cheap (what beats $9 pitchers?), making it the perfect place to prime before moving on to the Trasheteria for Retro 80s night. Most people are too plastered to realize that the DJ plays the same tracks, in the same order, every single week.

After this year-long frosh-fest, you'll likely be seeking something different. Two words: Hunter Street. Here you'll find The Sapphire Room, Peterborough's only martini bar, The Red Dog, Sidewinders, Gordon Best Theatre for live shows, and the (in)famous Only Cafe, appropriately named because it eventually becomes the only place Trent students go. The Only is small, dark, and smoky. Modern art covers the walls and ceiling. There's pinball, piercingly loud music, lots of attitude, and lots of people you know. You will complain about the service, you will complain about the prices, but all the griping in the world won't be able to keep you away.

If you find yourself seeking (temporary) refuge from The Only, and wish to have your pint elsewhere, try McThirsty's for imports, or The Peterborough Arms for microbrews. In the mood to dance? Try Sin City—but only on Mondays. Brave The Rooster or The Vibe if you dare, but expect a testosterone-charged meat market…and be careful: After a few beers everyone looks like prime rib.

Rainbow dances are regularly held at The Gordon Best Theatre. This is a great way to meet people in the queer community when you're new to the city.

If you enjoy live music, Peterborough has much to offer.

A Word to the Wise:

1. Live in rez for first year … it rocks. But move out after that! There are lots of cheap vacancies downtown.

2. Drink KLB.

3. Get involved, but don't let activism become your life.

4. Make the experience your own. Seek out new, funky places, attend obscure little concerts and events, study abroad for a year, dress freaky, and try new things.

Watch for posters and listen to Trent Radio for details; there are always shows going on. If you have an instrument of your own, keep an eye out for bars hosting open jams. For strumming a few tunes, you can usually wrangle a pint or two out of the bartender.

When all the bars are closed, check out the borough's late night eats. The Night Kitchen serves up gourmet pizza delights, and Pita Pit features lots of tasty choices. Both are open really late.

No matter where you choose to hang out, remember that in Peterborough, the quest for anonymity is futile. You will inevitably run into someone you know every time you leave your house.

ON PETERBOROUGH

At first, Peterborough is a difficult place to adjust to. The deserted streets on a Sunday afternoon can seem like something out of a Stephen King movie. But like no other place in the world, Peterborough grows on you. In first year you'll be grateful for any opportunity to escape, and by third year you'll never want to leave.

The downtown area is a haven for small businesses and lovely little restaurants with some of the best food in the world. There is no better procrastination technique then spending hours perusing the shelves of the tiny used-book stores, and there's always a place to hock your CDs when you run out of beer money.

When your OSAP installment comes in, be sure to opt out of rez food a few times; you'll be glad you did. For the best nachos you'll ever have in your life, try Hot Belly Mama's. Kick back on the comfy couches and enjoy the jazz as you indulge. If Thai food is your pleasure, treat yourself to a delectable dish at Cosmic Charlie's. For a delicious breakfast after a night of boozing, The Only is (as usual) the only place to go.

One of Peterborough's true gems is the Kawartha Lakes Brewery. KLB brews some of the tastiest beer you'll ever have the pleasure to try, and it's only available in Peter-Patch. I highly recommend the Pale Ale, but if you have a sweet tooth, the Raspberry Wheat is also quite popular.

Peterborough has a strong art culture. There are craft shows and markets, as well as strong support for community-based theatre. There's lots of opportunity to express yourself, and lots of great talent to see. Peterborough is a city with many hidden treasures. It's not much to look at initially, but if you seek out the nooks and crannies, the borough will find its way into your heart. Peter-Patch vets "Under the Attic" wrote a song about the city, and eventually you'll come to feel as though the words were written for you: "I thought we'd stay forever, but I guess we were just passing through."

University of Waterloo

By Mae Cantos

Waterloo. Not Napoleon's downfall, not the ABBA song. Waterloo, as in University of. Founded in 1957, the University of Waterloo (UW) lacks the rich heritage and history of some of the older universities, but it has something better than historic buildings laced with ivy—ugly architecture filled with brains.

The University of Waterloo is a concrete campus nestled in the bosom of the twin-city area of Kitchener-Waterloo, covering an area of 900 acres. UW is an average-sized university with an above-average reputation for science and technology and all else that is "nerdy." The university is slowly shaking that stereotype with its stellar sports teams and increasing involvement in extra-curricular activities.

UW is a collective meeting of the minds, where top students from all over venture to advance their education, and who can blame them? UW, sometimes hailed as the MIT of the North, is one of the best and most prestigious universities around.

Located smack dab in the middle of Mennonite country, UW lacks the city hustle and bustle of U of T, or the picturesque calm of UNB. Students here have access to downtown Waterloo and Kitchener, as well as a variety of parks and conservation areas close by.

The main core of the campus is surrounded by Ring Road, which acts as the only throughway for vehicles. Built in the sixties, the buildings are pretty drab and sterile. Many have looked at them and wondered, "What were they on when they built this?" And to accompany the acid-induced architecture are wonderfully creative names such as Biology 1, Biology 2, and, wait for it, Biology 3—just kidding, there's no Biology 3—but you never have to worry about forgetting the name of a building. There is a trend that your classes are never held in the building after which they are named—students typically have Chemistry in the Arts Lecture Hall, nutrition in the Math & Computer Building, and Biology in the Engineering Lecture Hall. As if that wasn't confusing enough, people refer to each of these buildings by their initials—EL, DC, AI, B1, B2, etc.

One famous UW landmark is the Dana Porter Library (a.k.a. the Sugar Cube) which acts as a beacon to lost frosh.

Rumour has it that this building is sinking due to the fact that the architect forgot to include the weight of the books into his plans. This library is one of the quietest places to study on campus—almost too quiet. The ninth floor, a favourite of many students, offers a great view of the university for people who have better things to do than study. The Dana Porter Library is known as the Arts library and Engineers and Mathies explain that that is why it is almost always empty and therefore almost always quiet.

The other library is located in the Davis Centre for Computer Science and Engineering. This building is designed to resemble a microchip from above, but really looks more like a gerbil playground with its brightly coloured pipes and tubing. The Davis Centre library is science and tech oriented, but don't expect to get any studying done. Davis Centre is more of a social place, where students go to chat, eat, or do anything but schoolwork under the pretence of "studying at the library."

Another building of interest is the Student Life Centre, and it is exactly that. This building houses all that you would ever need (or never need) as a student. There's plenty of food and drink, a pharmacy, a hair salon, a used-book store, a games room, quiet areas, not-so-quiet areas, offices, clubs, student services, and much more. The Turnkey Desk is a definite pit-stop, offering everything from condoms and coffee to munchies and magazines. It's open 24 hours a day, just like the Student Life Centre, and is a fountain of knowledge for students, staff, and everyone else.

For all your sporting needs, the Physical Activities Complex, affectionately referred to as the PAC (pronounced "pak"), and the Columbia Icefield Complex fit the bill. The PAC houses two multi-purpose gyms, a pool, two fitness studios, a weight and cardio room, activity areas, squash courts, and a bouldering wall. The facilities are dated and cramped—having been built over 20 years ago for a student population that has since quadrupled. Columbia Icefields boasts newer amenities, with an aerobics studio, a couple of gyms, baseball diamonds, a full-size hockey rink (hence the name "Icefields"), and more; it also houses many of the varsity teams change rooms.

Vital Statistics

Address: 200 University Ave. West, Waterloo, Ontario, N2L 3G1

Admissions office: (519) 885-1211

Website: www.uwaterloo.ca

Total enrollment: 21,693

Male-female ratio: 52 to 48

Average entrance grades: Arts: 72%; Science: 72%; Engineering: 81%

Tuition fees: $3,990 (regular); $5,160 (co-op)

Residence fees: $5,200 (including meal plan)

Spaces for students in residence: 3,300 (approx.)

Percentage of international students: 1.7% undergraduates; 13.7% graduates

Percentage of out-of-province first-year students: 7%

Co-op programs: 40 co-op programs offered through UW's six faculties: Applied Health Sciences, Arts, Engineering, Environmental Studies, Mathematics, Science.

Financial aid: Entrance awards, bursaries, and OSAP are available.

Facilities for students with disabilities: Office for Services for Persons with Disabilities.

Aboriginal students: Various student organizations.

Student services: Academic advisors, co-operative education and career services, chaplains, computer support, counselling services, health services, legal resource office, ombudsperson.

CAMPUS CULTURE

Contrary to popular belief, UW is not chock full of hard-core computer nerds or geeky engineers; UW is truly a multicultural university, consisting of students from all over the world. There are church colleges—St. Jerome's University (Catholic), Renison College (Anglican), Conrad Grebel College (Mennonite), and St. Paul's United College—as well as numerous ethnic and religious student groups. There's a club for every culture and area of interest, from the Ski Club to the Student Ambassador Association to the Swing and Social Dance Club.

The multiculturalism and diversity is as plain to see as the clothes people wear. There is only one word to describe the style of dress at UW: whatever. The fashion ranges from roll-out-of-bed to walk-down-the-runway. Garb also varies from faculty to faculty. Artsies definitely have the best fashion sense (they're in arts after all). Students in Applied Health Sciences favour track pants and sweatshirts and anything sporty. Science folk and Engineers pretty much look the same, except one group wears a lab coat more often and gets crappy co-op jobs. And then there are the Mathies, who manage to have a totally diverse look of their own—from preppy to punk to the pink tie that serves as their mascot (you have to see it to believe it). Basically the moral of the story here, kiddies, is "Whatever you wear, we don't care."

With so much diversity, it's hard to narrow down what being a UW student is all about. Some say career-minded, with reference to the realistic world of co-op; others say apathetic, noting the lack of involvement in areas such as elections, sporting, and social events. There is no one word to define the quintessential Waterloo student. They are smart, hard-working, mature (most of the time), and proud of their reputation. Most of all, they live up to it. To paraphrase one of the greatest motivational speakers of our times, "We're good enough, we're smart enough, and doggonit, people like us."

With all these people around there are all kinds of events and activities to take advantage of. The first official taste of university life will most likely come in the form of Frosh Week. This is the week before classes start, when the opportunity to redesign yourself exists. You make friends and enemies (but you won't find out who's who until it's too late), consume copious amounts of BEvERages, learn how to function on little to no sleep (a definite skill required for scholastic success), and recite cheers that would make a sailor blush. Slandering other faculties and parading around in your frosh shirt provides endless entertainment. Popular items on the list are streaking (or other forms of exposure), travelling to distant places, and "borrowing" other faculties' mascots—the Mathies' giant pink tie, the Artsies' boar statue "Porcelino," or the big wrench the Engineers call "Tool." The grand finale is a giant toga party—the biggest one in all of Canada.

Other big events at UW are Oktoberfest, St. Patrick's Day, and Homecoming. These festivities alone could support the local beer and liquor stores for the entire year. Oktoberfest is a great excuse to wear dorky German gear and party to polka music until you puke (from the alcohol or the music, whatever gets you first). The whole city of Kitchener-Waterloo gets right into the festive spirit, making Oktoberfest in Waterloo the biggest party outside of Germany. Wunderbar! St. Patrick's Day is another celebrated event, with the party held at the Bombshelter student pub. The green beer flows freely from the taps and people have been known to stay at the Bomber from open to close, only to leave with more green on their tongues than in their pocket. Homecoming at UW revolves around the pre-season Naismith Basketball Tournament. Alumni are invited back to recall their wonder years and the Big Tent party at Fed Hall is always a big hit for students, both past and present.

In the past, sports and athletics have taken a back seat to school and academics, but now with over 30 inter-university sports, and Campus Recreation offering a wide variety of activities, UW is home to a successful and ever-expanding athletic and recreation program. UW Warriors sport teams have consistently ranked high in their respective fields. The Campus Rec also provides ample opportunity for students to finally give their minds a rest and exercise some other parts of their bodies.

ACADEMIC ISSUES

Co-op is the lifeblood of the university and with 40 co-op programs offered, UW has the largest co-operative education program in the world. Each of the six faculties offers co-op programs except for Engineering, which is co-op only. Co-op students must pay an additional fee to participate in the program and maintain a higher average than their counterparts in the regular stream of study. Co-op is great for many reasons. First, you gain valuable experience in your field and hone your job-seeking skills, making you all the more marketable. Second, you can pay your way through school and make more money than you would working at a fast-food joint without ever having to say, "Would you like fries with that?" You can also make connections at various companies and start building your career network. Lastly, it looks really good on your diploma! There are those who hesitate to extol the virtues of UW's co-op program, citing crappy jobs and the lack of service from the department. Granted, the placement rate of co-ops is high (approximately 98%); the level of student satisfaction, however, is nowhere near that. Complaints about not getting interviews, missing classes and/or exams, resorting to setting up your own job, and fighting for a work placement credit are common woes of the UW co-op student. There is no guarantee that you will be given a job, or a good one. In this respect, UW is a school for the serious-minded and realistic student. There is a lot of tough competition out there; you just have to be tougher.

Having such a large number of students in co-op means that there's always life on campus. Depending on what stream you're on (four month or eight month) determines when you take your first co-op term (after four or eight months, get it?). Your stream will also determine the people with whom you will spend the rest of your university career. It's kind of like a parallel universe which is always four months behind. Needless to say, UW is a year-round school, which means going to school in the summer. Actually, it's not that bad—the weather's nice, people are more laid back, and there's always a game of beach volleyball and a cold brew waiting on the Bomber patio. Oh yeah, and there's that school thingy, too.

Aside from the recognized reputation for producing top students in technical fields such as math, computer science, and engineering, UW has a vast array of innovative and unique programs, such as Health Studies and Gerontology, Recreation and Leisure Studies, Science and Business, Urban Planning, Rhetoric and Professional Writing, as well as excellent professional schools in Optometry and Architecture. Regardless of the program you're in, a sense of recognition and accomplishment is generated for studying at a school with such a prestigious academic standing.

REZ LIFE

Going away to university should be exactly that—going away. One of the biggest things about the university experience is the opportunity to live on your own. Living away is a highly recommended experience if you can afford it, especially for first year. One of the most popular living arrangements among frosh is to live on campus in residence. UW assigns rez rooms based on a lottery system. The lesson learned is to apply to every possible form of student housing available, thus mathematically increasing the probability of securing a living arrangement for the upcoming school term. Aren't you glad you took finite? There are three main UW residences, and each of the four affiliated church colleges offer housing as well.

The Villages are by far the largest block of residence buildings and are divided into two main parts. Village I is a maze of glass and concrete and has gone through some major renovations. It now boasts a laundry, wide-screen TV, and Internet café. Village II is reserved for frosh and it's one constant party. There is always someone willing to go out and relive Frosh Week or help pull pranks on unsuspecting victims. There are same-sex, co-ed, or quiet floors but no guarantees for requests. Just don't embellish the truth on the roommate compatibility questionnaire. Fate has a funny way of sticking you with a roommate from hell.

All residences on campus have a meal plan, so prepare to gain the dreaded "frosh fifteen" on a steady diet of greasy breakfasts and potatoes. Oh, and be wary of the "mystery meat."

Columbia Lake Townhouses (CLT) are a good alternative

In a Nut Shell

The university in a phrase:
"Good school + good reputation = good pay, you do the math," or "Nerds of today are the millionaires of tomorrow."

Best thing about the university: Co-op (most students actually get great jobs).

Worst thing about the university: Can't seem to shake that nerdy reputation.

Favourite professors: Larry Smith (Economics), Diel-Jones (Biology), Bell (Health).

Most popular bird courses: Psych 101; Computer Science 100 (a lot of work, easy marks); Sex, Marriage and the Family (SMF); Health 101/102

Hot spots to study on campus: Davis Centre Library, comfy couches in the Great Hall in SLC, the Bomber (pub/patio), beach volleyball court/grassy hills around MC (in summer).

Quietest spots to study on campus: Upper floors of Dana Porter Library (the Sugar Cube), any empty classroom on MC, EL.

Need for car and parking availability: Everything is pretty much centrally located. There's lots of parking but you need a pass—so get one early to get the lot that you want. There's also pay-as-you-park lots. But realistically, unless you commute from home, you really don't need a car. Bike or rollerblades are more efficient forms of transportation (except that you can't rollerblade on campus).

Sexually speaking: All depends on how hard you look and how high (or low) your standards are. Popular myth: There are no good-looking datable women at Waterloo. Scary truth: there are tons of good-looking, datable women, but in comparison to the number of datable men, this ratio weighs heavily in favour of the male gender. GLLOW—Gay and Lesbian Liberation Organization of Waterloo.

Fraternities/sororities: They are not recognized as official clubs at Waterloo.

Athletic facilities: Physical Activities Complex, two multipurpose gyms, weight and conditioning rooms, activity areas, squash courts, indoor sprinting track, fitness studios, swimming pool, and a bouldering wall for practising climbing techniques, Columbia Icefield Complex

Library facilities: Library is adequate; if you can't find something, there's always Laurier.

Computer facilities: Excellent computer availability.

Weather: It's not called Waterloo for nothing. It rains and snows a fair bit here.

Safety on campus: Walksafe program; all over campus, direct phone lines to UW police; well-lit paths; safety van; 24-hour Turnkey Desk; UWCRT (University of Waterloo Campus Response Team).

Alumni: Denise Donlon, William Reeves, Martin Rutte, Jim Mitchell.

to your typical residence-style dorm. It is fully equipped with single rooms and a kitchen, and having only a few other roommates to deal with make these living arrangements ideal for some. On the other hand, there is the fact that the CLT is so bloody far from everything else. That seems to be the general theme for housing in Waterloo—nice place, nice walk. Speaking of housing in Waterloo, there are plenty of options other than residence. There are the Waterloo Co-operative Residences—built, owned, and run by students—or the Phillip Street Townhouses, both within spitting distance of the university. The university also helps out with house hunting by posting housing lists for the area (as well as Toronto and Ottawa for the co-ops). Start your search early or you could end up living in the Student Life Centre and showering at the PAC—hmmm, not a bad idea.

NIGHT LIFE

Waterloo is a great party town—think of it, you have two universities (Waterloo and Laurier) and a college (Conestoga), all within close proximity of one another. The town is always buzzing with things to do. You needn't leave campus once night falls, as there are many options for evening plans. Until recently, Fed Hall, billed as the largest student-run nightclub, sucked large, but now with the infamous "Boys 'n' Girls" night added to the roster it has climbed to the top ranks of the night life ladder as *the* place to be. Fed Hall is open to all UW students and is the only place that underagers can party with their legal friends. This is party central for froshies and exudes that downtown club feeling with pumping bass, flashy lights, long lineups, and a sardine-like squeeze. The Bombshelter—a UW favourite watering hole—is much like the beer they serve, an acquired taste. The Bomber is mostly populated with upper years and is more of a sit down and drink place but there's also dancing and pool tables for the clubbers, and cheap pub grub is available for even the stingiest of students. Wilfrid Laurier University—the high school up the road—also has a couple of cool on-campus hangouts; there's the Turret (the Fed Hall equivalent) and Wilf's (the Bomber equivalent). For those that aren't into the whole dance scene there are other alternatives. If you like

A Word to the Wise:

1. Guard your WATCARD with your life. This little piece of plastic with your picture on it will be the most valuable card during your stay at UW. This is your student ID, your library card, your photocopier card, and your meal card, and you can put extra money on it to use at various locations to buy food, stuff, and services. Have money on it at all times to serve as a means of emergency cash. It's convenient, it's durable, it's a WATCARD–don't leave home without it.

2. Buying books is a real hassle each term and long lineups to the bookstore are a familiar sight. Try looking around for used books–they're a lot cheaper and contain basically the same information–or check out the school library, as many textbooks are available through the reserve system.

3. Try and map out the quickest route from class to class, with occasional stops at the various C&Ds (student-run Coffee & Doughnut shops) for sustenance in the form of bagel and juice.

4. It's a good idea to plan alternate routes through the various buildings and underground tunnels for use during inclement weather (hey, it's not called WATERloo for nothing).

alternative music, the Revolution on Fridays is the place to be and Phil's is also pretty good. For those into the underground groove, check out Club Abstract and catch DJs spinning the latest in house, jungle, techno, and trance. Louie's and the pub-style Fox, located a five-minute walk from the university, offer ample entertainment whether you're looking for a jock-rock meat market (Louie's) or a nice pint of Guinness and a game of darts (the Fox). There are also clubs in downtown Kitchener—Lyric, Metropolis, Stages—that are just a quick cab ride away.

For those post-party munchies, there are plenty of places that cater to every taste. Mel's Diner is a favourite, fifties-inspired joint that has the best all-day breakfast around—the perfect hangover cure. The Pita Pit and Gino's Pizza are open late to serve up fast food that is sure to satisfy. For a quickie, drop into Farah's Foods—open 24 hours—and grab that twinkie you've been craving. Those seeking a more refined taste, or a coffee to sober up, can head to William's 24 Hour Coffee Pub, which is a popular hangout to eat, drink, talk, and study (or at least try).

If you want to go out, but aren't in the mood to drink or dance, there are plenty of other things to see and do. You could catch a movie, play bingo, shoot some pool, or go sing karaoke. Kitchener Sportsworld offers more than enough to keep even the most attention deficient individual occupied. In addition to the student club activities and recreational programs offered, each of the student societies within each faculty always has plenty of events planned. Whether it's a coffee house/talent show or movies shown in the student lounge, there is always something to do.

ON WATERLOO Waterloo seems like a quiet little town on the outside but is bubbling with vibrancy on the inside. Hailed as the core of "Canada's Technology Triangle," Waterloo is backed by UW's major computing and technology research centre and is the home of many hi-tech companies. But don't let that lead you to believe that the only thing to do for fun is hack the system. There is such a wide variety of things to do, you won't know where to begin. The Mennonite influence can be seen at the St. Jacob's Farmer's Market offering fresh fruit and veggies, meats and cheeses. Great deals can also be had at the Factory Outlet Mall just beside the market. There's a shuttle bus that goes from UW or you can take the scenic route with the Waterloo-St. Jacob's Tourist Train. There's Waterloo Park which has a mini zoo and hosts the "Sounds of Summer" concert and the "Wonders of Winter" light display. Waterloo has all the shops, restaurants, theatres, festivals, and perks of the big city without all the bustle. Waterloo's twin city of Kitchener offers a more city-like landscape and you are sure to find whatever it is you're looking for. If it's beer you're looking for, then look no further. Waterloo is a bonafide brewing town, with several local breweries and an abundance of cheap beer. Do you really need any more incentive to come here? Sure, Waterloo may not have the cosmopolitan flair of Montreal or the breathtaking beauty of Vancouver, but it's got a great history and heritage and one hell of a university (OK, Laurier's pretty good, too). It's a place where one can learn, a place one can love, and a place one can call home.

The University of Western Ontario

By Blair Trudell and Christine Ibarra

Originally founded in 1878 under the name of The Western University of London, Ontario, by Bishop Isaac Hellmuth and the Anglican Diocese of Huron, Western later changed its title to The University of Western Ontario in 1923. It also moved from the original Huron campus to its current location in north London sitting on the banks of the river Thames. Today the campus is largely self-contained, with a colonial touch (to be expected from a city named London and a campus located on the banks of the Thames). It is, to say the least, a beautiful campus complete with the stone and ivy and well maintained greens. Crossing through the welcoming gates is an awesome experience, invoking feelings akin to a larger than life experience, reminiscent of the day you were a doe-eyed high school freshman. Not to worry, however, for on every campus across the country on that fateful September morning, there will be thousands just like you, wondering just what the hell they've gotten themselves into and where the closest pay-phone is.

Many students choose to attend Western simply for its pre-eminent Business school. The Business facility is one of the main facilities on campus and has an international reputation. Its programs are the most heavily funded, best staffed, and, of course, the competition is fierce. Remember, all the students who are accepted into Western's first year will not necessarily end up in the lusty Business program—you can only be accepted after second year. This weeding out process helps maintain the high standards of this prestigious Business school. After all, it is consistently ranked as the best in the country and its reputation is deeply embedded into the psyches of the outside business community that recruit heavily from the school each year. As a result of this recruitment, graduates of the business school often find themselves in comfortable jobs upon graduation with high starting salaries and a secure future ahead.

Money is the key word to understanding Western. Whether you have it now, or want it in the future, Western is a kind of breeding ground for the Canadian business elite as well as the enclave of its offspring. With this in mind, the visible presence of fraternities and sororities make perfect sense. They are the networks of the future and create those old-boy alliances that become so beneficial down the road.

This said, Western is a big enough school to avoid the Business school scene if need be. Less than a quarter of the school is enrolled in Business and even fewer students find themselves "rushing" to fraternities. The campus supports an ethnically healthy and diverse student body that also boasts other popular faculties: Psychology, Biology, Political Science, Sociology, Kinesiology, Physical Therapy, Medicine and Journalism.

Apathy is not common at Western. The life of the student is bound in a myriad of events offered by the university. Whether it is the brotherhood or sisterhood of a fraternity or sorority that you seek, or wondering how well the Mustangs are doing, Western offers many opportunities for participation in a variety of different areas. The benefits are clear. Campus life is vibrant within the university, and this makes for a lively social scene. Because getting involved is all the rage at UWO, even the normally uninterested can be persuaded into becoming active participants.

CAMPUS CULTURE

Students can easily find their own niche amongst the vast roster of clubs and teams that Western has to offer. You can participate in intramural sports, from tae kwon do to ultimate frisbee. Inflate your ego—run for Student Council and manage multi-million-dollar budgets while rubbing elbows with the big wigs. For an out of this world experience, join the X-Files Club. Write for *The Gazette*, Western's daily campus newspaper, if you have a flair for writing (and don't generally suffer from writer's block). Join SALSA (Spanish and Latin American Students' Association) and learn how to do it, salsa that is, and wiggle

Vital Statistics

Address: London, Ontario, N6A 5B8

Admissions office: (519) 661-2111

Website: www.uwo.ca

Total enrollment (undergraduate): 19,017

Male-female ratio: 45.7 to 54.3

Percentage of international students: 2.9%.

Percentage of out-of-province students: 5.2%.

Average entering grade: Arts: 75%; Science: 75%; Commerce: 75%; Engineering: 75%.

Tuition fees: All first-year undergraduate programs (except Engineering): $3,515; Engineering: $3,860.

Residence fees: $5,206–$5,906 (in traditional-style residences and depending on size of mandatory meal plan).

Percentage of students in residence: 27% undergraduates (75% of first-year students live in residence).

Internship programs: Engineering Science, Computer Science, Physics, and Statistics and Actuarial Sciences.

Financial aid: Admission scholarships guaranteed to students entering with an 80% average or above; the top 100 students in Arts, Engineering, Science, Health Sciences, Science, and Social Science also receive four-year continuing scholarships worth $8,000; students with above 90% average can apply for the National Scholarship Program, with scholarships from $16,000-$24,000; bursaries, needs-based awards, and OSAP also available.

Facilities for students with disabilities: Disabled Students' Services is an agency set up to help with the concerns of disabled students.

Aboriginal students: Native Student Association.

Student services, Academic, career and personal counselling, student employment services, health services, housing services, legal aid.

---

your *assets*. Western students also have a lot of heart—each year they host Shinerama, an annual charity event that raises money and awareness for cystic fibrosis.

The Purple Spur Society has a long history of being the biggest, loudest, and craziest club at Western. There definitely is no lack of school spirit associated with this club. The Spurs have organized a poverty ball at the Ceeps, Mardi Gras, and trips to Casino Niagara to play with Lady Luck.

If you're considering Western to get away from your spoiled, bratty younger sibling, or to escape the dictatorship of your bossy, controlling big brother or sister, think twice. One big part of campus culture, love it or hate it, is Greek life. Sororities and fraternities are a strong presence on campus. During Rush Week, sororities and frats are at full force, trying to recruit pledges. You'd better brush up on your knowledge of Greek symbols. You will quickly learn that alpha, sigma, and pi are the first three letters of the Western alphabet. Students have skewed opinions about this, from loving it (those who rush) to antipathy. But even if you don't choose to join a frat or sorority, you will most likely find yourself at a few Greek-style keg parties at some point in your illustrious university career.

Like the Greek life associated with sororities and frats, Western remains much like its American counterparts. Western is a Rah! Rah! university complete with world-class cheerleaders, varsity football team, and king and queen contests at Homecoming time. Every fall, Homecoming Weekend draws large crowds and alumni come back to relive their memories of Western days gone by. This tradition at Western starts off with a Homecoming Carnival and Parade. Jump on the bandwagon and find yourself in a sea of purple and white faces. Kick off the game and cheer on the Mustangs. Go 'Stangs! Go!

ACADEMIC ISSUES
With a population of over 24,000 students and a faculty of 1,250 members, the university offers a wide range of undergraduate programs and degrees. It has been said of Western that it tries to be all things to all people. In the past, Western showed great testament to this, expanding undergraduate programs and degrees to cover a more diverse spectrum of studies available. Like everywhere else, the eighties' spending orgies collided with the nineties, and today, Western struggles to maintain this wide range at the expense of limited class space and over-populated lecture halls. The mega class is an all too common experience. The professional schools carry much clout. Many UWO students study in generic undergraduate waiting rooms in the hopes that it will soon lead to the fulfillment of a better life: acceptance into one of the professional schools. This, of course, is both beneficial and harmful. The prerequisite for the majority of the professional schools is completion of two years of an undergraduate degree, thus a Richard Ivey hopeful may well spend two years in Political Science or the Fine Arts before acceptance into this coveted establishment—the result is either victory or defeat. A student at Western is given time to play and explore the post-secondary environment before any major decisions need be made, but

In a Nut Shell

The university in a phrase: Major in yourself.

Best thing about the university: The amount of things to do, see, be part of.

Worst thing about the university: Size and exclusivity.

Most popular bird courses: Geology 020 (a.k.a. Rocks for Jocks), an easy science credit for those who require one but aren't in science.

Quietest spot on campus to study: Third floor of the DB Weldon Library.

Most social spot on campus to study: UCC Centrespot or Periodical A or B in DB Weldon.

Need for car and parking availability: Not a big need for a car as a bus pass is included in tuition fees, but 2,500 parking spots are allocated to students at $208.20 for the year.

Sexually speaking: In the words of Wayne and Garth: Ssshhhwing! Western is rumoured to have one of the most sexually active campuses in Canada. With all that partying and pep rallying, you're bound to hook up. Western also has an openly gay and lesbian population and is an accepting campus. Furthermore, it is possible to maintain some anonymity and privacy because of the size of the school.

Attitudes towards fraternities: A major love/hate division.

Weather: Nice fall/spring, snowy winter but bearable.

Sport facilities: Western has excellent sporting facilities that are well maintained and accessible. Sports are a major part of the campus culture and it is not hard to see why.

Library facilities: Eight to choose from.

Computer facilities: Numerous labs situated in different buildings around campus. There's usually a line-up to check e-mail during peak hours.

Safety on campus: Foot Patrol is available to escort students from place to place on campus; well-lit paths; Campus Crime Watch Program, UWO police force, student emergency response team.

Alumni: Paul Beeston, Roberta Bondar, Sheila Copps, Roberta Jamieson, Silken Laumann, Marnie McBean, Audrey McLaughlin, Alice Munro, Kevin Newman, David Peterson, Alan Thicke, Galen Weston.

---

can easily be left stranded in the "academic desert" if they fail to gain acceptance into one of the professional schools. A good lesson here is to have a working back-up plan, and to take advantage of the other faculties at Western.

This said, students will not find a lack of choice. Western offers all the generic degrees, such as Biology, Biochemistry, Political Science, and Latin. There are also rarities like an undergraduate degree in Film Studies or a degree offered in Media, Information, and Technoculture. These are shadowed, however, by programs like the Richard Ivey School of Business, or the highly competitive Bachelor of Education program and, of course, the concurrent HBA/LLBA, a program that grants both a law degree and an honours in business administration in six years.

Overall, the academia at Western is a mixed bag, offering a variety of undergraduate degrees and special programs that are the envy of the country. Students with poor academics will be crushed under Western's wheels, but those who excel will reap the benefits.

REZ LIFE

If living in rez conjures up images of *Animal House*, then you'll be in heaven at Western. All first-year students from outside London are guaranteed a room in residence, so take advantage of this great opportunity to live amongst the other 75% of first-year students who also choose to live in rez. After all, living in rez is the ultimate party experience, not to mention a great way to make friends and meet drinking buddies. Fate will determine whether or not you spend your time in rez on the border of insanity, since rooms are assigned based on a lottery system. Delaware Hall, Medway-Sydenham Hall, and Saugeen-Maitland Hall are traditional residences with mandatory meal plans. By far, the largest and wildest rez is Saugeen-Maitland, nicknamed "the Zoo," accommodating an energetic and enthusiastic 1,250 students. Essex Hall, Alumni House, and the newly built Elgin Hall are apartment-style residences. In addition to these resi-

A Word to the Wise:

1. Don't believe all the stereotypes you hear. Go with an open mind and you'll have the time of your life.

2. Make sure you pack some purple and white clothing for those Mustang games. Get a head start and get some face paint, too.

3. Try and be yourself. Western does have a lot of pressures to conform to standards. If you can avoid this you will surely feel empowered.

dences, each college has its own residence. Residences organize hall parties, jello-eating contests, pub crawls, pool and cosmic bowling nights, as well as other spur-of-the-moment events. Residences offer a great party scene, without the smoky atmosphere of a club since there is no smoking in any of the halls.

London has a wide variety of affordable rental accommodations. By second year, students have had enough of rez food and sharing bathrooms so they try to live closer to Richmond Street (a.k.a. Richmond Row), within stumbling distance to the various clubs and pubs.

NIGHT LIFE

Western and London night life are synonymous with one word: party. Western is one huge party. All you have to know is which parties to go to. Parties at Western can sometimes get out of control and you can easily lose your mind, or your underwear for that matter, so beware.

Right on campus, within crawling distance to the residences, are The Spoke, featuring retro-eighties music on Monday nights, and The Wave dance club. Off-campus bars and clubs are plentiful around London. A bus ride away, on Richmond Row, within a block of each other, is The Ridout, a seedy tavern/club (London's equivalent of Toronto's "The Brunny"), which serves cheap pitchers of beer and guarantees a great time. The Ceeps, a traditional Western drinking hole since the dawn of time, where everybody's grandfather came and drank excessively, continues to uphold the tradition and still draws large crowds. Here, preppy frat boys quaff beer, shoot pool, and engage in "intellectual conversations" at ancient, battered tables. The Mongolian Grill serves up a mouth-watering stir-fry, and up above, the Great Martini Bar markets to students as an Austin Powers rip-off. Somewhat off the beaten path, but still wildly popular, is The Drink, which spins the best in dance music, techno, house, and booty. Move your body at DV8 where you can dance off the alcohol you consumed earlier in the evening.

Other hot spots to check out are Barney's pub/patio and Jim Bob Rae's, which attracts an older crowd. T.J. Baxter's serves up great burgers and offers dancing on the third floor. For those wanting more elbow room, Joe Cool's, decorated with a revolving, fluorescent globe, serves up great-tasting burgers, perfect to start off the night.

ON LONDON

If there isn't a Mustangs game, and when you're not busy chugging a beer and are sober enough to be in seen public, you should take in the sights of this beautiful city. London is a medium-sized city with something for everyone, from a local bubble gum factory to country markets and comedy clubs. Hop on a double-decker bus for a tour of this "Forest City" and its attractions or cruise down the scenic and historic Thames River. You can practice your rollerblading wizardry or soak up the sun while sunbathing on the lush grassy lawns in one of the many parks. The Talbot Theatre hosts plays and musical events for music lovers. London Museum of Archeology is worth a peek; you can even discover a reconstructed prehistoric Indian village. There are various shopping centres located close by, great places to spend Daddy's money. You can also splurge and dine out at one of the many restaurants or trendy cafés close to the campus.

Wilfrid Laurier University

By Robin Whittaker

The Waterloo Lutheran Seminary boasted four students in 1911 when it embarked on a tradition of educating a small number of students exceptionally well. In 1925 it became affiliated with the University of Western Ontario, and in that year the top two graduates of the two-city school were from the Waterloo campus, thus beginning a three-quarters-of-a-century rivalry with UWO and proving the old adage "quality over quantity." In 1960 the school changed its name to Waterloo Lutheran University and cut its ties with Western (some would say the best thing it's ever done). In 1973 it was renamed Wilfrid Laurier University. Rumour has it that the name was chosen so the administration wouldn't need to change its WLU letterhead.

Laurier is concentrated in one city block, with three exceptions: University Place, an apartment building recently purchased as a residence for the expanding first-year populace; the infamously inconvenient 202 Regina building, which houses, most notably, the Registrar's Office and the Business Office; and the brand spanking new expansion campus in Brantford, which opened in September 1999.

Laurier's Waterloo campus is architecturally diverse and even mildly scenic, despite its brevity and urban locale. Most of the residences are brick boxes of the red and yellow variety, with the exception of the apartment-style Bricker Residence, which looks slick and contemporary. The library is a seven-floor brittle cement layer-cake with windows running around it on every floor. A chunk of the entrance-way came a-tumbling down a few years ago, but has since been reconstructed. The most talked about architectural phenomenon on campus is the Peters Building, designed by University of Waterloo architecture students some time ago to ensure that Laurier students would never find the same classroom twice. Only the faculty offices have windows, so the classrooms are relatively dreary things sporting state-of-the-art data projectors.

The campus's oldest building, Willison Hall (named after Reverend Nils Willison, who was the school's first graduate and one of the above-mentioned founding four students), is a brick box with a nice roof. At the centre of campus is the Dean Nicholls Campus Centre which includes the Students' Union, Student Publications, two campus bars, a small variety store called The Centre Spot, and the Food Court.

CAMPUS CULTURE

Laurier is renowned for its school spirit. The first day of Orientation (Frosh) Week has first-year students screaming, singing, dancing, and wearing the virtues of Laurier spirit. The small first-year contingent means that everyone can fit into the Athletic Complex gymnasium for scream-offs and activities that will literally introduce you to over 500 students by week's end. Lifelong friendships are made in the first week and the small campus size means that you'll recognize dozens of friends and acquaintances everywhere you go.

Sports are huge at Laurier. Either you're into the excitement they produce (especially Golden Hawk football) or you're not, and this can define your early years. Most importantly, $2.5 million has been thrown into Laurier Athletics this year. Newly hired Athletics Director Peter Baxter sums it up: "We are not aiming to be the best small school around, but to provide the best program in the country." Big-name football, hockey, and soccer coaches have recently been hired, promising to improve upon an already busty trophy chest.

While it is generally a tight-knit society, Laurier is hardly regarded, from within the student body at least, as ethnically diverse. My floor-mates in first year, for example, sheepishly

Vital Statistics

Address: 75 University Avenue West, Waterloo, Ontario, N2L 3C5

Admissions office: (519) 884-0710 ext. 3351

Website: www.wlu.ca

Total enrollment: 7,863

Male-female ratio: 46 to 54

Percentage of out-of province first-year students: 1%

Average entering grades: Arts: 76.5%; Science: 73%; Commerce: 85.5%

Tuition fees: $4,014.00

Residence fees: $2,643 (dormitory style) + $2,000 meal plan; $3,636 (apartment style) + $600 meal plan available.

Percentage of students in residence: 15%

Financial aid: Scholarships and awards ranging from $50 to $4,000. Bursaries and OSAP available.

Co-op programs: Anthropology, Biology, Business and Economics, Chemistry, Computer Electronics, English, Environmental Studies, Geography, History, Kinesiology (Physical Education), Math, Political Science, Psychology, Sociology.

Services for students with disabilities: Special Needs Office.

Aboriginal students: First Nations Students' Association.

Student services: Career assistance, counselling and study skill services, dean of students, health services, housing office, non-denominational chaplains, office for mature students.

---

dubbed our floor "Aryan Acres." Furthermore, there is relatively little out-of-province representation—a point that has baffled more than one student. There are, nevertheless, a variety of visibly successful clubs on campus that represent specific cultures: the Black Students' Association, Chinese Students' Association, Irish Students' Association, Jewish Students' Association, and South Asian Laurier Students' Association are a few.

Participation is the essence of student life at Laurier. Everybody's doing it to the point of being over-extended. One student belonged to four campus clubs; he wrote, directed, and stage-managed plays with the Laurier Fringe and the Laurier Theatre Collective; edited and wrote for the student newspaper *The Cord*; volunteered as a campus tour guide; and acted as a member of several school committees during his four years. And there's always someone who will proudly tell you they've done more. If nothing else, one graduates from Laurier with a sculpted sense of involvement and a strong idea of how much is too much.

There are political clubs on campus, but in general apathy is prevalent, especially with Laurier's own Students' Union where voter turnout is notoriously low despite a carnivalesque atmosphere in the Concourse (the centre of campus) on election day. And if people are feeling screwed by the administration (academic or student elected), they speak loudly amongst themselves, but cast no stones.

The average Laurier student tends to blend and shine, not stick out and shock. Non-status-quo appearance is usually filtered out by the end of first year, perhaps due to the close-quarters of residence and the immediate push to participate in all that Laurier spirit. Black remains the most non-conformist colour around and most students choose to flaunt a menagerie of WLU apparel. Biz-school stigma may be a factor with the conservative attire as well.

ACADEMIC ISSUES

Business, business, business. Your stay at Laurier will be defined, at least when academia comes up, by which side of the business fence you graze on: biz-knob or arts-whatever. The School of Business and Economics (SBE) is the administration's favourite child, if for no other reason than it garners millions of dollars in alumni and community donations. The SBE is one of the nation's top business schools, and its graduates have phenomenal placement rates upon graduation. The relatively large size of the faculty means that it can provide resources and connections to its students, and its small class sizes mean a quality learning experience. And besides, the SBE gets all the prime attention when there's a beef to be had.

The Faculty of Arts and Science offers a plurality of strong programs. Small class sizes (usually around 40 students and rarely more than 90) mean enviable student-faculty ratios. Professors are very approachable and sport impressive credentials. The downside to the small faculty, however, is the modest course selection offered by many departments, but courses are often available to Laurier students down the street at the University of Waterloo. Departments such as English, Anthropology, Phys-Ed, and History offer thorough and demanding programs. The Communications Studies (CS) program, however, presents yearly headaches for students who can't finish in three or four years because too many electives are granted to non-CS majors.

Everybody's hopping mad about significant cutbacks to all the departments, but most hold the Ontario government responsible for threatening the minds of its youth, and not the relatively unmotivated student population. There's a fairly relaxed vibe among Arts and Science students and professors, but if you've missed a class or three it might be wise to look around hallway corners in case your professor happens to be

In a Nut Shell

The university in a phrase: "One square block of school spirit where everybody knows your name." Or, "The high school down the street" (a favourite of University of Waterloo students).

Best thing about the university: Easy to meet people, and small classes.

Worst thing about the university: Hard to hide from people, and modest course offerings.

Favourite professors: G. Boire (English), J. Abwunza (Sociology), D. Black (Communication Studies), T. Copp (History), S. Jha (SBE), J. McCutcheon (SBE), L. O'Dell (English/Theatre).

Most popular bird courses: Love and Its Myths (RE103), Writing for the Media (EN227).

Hot spots to study on campus: The Concourse (if you dare, between classes it's like studying in a subway station); the newly renovated Torque Room; department lounges; SBE computer labs.

Quietest spot to study on campus: Seventh floor of the library; the Crystal Solarium; vacant classrooms.

Need for car and parking availability: A car in K-W is a convenience, not a necessity, and there's next to no parking on campus (unless you win the parking lottery, literally). Laurier students walk everywhere, but rarely stray far from campus. Taxis provide trips to downtown Kitchener, and for some reason only the locals trust public transit.

Sexually speaking: First year is a crazy romp of meeting people, baby! After that, some cool off, but not everyone. That's why the Turret isn't just a first-year hangout, and why Loose Change Louis' does such great business. Gays, Lesbians or Bisexuals at Laurier.

Fraternities/sororities: Either you love them because you're in one (a small but vocal minority) or you despise them and everything they swear they don't stand for. And don't try to start your own because, according to one student who had over 200 signatures, "the Students' Union reps told us we were giving a bad name to the Greeks."

Attitudes towards the administration: Everyone knows WLU also stands for "We Line Up," especially when OSAP and tuition issues are at hand. The Business Office (which does the money stuff) has taken heat recently over the curious ways in which they've informed students of their fees, but they're usually helpful when they mess up, as is the Registrar's Office, where you can expect to have to "clear things up" at least twice a year.

Athletic facilities: The Athletic Complex (AC) is a favourite among

coming your way. The downside to small class sizes is that your profs will recognize you outside of class and if you haven't handed in that paper yet, you're going to have some explaining to do.

The Faculty of Music is tops in its field, but its students tend to become isolated from the rest of the student body because of demanding courses, practices, and performance schedules.

Laurier's Business and Economics and Arts and Science co-op programs are highly competitive and well-respected off campus. On campus, however, students have traditionally been divided over their merits. While the office maintains contacts with top corporations, Arts and Science students are all to often presented with camp counsellor jobs instead of jobs where the chance of post-co-op promotion is high. Co-op students often complain about the footwork they have to do themselves, while paying $180 to $500 per term for résumé and interview workshops. And if you're offered that counsellor position, you'd better take it or you'll get the evil eye. That's no small factor in setting the Laurier co-op placement rate at 99% every year. Nevertheless, just as many success stories can be heard from students, especially Business students

(and Arts and Science students who argued until they scored Business-type placements), who have found their calling in nurturing environments.

Regardless of the faculty you choose, if you are admitted into Laurier consider that a crowning achievement in itself. The school boasts one of the highest first-year entrance cut-offs in the country. An undergrad school first and foremost, students enter first year better prepared than at other schools, and come out with a well-respected institution on their résumés.

REZ LIFE At Laurier, residence is all about the first-year student. And if you've applied before June, you're guaranteed a place to lay your head on campus. Lifelong friends are made with your neighbours down the hall. These are the guys and girls with whom you'll go to bars, eat meals, bare your soul, stay up all night, and maybe even study. Beverages, practical jokes, hangin' out with your sister or brother floor (assigned or adopted), and eating A&W four meals every weekend are all pastimes in which the average on-campus resident partakes.

In a Nut Shell *continued*

die-hard jocks and those who just want to tone up or play a game of squash every now and then. The Olympic-size swimming pool is a swimmer's dream. University Stadium is home to both the Laurier Golden Hawks and the University of Waterloo Warriors football teams. The stadium also has indoor athletic equipment. You should use these facilities because your student fees are paying for them anyway.

Library facilities: Laurier has a modest library collection, but a three-cornered inter-library loan system allows rapid access (usually within a couple of days) to the formidable holdings of the University of Waterloo and the University of Guelph.

Computer facilities: Again, the biz-knobs have it great. Fifty dollars gets them unlimited access to word processors, printers, a graphic Internet platform, and even scanners. Laptops are also available on a loan basis, though they become scarce when papers are on the horizon. For the rest of the student population, Laurier has finally emerged from the dark ages to provide on-campus computer and Internet access to those students not worthy of Biz School donations. Several new computer labs were set up across campus with e-mail, Internet, and word processing capabilities.

Weather: The K–W region has a climate unto itself. It can be a sunny 30 degrees an hour away in Toronto, but pour buckets for days in Waterloo. Winters are windy, frigid, and white, but when you're in residence on campus you laugh it off because class is at most a three-minute walk from your bed (and some buildings have connecting underground passages). Summers are beautiful for patio hopping.

Safety on campus: Laurier is proud of its safe campus. Foot Patrol, operating out of the Students' Union, is a walk-home service that will go anywhere a student lives to get him or her home safely, even if the Foot Patrollers, in volunteer teams of one guy and one girl, have to bike back! Campus Security is an omnipotent presence on campus all day and all night.

Alumni: Justice Janet Boland, Supreme Court of Ontario; Donald Campbell, Deputy Minister of Foreign Affairs; David Chilton, author of *The Wealthy Barber*; Dr. Michael Overduin, cancer researcher; Alan Pope.

Despite its one-block area, the Laurier campus sports a total of nine residences, all reserved for first-year students. Bricker and the newly purchased (off-campus) University Place offer comfy, real-life apartment-style housing where students, radically enough, cook their own food and live in comparatively greater comfort than they might in more traditional residences which require meal plans fitting various appetites. Conrad is the school's all-female residence and Little House is the all-male residence. The remaining residences are co-ed. MacDonald House was among Laurier's first co-ed habitats, and was apparently convincing enough to encourage recent switch-overs by Willison (formerly all-male and Laurier's mild answer to an Animal House) and Boukaert (formerly all-female and tidy). Euler and Leupold are the school's "quiet" residences (earlier lights-out). The traditional residences are as tidy, or as crazy, as the personalities of their occupants, but the dons (residence floor supervisors) always ensure that some degree of order is maintained. There's no real "favourite" residence, perhaps because personal interaction is so easily achieved outside one's own building. However, "What rez are you in?" is still a popular pick-up line, followed by, "I know this girl whose friend…."

After first year, however, you're left on the street to find a home and deal with rent, phone, cable, and dinner bills in the real world. Waterloo, at least at the north end, is a university town. With the University of Waterloo literally down the street, there's no shortage of student living if you start early enough. First-year students are encouraged to find accommodations as early as February if they want the prime locations close to the school. But there will still be desirable spots come May and June. Rent tends to be between $230 and $375, depending on your quality of living, distance to the university, number of utilities included, and, of course, the luck of the lessee.

NIGHT LIFE

Kitchener-Waterloo is the barfly's answer to a salt-lick, and for the dancin' machine in you, it's da bomb. Oktoberfest, the area's annual, internationally famous mega-drink-a-thon, sets the tone for the university student's stay at Laurier. As a first-year student you'll spend most of your party time carousing at the Turret, the school's formidable dance bar and meat market. By second year, students either come back to the Turret Thursdays and Saturdays to get their groove on, or head for the sit-down, rockin' atmosphere of Wilf's. There's no question these are the social venues of choice for Laurier students, especially in one's formative years. Alternately, check out the immaculate club-house feel of the Grad Pub, open to all.

But when you get tired of the same ol' scene (though not everybody does), there's a whole new world waiting for adventurous chicks and roosters willing to cross the road to get to

A Word to the Wise:

1. Don't miss out on the Frosh Week festivities. It's not actually possible to do so, but it's rumoured there are those who didn't sign up for it in August. These people should have gone elsewhere. The nightly events acquaint you with the city's hot spots, via school bus drop-offs and returns, so you'll know where you want to be every night, or for that matter where never to go again. Not everybody comes out of Frosh Week having had the best of times, but it will be the most hectic week of your life to date, and therefore among the most memorable.

2. Become active in campus life. Laurier's Dean of Students David McMurray, upon coming to the school a few years ago, commented that the level of student participation in extra-curricular activities was unbelievable. Clubs, sports, student politics, student publications (newspaper, yearbook, photography), do-it-yourself theatre, part-time employment and volunteering at the school, and getting involved as a student department representative or senate member are all opportunities that are rewarding and great to slap on a resumé.

3. It doesn't matter if you don't know what program really tickles your fancy coming into first year. Hardly anybody does. By second year you'll have a better idea. All you need to know going in is whether you're a biz-knob or an arts-whatever. The rest will come (even if it takes four years!).

4. Keep track of the courses you need for your degree. It's easy for students to lose track of required courses, and a few discover this too late and are forced to take another term or two to catch up.

5. Check out the "Bag o' Crime" in *The Cord*, Laurier's student paper. It sums up the week's on-campus misdemeanours, which tend to include the routine breaking of Laurier's only parking lot gate-arm and the occasional theft of campus patio chairs.

6. Go elsewhere in the summer if you can. The city shrivels almost to its locals-only size after exams. Laurier students are few and far between in the sunny months, though this does leave more patio space for the stick-arounders.

7. Residence life, and for that matter all university life at Laurier, is what you make of it. Get involved as much as you want, and you'll be happy. Don't, and hey, you still might be happy, too.

the other side. Laurier is situated at the crossroads of Waterloo's two main streets: University Avenue and King Street, each of which presents the late-night pedestrian with ample bar sampling opportunities. Right across from Laurier is Morty's, the small sit-down bar that always gains a loyal clientele due to its big-screen TV and wing nights. A little down the way, on University Avenue, the Fox and Pheasant quickly becomes a student's comfy hangout if a more spacious sit-down atmosphere is what you crave. Jose's Noodle Factory is right next door and willing to whet the patio hopper's whistle. One block from these is McGinnis Frontrow, the sports bar with a big screen and imposing memorabilia. In the other direction, on King Street, you can mingle with the locals or bring all your pals to the truck-stop atmosphere of Ethel's Lounge (a favourite Big Sugar hangout when they come to town), the humongous four-storey

haunt of the Huether Hotel/Lion Brewery/Barley Works, the merry ol' England fair of Kingsbridge Crossing, and the more modern décor of Time Square. Finally, the Fool on the Hill provides a super alternative to the Fox, mainly because of its ultra-friendly wait staff and hearty meals.

If the unce-unce-unce of the Backstreet Boys and the Village People is more to your liking, you've also come to the right place. Off campus, Loose Change Louis' maintains a reputation for tight clothes and light-headed, sweaty fun. For the more die-hard dancers, look no further than a $5 cab ride to the gigantic Revolution, or to downtown Kitchener's The Lyric Night Club, home of Chris Shepherd and arguably the area's craziest dance club. Across the road from The Lyric is the Metropolis, boasting three floors of competitive strutting. But for the more alternative crowd, Phil's is a sweat-box of loud, rockin' tunes (just don't have the misfortune to see the place with the lights on!). Club Abstract attracts those Laurier students who don't believe in dress shirts and subtle make-up 24/7; it's where the goths and the eclectics hide out.

Live music in Waterloo is the happenin' thing—the backbone of the city's tight creative community—featuring rock, folk, blues, reggae, jazz, jungle, and even a symphony orchestra. Bar bands abound, exuding enviable talent. The Lyric and the Turret are on the big-name band circuit, frequently hosting such acts as Big Sugar, 54-40, and The Tea Party. Lulu's, a distant but unique concert venue, hosts such icons as Colin James, Sass Jordan, James Brown, Trooper, and Kim Mitchell, though its biggest claim to fame is that it once had the longest bar in Canada.

Finally, for those who are not of age, don't fear. There's more of you than you might think. Frosh Week celebrations are for all, even the bar stuff: you'll just get a wristband at the door of the establishment indicating that you can't have alcohol in your hand. The same is true for campus bars throughout the year. And you'll appreciate the beverages even more when you do reach the magic 19.

ON KITCHENER-WATERLOO

The locals will have you know there's more to Kitchener-Waterloo than two universities and Oktoberfest, but you probably won't realize it for most of your university career. The scenery runs the gamut from shady Waterloo Park to seedy downtown Kitchener. Public transit makes everything convenient (when it's on time), and the train station and bus depot provide the automobile-deficient with a means to come and go as they please. From the quaint Princess Cinema to the leviathan Silver City, there's no lack of movie theatres from which to choose. And if live theatre is your passion, K-W can perform with the best of them. Big-city dwellers call Waterloo a small town, but farm folks and Smallvillians are often dizzied by the pace. K-W is close enough to the Greater Toronto Area (one hour) that employment connections for co-op and the summer, and pro sports games on weekends, aren't out of the question. But few students leave Waterloo on a regular basis because new friends are made every day in the small university atmosphere and you'll find it difficult to say good-bye.

University of Windsor

By Christine Ibarra

The University of Windsor is a medium-sized university on a medium-sized campus. The campus is situated in the middle of a residential area where it has an impressive view of the Ambassador Bridge and the Detroit skyline. You can literally get from one side of the campus to the other in 10 minutes and you can walk to downtown Windsor in about 30 minutes. The campus is attractive and the architecture is a blend of historical and modern styles. Windsor was established in 1857, originally founded as Assumption College by the Jesuits, and retains many old stone buildings covered in ivy.

Unfortunately, Windsor does not exude a sense of prestige like other long-established universities. During the early eighties, Windsor was dubbed "Last Chance U" due to its low entrance requirements and the fact that many students went to Windsor because it was the only school where they could get accepted. In the early nineties, it gained the reputation of "It Could Be Worse U." Over the past decade, the university has come a long way and its image is improving. Windsor has expanded its curriculum and offers innovative programs putting students in the driver's seat after graduation. According to a recent survey, 97% of Windsor graduates contacted from the class of 96 had jobs within two years after graduation. The survey also showed 100% of Nursing, Computer Science, Math, and Physical Sciences graduates were employed.

CAMPUS CULTURE

Windsor's student population is diverse on many fronts. Reflecting the diversity of the city, Windsor's student body is made up, in part, of first generation Canadians from a broad spectrum of cultural and ethnic backgrounds and children of blue-collar workers. There is a high influx of international students, particularly American students from across the river. Windsor draws the large majority of its students (just over 50%) from neighbouring counties: Essex, Lambton, and Kent. As a result, students come in pre-established cliques and tightly knit friendships before the first day of class. These circles are sometimes hard to penetrate, but there are lots of opportunities to make friends. Overall, Windsor students are a friendly bunch and the atmosphere is friendly and relaxed. Depending on whether or not you grew up in Windsor, your take on the city will be completely different. Windsorites enjoy the slower pace compared to their American Detroit neighbour. A lot of students who come from out of town form tight bonds with other students who don't go home on weekends. Compared to other universities that are ghost towns on weekends, U of Windsor is alive with activity.

Whether you're frosh or not, Frosh Week is a guaranteed great time filled with action-packed events, pub crawls, and dance nights. Swing Night is one of the highlights of Frosh Week (perhaps owing to Gap commercials and the newly founded following of the Brian Seltzer Orchestra). Whatever you do, don't miss out on Frosh Week. By the end of the week, you'll have made a ton of new friends and you'll know some of the ins and outs of campus life.

To see and be seen, students hang out at the CAW (Canadian Auto Workers Student Centre) which has everything you could ever need as a student—all under one roof. You'll find CJAM, the campus radio station, *The Lance* student newspaper, UWSA (the University of Windsor's Students' Alliance), The Pub, a games room, a travel agency, health services, a pharmacy, a used-book store, photocopy machines (to copy notes for those classes you skipped), and so much more.

There are dozens of clubs and student organizations to join, such as "Amigos" Hispanic Association, Music Therapy Association, and Investment Management Club, to name but a few. CARISA (Caribbean Students' Association) is also very active on campus and organizes "Sports Weekend," a cultural event that features a fashion show and action-packed basketball games. You can also get involved in intramural and recreation sports, from badminton and ju-jitsu karate to kayaking and swimming.

Windsor's sports facilities are world-class and in great shape. The Lancer men's and women's track and field teams have consistently placed in the top three in Canada-wide university championships. Sadly, the Lancer's success goes virtually unnoticed. With such great facilities and such an interesting mix of students, there's never a dull moment at

Vital Statistics

Address: 401 Sunset Ave., Windsor, Ontario, N9B 3P4

Admissions office: (519) 253-4232 or (519) 253-3000 ext. 3315

Website: www.uwindsor.ca

Total enrollment: 12,241

Male-female ratio: 46 to 54

Average entrance grades: Arts: 66%; Science: 66%; Commerce: 66%; Engineering: 70%

Tuition fees: $3,854

Residence fees: Quad $5,812.50–$6,212.50 (double room with meal plan); $6,547.50–$6,947.50 (single room with meal plan); Electa, Tecumseh, and Clark: $3,178.00–$5,287.50

Spaces for students in

residence: 1,650 spaces for single students; 1,000 spaces reserved for first-year students.

Percentage of international students: 3%

Percentage of out-of-province first-year students: 1%

Financial aid: Entrance scholarships and awards from $500 to $1,000 for one year. Renewable awards up to $12,000 for four years. Residence awards available to all high school students who live in residence and their average is 75% of higher. Bursaries and OSAP also available.

Co-op programs: Business, Computer Science, Earth Sciences, Environmental Biology and Geology, Great Lake Studies, Human Kinetics, Engineering (Civil, Electrical, Environmental, Industrial, and Mechanical).

Services for students with disabilities: Centre for Educational Difficulties; Special Needs Office and coordinator.

Aboriginal students: Aboriginal Legal Advisory Clinic, Aboriginal Education Counsellor.

Student services: Academic advisory centre, career services, counselling, computer centre, international students centre, housing, legal aide, ombudsperson, psychological services, religious services, tutoring services, writing centre.

Windsor. You'll find endless opportunities to stay active socially, culturally, and athletically.

ACADEMIC ISSUES

Windsor draws on its U.S. border location to its advantage. Being situated across the river from Detroit and on the junction of two Great Lakes has allowed Windsor to establish partnerships with institutions and corporations on both sides of the border. Windsor offers a university experience with a window on two dynamic cities—Detroit and Windsor, of course. Canadian students can participate in a co-op program with Wayne State University in Michigan and take courses in the States while only paying regular Windsor tuition fees. There are many opportunities for students to gain hands-on experience in various fields such as health care, automotive, and aquatics. Windsor boasts the Great Lakes Institute for Environmental Research which offers research and co-op opportunities for Environmental Biology students. The University of Windsor/Chrysler Canada Ltd. Automotive Research and Development Centre provides work-term positions for Engineering students.

Windsor is best known for Business and its professional programs in Law, Education, Engineering, Nursing, and Social Work. It is also noted for its Human Kinetics, Clinical Chemistry, Co-op Engineering, Sports Management, and Social Science programs. Windsor also has schools of Dramatic Arts, Music, and Visual Arts.

Class sizes are small, making the atmosphere less intimidating. There is a high level of interaction between students and professors. Profs are usually accessible and more than willing to help students. Many students benefit from this open-door policy and get individual attention to suit their needs.

S.O.S. (Students Orienting Students) helps first-year students adjust to university life. Peer advisors can give you advice on what classes to choose for first year. The Head Start program partners you up with a student volunteer who can answer your questions from a first-hand perspective. University 101 provides academic support to help first-year students manage their time and improve their study skills, making the plunge into university life much easier.

REZ LIFE

There are seven possibilities for residence life at Windsor. Students requesting to live in residence are more or less guaranteed a space. Rooms are assigned by random lottery but students coming fresh out of high school will undoubtedly be assigned a double room in one of the Quad residences: Cartier, Cody, Laurier, or Macdonald Halls. You can either choose who you want to room with or you'll be matched with someone based on your answers on a residence roommate questionnaire. This seemingly insignificant piece of paper determines who you are compatible with and what type of living arrangement you prefer (quiet/not so quiet, same sex/co-ed). (Mismatches occur from time to time, but don't worry it might not be you.) You can also request to live on a theme floor. Smoke- and alcohol-free environments can be found on Wellness floors. Academic theme floors bunch students in the same or similar programs together.

There is hard-core partying in Windsor's residences; however, the Quad residences are known to be the most spirited (Macdonald is the wildest and craziest of them all). All of the Quad residences are co-ed and they have institution-like rooms (Cartier was originally designed as a prison). Macdonald used to be an all-male residence. There are urinals on every floor and only four toilets per floor, whereas all of the washrooms in Laurier have toilets.

After you survive your first year, you "graduate" to a new level. Upper-year students can apply for apartment-style and townhouse accommodation. Don't make plans to live in Huron Hall, the motel-turned-residence with sliding patio doors that lead to a balcony that generally attracts people who like to party. Huron is going to be knocked down to accommodate a bigger customs truck depot. Tecumseh Hall offers apartment-style living and a quieter atmosphere. Clark Residence is the newest residence. Many students boast that life in this townhouse-style rez is just like a *Friends* episode. Electa Hall is reserved for mature clientele of upper-year and graduate students (you have to be at least 21 to get a room there). Electa has much-coveted single rooms with a shared bathroom and lounge area, and a kitchen on each floor, giving you the option to prepare your own meals.

If your residence requires you to purchase a meal plan, don't worry because the food isn't as bad as you think. Windsor offers a wide variety of food choices. You can taste the world at the Market Place food court in the Student Centre which features international cuisine.

Living in rez in the best way to get settled in and make friends. Resident assistants organize many fun and exciting events, from rock climbing and "rock 'n' bowl" to talent shows and movie nights.

For the past three years, the Residence Spirit Cup has boosted school spirit among the students living in rez. This year-long competition promotes healthy rivalries between residences. Floors/units try to "out spirit" each other and build up points for participating in events such as cheering on the Lancers and organizing food and clothing drives.

NIGHT LIFE

If excitement is what you crave then downtown Windsor is definitely the place to go. Fun knows no borders and sometimes spills over to Detroit. If quaffing ale and downing shooters are more your style then you should stay on the Canadian side of the river because the legal drinking age in Michigan is 21. Weekends are big nights for most bars and clubs. Reactor Nightclub is one of the newest additions to the club scene in downtown Windsor. Reactor goes full-tilt on Thursdays, Fridays, and Saturdays and guarantees an explosive time. On Sundays head to the Loop; it features retro, disco, and old-school tunes (be prepared to sweat a lot). Dominion House Tavern, a.k.a. the DH, is hot on Tuesdays and Thursdays, attracting students to its drink specials. Most people go to the DH to drink, but after a few hours, you can build up enough liquid courage to test out the brand spanking new dance floor. Windsor Music Café is *the* drinking, dancing, and pick-up spot. Rock Bottom Bar & Grill (mostly bar) features a sit-down atmosphere, tasty food, reasonably priced drinks, and the presence of at least a half-dozen of your closest pals. The Residence, Rush, and Don Cherry's are also favoured watering holes. Check out Woody's and Howl at the Moon, too. If you're looking for some action, look no further than Faces Roadhouse. Faces' prime location near campus (within stumbling distance from the Human Kinetics building and St. Denis Athletic Centre) pulls in many athletes and Kinesiology students who like to rock around the jock. Beer flows freely and cheaply at Faces, especially on Wednesday nights. The Pub is a favourite hangout on campus and Thursday nights feature good drink specials.

Students answer post-bar munchies at Dragon's Inn Chinese restaurant and the Pita Pit, which are open late. Other choice eateries at any time of day include Bubi's, Hurricane, and, of course, Mickey Dee's (McDonald's) and Harvey's.

If you prefer a quieter night, then catch a flick at a movie theatre or enjoy a healthy, mouth-watering meal at The Eclectic Café for vegetarians. Grab a java at a European-style café or chat online with out-of-town friends at an Internet café.

In a Nut Shell

The university in a phrase: Its unique location (and American influence) makes it an interesting place to go.

Best thing about the university: Fun and relaxed atmosphere. There's no pressure to fit in.

Worst thing about the university: Bad reputation; pollution spewing from Detroit; out-dated library resources.

Favourite professors: N. Biswas (Engineering); T. Flemming (Criminology); S. Towson (Psychology); J. Weese (Human Kinetics).

Most popular bird courses: "Rocks for Jocks"—Geology 101; "Bonehead Bio"—Intro to Biology.

Hot spots to study on campus: The CAW.

Quietest spots to study on campus: The library.

Need for car and parking availability: It's nice to have a car to visit Point Pelee and the States, but good luck parking it around campus. Biking and rollerblading are great alternatives since Windsor is flat.

Sexually speaking: Windsor is small enough to meet someone and big enough to keep your personal life private.

Fraternities/sororities: They don't have a strong presence on campus.

Athletic facilities: Windsor has one of the best indoor tracks in Canada.

Library facilities: Free library privileges at Wayne State University in Detroit, Michigan.

Computer facilities: All students are given e-mail and Internet access.

The Computer Centre features Pentium computers for assignments, e-mail to check grades, and more.

Weather: Hot and hazy summers; the air quality and pollution is bad in the summer, so if you're around then, make sure your place is air-conditioned and stock up on bottled water. "Mild" winters with little snow by many Canadian standards with temperatures between –1° and –5° Celsius (around 30s Fahrenheit).

Safety on campus: Walksafe program escorts students on campus as well as a few blocks off campus. Nightly foot patrols and campus police.

Alumni: Michael Bell, former Canadian ambassador to Egypt; Julie Kryk, Lilith Fair performer; Mark MacGuigan; Richard Peddie; Vicki Russell; Al Strachan; Anne Maria Tremonti.

ON WINDSOR

The City of Windsor is known as "Canada's Automotive Capital," and is home to the "Big Three" automakers and many ethnic communities. There is plenty to do in this blue-collar city, from art galleries and live theatre to wining and dining at the many restaurants that feature cuisine from around the world (Hungarian, Greek, Polish, Indian, Japanese, Chinese). Be sure to check out Via Italia (Little Italy), a half-mile row of small family-owned and -operated businesses—boutiques, cafés, and food markets. There are also lots of bars and coffee houses to enjoy.

Try your luck at the Casino. You could win enough money to pay off your student loan or just as easily dig yourself into even more debt. If money is starting to burn a hole in your wallet, join the many students who enjoy cross-boarder shopping. Gas, clothes, and groceries are much cheaper across the border in the U.S. of A. (although when you factor in the exchange rate, some things cost about the same).

Windsor is an easy four-hour drive (three and a bit depending on how fast you're going) to Toronto or Chicago. Sports nuts can zip across to downtown Detroit and cheer on Canadian teams when they play against the Detroit Tigers, Pistons, or Red Wings. Take a tour of the historic Canadian Club Distillery and see how good ol' Canadian whiskey is made. Rollerblade or bike along the waterfront. Venture a little farther and discover one of Ontario's thriving wine regions. Wine enthusiasts can indulge in wine making and wine tasting at the many wineries in the surrounding areas. Picturesque Pelee Island and Point Pelee National Park are a close one-hour drive away.

York University

By Lorraine McMeekin

"In 1959, we had no faculty, no students, no buildings—only President Murray Ross, and grand dreams. Forty years later we have more than 40,000 students, more than 4,500 faculty and staff and we have just completed a $108 million campaign—the largest in York's history."

—Dr. Lorna Marsden, President, York University

Welcome to York University at the turn of the century and the millennium. In 40 short years, the university has grown to become the third largest in Canada. It has built a reputation for world-renowned research, innovative teaching methods, and a community that is diverse in ethnicity and political beliefs. It is comprised of two campuses—Keele and Glendon—both offering a curriculum designed to carry on the tradition of a liberal arts education that was president Murray Ross's original mandate.

The Keele campus is located in northwest Toronto, north of Highway 401, off Keele Street, and is a neighbour to the "Jane and Finch corridor." This is not something you want to emphasize to your parents if they are nervous about your safety. A visit to the campus in the summer will leave a pleasant but misleading impression in your mind. Artistic landscaping in the Harry Arthurs Common seems designed to detract from the grey concrete that has been used to construct most of the buildings. Well-placed trees along the walkways create the illusion of nature on this mostly urban campus. Shortly after Thanksgiving, the green will fade and the rest of the academic year will be spent in a hazy shade of grey and brown.

You will soon become acquainted with the echo you create by stomping through the middle of the Vari Hall rotunda, the massive lecture halls in the Curtis Lecture hall building, and the offices and seminar rooms of the Ross Building. You may also experience classes in the Chemistry and Computer Science building, the Centre for Fine Arts, the Lumbers building, or any of the seven colleges—Founders, Vanier, Maclaughlin, Winters, Bethune, Stong, and Calumet.

Glendon College, York's original location, is nestled away in one of Toronto's most prestigious residential neighbour-hoods. This may be something you want to emphasize to your parents, if you are considering Glendon as an option. Overall, Glendon has a more traditional, collegiate feel to it. The community is small, and most people tend to know (or at least recognize) the students around them.

Your official introduction to life at York occurs during Frosh Week. The Orientation Directors strive to design a week of events that is as inclusive and accessible as possible. Your college will host an array of events designed to make you feel at home in your new surroundings.

Games, dances, and all-night parties all allow you to get to know your fellow frosh and to interact with upper-year students, who are more than willing to help you or answer any questions you might have. Get lots of sleep before you arrive—you won't get another good night of sleep until the following April.

A student body population of over 40,000 students may seem intimidating to a lot of new students. A certain amount of paranoia may kick in on the first day of class when trying to find lecture halls, a place to buy morning coffee, or a bathroom. As you begin to know your way around, the claustrophobia will disappear. You will learn to make your way through the throngs of people cruising through the Vari Link or congregating in the Student Centre. Soon, you will have picked out your favourite between-class hangout, the washroom with the smallest lineups, and you will even know where your classes are located.

CAMPUS CULTURE

Diverse is possibly the best word to describe the culture of the student body. Hardly surprising, however, when you consider that York is located in Canada's most ethnically diverse city. The experience of York's students is rich and unique because they are introduced to a variety of individuals whose ideas have been influenced by either their cultural and/or social backgrounds or their political experiences. Be prepared to leave a lot of preconceived notions at home, because they will limit your ability to learn from and appreciate the ideas of other individuals.

There are an endless number of student-run organizations

Vital Statistics

Address: 4700 Keele St., North York, Ontario, M3J 1P3

Admissions office: (416) 736-5000

Website: www.yorku.ca

Total enrollment: 36,885

Male-female ratio: 39 to 61

Average entering grades: Arts: 73%; Science: 75%; Commerce: 85%

Tuition fees: Arts and Science: $4,440.20; Schulich School of Business: $4,491.30; Glendon College: $4,363.50

Residence fees: Double: $2,681 +

(either) $1,800 or $1,200 meal plan; single: $3,561 + (either) $1,800 or $1,200 meal plan

Percentage of students in residence: 6% (including Glendon)

Percentage of international students: 4%

Percentage of out-of-province first-year students: 2%

Co-op programs: York offers several joint programs with various Toronto colleges. The newest addition is the Seneca @ York campus.

Financial aid: based on 1998–99 awards, approximately 3,800 entrance (application and automatic) scholarships are available.

Services for students with disabilities: ABLE York; Learning Disabilities program; March of Dimes; Office for Persons with Disabilities.

Aboriginal students: Aboriginal Students' Association

Student services: Academic advisors, career services, writing workshops, women's centre, daycare.

that will allow you to interact with others who share your interests. If you are a "politician," you may choose to represent your college constituency on the York Federation of Students (YFS), York's central student government. Each of the colleges also has councils that are constantly in need of people power. Other politically oriented organizations include OPIRG, the International Socialists, and the York chapters of the Young Liberals, the Young NDPs, and the Young PCs. Those who like to write may choose to become a member of the *excalibur* newspaper staff, or to write for one of the smaller papers (the *Lexicon*, and the *Vandoo*, to name a couple). Other organizations include TBLGAY (Transgender, Bisexual, Lesbian, and Gay), academic clubs (eg., the Astronomy Club), and clubs that represent various ethnic origins, such as the Jewish Student Federation and Sikh Students' Association. Adrenaline junkies can get their kicks by joining the Sky Diving Club.

For those that want to participate in sports but aren't varsity material, Sport York offers intramural teams that are geared to all levels of ability. Golf, broomball, inner-tube water polo, and bowling are popular and a fun way to meet new people, burn off stress, and keep the "freshman fifteen" under control. Points from these events are awarded to the colleges and the coveted "Torch" is presented to the winning college at the end-of-year banquet.

There is not a lot of York spirit to be found on campus. This can be attributed to the large student population and the fact that most students are commuters who treat their university experience with a nine to five attitude. Most residence students develop a strong loyalty to their colleges and participate in the activities that are hosted by them. Some attempts have been made to create a sense of York pride by promoting sporting events and having centralized Frosh Week events. The col-

lege councils have also been trying to organize events that promote interaction between students.

Residence students sport a more casual wardrobe than commuter students for classes. Bring hospital pants, tear-away pants, and baseball caps; it is almost impossible to live in residence for a year without participating in some activity. The somewhat remote location of the Keele campus certainly promotes involvement if you'd like to do anything other than schoolwork. The preferred hangouts of rezzies are the college pubs or the residence common rooms.

The favourite hangout for commuters is in the food court of the Student Centre. Unfortunately, many commuters miss the opportunities involvement can offer. They leave the university with a degree, but they have missed out on the social benefits that pub nights, intramural sports, and joining a club can provide.

ACADEMIC ISSUES

Students arriving at York (or any university for that matter) will learn very quickly that their high school courses did very little to prepare them for their first university assignments. Your guaranteed A or A+ paper in high school may only earn a C or C+ here. Don't panic—you didn't destroy all of your brain cells during Frosh Week. The academic standards have just gotten higher. Talk to your teaching assistant and ask how you can improve. This may seem intimidating, but it will definitely help to improve the grade of your next assignment.

Attempts have been made to control the over-population problem of first-year students experienced by so many universities today. The largest class for many first-year students will be the requisite (but ultimately useless) Natural Science course. This is known to be York's "bird course," and appears to be more of an annoyance than anything else. Although you can take it at any point during your stay at York, it is recommended that you take it in your first year.

If a more intimate learning environment is what you crave, Glendon offers smaller class sizes, where the opportunity to interact with professors and fellow students is virtually guaranteed. Glendon is a bilingual college and boasts strong programs in Translation and International Studies. Over the past years, Glendon emphasized a renewed focus in the areas of French, Business and Computer Studies. Unfortunately, however, not all departments at Glendon offer a balance of courses in English and French.

REZ LIFE

Living in residence in your first year is the easiest way to meet a lot of people. You will probably be socializing with your neighbours before you unpack your toothbrush or kiss your mommy bye-bye. The residence you live in is usually the one that is connected with the college that you have chosen to affiliate yourself with. Each college has a different "theme" and thus attracts students studying in an area that coincides with that theme. The theme of Bethune College, for example, is Science and Society—most of the students who live in Bethune Residence are from the Faculty of Science or the Faculty of Environmental Studies. This is not a hard and fast rule, though—a Fine Arts student may well find him/herself living in Stong Residence (mostly Kinesiology students) instead of the traditional Fine Arts residence, Winters. You will hear references to "Complex One" and "Complex Two" and wonder "huh?" It's very simple. Complex One is made up of the following residences: Founders, Vanier, Winters, and Maclaughlin (or Tatham Hall). Bethune, Stong, and Calumet residences make up Complex Two.

The Glendon campus has two residences—Hilliard and Wood. Most of the rooms are singles. This is an advantage for those who are night owls, have a significant other(s), or like to maintain a degree of privacy (warning: privacy, even in your own room, is minimal). Double rooms can be fun, provided you get along with your roommate. The floors are divided into "houses"—each house has its own common room and washroom. While we're on the topic of washrooms, by the way—most floors are co-ed (there are some all-female floors to be found) and therefore, so are the washrooms. The thought of showering or relieving yourself with someone of the opposite sex in the stall next to you may make you a bit nervous. Remember, if Ally McBeal can do it, so can you. Bethune, Stong, and Mac are rumoured to have the largest rooms. Both Glendon residences are reputed to also have nice-sized rooms. The walls in all of the buildings are made from bricks of concrete and are painted a most uninspiring shade of off-white. The paint has been coated with a substance that makes putting posters on them next to impossible. Many people have slept on the beds throughout the years, so they are not going to be as comfortable as your bed at home. Bring a couple of extra pillows, too, because the standard-issue ones have lost a lot of their fluffiness. You must also bring your own linens and towels—sorry, no linen service.

Most residence students are required to purchase a meal plan. Exceptions are made for those who live in Calumet Residence or the suite-style rooms in Bethune and Winters. The meal plan is most simply described as a debit card system. Your York Card can be used to purchase food at most of the food service establishments. You can decide to choose a steady diet of Wendy's or KFC for the year, or, if you are health conscious, Berries and Blooms, the Falafel Hut, and Great Canadian Bagel may become your favourite feasting grounds.

Glendon students have a more limited choice of food establishments. Glendon only has one cafeteria which closes quite early, an inconvenience for those who like to eat later in the day. The pub, Café de la Terrasse, serves snack foods that will help curb those late-night munchies. You should also bring a healthy supply of KD, Mr. Noodles, canned fruits, and your other favourite non-perishables. Why? Well, long before the inevitable disappearance of your meal plan sum, you will probably tire of the globs of grease you have been filling your body with.

Residence life is largely what you and your fellow housemates make of it.

The annoyances of a noisy neighbour, missing cutlery, and a messy washroom are outweighed by the friendships you will make. Do get to know the people that you live with. You may soon realize that you have become best friends with the person you never would have talked to in high school. Your housemates will be an incredible source of support during those crazy exam-cramming sessions and essay-writing all-nighters.

NIGHT LIFE

Students can satisfy their need to binge on beer and alcohol, dance away the stress of academic life, and flirt with other frenzied students at any number of campus pubs. Over the past few years, the most popular Thursday night (a.k.a. pub night) havens have been the Underground (in the Student Centre), On the Edge (Calumet), The Orange Snail (Stong), the Cock and Bull (Founders), and the Absinthe (Winters). The popularity of the pubs changes from year to year—one that had lineups one year may be empty the next. The pub scene will also be changing over the next few years because of changes to the pub licences. Rumour has it that the pubs listed will remain licenced, although nothing is definite yet.

JACS (Bethune) will be operating as a coffee shop, and the

In a Nut Shell

The university in a phrase: A corporate institution that attempts to create the illusion that it continues its original mandate of an accessible, liberal arts education—and fails to do so.

Best thing about the university: The opportunity to meet and interact with such a diverse group of individuals.

Worst thing about the university: The lineups for EVERYTHING—you will usually be sent to another one as soon as you get to the front of one; the Pepsi exclusivity agreement (bring your own Coca-Cola).

Favourite professors: Ian Smith (Linguistics), Ray Rodgers (Environmental Studies), Arthur Haberman, (Humanities), Paul Delaney (Sciences), all of the Philosophy profs.

Most popular bird courses: Any first-year Natural Science course.

Hot spots to study on campus: Any campus pub, residence.

Quietest spot to study on campus: An empty classroom.

Need for a car and parking availability: A car is a nice luxury, considering the location of the campuses. Parking is extremely expensive, and there are fewer spots than decals sold.

Sexually speaking: Lots of sex can be found for those who are into "free love." Residence and pub nights are good opportunities for finding intimate interaction. York is queer positive and TBLGAY hosts events for queer students.

Fraternities/sororities: They are not encouraged on campus—interested people usually join U of T chapters.

Athletic facilities: Tait Mackenzie has a fully equipped gym that offers personal training and a variety of classes. A shoe tag can be purchased for $5, which allows you access to all gyms. The Ice Gardens also has a gym that is available to students for a reasonable fee. Glendon also boasts great sports facilities, featuring the former home of the Toronto Raptors' practice sessions.

Library facilities: The main library is the Scott Library. It has five branch libraries, including the Law Library, the Map Library, and the Sound and Moving Image Library. The library at Glendon is Frost Library. All libraries are accessible to all students. The fines are outrageous, especially on reserved materials. If you can't find something, there's always U of T.

Computer facilities: The Steacie Science Building has 24-hour PC and Mac labs. All computer terminals have Internet access and all students are issued a York e-mail account. Many of the colleges also have small labs.

Weather: York is cold and windy in the winter. Wind-breaking ski jackets, hats, scarves, and mittens are a definite necessity to survive the winter climate.

Safety on campus: The Student Security service offers nighttime van and foot escorts to various locations on campus. The walkways are dark and the parking lots are even more so. Walk with a group—always.

Alumni: Neil D. Bissoondath; Mark Breslin; Rosemary Dunsmore; Edward Greenspan; Christopher Hume; Steven G. MacLean; Clayton Ruby.

Mac pub, Oscars, will remain closed. Friday nights are considerably more quiet on campus. Most students are still in recovery from the night before. On Saturday nights, the only pub you will always find open is the Cock and Bull. Many residence students will flock there to break the monotony of movie nights in the common room or to avoid looking at their study notes for the exam they have on Monday morning. The Bull has a noted reputation for being a meat market—if you want to find a partner for a shallow, meaningless shag this is a good place to start. Of course, these liaisons can be found almost anywhere you have a number of drunk young adults.

Entertainment can also be found on campus during the week. If you want to hear live music, the Grad Lounge (no, you do not have to be a graduate student to hang out there) and the Ab often play host to local talent. The Grad Lounge also hosts occasional poetry reading evenings.

Actually, the Grad Lounge is probably one of the "cooler" places to have coffee with your friends or to down a few pints when you are in the mood to procrastinate.

The Underground is York's version of a nightclub. It is a multipurpose facility—during the day it is a sit-down restaurant with a fabulous menu and friendly service. In the evening, it hosts club-style pub nights and periodically serves as a venue for concerts. The bands are usually fairly big names—this past year the Spirit of the West and Love Inc. entertained two full houses. Ticket prices are student friendly, and it is a great way to relax with a group of your new friends. Other events you may find yourself at the Underground for is a Battle of the Bands, weekend pub nights, or a mid-year or end-of-year college formal. Non-alcoholic events include the Friday night "Reel 'n' Screen" movie sponsored by the YFS. This is a chance to see fairly new theatre releases for much less than you will pay at a Famous Players, Cineplex Odeon, or AMC theatre. If you keep your eyes open, you will also find dance and theatre

A Word to the Wise:

1. On your first day of class, you will be handed your course outline—a class by class breakdown of the reading material, the assignment due dates, and the grading scheme for exams and assignments. Write down the important dates in your day planner (yes, this is ESSENTIAL to your survival). The reading list will probably look huge, especially if it is a Humanities or Social Science class. To avoid unnecessary expenditures on textbooks, look carefully at how much of each text will actually be used. If it is only a few chapters, photocopying is a great way to save some money. There is nothing worse than looking at your book shelf at the end of the year and realizing that there are about $200 worth of books that have never been opened. The money could have been put to a better use—buying booze or food, for example.

2. The academic issue that has had the most impact on students is the ever-rising cost of tuition. Many will try to avoid dropping classes because they will continue to rise in cost. For that reason, it is important to familiarize yourself with academic policy and regulations. Don't count on your professors or academic advisors to provide you with accurate information on your academic rights. The YFS has recently published a student rights handbook that will guide you through the Senate regulations regarding appeals, deferrals, drop deadlines, and refunds. It is probably a good idea to get a hold of one early in the year. This will avoid being sent around the campus to talk to that elusive "right person" and eliminate unnecessary stress. If you find yourself in need of help with a petition, the YFS also provides a Student Advocacy Service (S.A.S.). This service will help you with writing your petition and informing you about the necessary documentation to support the petition.

performances on campus. Many of the clubs also sponsor social events for members and friends. If you are worried that you won't be able to attend pub night because you're 19, relax. Pub nights are all ages. Most pubs operate on a wrist band policy which is meant to easily identify those that can (legally) drink from those that can't.

ON TORONTO

So, you want to come to school in the mega-city. The energy of downtown is (unfortunately) quite a distance from the Keele campus—Glendon students have the advantage of being only about 15 minutes away by car from the downtown core. Still, many Keele students find themselves exploring the streets of downtown shortly after their arrival. TTC buses come on to campus—hop on one and ride that rocket to the destination of your choice. Popular subway stops for shopping include Yorkdale, Osgoode, Bay (for Yorkville), and Queen. If you are in the mood to be cultured, check out the Royal Ontario Museum at the Museum subway stop or the Art Gallery of Ontario at the St. Patrick stop which offers a "pay what you can" entrance fee.

You will learn to be thankful for anything that gives a student discount. To cut the additional transit costs on a day of exploring, purchase the Day Pass (i.e., unlimited travel) and explore to your heart's content.

The downtown night life is well worth checking out. Nightclubs, pubs, martini bars, and raves are all weekly traditions for the youth of Toronto. Check out the Courthouse, My Apartment, Insomnia, Shark City, the Labyrinth, Paupers Pub, or the Devil's Martini.

For residence students, the main disadvantage is the distance between campus and downtown. You can take the TTC there, but you will have to leave well before "last call" to make the last subway home. Twenty-four-hour buses can get you most of the way, but really, who wants to be waiting around for a bus in the freezing cold? Cabs are an option, but can get rather costly. Making a bargain with the cabby may give you a flat rate as long as you promise a nice, fat tip. If you decide to stay downtown for the night there are plenty of 24-hour greasy spoon restaurants to drink coffee in until dawn. If you are still in the mood to party, Industry is a lot of fun, but expect to pay a heavy cover charge.

Bishop's University

By Andrea Gordon

An extraordinary location, a dedicated teaching faculty, small class sizes and a diverse student body combine to make Bishop's University one of Canada's premier liberal arts schools. Founded in 1843 by Anglican clergymen determined to offer to the country at large "the blessing of a sound and liberal education," Bishop's offers an architectural style largely inspired by Oxford and Cambridge. Located in the town of Lennoxville, just over an hour's drive east of Montreal, in the heart of Quebec's Eastern Townships, Bishop's University also grants students a wide range of recreational activities including great downhill skiing, bike trails, and golf courses.

A remarkable achievement of these past hundred years is Bishop's continuity of architecture. The architectural style of Gothic revival has prevailed, with even new edifices erected in the same style. The breathtaking campus is located on the shore of the Masawippi River. Inside the buildings, classrooms remain small and intimate, and just one classroom, Bishop's Williams Hall, has a seating capacity for more than 65. Many new additions were made to the campus in recent years. Bandeen Hall, among the largest projects, transformed an old gymnasium into a beautiful concert hall. Most recently, the Student Union Building was renovated, adding an atrium and a new on-campus bar, Jehosophat's Loft, named in honour of one of the school's founders.

CAMPUS CULTURE

Bishop's boasts a very regional as well as culturally diverse student population. Half of the students attending are from out of province, with Ontario and the Maritimes being the largest provincial contributors. A full 8% of students are categorized as international students. With Bishop's close proximity to the American border, every fall there is an influx of American students on campus. Luckily, the campus holds a sort of conformist, J. Crew look and feel so the American students do not feel out of place.

Once a student at Bishop's, you almost automatically become involved in Bishop's life. With roughly 1,850 full-time students, it's difficult not to participate in at least one extracurricular activity, but you'll find that most students participate in a wide range of clubs and activities. Intramurals and ath-

letics thrive on Bishop's campus. Approximately two thirds of the student population participate in intramurals throughout the year. Bishop's excellent sports facilities and numerous playing fields also contribute to the athletic feel and it's hardly a sight to see pick-up games of ultimate Frisbee, football, and soccer being played all over campus. There is a huge following for Bishop's sports, with football and men's basketball being the most popular teams. A weekend football or basketball game draws huge student attendance and of course encourages school spirit. Big Buddies (a big sister or big brother type organization) is the most popular club on campus. The campus radio station (CJMQ) also fosters student involvement (CJMQ is the only English radio station transmitting from the Eastern Townships). Recently, the listening area increased and programming has, in turn, become more diversified.

However, the mention of politics often makes students apathetic. With the recent establishment of a system of differential or discriminatory tuition, as students have named it, provincial politics are discouraging to any student. The average Bishop's student tends to be more community than provincially minded and the here and now of Bishop's remains the primary focus of students rather than events going on in the "outside" world.

ACADEMIC ISSUES

A small Anglophone liberal arts university located in Quebec definitely encounters problems with funding. As any small university must compete with larger, more technical-based schools, the merits of a liberal arts education are often discussed in meetings around campus. Humanities remains the largest division at Bishop's with the Faculty of Business following as a close second. The academic reputation of Bishop's has grown in past years. Small classes are Bishop's strength. The only teaching assistants you will find are in the faculty of natural sciences. Professors are readily available for consultation and information. Students are encouraged from the outset to speak with professors about any issues concerning their academic performance. On average, by a student's third or fourth year, the typical class will have ten to twenty students. The advantage of small class sizes

Vital Statistics

Address: Bishop's University, Lennoxville, Quebec, J1M 1Z7

Admissions office: (819) 822-9600 ext. 2681

Website: www.ubishops.ca

Total enrollment: 2,367

Male-female ratio: 49 to 51

Average entrance grades: (High school) Arts: 75%; Science: 70%; Commerce: 75%; (CEGEP) 70%—all

Tuition fees: $2,360 (Quebec students); $3,860 (out-of-province students)

Residence fees: Room and obligatory meal plan range from $4,568–$4,928

Percentage of students in rez: 35%

Percentage of international students: 8%

Percentage of out-of-province students: 48%

Financial aid: Renewable entrance scholarships from $1,500–$5,500 are awarded to outstanding students from high school; and from $750 to those not already on a scholarship, on completion of at least one full year of study with first-class standing. 10% of entering class, and 10% of student body, are on university scholarships in any given year.

Co-op programs: Japanese Language/Civilization course—joint with Université de Sherbrooke.

Services for students with disabilities: Special Needs Coordinator in Counselling Centre.

Student services: Athletics, campus security, counselling, health services, and a student's representative council.

is indisputable. Professors are quick to notice where your academic weaknesses lie and corrective measures are quickly taken to improve academic performance. Also, Bishop's requires students to sample a variety of elective classes from different divisions. For example, Business students must complete elective courses in the division of Social Sciences.

REZ LIFE

Nothing beats living at Bishop's for your first year of school. Bishop's is a residential university and it is highly encouraged that students live on campus for at least one year to acquire the full Bishop's experience. Roughly 520 students reside in one of five residences. Dewhurst is the main dining hall and all students are required to purchase a meal plan if living in residence. The food has improved in the past few years but choice is limited and the food remains pricey.

Mackinnon is the largest residence on "Old Side" and houses 140 students. The rez is dormitory style but also offers kitchens on each floor. Mackinnon has the largest reputation on campus. It normally attracts the not-so-quiet first-year students who come to Bishop's ready for a good time. The building is rather ugly in relation to the others but it is centrally located between the dining hall and classes.

Norton and Pollack residences are joined together and overlook the historic quad. Beautiful from the outside but quite cramped inside, they are the other two residences on Old Side. Purple-painted doors, narrow hallways, small communal bathrooms and two great TV rooms are usually what one thinks of when referring to Norton, the 80-room residence. Pollack, the smallest residence on campus, has larger washrooms than Norton. It houses 44 students on three floors with the third floor designated as an all-girls floor. Pollack is defi-nitely the quaintest residence, and being attached to the louder and larger Norton Hall, it offers all the benefits of crazy residence life while offering a quiet atmosphere when necessary.

There are three "New Side" residences that are identical in structure. "The triplets," Abbott, Munster, and Kuehner, are home to 260 first and upper-year students. Eight students live on each floor and students on New Side have the benefit of sharing a bathroom with one other person. Commonly called "the bog," the bathroom connects a pair of rooms together. Kuehner is the right choice for first-year students

A Word to the Wise:

1. Live in residence. It's the best way to meet people, plus you can't beat the "activities."

2. Get involved. There is something for everyone. No one comes to Bishop's to be left alone, so try everything from the rifle club to water polo. You just might find your calling.

3. Talk to your professors. Go see them and ask where you can improve in your performance. They want to help you. This will also help you when it comes time to ask for reference letters.

4. You will get bored at times but, as soon as you leave Lennoxville, you will want to come back and see the familiar sights and faces. Try to get away every two months or so to a peek at the outside then you will soon want to come home to Bishop's.

5. Dress warm, because it gets cold.

In a Nut Shell

The university in a phrase: You get a solid liberal arts education and a wicked hangover too.

Best thing about the university: Small size and location.

Worst thing about the university: Small size and location.

Favourite professors: B. Robson (Business), R. Harries (Drama), G. Tucker (Political Studies) S. McKelvie (Psychology).

Hot spot to study on campus: The Quad; University Centre (Jehosophat's Loft)

Quietest spot to study on campus: Basement of John H. Bassett Memorial Library.

Need for car and parking availability: A car in Lennoxville is not a necessity. However, you will soon become popular if you do have one, especially for students to travel into Sherbrooke for shopping, or to the grocery store. Parking is $70–$80 for the year and parking spots are rampant.

Sexually speaking: It's easy to meet significant others but at Bishop's it is hard to stay significant.

Fraternities/sororities: There are only four houses of the Greek persuasion. They are accepted on campus because of their charity work and they have great parties.

Athletic facilities: The John H. Price Sports Centre is a hub of activity on campus. Membership to the Plex is included in student fees at the beginning of each semester. Playing fields and the arena are all well maintained while Bishop's boasts a nine-hole golf course on campus and eight tennis courts.

Library facilities: John H. Bassett Memorial Library offers students a wide range of resources. Librarians are helpful and friendly and inter-library loans are encouraged but not often necessary. Chaplain College CEGEP also uses the library so allocations have increased.

Computer facilities: Internet access available to students. Residence rooms are wired for Internet access. Library catalogues are accessible online. Computer labs are available for course-related or general use.

Weather: Beautiful in the fall but watch out because winter lasts a long time. Lots of snow and good skiing but for those who shy away from the cold, you'd better live on campus and close to everything because you will freeze.

Safety on campus: Lighting is still an issue on campus and security phones are also needed. There have been minor incidents but the student patrol is highly effective in ensuring campus safety on rowdier nights.

Alumni: Edmonton Eskimos, Leroy Blugh, poet Ralph Gustafson, CBC's Don Murray, Larry Smith, Norman Webster

---

wanting more privacy than Old Side can offer. Abbott and Munster tend to house upper-year students, so if the first year experience is what your heart desires, then Kuehner is probably your best bet.

NIGHT LIFE

Lennoxville is definitely not a metropolis, but it does offer many entertainment possibilities. Jehosophat's Loft is Bishop's on-campus bar, operated by the Student's Representative Council. All profits generated from the Loft return to student life and interests. The Bishop weekend begins Thursdays and Thursdays are the Loft's most popular night. If you like dancing and seeing everyone you know, it's definitely the place for you. But beware: Because it's definitely a place where everybody knows your name, you'll soon find out that your actions will never go unnoticed.

If exploring downtown Lennoxville is your desire, the Golden Lion Pub is the most popular watering hole in town. The Lion has its very own microbrewery and offers the widest selection of beer. Acoustic Tuesdays are always popular with the university set, as somewhat drunken patrons eagerly display their musical talents to the crowd.

Sherbrooke also offers an exciting nightlife. Located a short five-minute drive from Lennoxville, la ville's big night is Friday night. Sherbrooke has a wide variety of bars and restaurants to suit every taste. Don't miss Le Well Pub on Fridays. A change from the closeted Lennoxville atmosphere is often necessary and Sherbrooke can provide just that. Ironically, most Bishop's students tend to end up in the same bar by the end of the evening, ultimately replicating an evening in Lennoxville.

ON LENNOXVILLE

Lennoxville is primarily a university town. There really isn't very much to do aside from hanging around Bishop's. Lots of students often make fun of the locals, they're a generally hokey bunch with a lot of personality. There is a rumour that the town is inbred, but hey, that just makes life even funnier. Be sure to check out the Hell's Angels' party pad. No one really knows what goes on in there, and if you get in you'll be the most popular person on campus. The best thing about Lennoxville is that it's close to being in the heart of nature. There are lots of trees and wildlife, and even a river, to make it a really pretty and picturesque campus to hang out in.

Concordia University

By Maggie Greyson

The history of Montreal can be read through the story of Concordia University. The school's origins are a result of an interesting hybrid between a Jesuit college and North America's first YMCA. Today the school is multicultural, politically active, diverse, and thriving. The students, staff, and faculty of the school come together from every corner of the province, country, and the world.

Loyola College, in Montreal West, was founded in 1896 as a liberal arts program for men. It was connected with the Jesuit College and, at the back of the campus, monks continue to reside even today. Any religious influences, however, have long since been eradicated, except the Loyola Chapel (c.1933), which, interestingly, houses two theatres in its basement. Women began attending in the late sixties, apparently to the chagrin of many of the male students at the time. Sir George Williams College and Loyola College are the two complementary halves that make up the university as a whole. Sir George Williams College, the downtown campus, started as evening classes offered by the YMCA. To get a better feel for the grass roots approach of Sir George Williams College, read a brief history of the YMCA found on the Internet.

The downtown campus has spread like a virus into dozens of unique buildings between the Molson Centre and the Montreal Museum of Fine Arts. The central terminal, affectionately referred to as "The Airport" by some, is a nine-story unholy terror that resembles a Borg ship from Star Trek, both inside and out. It was built in the 1960s; need I say more? Once you escalate past the fourth floor of the Henry F. Hall building, each Lego level is almost identical. The core of the building is deprived of natural light and covered by lockers. If you have an aversion to buildings without a soul, you're outta luck chum, because most faculties hold classes here. Concordia boasts about its new library building across the street on Maisonneuve, for obvious reasons. It was built in the

eighties and is much more feng shui: plenty of windows and an eight-story atrium. Many of the other buildings that Concordia has spread into have their own peccadilloes. The Visual Arts building on Rene-Levesque was once a car dealership and parking lot. The art studios maintain slab concrete walls, thus financially discouraging a desperately needed new ventilation system.

Rue Mackay, pronounced "mickeye," is a one-way street on the West side of the Hall building. This street separates the Hall building from old converted town houses that are now student-run spaces and faculty offices. Each of the last 25 years has seen an effort to "green" this street, but alas it currently remains blacktop scum. Aside from a temporary park on the corner a block away, this part of Concordia is a concrete wasteland. Geographically speaking, however, it's close to the mountain, shopping, and the infamous Crescent Street party scene.

Loyola is the antithetical spouse to the downtown campus. This campus is cradled in the cheap residential area of Notre-Dame-de-Grace. If you want that classic Ivy League university feel, you'll find it here, seven klicks from the hustle and bustle of the big city. Between the grassy fields, you beeline around a dozen large and variously designed buildings. The recently constructed Vanier Library is the first building you have to walk around once you get off the Shuttle bus. This library is so good McGill students have to be restrained from entering. The Performing Arts departments, Communications, and a myriad of other Arts and Science departments co-habit Loyola. Recently, interest has been shown in the lovely "satellite," thanks to Loyola alumni money.

The unfortunate who pick the hostel-type residence out there are confined to the shuttle bus schedule or tribulations of the city bus system to find any night life, for there is none around. There is also a lack of places to eat. So, be prepared for the love/hate relationship you will experience with both campuses.

Vital Statistics

Address: 1455 de Maisonneuve W, Montreal, Quebec, H3G 1M8

Admissions office: (514) 848-2424

Website: www.concordia.ca

Total enrollment: 24,272

Male-female ratio: 47 to 53

Average entering grades: Arts: 65%; Science: 68%; Commerce: 70%; Engineering: 75%

Tuition fees: $2,481 (Quebec students); $3,981 (out-of-province Canadian students)

Residence fees: $2,301 (shared room); $2,678 (single room); Meal plan: $1,625–$2,250

Percentage of students in residence: 4.8%

Percentage of out-of-province first-year students: 15%

Financial aid: entrance and in-course scholarships, bursaries, and loans

Co-op programs: Accountancy, Biochemistry and Chemistry, Computer Science, Economics, French Translation, Management Information Systems, Marketing, Mathematics, Statistics and Physics.

Services for students with disabilities: Services for Disabled Students Offices on each campus; accessible classrooms and wheelchair accessible inter-campus shuttle buses; special services, equipment, resources, academic support systems.

Aboriginal students: The Centre for Native Education offers support services and resources to Native students at Concordia. The Centre is a welcoming space where students can meet each other to discuss academic issues, and plan social activities, or just relax, have a cup of coffee, or meet a new friend.

Student services: Off-campus housing service

CAMPUS CULTURE

Montreal is an energetic city that allows anything to happen. Both school and town are a hot-bed of political activity and cultural invasion. Many of the students are part-time as the university does not want to discriminate or discourage anyone from studying. The average age is 26; aside from that statistic, classes are known to be filled with students from 18 to 81 years of age. The whole population is quite mature, especially due to the pre-university college certificate all Quebecers must pass. Concordia is seen as further education, so generally people attend in the hopes of coming closer to their dreams while slugging it out through homework, family life, and/or a job. School spirit translates into "How can I make life better while I live under the poverty level?" The Quebec Public Interest Research Group is one place many turn to for extracurricular involvement. The actions they create ripple and wave throughout the school, province, and country. They support Fair Trade Coffee, the non-profit health food store Le Frigo Vert, and Community Based Alternatives to Banks. The Concordia Student Union tries very hard to accommodate everyone's projects. While they aren't in a mess of their own they can be counted on for excellent support systems. The past years they have put on a huge all day outdoor Orientation concert and run a job and housing bank.

The university is quite multicultural and international. Each cultural group is quite proud, and one can find student associations from every corner of the world parked daily in the mezzanine level of the Hall building. International music blares and flags fly amidst the tempting smell of cheap dishes of foreign cuisine. It sure beats the standard cafeteria fare.

Once again, school pride is much like Canadian confidence in diversity. Concordia is the "other" English university in Montreal, and some students claim that they try damn hard not to be like their wealthy neighbours in order to be themselves. However, there are many students who wear knapsacks adorned with McGill paraphernalia on their backs. Both Engineering and Computer Sciences and Commerce students sport their colourful jackets with Stinger Pride. And anyone can spot the football and basketball teams because of their jackets, too. Concordia has some great athletes and wins a lot of games but it's not much discussed. A mega-athletic complex is in the works to replace the (t)rusty old Victoria Gym centre.

ACADEMIC ISSUES

Since Quebec has just increased tuition fees for those who come from out of province, the Student Union tries to rally everyone together on what feels like a monthly basis to argue against more cuts to education. By and large the students are generally more left-leaning, because they realize what it is like to live in a society where 11% of everybody, degree or not, is unemployed.

The university administration, not unlike many others, has begun to run the school like a business, thus endangering healthy class sizes and the wildlife in the Fine Arts Faculty. Various Arts and Sciences programs have been added to the endangered species list. So, if you want Concordia for a specific program, be careful what you choose. If you want Concordia for the city culture and its "open door" policy to finishing a general degree, relax; it will be around for a long time to come. Admissions are fair, but you'd better have a snappy portfolio if you want into Fine Arts. There is a very

In a Nut Shell

The University in a phrase: Concordia prepares you for your future, providing many interesting opportunities for personal growth and success in a culturally rich and affordable environment.

Best thing about the university: MONTREAL!!! And you can be part-time forever.

Worst thing about the university: The Hall building and the food.

Favourite professors: Norma Joseph (Religion); Charles Ellis (Music): Jean-Claude Bustros (Film Production)

Most popular bird course: There aren't any chickens crossing the street here.

Hot spot to study on campus: Quiet room on the first floor of the Webster Library.

Quietest spot to study on campus: Vanier Library.

Need for car and parking availability: Leave your four wheels at home and take the Métro everywhere. Montreal is very efficient (read relentless) at distributing parking tickets to the few metered spots around school. In the winter you'll spend more time digging your car out of snow banks than driving it. If you insist on driving, however, you may pay about $5/day to park nearby in a lot.

Sexually speaking: Whatever you are into or not into is welcome at Concordia. Graffiti in the bathroom stalls invite you to explore your options—safely of course.

Fraternities/sororities: They play a role here, like all groups do...but they generally blur into the noise with all the other communal events and projects. If you want to network with a group of movers and shakers, join a Commerce and Administration working group.

Athletic facilities: If you want to take some cheap classes get them while they're hot. Presently the Victoria gym is quite "low profile" shall we say. You may miss the sign for it when you walk by a dark high school building with weeds growing up through the concrete out front. In a few years a shiny new facility will be built for all of your athletic needs.

Library facilities: The Webster library downtown is conveniently located across the street from school. The Vanier is a wonderful resource as well. They both are topnotch in multimedia and modern facilities. Webster can get backed up with students, while Vanier always has an easy flow, reflecting its smaller-sized clientele. Montreal has three other universities, two of which are French, and transfers from their libraries are relatively simple.

Computer facilities: Over 200 public-access personal computers/workstations; time-sharing terminals; graphics and word-processing facilities

Weather: Summer is le gorgeous! Winter is l'enfer! Between December and March heat bills multiply exponentially. And if you aren't coming with knee-high winter boots, don't come at all. While Montrealers carry their load of snow, the wonderful summer is celebrated upside-down and backwards until the snow falls again.

Safety on campus: We have a model program of students who patrol the campus; however, they continue to elude detection, and there isn't much of a campus. Aside from the occasional national scandal, students and their belongings are safe.

Alumni: CBC's Hana Gartner; film producer Pierre Gendron; chairman of Hydro Quebec Jacques Ménard; authors E. Annie Proulx and Nino Ricci; president and CEO of Petro-Canada James Stanford.

---

broad base of undergrad and master programs in everything from Women's Studies and Political Science to Leisure Studies, Fine Arts Studies in Sexuality, and Hebrew. Concordia is known for its Commerce program, a large Geography department and the famous (newly named) Mel Hoppenheim School of Cinema. Apparently, mere acceptance into the animation department means a guaranteed job.

The Fine Arts department is comprehensive. Small-sized classes are taught in Jazz Performance, Ceramics, Design, Print Media, etc., etc. and etc. They even offer basket weaving in the Fibres Department. These artists command respect because they apply their training and the opportunity to create at quite a high philosophical level. The students run two of their own galleries in the building which are free spaces in many senses of the word.

The majority of professors are part-time, meaning a variety of things. Often they are experts in their fields who are passing through long enough to instill their passion in your heart. Often the traditional concept of the student-teacher relationship gets checked at the door. Dr. Norma Joseph, a professor in the Religion department, holds regular "Coffee with Norma" for anyone who wants to chat her up in Java U, the school's funked up café.

The school's motto is "Real Education for the Real World." This means Real Headaches sometimes in dealing with the administration. There are few loopholes to the complicated registration system. Plus, Concordia has so many interesting classes that some are offered from 8:00 p.m.–10:00 p.m. Monday's to Friday's or on Saturdays. So, the perfect schedule may be only in your dreams.

The school tries hard to accommodate those who speak French first. Presentations and exams can be handed in in either national language. In the halls you hear as many other languages as you can think of. The school is aware of the special needs of its students and makes every effort to accommodate where possible. Thus, there is no discrepancy between part and full-time programs. A large number of students do not graduate in the amount of time set out for them. Insane students can graduate faster, while others take longer to finish their degree.

REZ LIFE

They say that a dying city is at its cultural peak. Festivals and parties, art and culture ooze out of every neighbourhood. This said, don't live in residence: Experience Montreal. Higston Hall is located on the West end campus far, far, far from the fun stuff. The neighbourhood is quiet and settled. If your desire is convenience to campus life, live beside it. The rent is better and everything will be more convenient than if you live in a dorm. In a school of over 20,000 students, Higston Hall has trouble filling its 150 cells each year. Living out at Loyola means sacrificing a room with a view, your own kitchen, sleep, and privacy. The Concordia Ghetto, extending west of the Hall building, although priced about the same as rez, is in a thriving part of town. Chances are your building will be infested with students anyway, but hopefully critter-free.

The McGill Ghetto is more expensive and not as convenient but fits the term "ghetto" more aptly. A 20-minute walk down Sherbrooke is the most student "type" of life you'll get off campus. The streets are crawling with party animals 'round the clock. It is safer, however, to live in an area without drunk shenanigans, so look to the Plateau. Montreal's "main" street, St. Laurent, runs north into the first settling area for many immigrants. The Plateau neighbourhood is Portuguese, Jewish, and Italian. You may find a great apartment here to share for less than $250/month each. It's hard not to be within walking distance of a fresh bagel shop, deli, or fruit stand. Pizzadelic, gourmet pizza resto-bars, are springing up everywhere and are great for two—plus they deliver.

NIGHT LIFE

Your entire body pulses with the bass, while your ears are deafened. Images of flailing bodies, sequins and feathers are captured by strobe lights. The alcoholic potion pumping through your system alters the universe around you. Every object becomes a vital clue that defines the direction of the events unfolding. Hundreds of spaces and places transform your body and soul below the sunless sky. Montreal plays host to superior entertainment at friendly prices. If dress code is your thing, frequent any one of the late night resto-bars at the bottom end of St. Laurent. You may have to wait to eat in the dark bohemian Cafeteria or any of its neighbours if you crave sustenance past 10 p.m., and it will take you an extra 10 minutes to walk through all the bouncers and clientele that pose in the streets at midnight Thursday through Saturday. Great beginner bars include the Loft, Angels, and Café Campus, which all play music you will recognize, not to mention the people are fun. These places are very popular with the hip and chic locals. Mix these in with the upscale lounges and fast food joints and you've got every nighthawk's desire. Nicholas Cage was seen at Jello Bar on Ontario Street, which is famous for its live swing. For more serious entertainment, the Sphinx and Foufoune Electriques on Stanley street and St. Catherine's respectively are more hard-core alternative.

Although Montreal is very inexpensive, the nights are long. If you depart at 9 p.m., warm up your liver with some beer and wings at the Peel Pub on St. Catherine's. A cheap cab or metro ride will get you off the street famous for its strip clubs

A Word to the Wise:

1. Pack your lunch or a loonie. In and around the Hall building you can fill up on nutrition in many thrifty styles. Le Frigo Vert (enviro + socially friendly), Mother Hubbard's Cupboard (pay what you can Monday dinners), $0.49 Pizza, the Hall building mezzanine food fairs...

2. Educate yourself for free! Concordia has many interest groups who will gladly share food, knowledge, and music. Or, the Concordia Student Union has a list of phone numbers if you want to get involved!–religious, environmental, departmental, political, social awareness, sports and social groups all under the Big Top.

3. The cost of living is rock bottom in Montreal, so buy now. Rent, resto-bars, cab fares, admission fees and ticket prices, on sale at student rates.

4. If your apartment doesn't include heating, buy a lot of blankets–it will be cheaper.

5. Go to class. You'll never know what you might find!

and, for something classier, St. Sulpice used to be a private mansion on St. Dennis and will remind you of all those house parties of your youth, no cover and an awesome backyard. Shake your booty at any one of a dozen swanky night clubs on Crescent Street, one block away from the Sir George. It's not hard to find accommodation within stumbling distance from a super tavern, pub, or bar. The Concordia Ghetto funds Brewtopia, Hurley's Irish Pub, the Cock and Bull, and McKibens. They are all fun for happy hour or between-class liquid diets. The Concordia Student Union runs its own establishments on the premises. The Hive at Loyola was a dive/storeroom but doesn't have a license yet. Reggie's boasts surprising yet variable successes. Thursdays a DJ spins and the liquor flows at a great rate.

If you have a flare for experimentation, the village at Beaudry metro is wild and woolly, and so is Sky Bar for the gay scene. The Concordia Queer Collective is a big organization with a friendly office. Drop in to find out more of what Montreal has to offer in that respect.

ON MONTREAL

Montreal is a quilt of little business and residential areas that have been sewn together as the neighbourhoods slowly evolved. Any area below the Blue metro line and above the Orange is guaranteed to be convenient for every aspect of your scholastic life. Any farther out, you will have to compromise a 10-minute proximity to movie theatres, clothes shopping, malls, and pay larger cab fares from the bar.

The winters are freezing but apartments in Montreal are always uncomfortably hot so dress for the tropics all year round. You will be well prepared when summer comes and the city goes hog wild with its non-stop festivals. Look to the sky for fireworks, open your eyes to hundreds of jazz concerts, and open your mouth for the food and taste the world. Montreal has four free weekly mags that can help you plan every minute of your day.

If you become overwhelmed with activity you can always go to the park and stroll up the mountain. Mount Royal attracts visitors to its almighty summit every day (except when it is closed due to ice storms!). Every Sunday, weather permitting, organized vendors sell the usual dresses, jewellery, bongs, and hackay-sacks. These items are merely the sideshow though for dozens of tam-tams and sun lovers partying around the Angel. Have a late breakfast that day because they don't start until 1 p.m. Then, stretch out in the sun with thousands of others from all walks of life, and enjoy each other's differences in a peaceful and harmonious way. Let the sounds, sights, and smells lull you into a higher state of consciousness.

Montreal is a wonderful place to mature in. There are many influences and influential places, people, and things to become familiar with, not to mention the Francophone culture in your very own backyard. Escape to the Laurentian mountains for some camping, hiking, or rock climbing. The McGill Outing Club meets every Wednesday night on campus and plans trips for anyone who's got a little stash of cash.

Montreal is one the world's largest French-speaking cities, but you can live and study in Montreal without having to speak a word of French. Knowing French will definitely make your life more interesting, but, if you've never been so lucky as to learn it, you won't be alone. Most storekeepers have met someone like you before and are generally accommodating. Get to know the French areas of town! St. Dennis and Mont Royal are great streets for fine dining, and excellent furniture, clothes, and vintage shopping.

McGill University

By Jason Chow

Located adjacent to downtown Montreal and at the foot of Mount Royal, McGill lives up to its elite reputation even visually. Approaching the school from the main entrance, you'll find the Roddick Gates and the neo-classical Arts Building with its strong columns, exemplifying the history behind the institution. The Arts Building, the Redpath Museum, the Redpath Library, and the MacDonald Engineering Building are all nearly two centuries old. Covered in ivy, they lend an established, historic feel to the school.

McGill's alumni also add to its colourful and successful history. McGill has been the base for authors like Stephen Leacock and Hugh MacLennan, poet-musician Leonard Cohen, pioneer neurologist Wilder Penfield, and media mogul Conrad Black. The student centre is named after William Shatner, the Star Trek superstar who attended the school way back when. The many famous grads of McGill continue to perpetuate its good reputation.

When wealthy merchant James McGill passed away in 1813, he bequeathed 46 acres and £10,000 "for the purpose of education and the advancement of learning." In 1821, a Royal Charter authorized the new institution to be called McGill College. After numerous legal battles, the new college finally received the financial endowment and constructed the historic Arts Building and Dawson Hall, then opened its doors in 1843 as a part of McGill College. Later, in 1885, through a merger of McGill College and the Royal Institution for the Advancement of Learning, the name McGill University was officially adopted. Since then, the school has expanded to also include a second campus on the western tip of the island of Montreal. The suburban McDonald campus in Ste. Anne-de-Bellevue is used as the teaching grounds for the Environmental Studies and Agricultural Sciences programs.

Aside from the historic, ivy-covered mainstays, McGill also has its fair share of modernist concrete behemoths from the 1950s and 1960s. Among them, the MacLennan Library is the most frequented, housing the social sciences and humanities collections, and is used as a place of study by most during exam time. The McIntyre Medical Sciences building, resembling a giant concrete beer can, stands tall a little farther up the mountain. The student centre—the Shatner Building—is another concrete nightmare and has been deemed unsafe for big parties by fire inspectors. The Leacock building is a nine-floor Lego block that contains all of the Social Sciences. Fortunately, McGill makes up for the architectural nightmares with its compactness. McGill, although a school of 24,000 students, occupies a surprisingly small amount of space. Most of one's classes are confined to a small corner of campus, and even if one needs to traverse the entire campus, it is usually not a far walk.

Behind McGill sits Mount Royal Park, the city's playground. More of a hill than a mountain, the park and its many leafy trees turn into a beautiful yellow, brown, and red during the first month of school. And on its south side, downtown Montreal and all of its amenities are offered to the student. It is common for a student to go shopping, slip into a bookstore, or grab a caffeine fix in a downtown cafe in between classes.

CAMPUS CULTURE

McGill enjoys one of the most diverse student bodies in the country. Its reputation attracts many from Canada, the U.S., and beyond. Over 30% of students are from out-of-province and 13% are international students. Known as the "Harvard of the North," many Americans, primarily from the New England area, also partake of the McGill experience. It is also common to meet McGill students from different continents and hear many use English as their second language.

Cosmopolitan Montreal and its bustle of activity have rendered McGill students a generally apathetic bunch. Sports teams win and lose unnoticed, campus politics are ignored, and student involvement in clubs and societies is limited. The city offers many things to do, so students often involve themselves in other pursuits off-campus. Nevertheless, concerned students offer a plethora of clubs to join, and produce over ten student publications, while a comprehensive intramural sports program appeals to several tastes. And these clubs offer colour to McGill life, whether it is flag football on the lower field in the middle of campus in October, the McGill Drama Club's

Vital Statistics

Address: 845 Sherbrooke St. W., Montreal, Quebec, H3A 2T5

Admissions Office: (514) 398-4455

Website: www.mcgill.ca

Total enrollment: 21,069

Male-female ratio: 45 to 55

Percentage of international students: 6%

Percentage of out-of-province students: 38%

Cut-off grade for admission after first round: Arts: 78%; Science: 80%; Commerce: 80%; Engineering: 75%

Tuition fees: Quebec students pay $2,502 for Arts, $2,549 for Management, $2,507 for Sciences, and $2,708 for Engineering. Out-of-province students pay $4,002 for Arts, $4,049 for Management, $4,007 for Science, $4,062 for Engineering.

Residence fees: Rooms in any of the co-ed residences range from $5,200 to $5,750 and include a five-day meal plan. The all-female Royal Victoria College costs its tenants $6,500 and includes a seven-day meal plan. Rooms at Solin Hall rent for $4,750. Off-campus bachelor accommodations range from $350–$600/month; 1 bedroom from $370–$700/month; 2 bedrooms from $450–$750/month.

Percentage of students in residence: Roughly 7.5%

Co-op programs: Mining and Metallurgical Engineering.

Financial aid: Undergraduates at McGill receive financial aid through scholarships, bursaries or on-campus student employment. McGill offers an undergraduate bursary program, contact and apply through the Financial Aid office.

Student services: Counselling of all sorts including psychological, academic and employment counselling; student union and student council; financial aid; housing and employment offices; ombudsperson; health services; chaplaincy.

Drama Festival in January, or the McGill Daily's biweekly musings on campus issues and culture.

Even so, the new McGill student often feels alienated and lost in the shuffle. Classes in the first year are often held in 500+ auditoriums. The bureaucracy is large and impenetrable. Everything is registered under a student number. Most McGill departments have elaborate voice mail systems. Residence is big and can be uninviting. But eventually, an independent rhythm sets in, and the McGill student plods on at school, hangs out with his/her friends, and finds a niche. Classes eventually get smaller and you begin to adopt the atmosphere as your own.

ACADEMIC ISSUES

McGill has one of the most respected faculties in the country and is known for the strength of its many programs. Ninety-five per cent of its professors hold PhDs. A peek at the back section of the calendar shows their impressive credentials. Most of the time, they hold degrees from Ivy League schools or reputable universities overseas and within Canada and are recognized as being at the top of their fields. Most professors, aside from teaching, are highly engaged in research, adding to the calibre of the faculty.

To maintain its aura of elitism, McGill tries to impose stringent academic standards on its incoming students. The average entering grade is 85.7%. Moreover, McGill looks at the entire high school record of prospective students. And its academic reputation is bolstered by its students' suc-

cesses—McGill boasts a number of Nobel Prize Winners and Rhodes Scholars.

The average McGill student feels the pressure of school and the cram of midterms, papers, and labs. Grading is generally regarded as tough, with the average student holding a B average. In some departments (Political Science, for example), many students claim that it is impossible to obtain an A from a professor. Some classes in Management and Science are graded on the curve, restricting the number of students who are given good grades. Academics, in general, are held in high regard by McGillers.

Like all schools in Canada, McGill is also feeling the pinch of government fiscal austerity. Many professors have left, others have been cut, and those retired have sometimes not been replaced. Classes have been cut and programs shortened. The ubiquitous "black dot" in the McGill calendar (classes that are listed with a black dot are not offered in that particular academic year) seems to spread like a virus. Class sizes have grown. Often, students must sit on stairs or on the floor because all the seats are taken. The MacLennan library, which houses the collection for the humanities and social sciences, is notoriously known to have poor variety, and squeezed funding has only exacerbated that problem.

McGill is also known for its traditionalism and is slow to adapt to changing student concerns and needs. For example, while other schools have flourishing Creative Writing programs, McGill only has one class of such nature. There are no Fine Arts classes. Courses regarding gender theory and queer studies are few and limited. The African Studies department struggles to survive. Co-op programs are limited to Mining and Metallurgical Engineering.

The first-year experience for non-Quebec students is broad. (Quebec students with a CEGEP diploma are enrolled in three-year programs, as opposed to out-of-province students who are required to take four.) Science students involve themselves in a general program as do Arts students. These programs require them to take classes in any three of the major categories: Humanities, Social Sciences, Languages, and Sciences. After this general first year program, students are required to choose a major (or two) and a minor (or two). McGill's requirements for an Arts major program is only 36 credits and 18 credits for a minor program (the average 3 hr/week lecture is worth three credits), giving much room to dabble in your own interests outside of your own field of study. Honours programs are more intensive, requiring 60 credits and a thesis. Most of the students in Honours programs are ones who later further their studies in graduate school. Science, Engineering, and Management students are less fortunate. Their programs are more planned out and intensive, leaving little time for study in other fields.

In the Arts Faculty, McGill is especially strong in History and Anthropology. Somehow, the history department seems to be less affected by the budget restraints. Psychology, a huge department, is known to be a highly competitive and difficult program. English Literature students complain and complain of their department's lack of funding and the subsequent shrinking of course selection. Political Science is also experiencing similar problems. In the Faculty of Sciences, the most popular programs are Biology, Physiology (both of which are filled with students and their medical school aspirations), and Computer Science.

REZ LIFE Although McGill boasts a residence capacity of 1,540 in four co-ed halls, one all-female residence, and an apartment-style complex, many are denied a place. Because McGill is attended by many students not from Montreal, space is in high demand. If you do get a place in residence, most are similar in pace and style.

At the top of the hill, over-looking downtown Montreal, is where the co-ed halls are situated. Molson Hall, Gardner Hall, and McConnell Hall are identical nine-story complexes that encircle the communal cafeteria—Bishop Mountain Hall. Most of the rooms are single occupancy closets set on long corridors. An older, grey-stone building with hardwood floors, Douglas Hall is a smaller residence, situated directly behind the north stands of Molson Stadium. Most of the rooms in

> "No undergraduate shall resort to any Inn or Tavern, or place of public amusement without special permission of the Vice-President."
>
> McGill University, rules for students, 1840, quoted in Lena Newman, *Historical Almanac of Canada*, May 1967.

Douglas are suites, where a common living room is shared by three who each have separate bedrooms. The all-female residence, Royal Victoria College, is located directly across the street from campus. All five of the residences include meal plans at yummy cafeterias. After a semester of residence food though, you'll be devouring mom's cooking during Christmas break. The apartment-style Solin Hall residence is located in another neighbourhood, five metro stops away from campus. Solin, for better or for worse, doesn't offer a meal plan. Rather, it is an apartment building owned and operated by McGill. Many students choose to live there for its residence atmosphere while at the same time maintaining the freedom of having an apartment.

Even if you don't get a place in residence, McGill owns ten small apartment-style buildings where they house students who didn't get into rez and match them up accordingly. MORE— McGill's Off-campus Residence Experience—has accommodations within a short walking distance to campus at comparative market rates.

If residence isn't your kind of thing, finding an apartment has traditionally been easy, though recent years have seen a trend in the opposite direction. Montreal has generally been affordable for the McGill student, especially when compared to other Canadian metropolises. Quebec tuition rates have also been slower to increase as opposed to other provinces (although out-of-province students are still enraged by the 50% increase in 1997 when the government opted for a differential fee for in-province students and out-of-province students). Throughout most of the past decade, the poor economy has kept rents low and vacancy rates high, making it easy for the student to find a cheap apartment in most neighbourhoods. It has been typical of a McGill student to pay half as much in rent compared to their U of T counterparts, but recent economic upswings threaten the renter's paradise.

Most students who live off-campus live in the McGill Ghetto, a neighbourhood just adjacent to the east side of campus. Rent is more expensive in the Ghetto and in the other areas adjacent to campus. The students who live there often pay for the convenience of living close to school. A little farther east and north is the Plateau and its hipsters. This neighbourhood is cheaper, though the influx of Montreal yuppies and hipsters have started to raise rents and decrease vacancy rates. Some McGill students choose to live in Notre-Dame-de-Grace, or NDG. NDG offers very cheap rents but often requires a bus pass to get to school.

In a Nut Shell

The university in a phrase: Montreal.

Best thing about the university: The city and location.

Worst thing about the university: The bureaucracy, differential tuition for out-of-province students, libraries.

Favourite professors: Valentin Boss (Russian History), Rex Brynen (Political Science), Peter Gibian (English), David Harpp (Chemistry), Henry Mintzberg (Management), Tom Naylor (Economics), Gil Troy (History), Amanda Vincent (Biology).

Most popular bird courses: Art of Listening (a.k.a. "Clapping for Credit"); Space, Time and Matter (a.k.a. "Space, Time, and…it doesn't matter"); The World of Chemistry.

Quietest spot on campus to study: The Nahum Gelber Law Library. State-of-the-art facilities including Internet hook-ups for laptops. Almost too quiet.

Most social spot on campus to study: MacLennan Library or pretending to read on the steps of the Arts Building.

Need for car and parking availability: A car is not needed in Montreal. Parking is expensive and limited in downtown and most neighbourhoods. Public transit is convenient, efficient, and runs late.

Sexually speaking: McGill students are independent-minded individuals. Some are in relationships, some "pickup" often, most are single. McGill is also accepting of queer culture. Queer McGill is one of the most out-spoken and supported organizations on campus.

Fraternities/sororities: McGill is home to a handful of fraternities and sororities, all in the Ghetto. They organize some parties, but in general, operate without much fanfare.

Athletic facilities: Memberships at the newer fitness centre of the Currie Gym cost $15 a semester while all the other facilities are free.

Library facilities: The MacLennan Library is ugly, inefficient, and inadequate. Its collections are out-of-date and devoid of many newer publications. If you're in a pinch, go order the book through a bookstore or try to find it at Concordia's library.

Weather: Beautiful autumn days, dreary winters, and late springs. Winter consists of snow, snow, and more snow. Cold temperatures feel even colder with the humidity. And whenever the weather tempts and starts to melt the winter away, more snow falls. Temperatures don't rise until mid March, so be prepared.

Safety on campus: McGill is generally a safe campus. Students run a Walksafe program where students are accompanied home from campus during later hours. There are also security posts on campus that the student can use in times of emergency. Avoid walking behind Molson Stadium just in front of the residences, where muggings have been frequently reported.

Alumni: Leonard Cohen (poet-musician), William Shatner ("Captain Kirk"), Conrad Black (media mogul), Rudolph Marcus (Nobel Prize winner in chemistry), Julie Payette (Canada's latest astronaut), John Raulston Saul (author/philosopher).

NIGHT LIFE

Montreal is renowned for its great nightlife and bar scene. Whether it is sipping back endless pitchers of beer at the Biftek, dancing the night away with an inviting member of the opposite sex at Gert's (the campus bar), or partying all night (and morning) at after-hours clubs, Montreal has something for everyone.

If you want a sit-down bar, cheap drinks, and good atmosphere, the Biftek is the place to go. McGillers have flocked to this drinking institution on Boulevard St. Laurent for years. Another popular St. Laurent watering hole is Copacabana, where happy hour starts after 7:00 p.m. St. Sulpice on St. Denis and its large, comfortable back outdoor terrace is perfect for a warm night. For those who like to bust a move, a popular McGill hangout is Angel's club, also on St. Laurent, on Tuesday nights. Thursday's are popular at Gert's if tight shirts and pants is the style you're looking for. Ditto for Crescent Street hangouts—a street that is lined with dance clubs and their cell-phone talking patrons.

Montreal isn't only about booze and parties. Cinema du Parc, a repertory house, is in the heart of the student ghetto adjacent to campus, showing second-run movies and arty films at a reasonable price. Cafés are abundant and stray away from the Second Cup variety although the infamous coffee-chain is beginning to invade the city. For many students, the café is used as a place for socializing, studying, or simply for a caffeine fix. Mount Royal Park is perfect for a light stroll or long jog. The world-famous Orchestre Symphonique de Montreal offers its seats to students at a very low price. And quality theatre is cheap at the National Theatre School. The city truly has something to offer all tastes.

Despite its 21,000 students, the McGill community feels surprisingly small. Especially for students not from Montreal,

A Word to the Wise:

1. Avoid McGill bureaucracy if you can. Pay your bills on time, get the appropriate papers stamped, visit your advisors when you're supposed to, etc. Red tape has frustrated many McGill students. You don't want to be one of them.

2. Go beyond the student ghetto and the regular student hang-outs. Try cafés besides Second Cup. Try the bars and clubs on the more francophone strip on Rue St. Denis. Montreal's a great city, so try not to confine yourself to the usual McGill routine.

3. Live in residence–any of the residences. The meal plan isn't great, but you'll meet interesting people and make good friends.

4. Be curious. Don't be afraid to ask questions from your TAs or professors. They're there to help you even though they sometimes give the impression that they don't want to. At the same time, if you think your TA or prof is an idiot, he or she probably is. However, they mark the papers and exams; you don't.

5. If you're writing a research paper, get to the library as soon as you know your topic. Take out your books before the next guy in class does. The collections are limited and if you leave your research to the last minute, you won't find the sources you need or you'll be stuck with books dated at the turn of the century.

it is common to run into acquaintances and friends on campus and on the street in your neighbourhood. Students hang out in the same bars, cafés, and clubs. After a while, faces become recognizable from classes and campus activities. The size of the university and the city may be large, but the student community is not.

ON MONTREAL

While French may be the language of most Montrealers, English is still alive and well, contrary to the national media. It is very easy for unilingual anglophones from Saskatchewan or Ontario to make their way around the city. In most of the areas surrounding McGill, service is provided in both languages and usually in equal fluency. Many of the out-of-province students at McGill are unilingual and have encountered little difficulty in the city. If you think you're coming to Montreal to learn French—forget it. McGill is an anglophone school. Most Montrealers will often address you in English even if you know French.

Montreal is truly a metropolis, boasting a population of around three million. Its European flair adds a different style and chic when compared to Toronto or Vancouver. There is a certain joie de vivre, a sense of hedonism. Thursdays are considered part of the weekend. Whenever the weather is warm, Montrealers sip their drinks outside on *terrasses*. Every Sunday, the hippies of the city gather at the park and dance to the beats of tam-tam and bongo drums. Montrealers make the most of their time, in the name of fun.

If you're not from Montreal, try to find a job or take classes during the summer months. Montreal boasts numerous festivals, including the well-known Jazz Festival, the Just for Laughs Comedy Festival, and The Symphony of Fire—an international fireworks competition. People sit outside on terrasses, soak up the sun, and sip on their cold drinks at bars and cafés. The city comes alive during the summer months, in contrast to the dreary cold of the winter months.

Acadia University

By Rebecca Earle

Stand up and cheer!

Stand up and cheer for old Acadia!
For, today, we raise
The red and blue above the rest...above the rest
Our teams are fighting
And they are out to win the fray
Well, I should say,
We've got the steam...boom! boom!
We've got the team...boom! boom!
For this is old Acadia's day!

The sweet sound of this Acadia University song is familiar to any student or alumnus who attended Acadia at any point in time. Founded in 1838 by the Baptist denomination, Acadia has, and always will be, a school full of spirit and pride. Acadia is located just 100 kilometres northwest of Halifax in Wolfville, Nova Scotia, in the heart of the Annapolis Valley. The town has a population of approximately 3,800 people that doubles to accommodate the more than 3,700 students who arrive in Wolfville each September to begin their journey of a lifetime.

The story of Acadia during the last 160 years is a fascinating and impressive one. In 1828 a meeting with the representatives of the churches in the Nova Scotia Baptist Association was held in Horton, now known as the town of Wolfville. The discussion was to propose a "Seminary for Education" with the curriculum to include "instruction in the usual branches of English Literature, and of scientific, classical and other studies, which usually comprise the course of education at an Academy or College." The institution was to be open to "children and persons of any religious denomination." The proposal was enthusiastically approved and Horton Academy opened on May 1, 1829, in a farmhouse (imagine that) with 50 students! In 1838, it was decided to establish a college in association with the academy so that the young men would be able to obtain a college education locally. Finally the institution was named Acadia College and subsequently named Acadia University in 1891.

The university, which is situated on 250 acres of breath-taking land, overlooks the dyked meadows, better known as the "dykes," of the Evangeline country. A few buildings were erected in the early 1900s, with the present University Hall built in 1925. However, many of the residences along with the new Beveridge Arts Centre (BAC) were constructed in the sixties and seventies: self-explanatory for those who compare architectural works! But each one tells its own story. Old and new alike, the buildings on Acadia's campus provide a sense of pride, particularly when one drives by Main Street and looks up to see the white pillars of University Hall.

Since the introduction of The Acadia Advantage, the classrooms of Acadia University have become far from dull. The new classrooms are equipped with state-of-the-art swivel chairs, computer plug-ins, and even large video screens to provide students with the latest in education technology. Even the labs in Patterson Hall, (the biology building) are equipped with computer ports to calculate data analysis right on the spot! No more experiments with toads and frogs—unless they are of the virtual nature.

CAMPUS CULTURE

Acadia is home to 3,700 students from over more than 30 countries around the world. People come from near and far to become a part of the Acadia family. Whether you are an Upper Canadian looking for an identity, a Nova Scotia lass/laddie who just can't get enough of home, or a Newfoundlander who wants a taste of something other than screech, Acadia has got a place for you. When you drive into Wolfville, you will feel a sense of a special culture—a treat bag of sorts with many surprises. In time, you will recognize faces and say hello to everyone you pass on the street, because now you have something in common with these people—you are Acadia students. Acadia has been best described as "being small in size and idyllic in setting yet having a cosmopolitan atmosphere because of its eclectic mix of students."

Everyone finds his or her own niche and identity at Acadia. Some students contribute their time to clubs and societies such as the Sensory Motor Instructional Leadership Experience (SMILE), Students Maintaining Alumni Relations Through Teamwork (SMARTT), The Frosh Society, The Chinese Club,

Vital Statistics

Address: Acadia University, P.O. Box 1269, Wolfville, Nova Scotia, B0P 1X0

Admissions office: (902) 542-2201

Website: www.acadiau.ca

Total enrollment (including Acadia Divinity College): 3,799

Male-female ratio: 45 to 55

Average entrance grades: 70%

Tuition fees: $5,450

Residence fees: $2,475–$3,590 without meals. Meal packages range from $2,015 (15 meals per week) to $2,120 (19 meals).

Spaces for students in residence: 1,624

Number of international students: 259

Number of students from outside Nova Scotia: 1,333

Financial aid: Each year Acadia University provides over $1.1 million in scholarships, bursaries, awards, and, prizes in recognition of academic excellence. There is no separate application for those who wish to be considered for entrance scholarships. Loans and bursaries are also available to help those in financial need. There are approximately 560 assistantships and 1,200 hourly paid jobs

Co-op programs: Biology, Business, Chemistry, Computer Science, Environmental Science, Geology, Math, Nutrition and Food Science, Physics, Psychology

Services for students with disabilities: Acadia University welcomes students with special needs and will accommodate individual requests. Counselling, academic tutors, parking accommodations, student assistants, wheel-chair accessible buildings, residences (Cutten/War Memorial) and ramps are all available to students at the university.

Student services: Just to name a few...personal, academic, financial, and vocational counselling, student medical centre, chaplaincy programs, a career planning and employment centre, 24-hour security, a multi-level student centre, an athletic complex, a bookstore, convenience store, and two campus clothing stores.

and the Curly Haired Guys Club. Others choose to spend their time elsewhere. Denton Hall lawn is usually packed with music students between choir practices, (hackeysacks in mid-air). The first floor of the library is crowded with those who wish to socialize. Some students choose to occupy a piece of green space on the front lawn of U-Hall or a slab of steel on Tully's beach, while others are seen reading in the Student Union Building (SUB) or sleeping in Michener Lounge. However, when something, just about anything, happens at Acadia, each and every one of the students come together to be as one. Varsity games, pep rallies, concerts, student union events and campaigns, assemblies, reunions, and even memorial services for those who have passed on...everyone comes together. This is something that is very special about Acadia, something that no other school possesses. It is about school spirit and pride. Everything that happens on the campus means something, whether big or small. There is no typical Acadia student because each one is special. However, if one had to sum up Acadia students, one word comes to mind—camaraderie.

ACADEMIC ISSUES

With the introduction of The Acadia Advantage program, tuition costs have soared at Acadia, leading many people to second guess this school for

their undergraduate degree. Also, many people are angry that the IBM notebook computers are mandatory because some students may already own their own computer. Despite these factors however, students should note that Acadia prides itself on its academic excellence and The Acadia Advantage is just another step toward promoting this excellence. Classes are small and individual attention is the first priority. That means your professor will notice if you miss that 8:30 a.m. lecture (unless of course it is Intro Psychology held in Huggins 10—the largest lecture room on campus). The cons: you may have to catch up on your sleep some other time. The pros: you'll be socializing at the AXE with your professor at the end of the year and speaking to him/her on a first-name basis.

Acadia offers more than 200 different curriculum choices leading to degrees, diplomas, and certificates. Many of the professors at Acadia are at the top of their field in research and many take students under their wing to expand on their work. Biology and Chemistry see major advancements in research, with NSERC grants being offered to deserving students. The

Science program is impressive and attracts many students each year, with most choosing Biology as a major. This program can be tricky to get into; the cut off is usually 80 students per year. For those who are unsure of what they want to do but did well in their high school gym class, Kinesiology is an option. This degree is becoming more popular and can be done in conjunction with Nutrition and Biology. One word of advice: Lose 10 pounds before you sign up. There are mandatory aerobics and dance labs.

Co-op programs provide students with classroom study and paid on-the-job training. These programs are available in the areas of Science, Business and Math. This option proves to be a valuable one in that it gives students an experience that they may not otherwise have the opportunity to get. Also, Masters programs (e.g. Clinical Psychology) usually require experience, and this would put you ahead of the game.

The Faculty of Arts proves to be another popular degree, with options in areas such English, Sociology, Philosophy, Music and Drama. The Acadia Theatre Company produces and performs many successful plays throughout the year with the Acadia music ensembles following in step. These Arts degrees have become increasingly popular in the last few years. Some advice to those who are considering English…that 97 on your transcript in Grade 12 doesn't mean that university English will be a joke. The classes are tough and you have to read up to 12 books a term in some slots. Best of luck to those who brave this degree!

Although Acadia does not offer professional studies other than Business, Education, Kinesiology, and Recreation Management, the curriculum prepares students to pursue futures in health professions such as Medicine, Dentistry, Physiotherapy, and Occupational Therapy. Students interested in these programs should talk to the health science advisor at Acadia.

REZ LIFE

Get ready to serenade the male frosh, make human sundaes, eat at the meal hall with no utensils while tied arm and arm, and see which residence beats the other at Play Fair. These are just some of the things that happen during Welcome Week at Acadia, and it only gets better (or worse) if you live in residence. Because Wolfville is such a small town, this is where Acadia's biggest parties happen…all

year long. This is also where you will meet the friends that will stick with you for life.

Acadia has ten residences to choose from depending on your style—all girls, all guys, and even co-ed, so you can be near your secret crush. Each residence offers something different to suit your needs, so be sure to apply for a room early to get a spot in the one you'd like. All rooms have a phone and voicemail, so when you are out partying or studying, Mom and Dad can leave a nice message. Also, all rooms are fully equipped for your notebook computer (i.e., Internet access), and that means no excuses about homework.

The most predominant residence on campus for females is Cutten House. It holds 298 girls and tends to be a touch "catty." Although the guys tend to be a bit rude when speaking about the Cutten girls, things are actually pretty conservative inside, with rules enforced for quiet hours and male guests. The building is a maze manor, in which colour-coded walls are used to indicate where one has ended up or where one needs to go. There are five floors and each section of the house has its own lounge with cooking facilities and couches. The rooms are a fair size, especially if you are lucky enough to get a corner one. This is the newest and biggest residence on campus, so many girls get stuck here. It has a big lounge and a large screen communal TV. It also has a poor excuse for a gym, so make the trek down to the arena if you really want to get in shape. Hey, the walk UP to Cutten is exercise enough!

The other female rez is Whitman House, a.k.a. Tully. This is a very old residence and if you like ghosts and wooden floors that creak—you've come to the right place. This is a very nice residence with a lot of history. It houses 96 girls, all of whom seem to stick closely together. They have a lot of spirit and tend to outdo Cutten in this respect. If you like the sun, Tully also has a beach. A beach at university? You'll just have to come to Acadia and see for yourself…

The male residences are extreme opposites of the "conservative" Cutten House. They are animal houses to say the least—typical of most male dorms at any university. Chipman holds 116 breeds while Eaton rings in at 194. They were built directly beside each other, a situation which tends to cause some tension. Both residences have a lot of spirit and try to outdo one another at the Cheatin' Cup, an annual hockey game between the two residences. Chipman is the nicer residence inside and has big rooms with beds built into the walls. It also holds the biggest pubcrawl of the year.

In a Nut Shell

The university in a phrase:
Simply the best.

Best thing about the university:
Small town family atmosphere.

Worst thing about the university: The tuition cost.

Favourite professors: Perry Johnson-Green (Biology), Hilda Taylor (Biology), Dan Toews (Biology), Guadalupe Puentes-Neuman (Psychology), Joan Allen Peters (Retired—Nutrition)

Most popular bird courses:
Chips for dips—Computer 1813; Rocks for jocks—Geology 1033; Clapping for credit—Music 1033. The only thing you'll memorize from these courses is your friend's ICU chat line address.

Hot spot to study on campus:
First floor of the library.

Quietest spot to study on campus: Fourth floor of the library.

Need for car and parking availability: Having a car in Wolfville is definitely not a necessity because even the boundaries of the town are within 5–10 minutes walking distance. However, a car can come in handy on those free days when you want to head into Halifax or go to see a movie in stadium seating—the Acadia Theatre certainly doesn't have this! It costs approximately $60/school year for a permit to park on campus so you decide if it is worth it.

Sexually speaking: By the time Acadia students are in their senior year, most have settled down with a significant other. A word of advice to those who are looking—wait in the lineup at the Anvil!

Fraternities/sororities: These do not exist at Acadia.

Athletic facilities: There is no excuse not to get in shape or enjoy a sport you love at Acadia. We all pay into the War Memorial Gym, so why not get off your lazy butt and take advantage! It is equipped with three gyms, a 6 lane 25-metre pool, an Olympic-size rink, squash and racquetball courts, weight rooms, and even an indoor track so you don't have to run outside in the winter. The only thing lacking at the gym are treadmills and some up-to-date bikes. Hopefully the budget will allow for this in the near future.

Library facilities: The Vaughan Memorial Library is a wonderful place to sit your bum down and read in a big comfy chair overlooking the lawn of University Hall or to plug in your notebook computer to surf the Net. The library also houses more than 800,000 volumes and holds a number of special collections. The library provides study carrels equipped to plug in your computers, wired group study rooms, and an electronic database, which allows students to obtain information about resources at other universities across the province.

Computer facilities: Notebook computers are integrated into undergraduate courses. Students can download class notes, e-mail profs and take part in chat groups.

Safety on campus: Acadia provides many services to ensure that students are in a safe and relaxed atmosphere. The blue lights, 24-hour security, and walk home service are there to meet students' needs. And if you are feeling tired after a night of study at the library or simply don't want to walk home from a friend's apartment, call John and he'll rescue you in the U-Hall van!

Weather: Pack your bathing suit and shorts to go tubing down the Gaspereau River in September. You'll need this attire well into October. Because Acadia is situated in a valley, the temperature always tends to be about 5–10 degrees warmer than most areas in the province. However, when winter rolls around, get out your parka. We've had snow before in May. This is when you'll curse those who built the university on a hill!

Alumni: Dr. Charles Huggins '20 (Nobel Prize recipient for cancer research), Dr. Enid Johnson MacLeod '32 (anesthesiologist, one of the first in Canada), Mr. John Nowlan '64 (with CBC-TV for 35 years and producer of Street Cents—the five time Gemini Award winning program), Dr. David Levy '72 (world renowned astronomer and author).

For those who want a co-ed atmosphere, there are many places to choose from. Chase Court is a maze of sorts made strictly of bricks. Crowell Tower was supposed to be twin towers (male and female connecting) and is now ready to fall. War Memorial House, a.k.a. the Barrax, is where most of the Upper Canadians stay, and Seminary House is almost impossible to get into since it is probably the nicest residence on campus. Raymond House is for mature students and La Maison Française is for those who wish to be in an all-French environment.

Anywhere you live on campus will prove to be an adventure—but not too much of one that will take you far from class. Each residence is within walking distance to class and the new meal hall. Just roll out of bed, throw on the slippers, and head on down to the dining hall to gorge on some grub with the other bed-heads. With the new Wheelock dining hall (opening Sept. 1999) fresh, restaurant-quality food will be prepared right in front of you. If the caf-food is not your thing, then you may want to rent a mini-fridge for those late

A Word to the Wise:

1. Live in residence once but be sure to wear flip-flops everywhere you go–no one knows what lives on those floors.

2. Live in residence twice and try the RA thing but be sure to buy a pair of earplugs and a sign saying "Babysitter is out" if you ever want peace and quiet.

3. Don't eat anything at meal hall that has a name you can't pronounce.

4. Take at least one bird course in your four years–it's fun to say that you spent $5,000 to take a course known as "Chips for Dips."

5. Ask your prof lots of questions and make yourself seem smart even though you have no idea what the #$*&%! is going on–this is how you get extra marks (guaranteed!).

6. Paint your face red, white, and blue, dress up like a cheerleader (this is fun especially for guys), and spell AXE with your bum at least once at a varsity game.

7. Groove with the AXE dancer on a Friday night and try to get an autograph, if possible.

8. Do sled down U-Hall on a meal hall tray in a snowstorm.

9. Whatever you do–don't sled down the mud on the dykes on a meal hall tray–you're bound to get lost.

10. Come to Nova Scotia and be a part of the Acadia tradition…after all that has been said, Acadia promises that you'll have the four best years of your life!

night Cheese Whiz creations. And for those who may want an apartment in Wolfville…start looking early as leases are signed a year prior to renting.

NIGHT LIFE

If you think of bars when you think of nightlife, boy are you ever going to be disappointed. There are slim pickings when it comes to these establishments at Acadia, with only two to choose from. And if you are used to going out late and coming home early, it's time to set your watch to Acadia's hours. Before you know it they are yelling last call and you are snuggled into bed by 1:30 a.m.

For you eager frosh ready to use your pick-up lines and fake IDs in September, the Anvil is the spot to shake your "thang."

This place is known for its 25¢ draft during "Power Hour" and post-game varsity athletic parties. So if you're looking to put the moves on that football star you've been eyeing, or just want to drink yourself sober (and do it really cheap), this is the place to go. The other alternative is the AXE, the campus bar located in the basement of the Student Union Building (SUB). This offers a relaxed atmosphere where you can grab a beer, shoot a game of pool, or sit out on the new patio to enjoy a cool breeze. Don't try to use your fake IDs here because campus IDs are needed to get in. Here you will find a mix of mostly third and fourth year socials consisting of couples or cliques of close friends. This is the place to head on Friday nights if you like to dance, Wednesday nights if you like the alternative scene, and Monday nights to relax and enjoy a coffee with live entertainment. Be sure to come early on the weekends if you want a seat.

Although there are only two bars to choose from, Acadia is nothing short of a party school. The SUB is home to many wet/dry super-sub parties where underaged frosh can also enjoy the feeling of being truly out on their own. This is where you'll get a chance to enjoy a set from a big name band or if this doesn't tickle your fancy, there's bound to be a house party down the street or a gathering of drunks at Subway after the bar. If the kegs are dry and your fridge is empty, Joe's offers a pub style atmosphere where you can keep on chugging after 1 a.m. it's also the place to grab the famous Acadia Scot Skins for just $4.00. Of course there's also the usual pub-crawls that make their way to Halifax when things are getting slow in Wolfville. And if all this doesn't suit your party style, head to the Barn with the first carload of people you see, have your own party in your dorm room, or just stop "sooking" and go to Dal!

ON WOLFVILLE

You certainly have to love a small-town atmosphere to come to Acadia. Wolfville is home to 3,800 people, with one main street and no traffic lights! However, as small as it may be, Wolfville offers a culture that is unique. Beautiful elm trees and historic century-old homes line Wolfville's Main Street. Stay a night at one of the many elegant bed-and-breakfasts, catch a show at the Atlantic Theatre Festival, do some shopping in the specialty shops downtown, or take part in the world famous Apple Blossom Festival. Nature enthusiasts will love to walk, jog, or bike the dykes and perhaps catch a glimpse of the world's highest tides. A hike to Cape Split is definitely a must for anyone who enjoys scenery and a bit of adventure. And if meal hall is turning your stomach, the Main Squeeze is the best spot to grab a quick pita and become famous…they take everyone's picture and post them on the wall. You will never feel out of place in this small town with its friendly atmosphere—and if you get bored you are only one hour from the city!

The University College of Cape Breton

By Kris Magliaro

The University College of Cape Breton (UCCB) is a rather contemporary institute of higher learning compared to other institutional "dinosaurs" of Atlantic Canada such as Acadia, St. Francis Xavier, or Dalhousie. Created in 1974 with the merger of the Eastern Institute of Technology and Xavier College, UCCB's humble roots stretch back a mind-boggling 25 years. Considered the "pride of the island," UCCB is found on beautiful Cape Breton Island and, more specifically, just off the Sydney-Glace Bay highway. Capers (Cape Bretoners) refer to this location as the "middle of nowhere." It is a ten-minute car ride from downtown Sydney on a treacherous piece of highway where even Mario Andretti could have serious competition from local speed demons.

The campus itself is known among staff and students as being both accessible and aesthetically pleasing. In 1997, UCCB underwent such major reconstructive surgery that, in September of that same year, new and returning students were shocked at all the improvements. There was a state-of-the-art lecture theatre, new student union block, and an exquisite art gallery that, among the items in its permanent collection, boasts a sketchbook from none other than Pablo Picasso. This Student Culture and Heritage Centre also includes an expanded cafeteria, complete with loud, obnoxious music piped through all day long by CAPR—the campus radio station more familiarly known as "CRAP." The most prized area is the Great Hall, impressive from both inside and outside.

The one thing UCCB thrives on is its accessibility. The design of the campus is that of one "super-building" that contains everything a student could need under one roof. There is no need to walk outside to get to either classes, meal halls, the library, or computer centre. The one exception is the residence, which is about a one-minute walk away. The Deans' offices are close by, as are the faculty offices, the labs, and the Registrar's office. Students with small children will enjoy the Daycare Centre, also conveniently located on campus. UCCB, being primarily a commuter campus, has enough parking areas and overflow parking areas to accommodate a small foreign country. The words "car pool" have no meaning here, as it seems that every second student drives a car to class each day. Recently, paid parking was implemented, which ignited a frenzy among the students who were angered at having to pay a dollar per day. The penalty for not paying the daily parking fee is a handsome parking ticket from the "pitbulls of the parking lot."

CAMPUS CULTURE

Many UCCB students are from the local area, that is, Cape Breton Island or mainland Nova Scotia. Out-of-province students make up a small percentage of the student population and international students, an even smaller percentage. Newfoundlanders make up a large chunk of these out-of-province students, mainly because of the articulation agreements between UCCB and Newfoundland institutions that make many courses transferable. The cultural similarities are also quite stunning; both Capers and Newfoundlanders are notorious for their drinking efforts and friendly dispositions.

Nonetheless, all foreigners soon find out what it's really

Vital Statistics

Address: University College of Cape Breton, P.O. Box 5300, Station A, Sydney, Nova Scotia, B1P 6L2

Admissions office: (902) 539-5300

Website: www.uccb.ns.ca

Total enrollment: 3,500

Male-female ratio: 45 to 55

Average entrance grades: 60% average, but, space permitting, will accept even lower.

Tuition fees: $3,963

Residence fees: $2,200/double; $2,500/single

Percentage of students in residence: Around 4%

Percentage of international students: 3.5%

Percentage of out-of-province students: 15%

Financial aid: Provincial and federal loans available. Entrance and in-course scholarships and bursaries also available.

Co-op programs: Virtually all technology programs and hospitality programs. Environmental Health, Environmental Engineering Tech, Civil, Electrical, Mechanical, Chemical Tech, etc.

Services for students with disabilities: Lots of ramps and elevators.

Aboriginal students: More natives, from the two local reserves (Membertou & Eskasoni), are attending UCCB each year. They have representation on the Student Representative Council and a program for all students called Mi'kmaq Studies. Mi'kmaq Student Services Centre also in existence.

Student services: Athletics, career education and placement centre, chaplaincy, counselling services, health services, on-campus childcare, reading & writing development centre, residence, tutoring.

like to be a Caper for a few short years. The only prerequisite students need to fit into this subculture is vast alcohol consumption. Aside from their impressive drinking abilities, Capers are known for their contagious twang which always contains the words "eh" and "bie." True Capers combine the two. There is also tarabish, the official card game of Cape Breton and UCCB. This game has been responsible for more "Christmas graduates" than any other and is ideal for those first-year students who plan on doing nothing but boozing, eating pizza, and sleeping.

The university itself exudes coziness and a small town atmosphere, which most find comforting and enjoyable. There is no pressure to get involved with athletics or extracurricular activities, although the number of people who do participate in campus life has been steadily escalating over the past few years. The reasons are twofold: First, there is a diverse range of societies, committees, and clubs in which students may wish to get involved, including the International Students Society, Students' Union, and The Biology Society to name but a few. Second, getting involved keeps the weekly alcohol consumption at a relatively reasonable level because, as first- and second-year students will attest, Capers will come up with just about any excuse to drink. Your senile, 86-year-old grandmother just got her driver's licence? Let's get some beer and celebrate.

> "I have travelled around the globe. I have seen the Canadian and the American Rockies, the Andes and the Alps and the Highlands of Scotland, but for simple beauty, Cape Breton Island outrivals them all."
>
> Alexander Graham Bell, inventor, resident of Cape Breton Island, N.S., quoted by Wes Ratoushk in *Silver Highway: A Celebration of the Trans-Canada Highway* (1988).

School spirit is not particularly high. Basketball is currently somewhat more popular than most sports, probably due to the back-to-back AUAA championships, that the Capers won in the 1993–94 and 1994–95 seasons. The low turnout for athletics can largely be attributed to Capers' indifference toward organized events, and their perpetual need to hang around the football-field-sized cafeteria all day long. Other spirited Capers opt for the Pit Lounge, the on-campus pub that opens its doors early in the morning for those social misfits who enjoy doing last minute assignments or papers. The afternoon crowd can enjoy some biting, kicking and punching, while watching the latest cat fight on *Jerry Springer*.

ACADEMIC ISSUES

As both a university and a college, UCCB offers a diverse blend of programming for all students. There are degrees, diplomas, and certificates available in science, arts, trades, and leading edge technology. UCCB's reputation as a community- and business-based institution is clearly on the rise, especially since it is the only university in the area which offers technology programs such as Environmental Health, Engineering Technology, Business Technology, and most recently, with the advent of the Sable Island Gas Project, Petroleum-based Technology programs. The only significant problem with the otherwise top-notch

In a Nut Shell

The university in a phrase: "A community- and technology-based institution with a diverse array of programs."

Best thing about the university: Small and closely-knit, with a great deal of student-professor interaction.

Worst thing about the university: Location. It's just not close to anything.

Favourite professors: Katherine Covell, Psychology professor: cool, witty and a little sarcastic. Barry Moore of the BACS department: students love this friendly and helpful guy. David Sneddon—Chemistry prof: organic chemistry was never dull or unorganized with this cat. Michael Manson of the English department: raw and sassy with very student-directed class discussions. John Coldwell of the Biology Faculty is hilarious at 8:30 a.m. Microbiology.

Most popular bird courses: Humanities courses. Introductory Sociology classes. Fine Arts courses. Some of these classes do not even require a brain.

Hot spot on campus to study: The Cafeteria. You can't even hear yourself talking most times, but some still try studying in this area.

Quietest spot on campus to study: Cubicles on the second floor in the library or anywhere on campus after 8:00 p.m.

Need for car and parking availability: Car is a must and lots of parking space for everyone, including another town.

Sexually speaking: To quote Austin Powers: "Shagadelic, baby!" The bars downtown are all about scooping and getting randy. UCCB's Psychology Faculty also offers "Human Sexuality and Sex Education" with Peter MacIntyre. An absolute must for all students. Homosexual students, however, may find that UCCB is not as receptive to same-sex love as other campuses and anonymity is difficult to come by.

Fraternities/sororities: There aren't any at UCCB.

Athletic facilities: Capers' Basketball games are played at the Sullivan Field House. There's also a new gym for all students. Canada Games Complex was a good spot for the now axed Capers hockey team.

Library facilities: Definitely not the bright spot about UCCB. Students are always complaining about the lack of books, new journals, and periodicals. Aside from the books, the library is a great spot to study. There are study rooms for groups and individual rooms for the bookworms. Library hours are utterly ridiculous and the source of much confusion among students.

Computer facilities: Five computer centres, though four of them always seem to be booked for classes when you need them. The one reliable one is usually packed during the day, but still manageable. New printers are available.

Weather: Erratic weather most times. Sunny one minute, cloudy and raining the next, then hailing or freezing rain—a meteorologist's nightmare.

Safety on campus: Well-lit campus and parking areas. Students' Union even has a "walk you to your car" service for those students who leave campus late.

Alumni: Some 8,000 to date including Major-General Lewis MacKenzie, former chief of staff for peacekeeping forces in Bosnia; W. A. Alex Morrison, president of the Pearson Peacekeeping Institute.

Science and Technology Department is the lack of a four-year major program in Chemistry, Physics, and Geology. Students can take the first two years of such programs at UCCB, but then must transfer to another university for the remaining two years. This approach is rather futile, making the choice of Psychology or Biology the prime one for most Science students. Many of the instructors are world-renowned researchers who conduct major research at UCCB.

There are also college diplomas and certificates available to those who prefer a less stringent approach to an education. One of the main reasons for UCCB's relatively poor funding from the provincial government is because of this blend of programming, which the government seems to view with contempt. Thus, funds are insufficient in comparison to other universities in Atlantic Canada. The Student Union at UCCB has made a strong voice against such neglect by the government of Nova Scotia and, in the process, has gained a status similar to David versus Goliath.

UCCB also offers another unique degree: BACS or Bachelor of Arts Community Studies. Students in this program take volunteer work placements somewhere in the community, as part of the curriculum. "Volunteer placements," however, means no pay for these students who must put in 160-hour work terms.

The Business and Arts faculties are equally popular and well-received by students. The Anthropology/Sociology, Political Science, and English departments offer the best array of courses within the Faculty of Arts.

Co-op programs are very much a part of the UCCB experience. Students enrolled in virtually any of the technology programs—whether business tech, civil engineering tech or numerous others—will have the opportunity to get practical work experience and a cheque for their efforts. These programs usually offer three alternating work terms, in addition to a heavy course load, in order to achieve a Bachelor of Technology. Making the pot even sweeter is the fact that many or all of the job placements are taken care of by the Co-op office and provide invaluable experience for students. It is little wonder why the tech programs are among the most popular at UCCB.

REZ LIFE

Students applying for a spot in residence at UCCB are advised to do so as soon as possible because they tend to fill up quickly. There's a *wide* variety to choose from: MacDonald Residence or MacDonald Residence. Some lucky ones will even manage to get into MacDonald Residence. That's right, there's only one residence. However, do not make the mistake of thinking that one lone residence cannot possibly provide a memorable time. The partying and socializing at "MacRez" is second to none. This one residence issue actually works in favour of the students. There is more of an opportunity for networking and forming tight bonds with fellow Rezmates of both the female and male persuasion. A common complaint, however, is the Brinks-like security. Gaining access into Fort Knox would be easier than trying to get an overnight visitor into MacRez.

The residence houses approximately 150 students. Being only a hop, skip and a jump from the university, MacRez is convenient for the late night "staggers" back from the Pit Lounge, but the university is about the only place residence is close to. Aside from that, rez students are not in walking distance from anything but a gas station and a cable company. Everything worth doing or seeing is a seven to 10-minute car or cab ride away unless you have an affinity for comparing petrol prices or want to sabotage Cape Breton's cable.

Though there is no *inter*-residence rivalry here, there is *intra*-residence rivalry. This may take the form of one floor versus another or one wing versus another. What better way to get to know your fellow residence pals than to insult and mock them during a competitive conflict? This provides the foun-

dation for a wonderful love-hate relationship that will fester during the entire year.

Some students choose the apartment option for accommodations. Sydney has a fair amount of apartment space for rent if you don't mind taking the bus or driving back and forth from the university every day. One popular location is Rockcliffe, a mere five-minute ride from UCCB and often called UCCB's second residence. It is near all the necessary fast food chains prized by the prototypical student. Start carving another notch in the old belt.

NIGHT LIFE

Let the boozefest begin! Being a newly recruited UCCB student entitles one to certain responsibilities that must be fulfilled in order to achieve a successful metamorphosis into a true Caper. This transitional period takes roughly eight months to complete. Some can't take it. The first step in this program is to familiarize yourself with the campus pub. Newly renovated in 1997, the Pit has all the bases covered: big screen TV, pool tables, arcade games, cheap draft, and great local beer. This destination is ideal for MacRez students and packs quite a crowd on Friday nights for cheap drinks. Another highlight for Friday night boozing is the "crazy train" bus ride offered to downtown bars at 1:00 a.m., leaving from the Pit and comparable to a Simpsons' school bus trip. All in all, the Pit is basically for amateurs just warming up to Caper life and is not considered one of the big stops along the professional drinker's route.

The heavy artillery are Daniels, The Capri Club, and Smooth Hermans. All three are located in downtown Sydney, and all are a relatively short distance from one another. The Capri Club is among the first stops in a series for students on a typical liquor hunt. Good prices, great tunes, the occasional live band, and plenty of gals and guys for everyone. Sometimes dubbed the "sweat factory," first-timers always make the mistake of loading up on clothes when entering this liquor sauna.

Other brave souls try their luck at Daniels for cheap pitchers and great local bands on the weekends. On a packed

A Word to the Wise:

1. Avoid buying food at the cafeteria as much as possible. Even Bill Gates could not afford to buy the chicken fingers and fries there.

2. Study in the library and not in the cafeteria.

3. Try and get an apartment at Rockcliffe in second or third year.

4. Having your own car or knowing someone with a car will definitely be an asset. If this doesn't work, get to know the bus route, which is reliable and handy.

5. Tuesday night is Daniels; Friday night is the Pit and Chandler's; and Saturday night is Hermans.

6. Get used books at Bookmarks first (which is run by the Students' Union) and the UCCB Campus Bookstore later–when you become a millionaire.

7. Get involved with campus life. Nothing is taken too seriously and you can earn some valuable drinking money from some activities.

8. Try and get many of your classes in the same building or wing. Some wings are freezing (CE) while others are boiling (B). It's a lot like walking from the Arctic to Hawaii in two minutes.

9. Don't believe the infinite wisdom scribbled on the walls of the bathroom stalls concerning BA degrees; it's just not true.

Tuesday or Saturday night, moving around in there is a task in itself and is equivalent to trying to cram everyone in Cape Breton into your bedroom for a beer. This bar is sassy and naughty for the average liquor swine and does not disappoint. The downstairs bar is like drinking in a smokestack, but still delivers the goods with a knockout punch.

After everyone is all primed up, or after one in the morning, it's time to visit the "big bad boy" of the downtown area—Smooth Hermans. Trying to describe this bar to someone is like trying to sell a vacation package to Kosovo—an interesting experience, none the less. Hermans is better known by its motto: "Get drunk, puke in our toilets, have a hotdog outside and beat the snot out of someone." People get thrown out of this bar more than WWF wrestlers get thrown out of the ring. Do not be alarmed; it's merely providing the nightly entertainment. Once inside, it is easy to see why everyone saves this bar for last. It's spacious, air conditioned, and has ample dancing room for the Caper-to-be. This cabaret is open till 3:30 a.m. with live bands year round.

Those who prefer alternate bars, or more contemporary places of drink and merriment, should visit Bunkers, Chandler's, or Fiddler's Pub. Chandler's, especially, is starting to gather some Friday night momentum that could eventually, launch them into contention with the "Big Three."

ON SYDNEY Cape Breton Island is an artistic masterpiece. Located on the east coast of Canada, tourists flock from around the globe to gaze at her natural beauty and enjoy her friendly folk. Alexander Graham Bell, upon travelling around the world, once stated that "for natural beauty, Cape Breton out-rivals them all." Rent a car and drive around the famous Cabot Trail for breathtaking views, or swim at popular Ingonish beach. Take a whale watching tour or see photos of the Cape Breton Giant at Giant MacAskill's Museum in Englishtown. In Sydney, take a late-night stroll down the boardwalk, feed the ducks at scenic Wentworth Park, or try your luck on the "one armed bandits" at the Sheraton Casino. Celebrities also flock to the Island on a regular basis. Mel Gibson had his yacht by the government wharf, and Jack Nicholson, a frequent visitor to the Keltic Lodge in Ingonish, is even rumoured to have a cottage somewhere in the highlands. The historian types will enjoy the Fortress of Louisbourg, an authentic replication of the original French settlement of 200 years ago. Shop downtown on Charlotte Street or have a Napoli pizza, "the best in Sydney." Cape Breton has a distinct culture from that of mainland Nova Scotia. It's a subculture which is inviting and supportive of its university students, whom they view as the "Pride of the Island."

Dalhousie University

By Blair Trudell

Founded in 1818, Dalhousie University is regarded as the "academic powerhouse" of the Maritimes. Situated in Halifax's southern peninsula on the east coast of Canada, Dalhousie is concentrated in 10 city blocks and can be easily traversed in 15 minutes. Dalhousie is one of Canada's oldest universities, conceived early in the nineteenth century by George Ramsey, the ninth Earl of Dalhousie and lieutenant-governor of Nova Scotia at the time. His goal was noble: To create a college where all were welcome, regardless of class or creed. His means were equally noble: he deployed some navy boys and their boats, directing them south to Maine where they attacked a small port town named Castine. Sifting funds through standard practices of conquer and tax, the Lieutenant-Governor harvested the necessary capital and, from the spoils of war, Dalhousie was created.

Today the campus is architecturally diverse, mixing the old with the new and the beauties with the beasts. Buildings such as the Arts and Administration (referred to as the "A & A"), the Dunn buildings, and the University Club (reserved for professors) exude an ivy league feel. Amidst these buildings constructed of stone and blanketed in ivy, it's hard not to feel corny sensations of academic motivation and at least an inkling of school pride. That is, of course, until you enter—at which point these sentiments quickly vanish into the dull, yellowing walls and unadorned, cosmetically, neglected classrooms. One is quickly reminded then that Dal is, indeed, an institution.

Challenging the beautiful antiquity of buildings such as the "A & A" and the Dunn buildings are the concrete beasts known as the Killiam Library and the Life Sciences Building. If one could ever describe a building as bureaucratic, Life Science is its prime example. Constructed of what seems to be a single solid piece of concrete hollowed out into cavities and corridors, the building is a complicated cave-maze in which basic principles of logic have been excluded. Run-ins with Hades are not uncommon here, nor are those with students who claim to have been wandering the maze for countless years in search of their first-year French class. Offer them water or point them in the direction of the Styx, but be kind. You could be next.

The Killiam is equally ugly, though somewhat less sombre. At least there are windows and a spacey atrium in the middle of the building where procrastinators can socialize, sip coffee, and conspire in the shared lie that they are truly accomplishing some work. It brings to mind the advice George once gave Seinfeld: "Remember Jerry...It's not a lie if you believe it." Students are forewarned however; you will get more studying done at the nicer, quieter library of King's, not to mention the benefits of the softer, fluffier and higher quality toilet paper, a prize coveted by campus thieves.

CAMPUS CULTURE

The student body is culturally as well as provincially diverse. Dal has consistently boasted one of the highest percentages of out-of-province students and offers a wide variety of cultural and ethnic societies and clubs. Torontonians may find the opposite and often feel that the campus is thoroughly white. To a Glace Bay native, however, it is New York City. All in all, the student body is a cosmopolitan of sorts. Whether it is a meeting with the Chinese Christian Fellowship, a game of ultimate Frisbee with some "Upper Canadians," or mass consumption of alcohol with the "Capers," one can find their niche or even choose to dabble in them all. It is difficult, therefore, to pinpoint the average Dal student though there are some consistencies. The active and involved, generally found lingering in the Student Union Building, are known as "sub-rats." Unfortunately, they represent a small minority and the rest opt for boozy nights, introversion, or remain within their chosen groups. In a word, the majority of Dal students tend to be apathetic. Politics do not flourish here, nor do sport team advocacy or any form of school spirit for that matter. Pep rallies go unattended and voter turnout is consistently meek. It takes a

Vital Statistics

Address: 1236 Henry Street, Halifax, Nova Scotia, B3H 3J5

Admissions office: (902) 494-2211

Website: www.dal.ca

Total enrollment: 12,570

Male-female ratio: 45 to 55

Average entering grades: Arts: 81%; Science: 87%; Commerce: 82%; Engineering: 87%

Tuition fees: Arts and Social Science: $4,045, Science: $4,610

Residence fees: Rooms in dorm-style residence range from $2,730–$3,315; room and board $4,780–$5,440. Off-campus bachelor accommodations range from $325–$560/month; one bedrooms from $370–$700/month; two bedrooms from $450–$700/month.

Percentage of students in residence: 16%

Percentage of international students: 6%

Percentage of out-of-province students: 38%

Financial aid: 25% of undergraduates at Dal receive financial aid through scholarships, bursaries or student employment. Dal offers an undergraduate bursary program; Contact and apply through the registrar's office.

Co-op programs: Architecture, Biochemistry, Chemistry, Commerce, Computer Science, Costume Studies, Earth Sciences, Engineering, Environmental Design, Marine Biology, Mathematics, Physics, Statistics, Urban and Rural Planning.

Services for students with disabilities: Disabled Students' Student Union Researcher, wheel chair accessible buildings and ramps, specially designed residences, advisor for students with disabilities, physical accessibility committee.

Student services: Counselling of all sorts including psychological, academic, and employment counselling; student union and student council; housing and employment offices; ombudsperson; health services; writing workshops; chaplaincy.

---

bread and circus approach of free hot dogs and beverages to initiate any form of student assembly.

This said, there is ample opportunity to participate at Dalhousie and to get involved at a relatively relaxed pace. The extra-curricular activities provide a perfect opportunity to beef up résumé content and to achieve impressive titles without overwhelming responsibility. Keep in mind that there are few at Dal who take such initiative, if any at all, and sometimes it can be as easy as writing your name on a list. Overall, Dal students are independent. They frown upon fraternities, don't care how the Dal Tigers are doing, choose their own scene, prefer drinking downtown rather than on campus, probably don't belong to any societies, respect the independent and opinionated thought of the *Gazette* and view Dal as a means to an end.

> "Haligonians share the secret, and the secret is the sea. They don't think about the ocean all the time, but it shapes the city's character, keeps its pride of history fresh, and makes its people closer to one another than city folk usually are."
>
> Harry Bruce, essayist, "Halifax: The Best Town I've Ever Known," *Down Home: Notes of a Maritime Son* (1988).

ACADEMIC ISSUES

The abundance of universities in Nova Scotia means slim funding and tight budgets for Dal. For this reason tuition is high and has forced the amalgamation of Dalhousie with Tuns (now known as DalTech), a technical university with a focus on Technology and Computer Science. Limited funding has also forced Dal to specialize in the areas of science and post-graduate studies, leaving many undergraduates feeling neglected, unwanted and even parasitic. Despite this, Dalhousie prides itself on its excellent academic reputation. Dal offers a wide range of undergraduate degrees with impressive faculties. Its professors are involved in top research and have acquired some of the biggest grants in Canada, particularly within the areas of Physics, Computer Science and Chemistry. Biology and Psychology, however, are lacking. Recently, Biology classes have become overpopulated, underfunded and understaffed, leading to mega-classes (conducted in the Rebecca Cohn theatre) characteristic of those at U of T or UBC. The Psychology Department, on the other hand, has continually allowed more people to declare this major than they have made class seats available. The second-year Psych requirement is nothing short of a nightmare to get into, and many don't, leaving them in academic limbo. For first year Science students, Dal offers an impressive, but work-intensive foundation program in Integrated Science. DISP (Dalhousie Integrated Science Program) is a hybrid study of Science, putting emphasis on problem solving and group work.

Dalhousie also boasts several co-op programs in virtually all areas of science as well as in Economics and Commerce. Consisting of four alternating work terms, co-op is certainly

In a Nut Shell

The university in a phrase: "It's the place where slackers come to be intelligent, and where the intelligent come to slack."

Best thing about the university: The city and location.

Worst thing about the university: The excessive bureaucracy.

Favourite professors: M. Cross (History); R. Bleasedale (History); G. Taylor (History); Hildi Konok (French); J. Brown (French); L. Choyce (English); S. Cameron (Chemistry); D. Black (Political Science).

Most popular bird courses: Geology 1000; German 1010 writing requirement

Hot spot to study on campus: Killam Library atrium.

Quietest spot to study on campus: King's library is by far the best place to get some work done and after that closes head over to the Life Sciences building for the wee hours of the night.

Need for car and parking availability: A car in Halifax is definitely a luxury but not a necessity. Parking is available on campus for $100+ a year but Dal always issues more spots than they have available so parking is a chronic problem. Don't try

and beat Halifax's finest. They're well aware of the limited space in Dal lots and prey on those desperate to park.

Sexually speaking: It is easy to meet those significant others around campus but most get their libidos tamed after first year and then pick and settle. You will find that Dal is definitely not into the wild and crazy but opts for the stable and steady. Despite its overall conservative nature, Dalhousie is open-minded toward same sex love and has several societies supporting homosexuality, most notably the Bi, Gay and Lesbian Association of Dalhousie (BGLAD).

Fraternities/sororities: They do exist at Dal but you wouldn't know it and most don't care either way.

Athletic facilities: Dalplex is a dome-like facility that has all the amenities the enthusiastic athlete seeks. This modern structure is one of the rare successes in recent Dal architecture. Students often cite it as their most treasured prize at Dalhousie—so use it.

Weather: You heard it here first: Students do not go to Dal to soak up the rays or enjoy the mild winters. Fact remains that it will rain often and in winter, too. You might think that rain in winter implies a mild climate. Well think again, friend. Rain in Halifax

travels horizontally and is always teamed with a brisk wind that packs a Jack Frost punch. If you think those 30-below days in Montreal were bad, try 5 below and soaking wet. I can guarantee you that the latter is much worse.

Library facilities: Despite its ugliness the Killiam Library is well maintained and offers students all the needed resources. The cataloguing system (known as NovaNet) links the Killiam with other university holdings around Nova Scotia, allowing access to Mount Saint Vincent, Saint Mary's, and other libraries across the province. It is a resourceful and efficient library, but is facing budget cuts which are doing their share to lower the quality.

Alumni: John Crosbie (Former P.C. cabinet minister famous for saying everything wrong or everything right, depending on who you ask); Alexa McDonough (Leader of the federal New Democratic Party); Robert Macneil (journalist); Kathleen Sullivan (NASA astronaut).

Campus safety: Dalhousie is a safe campus and offers several agencies to insure this. The Tiger Patrol is a walk-home service or drive-home service offered to students, and there are alarm posts situated around campus which students can ring for assistance.

worthwhile for gaining work experience and some cash, but can be exhausting and long as students are asked to give up their summers. There are also detrimental consequences if a student cannot find a job. Dal job lists are limited and often students are on their own to find placements. Be forewarned that the absence of a work term could place you alongside those second-year Psych students in the waiting room of academic limbo.

In the Faculty of Arts and Social Sciences, English and Political Science are rumoured to have the best faculties and overall reputations. Both offer impressive instruction and a good variety of classes. Students of either are rarely disap-

pointed. History and Philosophy also have impressive faculties. However, History has become a little watered down and is slowly acquiring a reputation of being a "bird degree." Despite this, the professors are top notch and are among the most interesting found at Dal. In the area of fine arts Dal offers undergraduate degrees in Music, Theatre, Stage Design and a unique degree in Costume Studies.

The highly competitive health professions are well funded and very much alive at Dal. Physiotherapy, Occupational Therapy, Nursing, Pharmacy, and Dental Hygiene are all available as undergraduate degrees, but have very high admission requirements, sometimes exceeding those of medicine.

REZ LIFE Strap on your party booties and numb yourself to animal house culture 'cause rez life at Dal is a socially active one. In many ways, the residences at Dal pick up where fraternities and sororities never really began—providing parties, friendships, and even an identity. Seekers of the stereotypical university experience will not be disappointed and will find plenty of what they are looking for. From spontaneous booze fests, to room pranks, to just loungin' around, residence is all about sociability.

Dalhousie residence is limited, so apply as early as possible. Correctly fill out your forms and pay your deposits on time or you may find yourself searching for accommodations around Halifax, which has about a 1% vacancy rate and is very expensive. If you can, save this enterprise for the following year when you know the city a little better and have the resources to find the gems.

Dalhousie has five residence lifestyles to choose from, with Shireff and Howe Halls being the most predominant. Howe Hall is an H-shaped building divided into four houses (Bronson, Cameron, Henderson, and Smith) which surround the common dining hall. The detached building hubbed in the Howe Hall parking lot is another residence, named Studley House, that is also considered part of Howe, and uses the same dining hall. Bronson, Studley, Henderson, and Smith are all co-ed dorms while Cameron is all-male. Cameron and Henderson have, by far, the biggest rooms compared to those of Smith and Bronson, which are barely livable shoe boxes and are considerable candidates for human rights violations.

The all-female residence known as "Hotel Shireff" is divided into three houses (Newcombe, Old Eddy, and New Eddy), and offers a cleaner, quieter habitation, not to mention special amenities such as a Victorian reading room, water closets, sinks, and better food. However, Shireff tends to be a little more conservative than its Howe counterpart and has stricter conditions, such as mandatory male sign-ins and quiet hours.

The newest of Dal's abodes is Eliza Ritchie, which is a townhouse-like complex consisting primarily of single rooms. Its occupants are mainly from the professional schools. Residents are forced to dine at nearby Shireff, as Eliza does not have a common dining hall.

For braver students, or more accurately, for those left with no other option, there is the concrete disaster-waiting-to-happen known as Fenwick. A massive apartment building complex which is a lengthy 15-minute walk from campus, Fenwick is yet another example of an architectural nightmare. Rumour has it that when the pool, located on the top floor, was filled it sent pressure cracks throughout the building. It turned out that the chief architect forgot to add the weight of water in his calculations—a small mistake that ended up costing him his license. Remember: Understanding the logic behind Dal's modern structures is as futile a practice as having a quick coffee with a Philosophy major.

Glengary apartments, located on Edward Street, are a convenient two blocks from campus. They are perfect for those sleepy-eyed pyjama dwellers who can't seem to make it to those eight o'clock red-eyes. They consist of twelve four-person apartments and four single rooms. Preference is given to senior students and those who apply in groups of four.

NIGHT LIFE Halifax is nothing short of a party town. Rumoured to have the most bars per capita in the country, it is easy to see what Maritimers enjoy the most. There is no lack of drinking dens nor is there a lack of diversity. On campus there are two bars, The Grad House and the Grawood. The former tends to attract an older crowd, mainly students of the post-graduate schools, and is a great place to catch a quick game of pool and a beer between classes. Rarely does the Grad House get wild and out of control, for dwellers of this abode are well into their "Carlsberg

---

A Word to the Wise:

1. Use the Dalplex. The facilities are the best offered east of Montreal. You might as well, seeing as you'll pay for it anyway.

2. Check out Nova Scotia. A super hip province with a ton of things to do.

3. Try and live in residence, especially Howe Hall. It is an experience you will never forget and the best place to meet those life-long contacts.

4. Kiss your TA's behind. Remember it's they who mark your papers and keep in mind that everyone else in your class is applying to Law school too. You'll need all the help you can get.

5. Bring a raincoat. The weather sucks.

years." For something a little wilder, look no further than the Grawood. Located in the basement of the Student Union Building (just follow the trail of puke or passed-out frosh), this is where first-year students do their best to prove that they are finally on their own—free from the chains of Mom and Dad. Thursday is the busiest night and the Grawood is usually packed by 9 p.m., after which long line-ups are sure to be found.

Downtown is by far the best place to drink. Dalhousie is a ten-minute walk from the centre of Halifax and thus plays an integral role in its student culture. After first year, it is likely that you will never see the Grawood again and, instead, the bars of Halifax will become your second home. There is an infinite number of choices in Halifax, and a bar exists to please every preference. There is everything from your standard pubs to meat-market clubs, and everything in between. For quieter beers and some great food, or a great place to start off the night, try Maxwell Plum's or the Thirsty Duck, both English-style pubs. For a truly Haligonian experience, try the Lower Deck or the Split Crow; both feature live maritime folk and guarantee a great time. You leave yearning to be a sailor and proud of your newly-discovered Haligonian roots; both clubs are standard sites for the mom-and-dad-visit tour. For couch lounging, great ambiance and pool, the Speak Easy is unbeatable and, arguably, the most popular bar amongst Dal students. For live music try the Tickle Trunk, where Johnny Favourite and the Swing Kings got their start. Go early for some pre-pints and a game of Risk; the Trunk is unique but fluctuates in popularity. For Jazz, Jazz Fusion or disc spinning the Velvet Olive offers a trendy L.A. feel. Smoke cigars and sip some high balls and feel like you're "money" all night long. To satisfy the liquor pig in everyone, J.J. Rossy's is the trough. With offerings of super cheap, recycled draft and cocktails, it is easy to debauch yourself and boogie to some beats. Try your

pick-up lines here or try and fend them off; Rossy's is the arena of fidelity. For Kim Mitchell look-a-likes and the latest in mesh cap designer wear, the Liquor Dome is your place. A four-bar multiplex which offers laughter and dance under one roof, it is definitely worth a visit, if only once. For late nights, try the Palace, yet another trough open till three a.m. and the den of last chance desperation. Its clientele is the most diverse in Halifax, ranging from those Liquor Dome Kim Mitchell types to university prepsters to b-boy bad asses. It is, nonetheless, a blast that quenches a certain thirst.

ON HALIFAX

History-rich Halifax is the little-big town that offers the excitement of a large city with the charm of small town Canada. As the urban centre of the Maritimes, it is the ambassador of the East Coast, offering its own unique culture. Haligonians are friendly, indulge in quiet civic pride, and happily offer their city to all who choose to come. Despite its size, Halifax offers a large number of festivals, restaurants and things to do. Stroll in the breathtakingly beautiful Point Pleasant Park, take in some history at the old harbour, try your luck on red or black at the Casino, get some shopping done on Spring Garden Road, or lay some flowers and shed a tear for Jack Dawson's *Titanic* grave. While there is plenty to do in Halifax, the entire province of Nova Scotia teems with interesting sites. Rent a car, or make a friend who has access to one, because places like Peggy's Cove and the Cabot Trail are gems not to be missed—not to mention the many undiscovered beaches and villages that dot the province. Overall, Dalhousie is located in an ideal setting for a university environment, a setting that offers excitement without speeding up the pace, sociability without invading solitude, and exploration without homesickness. After leaving, you may find that you subconsciously cite Halifax as your hometown.

University of King's College

By Blair Trudell

If you are looking for a small Canadian version of Oxford or Cambridge, look no further than King's. Nestled in a sovereign corner of Dalhousie's campus it offers all the tradition, pretension, and academic elitism which you seek. Here, laughs come at the expense of Dante, Descartes, or Dostoyevsky. Practice your grovelling "Ha-Has" and your "good fellow" dialogue. They will be much needed at those bi-weekly formal meals, during which students and professors alike rub identically adorned black-robed shoulders, sip some sherry, chow down on several course meals, chit chat with guest dignitaries, and then call it a day. In short, you will either love or hate King's, (the latter coming naturally to any Dal student), so prepare yourself for the best or worst experience of your life. Students can come to King's and either bathe in its aristocratic waters or drown in its rapids.

Founded in 1789 in Windsor, Nova Scotia, by Anglican Loyalists in the wake of the American revolution, King's was the first university to be established in English Canada and is the oldest English-speaking university in the British Commonwealth, outside of the United Kingdom. In 1920, fire destroyed the Windsor location, forcing King's to relocate in Halifax and amalgamate with Dalhousie University. Like a cautious province entering the Confederation, King's sought protection of its identity and amalgamated on the condition that it would never offer the same degrees. Today that identity is stronger than ever and despite its close proximity to its larger neighbour it has become an island unto itself.

Spanning all of two square city blocks, King's campus is quaint but utterly charming. The campus is indeed reflective of King's mentality. As in a walled city, the library, residences, arts building, and chapel surround a common quadrant, which appears to guard the campus from outside intrusion. It is a pattern that certainly symbolizes the vigour with which

King's celebrates its uniqueness. All buildings face inward and entrances are only accessible from within the quadrant. A concrete path may be followed through King's to get to Dalhousie, as if to suggest to commuters that crossing through is acceptable, but staying is not. Its buildings are, to say the least, traditional. Built under Georgian and Anglican influence and constructed of stone, and the buildings ooze an air of history and prestige reminiscent of the Old World. Even the newly constructed library cleverly blends into the campus, testament that King's is and forever will be an institution of tradition.

CAMPUS CULTURE

King's was once described as the "Quebec of Dalhousie." If there is a better description, it remains undiscovered. This analogy still rings true: There will, and always has been, a rivalry between Dal and King's. Ask Dal students and they will tell you that King's students are pretentious and snobby. Ask King's students about Dal and they will tell you that Dal students are peasants—inferior beings whose jealousy of King's drives their resentment. The rivalry is a constant presence within both student cultures and exists more in fun than anything else. Don't expect it to come to blows in a bar or unfold into campus chaos. The truth is, social circles of Halifax overlap too much for this to occur, and chances are that no matter which university citizenship you choose, you're both from Toronto anyway and went to the same summer camp.

If it's cultural diversity you are looking for, choose U of T, because King's is whiter than Santa's beard. This aside, King's encompasses astoundingly diverse ideologies. King's is a place where left-leaning activists,

Vital Statistics

Address: 6350 Coburg Road, Halifax, Nova Scotia, B3H 2A1

Admissions office: (902) 422-1271

Website: www.ukings.ns.ca

Total enrollment: 862

Male-female ratio: 43 to 58

Average entering grades: Arts: 81%; Science: 86%

Tuition fees: $4,131–$5,291

Residence fees: $4,885–$5,250 (including meals).

Percentage of students in residence: 31%

Percentage of international students: 1%

Percentage of out-of-province students: 48%

Financial aid: Undergraduate entrance scholarships from $1,000–$6,000 available based on marks and essay submission. Approximately 15% of student body receive scholarships. Dr Carrie-Best award is open to competing applicants of Afro-Canadian or Aboriginal origin. Bursaries are also awarded to students at the end of the academic year according to demonstrable need. Bursaries are also given to exceptional students who carry a Canadian student loan at the end of graduation.

Co-op programs: Available internships in journalism, co-op programs at Dal: BioChemistry, Chemistry, Computer Science, Earth Sciences, Marine Biology, Mathematics, Physics, Statistics.

Services for students with disabilities: King's Library is fully accessible. Other buildings are poorly facilitated because of their age.

Aboriginal students: Aboriginal applicants are given priority. Aboriginal student services available at Dalhousie. Dr. Carrie-Best Award open to aboriginal students.

Student services: King's does have its own student union, newspaper, academic advisors, and chaplaincy. Other services are provided by Dalhousie University and used by King's students.

social anarchists, and deficit-debt obsessed, right-wingers peacefully co-exist within the comfortable confines of their liberal arts dwelling. There is something to be said in this. Whereas the most diverse schools such as U of T offer a multicultural mosaic, King's guarantees a multi-ideological stew.

Because of its small size and limited ethnic presence, King's features few culturally based societies. Its most notable is that of the school medium, the *Watch*, a clever and brilliantly written campus paper which is lacking in hard news but undeniably entertaining. It gets interesting when the *Watch* and the *Gazette* (Dal's paper), square off in literary battle, initiating bleak murmurs of school spirit and a multitude of laughs. The King's theatrical society is another distinguished society which produces plays and other events throughout the year. The plays are always well received and impressive. Even Dal students have been known to cross the border in order to share in the mutual appreciation of the productions (after denying to friends that they ever really attended). Despite the limited number of students, King's wins the prize for the most unique clubs. The clubs and societies stay well within the cultural sphere, which is to say that they are intellectually based. The Haliburton, for example, is a very old literary club where students gather to read and discuss their favourite works and even some of their own. There is also a humour-packed

night dedicated to bad literature. Outside the sphere of intellectually based clubs and societies, King's does have several more socially conscious clubs—the KWAC (King's Women's Action Committee) and the King's Environmental Group to name a couple.

King's students tend to be a lot more patriotic towards their school than the apathetic Dal students. Although most students attend King's for only one year, they will continually state King's as their place of origin. Thus, there is a strong bond and lots of cash from alumni rolling in. Overall, King's is definitely not for everyone. It is a unique abode in which academia, prestige, and aristocracy rule. Those people uninterested in these terms need not apply.

ACADEMIC ISSUES

Despite its pretentiousness, King's offers one of the best and most challenging first year liberal arts programs in Canada. FYP (Foundation Year Program) amasses a giant reading list of classic to contemporary literature from politics to poetry and everything in between. Consisting of six sectioned epochs, FYP starts in the ancient world with Homer and runs through the Middle Ages into the Renaissance and Reformation. It continues through the Age of Reason, and the era of revolutions and finally lands in the contemporary world. The program is not easy, but definitely rewarding. Often, it is King's

In a Nut Shell

The university in a phrase: "It's a lot like a Monty Python skit: frightfully British, and unlike anything you've seen, full of intriguing and absurd characters. You either really like it or fail to understand what all the fuss is about."

Best thing about the university: FYP and the close-knit community—one big happy family.

Worst thing about the university: The close knit-community. There are no secrets in this family.

Favourite professors: Dr. Crouse (Classics, Dante); Dr Kierans (FYP director); Margaret Daly and Eugene Meese (Journalism).

Most popular bird courses: Rough Justice 2221 and 2222. The study of Canadian pop culture from movies to drugs to the history of those women your mother warned you about. Great profs, great laughs, great fun (make a point of asking about the course title's significance, it could be an essay question—no joke). History 2335 Modern American Culture. Along the same lines as Rough Justice but a thorough unit on game shows.

Hot spots to study on campus: Main level of the King's Library where quiet conversation occurs, or, if you really don't want to get anything done, the basement of the Arts and Administration is the place to accomplish such ends.

Quietest spot to study on campus: In the bowels of the beautiful King's Library.

Need for car and parking availability: A car is a privilege and can be an advantage for those weekend escapes but it is definitely not a necessity. Parking is available at Dal or at King's for about $100 a year and escalating. Parking can be a nightmare during daytime as more parking passes are issued than spots are available.

Sexually speaking: Yes, it happens, but not without everyone finding out. Many ladies and gents are caught in the early morning "walk of shame." It takes super-stealthy slick-like-a-puma methods to keep your affairs private. Homosexual love is accepted but not private. Remember, there is a semi-voyeurish aspect that exists in such a small school. Shyer gays can find more anonymity at Dal in BGLAD (Bi-sexual, Gay and Lesbian association at Dal). This always has a significant King's contingent.

Fraternities/sororities: King's is a fraternity.

Athletic facilities: King's does have its own gymnasium and some sports teams. Otherwise the facilities at Dal (Dalplex) are open to King's students and are top-notch.

Library facilities: The King's Library is stunning and has the feel of a museum complete with artifacts and knick-knacks of interest encased behind glass. However, the resources of the library are also rather museum-like and are geared towards FYP. For more modern resources it's off to Dal you'll go.

Computer facilities: For the most part, the computers available at King's are reserved for the journalism students. However, at times, it is possible to slip in unnoticed to use the facilities. Your best bet is to use the computer facilities at Dalhousie in the basement of the Killiam Library or in the Commerce building.

Weather: A meteorologist's wet dream. Walk down the street and it's possible to be exposed to a complete cross-section of weather in just one day. It is, to say the least, sporadic and irregular: Snow one minute, hail the next, sunny skies and then on to visiting hurricanes.

Safety on campus: The Dal Tiger Patrol offers on-campus alarms as well as walk-home programs and roaming patrols. Altogether, a very safe campus.

Alumni: Charles G. D. Roberts, Rowland C. Frazee, Roland Ritchie.

alumni who walk away with the majority of awards at the convocation ceremonies at Dalhousie. The program is equivalent to four first-year credits at Dalhousie, and thus King's students must attend one first year Dal class (usually the language requirement). The program is perfect for those lost high school graduates who don't have a clue what to study. It offers students a chance to dabble in a little of everything while arming them with an eclectic background. Another benefit of King's is the quality of its lectures and professors. Lectures tie in art and music with literary works, so don't be surprised if one day you walk by and hear Wagner's *Ring of Fire* blasting from the lecture hall. It's all part of the King's experience; no corners are cut in the shaping of the young intelligentsia. And, as with any great lecture, a great professor is never far behind. King's offers some of the most knowledgeable professors in the field. Rumour has it that Dr. Crouse, the esteemed authority on Dante, is advisory to none other than the Pope. Needless to say, the professors can be a little intimidating. This is something that you will quickly have to overcome due to the two sets of oral examinations at Christmas and at the end of the year. Furthermore, getting an A on a paper is no small task. There is a hierarchy of meetings and reviews which precede such an honour. Remember: The key word to understanding King's is pretentious.

After first year, the majority of King's students say their farewells and then it's off to Dalhousie. For those who just can't get enough, however, King's offers a degree in contemporary studies, an extension of the FYP program which is "officially" open to Dal students, though not necessarily welcoming of them. Once again, this is a challenging program and carries with it all the academic trappings and tradition of the King's mentality. It creates nonetheless an interesting experience for curious Dal students who wish to see the inner workings of their estranged neighbour.

King's also offers a Bachelor of Journalism program for which completion of FYP is a requirement. Though the program is not accepted as a post-graduate equivalent, it is designed for those students who wish to enter the media immediately after graduation. King's also offers a post-graduate degree in journalism, which is both highly competitive and intensive. The good news is that it only takes one year, but be prepared to eat, sleep and sh...well, you know—journalism.

REZ LIFE

All of King's residences are dorm-style but don't think you will be roughing it like those other unfortunates at say...Dalhousie. The accommodations at King's are luxurious and spacious by general residence standards. There is adequate privacy, even in the double rooms which have a door separating the two entities. If you get along with your roommate, then one of the two rooms almost inevitably becomes a lounge, and if you can't stand your roomie, well, just shut the door and ignore each other. Remarkably, King's residences come equipped with maids. Yes, that's right. Maids. So don't worry about dirty linens or the ball of clothes in the corner—all will be taken care of. You must rest that mind of yours and avoid such silly, all-consuming projects such as cleaning your room.

There are three residences at King's. Alexandra Hall is all female and is often referred to as "the Nunnery." The student union handbook went as far as describing it as "a modern day chastity belt." There are rules against the male presence, such as curfews and sign-ins. Across from Alexandra Hall is the all-male residence called The Bays. The Bays is divided into four wings: Chapel, Middle, Radical, and North Pole (no they do not assume political beliefs). These digs are less conservative and less posh than those of Alex Hall and are often cited as being the most fun to live in.

Cochran Bay is the third residence and is co-ed. It is con-

sidered a place of privilege and reserved for upper-year students and those with good academic standing. It is less conservative than "the Nunnery" and operates on the same rules as the male residences.

For off-campus housing, all of the Dalhousie residences are available. King's students rarely have a problem getting into residence and thus, this is generally a last resort. For second year students and others wishing to leave the King's dwellings, you are left to your own devices. The Housing services at Dalhousie are available but, more often than not, useless. You will quickly discover the fierce competition that exists in Halifax for student housing. Sorry to say, but it's all in the connections. Keep your eyes and ears open; any information in this regard will be of use. Most likely, you will follow your elders and end up on Larch street, a mini-King's student ghetto and FYP alumni refuge.

NIGHT LIFE

Far and away the most popular social spot for all King's students is the Wardroom. Located on campus in the basement of the arts building, always smoky and packed, the Wardroom is the starting place to be on Thursday and week-end nights. Closely resembling your buddie's basement during high school, the Wardroom is just the place to gather and drink. Adorned with tacky, base furniture and flimsy card tables, there is nothing prestigious or pretentious about this place (except of course, the requirement of a King's student ID card for entrance). Dal students are allowed entrance only with a signature from a King's student—easily obtained and thus, many Dal students choose this establishment over the Grawood if only for the economical draft.

After this initial debauching, it's off to downtown Halifax or a bash on Larch street. King's students prefer the popular pool lounge, the Speakeasy, on Monday nights, and also flock to the Velvet Olive and the Blues Corner for live music. Halifax is by no means limited in its drinking facilities; in fact they are one of the few economic inputs of the Maritimes that refuse to dwindle. From breweries to bars, Halifax has it covered. Take advantage of the brewery tours offered by Keith's and Moosehead. Don't expect to learn about the fine art of brewing and the selection of hops; the only thing you will learn more about is how to drink harder, cheaper, and within a certain time limit. After this experience, it is most likely that the only tanks you will remember seeing are the ones provided by the Halifax Police Department.

Mount Saint Vincent University

By Christine Ibarra

Hundreds of radical feminists and nuns at every turn—this is the myth of the Mount. Yes, Mount Saint Vincent University, founded in 1873, declares itself an institution that is "committed primarily to the education of women." And yes, it attracts a lot of feminists. But no one burns her bra here and most of the Sisters of Charity—the nuns, who, at one time, ran the joint—keep mostly to themselves in the mother-house.

So what is MSVU all about? The first thing you should know is that the Mount has an out of whack female to male ratio of students: 85 to 15. That's right. Of the 3,500 students who attend the Mount each year, at most 500 are male (for the women this does indeed mean that the between-class washroom line-ups are a killer). Originally the school was created by nuns who wanted to provide a place for women to receive a strong post-secondary education. Today, the university continues this tradition of devoting itself to the educational needs of women. "The fact that it's a school for females is great," says a first-year Women's Studies major. "I feel like a first-class citizen here."

Because of its small size, however, and the orientation toward women, the Mount has not always received the respect it deserves. Students at larger Halifax universities like Saint Mary's and Dalhousie claim the Mount isn't a "real" university. "We've been dubbed a girl's school, Pill Hill, and a lesbian's paradise," laments one undergrad. "Just because it's mostly women here, the school keeps getting dumped on," says a philosophy student. "But the Mount is just as good as Dal, SMU, or King's. In fact, it's probably even better."

The Mount is one of Canada's most innovative universities, noted for its unique programs, including Tourism and Hospitality, Child Studies, and Public Relations.

Unlike other universities in Halifax, the Mount, located in suburban Halifax, is not in the centre of the city. A direct bus line downtown does pass the university's main building, but even still, students with their own modes of transportation are well loved. On the up side, the campus, which has lots of trees, is by far the prettiest in town. Located on a hillside overlooking the Bedford Basin, the university makes it hard to keep your eyes off of the ocean.

ACADEMIC ISSUES

In essence, Mount Saint Vincent is a women's university. It offers an academic experience from a woman's perspective. Unquestionably, this has had an effect on the level of achievement of female students at the Mount, particularly those in the university's science program. MSVU also attracts students for its innovative and atypical course offerings. Not only does the Mount have a strong program in Liberal Arts and Science, but it also teaches Business Administration, Child and Youth Studies, Human Ecology, Public Relations, Tourism and Hospitality Management, and of course, Women's Studies.

Students in Business Administration, Dietetics, Human Ecology, Information Management, Public Relations, and Tourism and Hospitality Management have the option to enter a co-op program. "It's an amazing experience," says one public relations co-op student. "In one work term, I learned more than I'll probably learn in four years of sitting in a classroom." Take advantage of this opportunity to earn while you learn.

MSVU boasts small classes so it is much easier to get acquainted with professors and other students. There are times, however, when you may wish that the prof didn't know you quite so well— such as when you're skipping classes.

CAMPUS CULTURE

Although MSVU scores high in the category of campus aesthetics and beauty, it barely gets a passing grade for excitement. This university is not Party Central. Students at MSVU are wide-ranging in age and maturity. Two-thirds of the student body are mature students (24 and up) with real life experience. These students are generally aiming to upgrade and re-enter the work force, and more than half of the students (close to 1,500 out of 3,500) are part-

Vital Statistics

Address: 166 Bedford Highway, Halifax, Nova Scotia, B3M 2J6

Admissions office: (902) 457-6128

Website: www.msvu.ca

Total enrollment: 3,500

Male-female ratio: 15 to 85

Average entrance grades: Arts: 65%; Science: 74%; Commerce: 69%

Tuition fees: $3,725 (ancillary fees $311–$346)

Residence fees: $4,445–$5,035 (room and board)

Number of spaces in residence: 242

Percentage of out-of-province first-year students: 16%

Financial aid: Entrance and in-course awards ranging from $50-$3,000 per year and bursaries. The Mount also offers a "Tuition-Driven Bursary" plan with awards based on documented need for which any registered student may apply annually. Short-term emergency loan program and Student Employment Bursary Program are also available.

Co-op programs: Business Administration, Dietetics, Human Ecology, Information Management, Public Relations, and Tourism and Hospitality Management

Services for students with disabilities: Students with special needs should consult the Dean of Student Affairs and Counselling Services.

Student services: Academic, career and personal counselling, career placement centre, chaplaincy, childcare centre, health office, writing resource centre.

time. More often than not, these people have off-campus commitments and thus don't have the time to get heavily involved with the face-painting shenanigans of university life.

These "non-traditional" students come to Mount Saint Vincent for many reasons. One says she enrolled at the Mount because of its child-care facilities, another says she chose the university for its Sixty-Plus Program (free classes for persons 60 years old and up). Also, because of the unusual spectrum of studies, many defensive students (particularly male) can be heard to say, "I'm just here for the program."

A lot of students come fresh out of high school. Many of these students choose Mount Saint Vincent because of its small size and intimate atmosphere. Because of its smaller campus, students sometimes feel a high-school-like claustrophobia, but overall, MSVU offers a relaxed and laid back atmosphere.

The one thing to note about Mount Saint Vincent's general atmosphere is that it is most definitely a university of cliques. The students rarely mix and mingle outside of their circles. The most notable cliques on campus are the athletes, the P.R. (public relations) students, the mature students, and the student council members.

Rosaria is the closest thing MSVU students have to a Student Union Building. It houses the bookstore, games room, student council offices, the dining room, Corner Store, and best of all, Vinnie's Pub. Thursday nights at Vinnie's Pub is the only event (other than convocation) where members of the different groups come together. Don't miss the beach parties and pub nights sponsored by the Athletics and Recreation Society.

MSVU offers a bite-sized sample of different clubs and activities to join, from the International Students Society, Business Society, and Tourism Society, to things like the Outdoor Club and *The Picaro* student newspaper. The MSVU athletics department offers intramural and competitive sports for women and men. You can choose from women's and men's basketball and badminton to women's soccer and women's volleyball to name a few.

REZ LIFE The Mount offers two different residence lifestyles. Wait! Before you read on, to quell rumours that there is an alcohol ban in rez—the alcohol ban has been lifted. Now that your worst nightmare is over, drum roll please. Behind door number one, Assisi Hall, a 12-storey co-ed high rise with mostly single rooms. This traditional style residence comes with 142 spaces, a comfy lounge, and kitchen and laundry facilities. Don't let the fact that there's a kitchen fool you—you still have to buy a meal plan. Don't worry though, the food's not that bad. Just don't be afraid to dig in and try the mystery meat.

Behind door number two, The Birches co-ed townhouses. There are five townhouses and space for 20 students per townhouse in single rooms. Students at the Birches sometimes feel like they're living in an episode of *Friends*. Complete with kitchen facilities, lounge, and laundry, students at the Birches must also buy a meal plan—except if you live in one of the Birches townhouses reserved for International and Mature Students. These lucky ducks are excluded from having to buy a meal plan. Speaking of ducks, The Birches are built around a natural pond where families of ducks and goldfish make their home. And, as you may have guessed, the townhouses are surrounded by a grove of birch trees.

If either of these living arrangements sounds like it may be for you, beware that residence space is assigned on a first-come, first-served basis, so apply early.

In a Nut Shell

The university in a phrase: The only university in Canada devoted to teaching women, MSVU offers its students a rare educational experience.

Best thing about the university: Small classes and personal attention from profs.

Worst thing about the university: The animosity between groups. Cliques don't tend to mix and mingle.

Favourite professors: P. Beaudette (Religious studies); T. Glanville (Nutrition); R. Warne (Religious Studies); J. Young (Business and Tourism).

Most popular bird courses: Computer 150 is a no brainer.

Hot spots to study on campus: Rosaria Centre; Sacateria (Seton Academic Centre's cafeteria).

Quietest spots to study on campus: The study carrels in the library. Around exam time, however, procrastinators come out of the woodwork and the library becomes more of a social hangout.

Need for car and parking availability: It's hard to find parking during peak hours.

Sexually speaking: Sex is not openly discussed on campus.

Fraternities/sororities: Take a guess. This is a campus with strong feminist sympathies.

Athletic facilities: Gym, dance/exercise studio, saunas, weight and conditioning centre, fitness classes.

Library facilities: If you can't find what you're looking for here, use the Novanet to access the holdings of all the libraries in Nova Scotia. You'll be able to find out who has what book— from the University of Cape Breton College to Dalhousie University.

Computer facilities: Several computer labs across campus. Students have access to Internet and Novanet.

Weather: Cold and wet. Whether it's precipitation in the form of rain or snow, Halifax can get pretty bad storms. Bring a parka, bring a good pair of waterproof boots, bring an umbrella, wear layers, and bundle up.

Safety on campus: A walking service escorts any student after dark across campus or to a bus stop.

Alumni: Dr. Nuala Kenny, director of Bioethics Education and Research at Dalhousie University; Elizabeth Roscoe, first woman justice of the Nova Scotia Supreme Court's appeal division; Dorothy Wills, founding member of the National Black Coalition of Canada; Joanne Thomas Yaccato, author.

NIGHT LIFE Halifax is a party town. In fact, it's rumoured to have the most bars per capita in Canada. On campus, it's the infamous Thursday night pub nights at Vinnie's Pub. This evening even attracts students (mostly male) from Saint Mary's and Dalhousie. As the night progresses, liquid courage levels increase and people start to pack the dance floor. If you've never felt what it feels like to be a sardine, you'll soon find out here. Vinnie's can also get pretty hot—so be prepared to sweat. For more elbow room, but an equally happening scene just the same, check out Merrill's CafT and Lounge.

Downtown there is everything from your standard pub to beer drenched abodes and everything in between. You can always start off the night at places like Maxwell Plum's or the Thirsty Duck, both English-style pubs with good food and a nice relaxed atmosphere. For live music try the New Palace. For a truly Haligonian experience (and for more of the male persuasion), try the Lower Deck or the Split Crow. Both feature live Maritime folk and guarantee a great time.

ON HALIFAX Halifax is a wonderful little town that offers not only the charm of an east coast village, but as the urban centre of the Maritimes, it also offers bigger city attractions. It is a city that is also rich with history so there are lots of places to see and visit that will give you a larger sense of Canada's history. The native Haligonians are extremely friendly people and are always happy to open their town to university students and their families alike. There are lots of festivals, like the annual Mardi Gras festival where everyone dresses up in costumes, drinks copiously, and marches up and down the streets. There are also great restaurants and lots of things to do. There is the beautiful Point Pleasant Park that ends up right on the ocean. There's a casino, if you're interested in squandering whatever little pocket money you may have, and there's even a *Titanic* gravesite. In addition to Halifax, there are lots of beautiful places to visit in greater Nova Scotia, like Peggy's Cove and the Cabot Trail.

A Word to the Wise:

1. Profs make a point of remembering your name— and remembering when you skip their lecture.

2. The Mount is a small campus. You'll be amazed at how fast bad news (a.k.a. gossip) travels. Watch out.

St. Francis Xavier University

By Tyler Hellard

Founded in 1853 (relocated to Antigonish in 1855), St. Francis Xavier University has had many reputations in its long history. It has been viewed as a haven for devoted Catholics, a school for bagpipers and highland dancers, and a school for boozehounds. How one university could develop such varied stereotypes is unknown, but it is clear that all three groups and more have their presence at St. F.X.

St. F.X. has its religious ties, to be certain. But your average student is a far call from a regular Charlie Church. St. F.X. has been successful in maintaining a religious atmosphere for those seeking such things, while being a place to avoid church on Sunday for those who don't. With its location in Antigonish, annual host to the Highland Games, there is a strong Celtic presence, but again only if you're looking for it. And of course, St. F.X. has long been known as a school where the students drink themselves into a stupor five or six nights a week and party until dawn. This fact, like the others, can't be denied.

Antigonish is the last stop before Cape Breton (and the last chance to turn around). The St. F.X. campus has grown modestly over the years and has seen few major changes in the last 20 or so years. The residences were originally built when St. F.X. had half the student population it does today, but times are finally changing on campus. The University is investing $52 million in major renovations, including the removal of the physical plant and its smokestack, located almost exactly in the centre of campus. Trees once ripped from the ground on account of Dutch Elm's Disease are being replanted, and in ten years, the nice but worn-down campus will be one of the most beautiful in the country. In the mean time, there's a lot of construction to capture your attention.

The buildings at St. F.X. vary greatly. Nicholson Hall, currently home to most Arts and Business classes, was state-of-the-art when it was built back in the 1970s. Unfortunately, state-of-the-art in the 70s didn't include windows and no classroom has one. The Annex, a hold-over from St. F.X. of many, many years ago, looks more like a refurbished elementary school, complete with men's urinals that are not quite high enough. Bloomfield Centre, home of the Students' Union (St. F.X. having one of the few SUs that don't actually own their own building), is sliding down the hill. It was built at a pace that should leave it in a heap at the bottom of the hill in about 50 years. But these problems are things students learn to cope with, and they are small prices to pay for the general beauty of the St. F.X. campus. The campus has some outstandingly gorgeous architecture, most notably on lower campus (Morrison, MacKinnon, and Cameron Halls), a lot of grass to walk on and, most conveniently, buildings that are close together for those who don't get out of bed until five minutes before class.

CAMPUS CULTURE

St. F.X. has a little bit of culture for everyone. The Coady International Institute brings many foreign students to St. F.X. every year, and other students are encouraged to get to know and interact with them and share in each other's cultures. The campus also boasts its own art gallery. The gallery brings in a variety of exhibits throughout the year, including the St. F.X. Student Art Show as a traditional end to the academic year. Several art classes are taught at St. F.X. and students are urged to prepare work to be showcased.

St. F.X. has the disadvantage of not being in an urban cen-

Vital Statistics

Address: P.O. Box 5000, Station Main, Antigonish, Nova Scotia, B2G 2W5

Admissions office: (902) 867-2219

Website: www.stfx.ca

Total enrollment: 4,100

Male-female ratio: 44 to 56

Percentage of international students: 4.9%

Percentage of out-of-province students: 27.7% (14.0% other Atlantic provinces)

Average entrance grades: Arts: 70%; Science: 70%; Commerce: 70%; Engineering: 70%

Tuition fees: $3,965

Residence fees: $4,835–$5,395 (double room with meal plan); $4,440 (apartment-double)

Percentage of students in residence: 30% (approx.); 1,300 residence spaces

Financial aid: $625,000 is available in entrance scholarships or in-class bursaries. Approximately 20% of the student body have received assistance in the form of a scholarship, award, or bursary. 100 students receive scholarships directly out of high school. In addition St. F.X. employs over 750 students with part-time jobs.

Internships: Aquatic Resources, Education, Nursing, Service Learning.

Aboriginal students: Aboriginal Student Advisor; Aboriginal Student Lounge.

Services for students with disabilities: Very limited and poorly facilitated. Many of the buildings are not wheelchair accessible. St. F.X. does have a counsellor designated to assist students with disabilities and there are flexible room assignments as well as wheelchair-friendly washrooms located across campus.

Student services: Academic and career counselling, social counselling, chaplaincy, childcare, employment services for graduates, health services, international student advisor, writing centre.

---

tre, but at least good music is never hard to find. St. F.X., well known for its music program, often has students playing all over Antigonish in various genres. The Orient Lounge (a.k.a. the Dirty "O") provides frequent jazz shows throughout the academic year. Pat's Place, another local bar, has bands weekly, both from St. F.X. and elsewhere. The Students' Union also brings in big name bands to play St. F.X. Super Subs. Recent years have seen bands like Big Sugar, I Mother Earth, Matthew Good, Great Big Sea, the Watchmen and many more play the Mackay Room in the Student Union Building. The campus bar, the Golden "X" Inn, also brings in great Canadian music like Signal Hill, Weeping Tile, and the Killjoys for bar shows. The campus radio station CFXU holds its annual Adventure in Playland festival shortly after the Christmas break. The two-day event sees some of the Maritimes most talented indie bands and DJs crank out tunes. This event is entering its fourth year and is continuously drawing in bigger crowds. St. F.X. also has many societies to join, in a multitude of areas. It is a guarantee that there is something on campus for everyone. In the end, all of these diverse students have one thing in common—a really cool ring.

ACADEMIC ISSUES

St. F.X. is a well-known undergraduate school for academics. Science students and faculty frequently win awards and grants. The school is introducing a new St. F.X. School of Business and Information Systems to boost the profile of the already excellent, yet under-rated Business and IS programs. The Arts Faculty at St.

F.X. is distinguished in almost all fields including English, Sociology, Philosophy, Political Science, and Women's Issues. St. F.X. is also noted for its Aquatic Resources, Nursing, and Music programs. St. F.X. is one of the few schools that doesn't offer a student their GPA. Nobody seems to know why; it just happens that way.

If there are any academic issues that need addressing at St. F.X., students are given the opportunity to make them known. Each year the administration and faculty hold the Speak Out Forum, a place for all students to voice their concerns directly to the powers-that-be, and get an answer. The president of the university, the deans, and many more people, including a number of professors voicing their own academic concerns to the administration, are present.

St. F.X. has always been a school where the value of personal attention isn't ignored. Most professors make themselves readily available to students to help them get the most out of their academic opportunities. Department heads, the deans and individual professors are also readily available for academic counselling.

Among the many achievements you can aim for at St. F.X. is the X-ring. This is something that is truly achieved, but there's more to the X-ring than a "not-too-shabby" finger decoration. While at other schools a degree and a ring represent the fact that a person went head to head academically and survived, the X-ring means a little more. A person with an X-ring went head to head while drinking "upside-down margarita shots" and succeeded. A noteworthy accomplishment without a doubt.

In a Nut Shell

The university in a phrase: If you think that it was raw politics that led Brian Mulroney to his indulgence in cronyism, think again. It was all groundwork laid by St. F.X., Canada's old boys' university.

Best thing about the university: "The Ring."

Worst thing about the university: Slow moving administration.

Favourite professors: Gary Brooks (Psychology); Charlie Gallant (Women's Studies); Barry Wright (Business Administration); Grant Milman (Biology).

Most popular bird courses: English 201—Narrative in Fiction and Film; Geology 170—Understanding the Earth.

Hot spot to study on campus: Sorry to say but it is the library.

Quietest spot to study on campus: Any classroom in Nicholson Hall, the Oland Centre or Bruce Brown.

Need for car and parking availability: Having a car is not necessary in Antigonish. Everything is easily accessible via the shoelace express. A car is an advantage, however, if you want to escape the little town atmosphere and explore "Canada's Ocean Playground" a little. Parking availability is quite limited on campus.

Sexually speaking: St. F.X. is all about "mature love." Many are hitched or not interested in those very short-term relationships after first year. Since Antigonish is a small town and St. F.X. is a school founded on Catholic values, it's not exactly a hotbed for those alternative lifestyles. Several students tried to form a gay, lesbian, and bi society but it was not ratified by the university.

Fraternities/sororities: St. F.X is a fraternity.

Athletic facilities: The Recreation and Athletic Centre has seven squash courts, two gyms, a full-size fitness room, an elevated track, a 25-metre pool, a dance room, and ping-pong tables. The Hockey Arena is on its last legs, however, but what's hockey if it's not played in an old barn?

Library facilities: Most students feel that the Library provides efficient resources and, thanks to Novanet, this is finally true. Because Novanet links allow access to all university libraries in Nova Scotia, students no longer have to make weekend trips to Halifax for badly needed resources.

Computer facilities: There are nine computer labs and over 300 PCs across campus. The unique WebFX program combines cutting edge technology with innovative teaching. Every student and prof get a web account; 24-hour access to e-mail and the latest software, course materials, as well as Internet, are available.

Safety on campus: The small town atmosphere and Catholic roots insure a safe campus. The Student Union offers a walk-safe program which escorts people home at night.

Weather: Wet, windy, and often uncomfortable. The Maritimes is…well, the Maritimes. Bring a yellow full-body raincoat.

Alumni: Brian Mulroney (former prime minister), Frank McKenna (former premier of New Brunswick), Larkin Kerwin (former president of the Canadian Space Agency).

REZ LIFE

Insanity is key in St. F.X. residence living. Students entering a community-living atmosphere for the first time tend to go through a bit of a culture shock. Sure, *Animal House* was an exaggerated view of rez living, but not by much. Toga parties are more than annual, and many students often find themselves nursing a hangover instead of attending class on Fridays. (Note to Arts and Business students—you can actually avoid taking classes on Friday in your second, third and even fourth year if you work your schedule properly; Science students—you will be loaded with early morning classes). At St. F.X., in-house orientation (just a replacement term for "initiation," which was scrapped by the university years ago) can be delightful at times, and delightfully disgusting at others. You may be at St. F.X. for all of six minutes before someone calls you a "stupid freshman" (a term that will stick for the duration of your freshman year).

St. F.X., being a very traditional institution, has initiation rituals that have been a part of the school for more years than people would care to count. MacIsaac will wallop you on the keister with a large whale bone right before you sign it, thus adding to its long legacy; MacNeil has its now 30+ year old "Walk of Life" (renamed from the "Walk of Fate" when Dire Straits released the song "Walk of Life," which every MacNeil Marauder will hear more times than his sanity can bear), and of course there's Fraser and their sheep. What is done to the sheep in initiation into Fraser cannot be published in good conscience so you'll have to find out for yourself (but don't worry, they stopped using a real sheep a while ago).

Rez life is also a time of intense house rivalries. The most noted is the fiercely contested, and often amusing, rivalry between MacIsaac and Burke. This is topped off by February's annual BurMac hockey game, an event that has a whole weekend built around it (and an event that was once listed in David

A Word to the Wise:

1. Get your finger fitted for that glorious ring.

2. Bring some formal attire for the Christmas ball. Students often forget to do so.

3. Take advantage of the used book sale offered by the Student Union.

4. Prepare yourself for the first snowfall. Keep your head up; students partake in a full-scale snowball brawl.

Letterman's Top 10 University Parties in North America). People come from all over and the campus size nearly triples (though in recent years, the university administration has taken steps to put the kibosh on all the fun; for the most part, it has been unsuccessful). BurMac is more than just a game between house rivals and their residents. The whole campus takes part in this drinking binge and lives it up in true St. F.X. style. As a result, the local liquor store keeps an extra person on hand for the entire weekend specifically to restock the beer fridge and prevent the supply of Keith's (or Vitamin "K" as it is affectionately called), from running out.

Residence is full of surprises. Ever boogie-boarded down a hallway on two inches of soap and water? It has happened and will no doubt happen again at St. F.X. But mainly residence is where you meet, greet, and develop friendships that will last a lifetime. Even if you're being covered in god-knows-what and are being publicly humiliated during initiation, you do it as a group. If that doesn't promote closeness, nothing will. As cheesy as it sounds, there really does exist an X-Family (and it has absolutely nothing to do with super heros who have mutant powers—although that would be cool, too). X-Spirit is strong and people take great pride in the fact that they go to, or graduated from, St. F.X. A known fact is that a higher percentage of St. F.X. graduates marry other graduates, compared to any other Canadian university. Alumni return year after year to regale each other with stories of their times past at St. F.X. No one can deny that the X-Spirit is something that sticks.

The X-ring can certainly be a deciding factor when choosing a university. Let's face it, for the most part people's university experience will be similar, no matter where they go, but at St. F.X. you get the famous X-ring. This ring has even seen fame as part of a question on Jeopardy (placing third behind the Superbowl and the Pope's ring as most recognizable finger trinkets).

Residence life is the foundation for this family. It's where the majority of people in the X-Family started. Not only that but the year(s) you spend in residence are, more often than not, some of the most memorable of your life.

NIGHT LIFE Being located in a small town handicaps St. F.X., and the nightlife can often be predictable. The big nights are Thursdays and Saturdays, with a minor night on Friday. People can usually be found starting at the Golden "X" Inn and moving on to the Piper's Pub (the local meat market) between midnight and 1:00 a.m. But there are more options than that. If live music is your thing, then Pat's Place is the place to be on Friday nights. Once in a while, Chuggles puts on a special night and many students can be found "getting jiggy" there. To compensate for the lack of drinking establishments, house parties and pub crawls to Halifax along with other drinking festivities are a more than common thing. If you aren't up for boozing and dancing, you may be out of luck. Antigonish is desperately lacking in entertaining things to do (which is why boogie-boarding in residence is such a frequent thing). The town has one decent movie store, with a few not-so-decent ones in case your late charges are more than you can afford. If that wasn't bad enough, there's only one movie theatre with one screen (and movies like *Titanic* tend to occupy it for months on end). The university does have Sunday and Wednesday movie nights that show movies newly released on video on the big screen in Nicholson Hall (and the sound quality is much better than the theatre). Other than that, Antigonish offers a bowling alley. End of list. Being creative when coming up with something to do (or having a strange bowling fetish) may be what saves your sanity.

ON ANTIGONISH Antigonish, Nova Scotia, is a small town with a long history. It's called Antigo "nowhere" for two reasons: 1) It is not located near anything and thus can be defined as nowhere, and, 2) people who come to Antigonish want to go nowhere else. The Antigonish RCMP is one of the last in Canada that nobody has ever requested to be transferred away from. The town prides itself on its cultural heritage, and bagpipers, fiddlers, and highland dancers are common. Antigonish also plays host to the annual Highland Games—established over 160 years ago, the longest consecutive running event in North America.

Saint Mary's University

By Ayesha Adhami and Colin MacMillan

Saint Mary's—the jock university. The image that usually comes to mind is a bunch of football players going to class in Spandex and shoulder pads, sitting on long benches and being taught by wrinkly guys in baseball caps with whistles around their necks. Lots of sweat, grunts, and Gatorade. But wait, there's a lot more to this school. Saint Mary's University (SMU)—located minutes away from the soothing sounds of downtown Halifax—is loved for its excellence as a business school and for its small, closely-knit community. "It's not like Dal where you're just a number in a huge class. It's not like Mount Saint Vincent either, where you get the impression that nobody's going to talk to you if you're not a brilliant radical feminist," says one Arts major. "SMU is very...down to earth."

Saint Mary's started out in 1802 as a Roman Catholic men's college aiming to provide an opportunity for higher learning to the young men of Halifax. In 1913, the university was "adopted" by the Christian Brothers of Ireland (upon the request of the Archdiocese of Halifax), before being entrusted to the Jesuit priests in 1934. Finally, in 1970, through the act of incorporation, legal status was given to the board of governors and senate, which assumed responsibility for SMU's educational policy. While there have been some drastic changes to the old Saint Mary's (and let's not be stereotypical, co-education came in during the reign of the Jesuits, not after), it still retains many of the religion-based values of its inception. No, students aren't seen carrying hymnbooks and rosaries to class. But the institution does foster a "family" atmosphere, dedication to the welfare of the larger community, and an emphasis on learning in the broader context: As one English major explains, "It's an education which is applicable to the real world, and not just some musty corner of the library."

One of the reasons why SMU students agree that they're getting a "big city education" with a "small-town feel" is because of the university's size. "The campus covers only one city block," says an accounting major, "so if you're looking for a big school, try the University of Manitoba, where it takes a bus to go from one end of the campus to the other. Here it'll take you... well, in a blinding snowstorm with a dozen books and a kit bag with a pair of sneakers... about 10 minutes tops."

The campus has a modern look, with the exception of the McNally building, which has housed the entire institution for almost 30 years. McNally is an intriguing piece of architecture; it provides ivy for the intellectuals and houses a maze of floors capable of confounding even the most astute trooper. Many people say that the evidence that SMU is a "jock university" is the Huskies Stadium, the home of almost all the sporting events, which is located in the middle of the university. This, however, is not true, as it is actually situated just off-centre of the campus, beside the Tower Fitness and Recreation Centre. A lovely stretch of grass and trees is really the heart of the campus.

ACADEMIC ISSUES

Saint Mary's is primarily an undergraduate-focused institution that offers a wide range of programs and disciplines. Its professors are respected and approachable and many students, especially within the smaller faculty of Sciences, find themselves employed by their professors after graduation. The intimate relationship between students and their instructors is perhaps one of the aspects the university is most proud of. However, with recent budget cuts and the increased student population, this relationship is being threatened and has caused some classes to

Vital Statistics

Address: 923 Robie Street, Halifax, Nova Scotia, B3H 3C3

Admissions: office: (902) 496-8100

Website: www.stmarys.ca

Total enrollment: 7,235

Male-female ratio: 51 to 49

Percentage of out-of-province first-year students: 16%

Average entrance grades: 68%

Tuition fees: $4,026–$4,145

Residence fees: $4,450–$5,350 (single with meals); $4,020–$4,920 (double with meals); $2,105 (room only)

Percentage of students in residence: Approximately 15%.

Co-op programs: Computing Science and Business Administration, Geology, Geography, Small Business and Entrepreneurship.

Financial aid: There is a total of $800,000 in undergraduate awards offered at Saint Mary's including entrance scholarships ranging from $200-$2,000 and presidential entrance awards from $4,000-$5,000. After completion of first year at Saint Mary's there are achievement awards, named trusts, and bursaries available for continued student assistance.

Services for students with disabilities: Saint Mary's provides excellent facilities and accessibility for students with disabilities. Available are computers, Kurzweil reading machine, learning disabled student lab, and the Ferguson Tape Library. The campus is entirely wheelchair accessible and there are residence rooms available equipped to meet the needs of disabled individuals. The Atlantic Centre of Support for Disabled Students provides academic services for students with disabilities including its own FM service, tutors, note taking as well as visual language interpreting.

Student services: Academic and career counselling, social counselling, employment services, child care and health services

---

become cramped and overpopulated. The Business faculty, for example, has had to increase the number of classes it holds, so that now they stretch well into the night in order to accommodate these pressures.

Saint Mary's has recently re-invented itself, dropping its parochial ways and opening its arms to the national and international community. It now actively recruits prospective students from across the nation and around the world. One of its major academic attributes are its degrees in Japanese and Chinese studies. The school offers one of the few exchanges to Beijing, which, despite its slow start, is growing in popularity. Saint Mary's has also left its mark in the area of International Development Studies by sending several of its professors to Gambia, where they have been attempting to give that society the tools to develop its own university. In the past year, a group of Gambians were awarded degrees from St. Mary's.

Other impressive degrees in the Faculty of Arts include a degree in Irish Studies, a highly popular Major in Criminology, and recent additions like Atlantic Studies and English as a Second Language.

Saint Mary's also has a long-standing reputation of having the best and biggest school of business in Atlantic Canada. With the recent addition of the 18 million dollar Sobey building, this reputation seems secure. Saint Mary's has long offered an impressive co-op program within the business school which gives students an opportunity to make a few dollars while receiving first-hand experience. The business school also offers a wide range of majors, such as Accounting, Business Administration, Economics, Computing Science, Global Business Management, and Small Business and Entrepreneurship.

> "They say Nova Scotians spend the first twenty years of their lives trying to get away and all the rest of it trying to get back."
>
> Kelvin Ogilvie, quoted by Kelly Toughill in *The Toronto Star*, 15 April 1990.

Despite the success of the Business School and the Faculty of Arts, the Faculty of Science plays a weak second fiddle. Though most students do not attend the university for Science, it is, nonetheless, neglected. It lacks the facilities and the resources of other Atlantic Canadian universities such as Dalhousie, and it looks as though little will change. Saint Mary's has prioritized elsewhere whether its students like it or not. Part of the problem is the lack of research that occurs at Saint Mary's. As the president has explained in the past, Saint Mary's is a school that is student focused and community driven and thus concerns itself with these matters first. Despite its neglect, however, the university does make up for some of the loss by offering many co-operative degrees in areas such as Geology, Geography, Mathematics, and Computer Science.

CAMPUS CULTURE

Saint Mary's has made drastic changes in the last 10 years. It has sought to re-invent itself and shake its image of a football-crazed jock sanctuary. The result has been a more diverse student population. With

In a Nut Shell

The university in a phrase: "It's not Dalhousie or Acadia.... Thank God!"

Best thing about the university: The sense of community and school spirit.

Worst thing about the university: For many, it's that dreaded pigskin game. Love to hate it or hate to love it...Go Huskies!!!

Favourite professors: Stephen Davis (Anthropology), Malcolm Butler (Astronomy), Mike Larsen (English), Ellen Farell (Management).

Most popular bird courses: Religious Studies 351, "Love," and 352, "Death," are two of the favourites. Get a credit for expressing your feelings.

Quietest spot to study on campus: The Library is a place where you can actually get something done. Avoid the clusters of social acquaintances though or you can easily reverse its effect.

Hot spot to study on campus: The Student Centre Cafeteria. Studying here is like trying to get work done in a shopping mall.

Need for car and parking availability: There is no need to having a car in Halifax and quite often it can become more hassle than benefit. Although, if you're the restless type, a car can be a valuable asset for frolicking around Nova Scotia. Parking availability at SMU is quite limited. Get there at 8:00 a.m. if you want a spot.

Sexually speaking: At every party school there is always opportunity to find exactly what you are looking for. Saint Mary's, however, is less vocal about the subject. Mature love seems to be the norm and many are participants in long-standing relationships. For gay and lesbian students Saint Mary's is not the most liberal of campuses. However, thanks to the work of two former students who worked with Student Services to create the Student Outreach Society (S.O.S), the campus has become more accepting of the gay and lesbian presence. Homosexual students do not have to worry about being threatened or harassed for their sexuality but they may have to deal with the fact that it is hard to stay anonymous in such a small school.

Fraternities/sororities: SMU does not have any official frats or sororities. Most Saint Mary's students who yearn for the Animal House culture join the slim pickings at Dal.

Athletic facilities: The Huskies aren't a sports dynasty for nothing. Saint Mary's offers excellent facilities including Husky Stadium and the Tower, which contains four squash and two racquetball courts, a field house, a multi-purpose/aerobics room, weight room, sauna, steam room, hot tub, pro shop, and Sports Medicine clinic. As well, there is an all-weather track and field.

Library facilities: The Patrick Power Library is well maintained and houses over 500,000 volumes, periodicals, films, and audio-visual material. This combined with the services of Novanet (a library network system that allows access to holdings of all university libraries across Nova Scotia), makes the Library well resourced. The Library also contains the Ferguson Library for the Print-Handicapped where students with disabilities can get audiocassettes and large-print articles.

Weather: Horizontal rains even in winter. Bring a raincoat and some rubber booties.

Safety on campus: Saint Mary's is a safe campus, located in a safe city. The campus Security Force run by the students patrol the grounds and offer accompanied walk-home programs.

Alumni: Terry and Arthur Donahue (politicians), Andy Jones (comic), Wayne Gaudet (former Nova Scotia minister of education), Irwin Simon (CEO of Hain Food Group Inc.).

the new initiatives to recruit prospective students from across the country and major attempts to put Saint Mary's on the global map, the campus has become more and more cosmopolitan. The bulk of the student body, however, is still local, and the majority are either from Halifax or native to Nova Scotia.

Saint Mary's is unique from other campuses across Canada. There is a substantial amount of school spirit and little apathy. The majority of students are intertwined and aware of their university and the goings on. There is a strong sense of community on the campus which is reinforced by the Huskies sports teams. The fact that many of SMU's students opt for residence living over off-campus housing is testament to the way they regard their university. "On other campuses most flee residence after second year like a naked man from the cold...at SMU, many of the students stay in residence so long they begin to resemble the furniture," says one student.

Further testament to the abundant school spirit are the number of societies and clubs offered at SMU, and even more importantly the amount of participation that occurs in them. There is no shortage of choice at SMU and something to please just about everyone. There is the Environmentally Concerned Student's Society, the Saint

Mary's University Drama Society (SMUDS) (which puts on a full-scale production every semester), or one can choose to write for the *Journal*, SMU's student newspaper. There are also numerous religious- and ethnic-based societies such as the Bermuda Triangle Society, the Egyptian Students Association, the Christian Fellowship Society, and the Arab Society, to name a few.

REZ LIFE

Because a substantial number of students at Saint Mary's are locals, it's not difficult to get into SMU residence.

The 22-floor Loyola Residence contains almost 400 rooms; on each floor there are four suites, with one double room per suite. Each suite has a room for showering and a separate toilet area. There are no cooking or laundry facilities on the individual floors, although washers and dryers are located on the third floor of the high rise. This is undoubtedly the rowdiest residence, and students rooming here are in for quite a ride.

Vanier is the only all-female residence. Living quarters are almost the same as those in Loyola, but the showering and toilet areas are combined into one room—which means that you have to leave the door open if you're showering so your floormates can wash up. "It's okay," one resident says. "I've seen places around town that are worse."

Rice Residence has six apartments per floor—two small, two medium, two large (all at the same price). Apartments are for four people and contain one cooking facility and one bathroom. This is the calmest of the three residences, because all the units are separated. The very worst that could happen is a loud party next door, or being woken up by the exterminator. One hint: bring some extra-strength Raid. Also, try to get into 01 or 04 units—they're the largest.

For off-campus housing the best bet is to check the Off Campus Housing Office at both Dalhousie and SMU, or use the local newspaper. Remember, housing in Halifax does not come cheap and easy, and the best way to find out where to live is through the grapevine. Find out where other senior students live and try to get first dibs on their apartment or house. Halifax is not the place to be looking for cheap places to live in September. You may find yourself dependent on the charity of others or even on the first flight home.

NIGHT LIFE

Everyone at SMU turns up for the Atlantic Bowl, including alumni from P.E.I., Cape Breton, and New Brunswick. The game is shown at every pub in town and the whole city shows that "Husky Spirit." People start drinking around noon and continue throughout the game. Then it's downtown for the victory party or the "Let's-get-drunk-and-feel-better-Social." Recuperation periods run between two and five business days—so if you don't see people for a while, don't worry.

Oh, and one word of advice—whether you're a football fan or not, please understand that if you come to SMU the sport *will* affect your life. As a defender, a critic, a player, an enthusiast, or just someone who is trying as hard as possible to get away from the pigskin mania that haunts the campus every football season, you will learn to love it.

Between classes, after classes (and as some self-styled intellectuals will tell you, even instead of classes) there are numerous places around Saint Mary's to while away your time. Members of societies, teams, and residences tend to congregate in the campus pub, the Gorsebrook Lounge, where most of the schmoozing happens. A good mix of the students can be found in the Student Centre cafeteria—the bookworms, the jocks, the politicians, the alternative crowd, and the average Husky. The very artsy have found their way to the "cage." Located on the main floor of the Loyola Residence building, the "cage" is an area that seats approximately 50 right in front of Tim Horton's and Grab 'n' Go, which is fenced off from the main hallway by chain link walls.

And of course they don't call Halifax one of the best tourist spots in the Maritimes for nothing. There are numerous bars, pubs, and restaurants to satisfy even the fussiest connoisseur on the tightest budget. Go to the Liquor Dome (that's Cheers, the Atrium, My Apartment, and Lawrence's under one roof) on Argyle St. After all the other bars close up, the crowds weave their way to the Palace on Brunswick St., which shuts down at around 3:00 a.m. Even though SMU is a party school, you can get away with going out and not drinking—then you become the major endangered species, the designated driver, and gain new popularity at every social event and outing.

A Word to the Wise:

1. Watch a little football before you come to get into the spirit of things.

2. Get your registration finished early. It is done by mail, so many people do delay and end up without their classes.

3. Get course book lists early so you can take advantage of used text books. The extra coin you save will enable you to escape the mandatory meal plan every once and a while.

4. Bring some shorts and a couple of Tees. Saint Mary's can be traversed by tunnels that allow students to ignore the harsh Haligonian climate.

5. Know that citizens of Halifax are not known as "Halifaxians," they are known as Haligonians. The use of the former may cause you to be labelled as an "Upper Canadian" (Ontarian). Whether you are or not, the title is not looked upon warmly in the Maritimes.

ON HALIFAX

History-rich Halifax is the little-big town that offers the excitement of a large city and the charm of small town Canada in one. As the urban centre of the Maritimes, it is the ambassador of the East Coast, offering its own culture. Its inhabitants are friendly and indulge in their quiet civic pride but still offer their city to all who choose to come. Despite its size, Halifax offers a large number of festivals, restaurants, and things to do. Stroll in the breathtakingly beautiful Point Pleasant Park, take in some history at the old harbour, try your luck on red or black at the Casino, get some shopping done on Spring Garden Road, or lay some flowers and shed a tear at Jack Dawson's *Titanic* grave. There is plenty that one can do or find within the city's walls. But Halifax is only the beginning, because Nova Scotia is teeming with sites. Rent a car or make a friend who has access to one because places like Peggy's Cove and the Cabot Trail are gems not to be missed, not to mention the many undiscovered beaches and villages that dot the province. Overall, Saint Mary's is located in a city and a province that is an ideal setting for a university environment—it offers excitement without speeding up the pace, sociability without invading solitude, and exploration without homesickness. After leaving, you may find that you subconsciously cite Halifax as your hometown.

Mount Allison University

By Caitlin Hayward

From its earliest incarnation as a school for boys, founded in 1843 by a Sackville merchant named Frederick (no surprise) Allison, to its addition of a Ladies College in 1854, to the granting of the first degrees in 1863, to the current day, Mount Allison has prided itself on being a small, liberal arts and science undergraduate university. With a little over 2,200 students, the small part is understandable. As for the undergraduate part, with only two Masters programs (and about that many Masters students), Mount A is definitely focused on the undergrad.

People who come convinced of its "quiet conservatism" can live out their university career without fear of massive student movements, riots, and a "crazy" metropolitan lifestyle. Sackville is, after all, a town of 5,500 people—including Mount A students. But don't let the facade fool you; within the picturesque campus are some serious radicals. Though Mount A draws the large majority of its population from the Maritimes, don't come thinking that it's a hick university. A large and active artistic community, the large number of gay/lesbian students, environmental activists, and various community groups ensure that the Sackville bubble is "popped" on occasion.

"Pretty" is the most common word associated with the Mount A campus; the red stone buildings and Swan Pond give

the campus a picturesque feel. Hart Hall and Trueman House are two of the oldest buildings, with ghost stories and furniture to match their histories. Much of the original campus was built with sandstone from the Sackville quarry, giving it special significance to the town, though there are some newer buildings that are either tucked away or designed to blend with the older ones. Mount A isn't without its eyesores; however, the Physics and Engineering Building (the PEG) was started over twenty years ago and still isn't finished. It stands next to Centennial Hall, the main administration building, built in the late nineteenth century. A reminder of what the administration would do if it could ever decide to spend the money.

The facilities at the university can best be described as adequate. The basic athletic necessities are around, including a pool, a few fields, and a gym. The pride and joy of the athletic department and alumni remains the football team, consistently ranked among the best in Canada over the past decade. Though a popular fall activity is watching the games, still more popular is the griping about the rumoured 35% of the athletic budget that the team garners. The ice rink, home of the now defunct men's hockey team, is literally falling apart, and the school is waiting for the town to build a new civic centre before tearing down the building.

Vital Statistics

Address: 65 York Street, Sackville, New Brunswick, E4L 1E4

Admissions office: (506) 364-2269

Website: www.mta.ca

Total enrollment: 2,150

Male-female ratio: 43 to 57

Percentage of international students: 4%

Percentage of out-of-province students: 65%

Average entrance grades: Arts: 75%; Science: 75%; Commerce: 75%

Tuition fees: $4,220

Residence fees: On-campus residence range from $5,625 to $6,365. Off-campus bachelor apartments range from $300–$420/month, while two or more rooms usually break down to $250–$350 a month per room.

Percentage of students in residence: 50%

Co-op programs: None.

Services for students with disabilities: The Meighen Centre is specially designed for students with learning disabilities. Several residences are wheelchair accessible. Unfortunately, Mount Allison is indeed built on a hill, making steps an integral part of the day for almost everyone.

Student services: Counselling of almost every kind, including psychological (both peer and professional), academic, career, and for international students; student union and student council; housing; writing workshops, campus tutor pool; learning disability centre; chaplaincy.

ACADEMIC ISSUES

Priding itself on academic excellence, Mount A boasts the highest entrance average for frosh, and more Rhodes scholars per capita than any other university in the Commonwealth. This means that there are a lot of keeners on campus. But after the first semester, reality tends to set in; with such high competition, the true keeners come out and the rest of campus falls into place somewhere in the middle. With the emphasis on undergraduate education, teaching is a high priority with faculty; though they are expected to continue research, you're more likely to have a good teacher than the latest expert on ethnic warfare in central Africa.

Some very serious financial problems in the 1980s led to a "bare basics" attitude for a while. The sciences have been hit pretty hard; with fewer profs and limited lab space, departments have been forced to limit enrollment in many classes. Onus is on the students to strategically plan their classes, with some being offered only every two years and, others being limited to majors and honours students. If you don't know what you're doing in second year, you could spend the next three years making up for a first-year registration mistake. The Arts and Social Sciences have their own problems—with fewer profs come fewer classes. Potential students will not be wowed by the sheer number of courses offered; by the time you hit third and fourth year, options are seriously limited. And don't always believe the Calendar; like all universities, Mount A lists courses it hasn't taught in years. The financial situation also led to a series of outright cuts over the past decade, including the controversial decision to eliminate the Education and Engineering programs in 1997. Mount A is now slowly starting to rebuild programs after years of trimming back; it is re-arranging its Environmental Studies/Science and International Relations programs, and has added Women's Studies and International Business & Economics recently.

While Mount A has had a balanced budget for several years, the price has been high; the events and decisions of the past two decades have effectively poisoned faculty-administration relations. Two faculty-union strikes in seven years attest to some serious undercurrents of tension between the current administration and the teaching faculty. Even the staff association took strike action in 1993.

The Fine Arts department gives the university bragging rights, with painters like Christopher and Mary Pratt as alumni. Alex Colville is a former instructor (his depiction of the administration on a prominent mural is not to be missed—there is a large horse's ass in the middle of the picture!) and one of the oldest university art galleries in Canada sits on campus, and includes originals from many prominent Canadian artists. The Music department also has a great reputation, but tends to breed insularity in its students; their hectic schedule and the department's obscure location dissuade all but the most enthusiastic Music majors from joining the rest of the campus much of the time. The constant recitals and concerts however, add to the culture, and non-music majors are encouraged to join various groups.

Theatre, incorporated in the English department, is a popular program and extra-curricular activity. Again, theatre people can sometimes be vaguely insular as the time commitment

In a Nut Shell

The university in a phrase: "The biggest little university in the world." Cheesy, but there's a reason for it—just check out Homecoming!

Best thing about the university: Its small size—you know almost everybody and they also know you.

Worst thing about the university: You know almost everybody and they also know you.

Favourite professors: P. Bogaard (Philosophy), R. Hawkes (Physics), A. Fancy (French & Drama), P. Bryden (History), E. Steuter (Soc/Anth), R. Lapp (English).

Most popular bird courses: Astronomy 1001, Human Biology, Music 2000 ("Clap for Credit"), Intro to Sociology.

Quietest spot on campus to study: The departmental libraries are rarely used by students, perhaps because they close by 9 p.m.

Hot spot on campus to study: The library "Rail"—the place to see and be seen. Never mind the fact that flirting can serve as an incredibly effective procrastination technique.

Need for car and parking availability: Everything in town is a ten-minute walk or less; a car is only useful for mid-winter stress relief and driving to see any movie released in the past three months.

Sexually speaking: The small population on campus means that you can get a reputation pretty quickly, if you're not careful. On the other hand, no one is a complete stranger; even a random "hook-up" is probably a friend of a friend. The residences, the library Rail and the campus pub are probably the biggest pick-up joints; in-house "incest" is a popular pastime. But beware—it's almost impossible to completely avoid someone on this campus, especially if they live down the hall!

Fraternities/sororities: Why? The houses provide the close-knit support system frats/sororities vow to have.

Library facilities: A popular hang-out (have we mentioned the Rail?), the library is known more for its location than its academic uses. Adequate might be the best word to describe the latter category. Though the brochures claim that it has one of the best book-to-student ratios around, students tend not to use the massive amounts of late nineteenth century periodicals which sit in the basement. Students are advised to check out the selection before picking a paper topic, though profs have become quite adept at suggesting topics which have some relevant holdings. On the positive side, most of the Maritime universities are involved in an inter-library loan program, so finding a specific book is not necessarily so hard. But beware—books travel slowly, and if you want to use this system, you have to be prepared to plan ahead.

Safety on campus: Though campus security has been a hot topic on occasion, Mount A and Sackville are generally agreed to be very safe places, especially if compared to larger schools and towns. The Student Council's Walkhome program operates every night during the year, though it is rarely called and campus is patrolled until only 2 a.m. by a security officer, a fact which concerns some students.

Weather: Beautiful in the summer, when no one is around, but a New Brunswick winter is something to experience. Sackville is notorious for huge snowfalls; it's not unusual to have over a metre on the ground in January and February. Being next to the Tantramar Marshes and the Bay of Fundy guarantees some serious winds, but all and all, it's not that much colder than the rest of the Maritimes or southern Ontario.

Alumni: Christopher and Mary Pratt (artists), Ian Hanimansing (journalist), Margaret McCain (former Lt-Governor of New Brunswick), Grace Annie Lockhart (first woman in British Empire to earn a degree).

dictates giving up all pretences of a life when a show is being put on. But the shows are worth it, and belie the conservative image of the school.

REZ LIFE Residence life forms the basis of most people's social existence for their first year or two. Over 95% of entering students choose to live in residence, moving into a "house" on either the North or South side of campus. Houses vary in size, with Trueman, Harper, and Windsor houses having approximately 200 residents each, and some "satellite" residences, located just apart from the main cam-

pus, having as few as eight people. Most students live in houses of approximately 85 people, creating a pretty close-knit community. This is where most folks find their social niche, at least for the first tumultuous year. The actual buildings themselves are not in great shape; Palmer Hall, an all-girls residence and one of the oldest buildings on campus, looks great on the brochure but needs a major overhaul to try to bring it into even the late twentieth century. The same goes for Trueman House, one the largest and most spirited houses on campus, and home of the infamous Marriott smell (it's right above one of the two meal halls on campus). Bennett, Bigelow, and Hunton houses, each containing around 85 stu-

A Word to the Wise:

1. Live in residence. Like Cheers, it's the place where everybody knows your name. Everyone, from the almost-alcoholic party animal to the academically obsessed hermit, will find a house where they belong. This is where your social life begins in the first year.

2. Get involved! In a lot of ways, you learn more outside the classroom than within, so make the most of the surprisingly large number of extra-curricular options.

3. Explore Sackville (and the Maritimes if you're not from 'round here). Small as it is, there are hundreds of things to do, if you look beyond the obvious.

dents, were originally built to accommodate the influx of post-war students, and haven't been changed much since. A relatively unique feature in the residence system are the "satellite" houses: several old family homes converted into residences, holding anywhere from eight to fifteen people. Though they are probably the most interesting and distinctive houses, they are also in varying states of disrepair.

Though each house has its own distinct personality, nurtured as a tradition to rake up house spirit, they are not monolithic fraternity/sorority-like dorms; the small number of students in each residence ensures that few are left out of any activity unless they deliberately try to be. But if you are someone who values personal space in a big way, choose your house carefully; some houses can be claustrophobic if you're not into the regular university social scene (read "parties"). But each house does have a certain set of rules, and floor monitors and assistant dons generally make sure things don't get out of hand. The satellites are often home to the "alternative" crowd, for those interested in saving the world through recycling or in just avoiding living with eighty-five 18-year-olds.

NIGHT LIFE
This, brings us to the difficult topic of trying to explain Mount A's social atmosphere. This is not a campus for club-hoppers; with four bars in town (five if you count the pool hall), weekend (or weekday) drinking options are limited. Social options are similarly limited. Tim Horton's, a daytime favourite for caffeine junkies, closes down by 9 p.m., and Sackville offers few big city excitements. A coffee shop did open up a few years ago, though most students generally find themselves gravitating toward one of the three "main" bars in town.

The Pub, the more affectionate name of the Tantramarsh Club, is the only on-campus bar, and tends to be the final stop for those doing the rounds. This isn't a pub in the British style, but a casual bar with a couple of pool tables, foozeball, and a decent-sized dance floor. Timing is everything here; packed on Thursday and Saturday nights, this is probably the only time students actually line up at Mount A. The Pub's rival establishment, the Duke, offers much of the same atmosphere, only with significantly more football players. One other difference is the Duke's Open Jam night, at which the local Sackville and Mount A talent come out of the woodwork, and really should not be missed. Those who love live music tend to gravitate towards Duckey's, the third of the main Sackville triumvirate. Arguably the more "mature" bar, Duckey's is known as a good place for conversation, intellectual or otherwise, provided a live band isn't playing. Considering there's a band pretty much every weekend though, this bar's reputation as the more mellow bar may be built solely on the fact that it is the only bar in town where students, "townies," and profs all fight for the same bar stools.

Sackville does have its share of culture, however. The Struts Gallery is just downtown, and Mount A and the town jointly work on the Performing Arts series, which has brought anyone from the BC Ballet to the Gryphon Trio to Convocation Hall.

ON SACKVILLE
Sackville itself is a small community, and the downtown core consists of the only stoplight in town (yes, that makes it a one-stoplight, two-Tim Horton's kind of town!), and the surrounding couple of blocks of businesses. Where food is concerned, the downtown options are limited to Subway, Tim's, and Joey's, a great pizza joint and a big Mount A supporter. Places to take your parents, or to visit on Valentine's, include the Marshlands Inn and the Vienna Coffee House, both of which have great food, though not if you're on a student budget. Up near the highway (the Trans-Canada splits Sackville into upper and lower parts of town), is where the other Tim's is located, along with McDonald's and Wendy's. Patterson's Family Restaurant, a favourite for post-Saturday night breakfasts, is also near the highway, making it difficult to get there if the night before was particularly fun.

Though there is a distinction between "town and gown," Sackville is definitely a university town, and the businesses and townspeople are almost always super-friendly to students.

University of New Brunswick

By Michael Edwards

The University of New Brunswick (UNB) has been around since 1785, making it one of the oldest existing universities in Canada. Originally known as the College of New Brunswick and then King's College, it was a small affair until the 1920s, when the campus started to expand. The expansion continued throughout the years, culminating in a separate campus being built down in Saint John in 1964.

The Fredericton campus is comprised predominantly of red brick buildings—even newer buildings have been built in a similar style in order to blend in. One anomaly is The Old Arts Building, the oldest university building in Canada still being used today—history is an important part of UNB's existence. The Student Union Building is one of the newer buildings on campus, and is allegedly going to be expanding soon. But that's something that is discussed every few years, so don't hold your breath.

The campus is situated in the middle of the city, sort of like a town within a town, with everything within walking distance of everything else. One problem though—the whole campus is built on a hill. The joke is that we have unidirectional wheelchair access, and it makes traversing the campus from bottom to top more of a chore than a pleasure.

CAMPUS CULTURE

After spending a small amount of time in Fredericton, the overall conservatism will hit you squarely in the face. And that, not surprisingly, is also reflected in the university where the "normality" of the students is pretty obvious—expect to see an awful lot of UNB sweatshirts unless you hang out in the less popular parts of the campus.

UNB also has an uncanny knack of attracting students from all around the world (73 countries are represented) and the cultural diversity is very apparent in many facets of university life—from special cultural events to the many ethnic shows on the campus radio station.

Socially, there is a lot to choose from and a wide variety of clubs and societies that cater to anyone's tastes or interests. Even outside the formal clubs, it should be possible to find something to do—those seeking other folks to enjoy a game of magic or go to The Gathering can check out The Blue Lounge in the SUB, while sportier types can try out some of the merely adequate sports facilities.

Turnout for student elections is usually rather meagre, but referendums seem to bring out the politician in most people—students have recently voted against starting up a university football team, but voted for keeping CHSR-FM, the campus radio station. Interest in the many sporting teams isn't too high, either, but the success of the men's hockey team of late has rekindled that rarest of beasts, school spirit. Don't expect any pep rallies just yet, though.

Recent years have seen an ongoing battle of wits between the Student Union (SU) and the campus media outlets concerning funding. It all came to a head last year with money being withheld and a referendum held, but the eventual outcome was a lot more civilized—now students contribute directly to CHSR-FM and *The Brunswickan*, keeping the SU out of the loop and in that way ensuring unbiased reporting of all campus goings-on.

ACADEMIC ISSUES

If you follow annual university surveys in less reputable publications, you'd think that the University of New Brunswick was down near the bottom of the pack. But it really isn't all that bad—like every university, it has both strengths and weaknesses. UNB is feeling the pinch from reduced funding, but it is expanding its horizons with co-op programs available in both Computer Science and Business Administration, and with cutting-edge research into the advancement of satellite technology and the prevention of family violence.

Many of the first-year courses offered have ridiculously large classes, and that can mean that it doesn't take much for some students to fall through the cracks. That does, however, seem to be the general idea because it would be impossible to sustain such large classes in second-year subjects—think of it as a filtering system. Large classes also translate into a less hands-on approach to teaching, but the university still boasts that nearly half the first- and second-year courses offered have fewer than 25 students per class.

Vital Statistics

Address: P.O. Box 4400, Station A, Fredericton, New Brunswick, E3B 5A3

Admissions office: (506) 453-4865

Website: www.unb.ca

Total enrollment: 11,551

Male-female ratio: 50 to 50

Average entrance grades: Arts: 60%; Science: 60%; Commerce: 65%; Engineering: 65%

Tuition fees: $3,436

Residence fees: $4,450–$4,590 (double room with meal plan); $5,255–$5,395 (single room with meal plan)

Percentage of students in residence: 8%

Percentage of international students: Approximately 23%

Percentage of out-of-province first-year students: 17%

Financial aid: Entrance scholarships and awards to returning full-time students based mainly on academic achievement; emergency loans, bursaries, and government student loans are also available; financial counselling.

Co-op programs: Business Administration, Chemistry, Computer Science, Engineering, Forestry and Environmental Management,

Hospitality and Tourism.

Services for students with disabilities: Coordinator of Services for Students with Disabilities assists students with special needs.

Aboriginal students: Special services for aboriginal students including academic counselling and tutoring; Micmac-Maliseet Institute; Bridging Year Program.

Student services: Academic, personal, and career counselling, campus ministry, daycare, health services, international student advisor, off-campus housing office, student employment centre, writing and math centre.

The peak time for expansion at UNB was the late sixties and early seventies—fast forward 30 years, and there are about half as many professors as there were then, despite the fact that enrollment is way up. It's the same kind of story with many other universities—the older profs are being put out to pasture (early retirement is being encouraged) and they are not being replaced at the same rate. There are some attempts to recruit younger, more exciting professors who will make the university attractive to a whole new generation of students.

Even in its current state, UNB has some departments with reputations that are second to none: Engineering's Geodesy & Geomatics is rumoured to be one of the best in the whole world, and the Forestry department offers an incredibly impressive rate of employment after graduation. The Law faculty is one of the best in the entire country, too, and there is an incredible amount of competition for the small number of places it offers. As for the less impressive departments...like any university, UNB has its share, but there is normally at least one redeeming prof in each department. By the way, it is impossible to escape the bad courses in your early days, but luckily by the time you have picked your major, you will know just who to avoid like the plague.

REZ LIFE

For students moving away from home for the first time, residence life offers a certain amount of security and the opportunity to jump right into the party world (though this can come back to haunt you when it is time for finals). Residence life isn't cheap—having to buy a meal card pushes the price up above that of living off campus, but the

social life and convenience is very attractive to a lot of people. So much so that there is usually a waiting list to get into the on-campus residences, and a hotel off campus is used for the overflow until things settle down during the first term.

UNB has 12 residences on campus—the one off-campus residence (Maggie Jean Chestnut) was closed last year because of dangerous wiring and won't be reopened. That means that every student in residence has to buy a meal plan from Beaver Foods; their food isn't the most appetizing, but there is always a salad bar in case you can't face fried food anymore. Every residence (apart from McLeod House and Lady Beaverbrook Residence) is within a stone's throw of the others, so there isn't really a lot to pick between them, apart from the sexual make-up of the residents—male only (Aitken House, Jones House, and Neville House), female only (Lady Dunn Hall and Tibbits Hall), or co-ed (MacKenzie House, Bridges House, Harrison House, Joy Kidd House, Neill House, McLeod House, and Lady Beaverbrook Residence).

Each house has its own community, and with that goes all kinds of parties and special events which range from mud dives to pumpkin sacrifices. Most residences were built at around the same time, so the actual buildings and rooms within are interchangeable. Exceptions to the rule are the following: Lady Dunn Hall, Tibbits Hall, and Joy Kidd House are all in the same complex, and are the newest on campus (although they date back to the sixties). They have their own dining hall, so you can sneak down to eat in your pyjamas (everyone else has to go to the communal McConnell Hall).

McLeod House is a tower block at the top of campus, and features corridors that bear a striking similarity to the mazes

In a Nut Shell

The university in a phrase: Not a bad little university.

Best thing about the university: Relatively low tuition, some reputable departments, and an attractive campus.

Worst thing about the university: The fact that the campus is built on a hill—you'll really notice it when you have to rush to your next class.

Most popular bird course: CS 1045: Introduction to Computers; ED 3361: Internet Literacy

Favourite professors: Dimitri Triphonopoulos (English), Tillman Benfey (Biology), Bruce Balkom (Physics), Sandra Byers (Psychology), Gillian Thompson (History), Adam Chrzanowski (Engineering), Patricia Hughes (Law).

Hot spot on campus to study: The SUB Cafeteria.

Quietest spot on campus to study: The deep, dark corners of the Harriet Irving Library.

Need for car and parking availability: Fredericton is a small town, so walking is always an option, and the buses only run once an hour (at their most frequent), so make sure your watch is working. Parking permits cost $60 for two terms, and

you could still end up doing a lot of walking.

Sexually speaking: Things can get a little wild in the residences during the first few weeks, but everything calms down eventually. You could find a mate for life, though.

Fraternities/sororities: Not on our campus, thank you very much. And that's a good thing.

Athletic facilities: Sporting facilities could really do with an overhaul at UNB, but what is there is at least satisfactory. The Lady Beaverbrook Gymnasium offers a cardio training room, a climbing wall, an equipment room, a swimming pool, squash courts, and gyms which are used for intramural sports. In addition, there is the Aitken University Centre (home of the men's hockey team and also one of the more pleasant places to go walking during the winter months), tennis courts, and a couple of sports fields used by the university teams.

Library facilities: The Harriet Irving Library offers all the normal resources needed for studying, and an agreement with the University of Alberta to deliver books and journal articles quickly helps to plug any gaps in their collection. Smaller, specialized libraries (the Science Library, the Engineering Library, and the Law

Library) deal with their associated topics, but can have frustratingly reduced hours at times.

Computer facilities: Six computer labs with approximately 150 PCs. Access to e-mail, Internet and printers.

Weather: The summers can get terribly hot (30°C) and with the humidity, you'll be longing for air conditioning. The winters can get terribly cold (minus 30°C). Fortunately, there isn't much in the way of wind most of the time, but when there is, cover all your exposed flesh or else you could get frost-bitten. Take a varied wardrobe.

Safety on campus: There is now both a Safedrive and Safewalk program, and as long as you want to go home at the hours they are operating, you'll be just fine. There are problems with lighting in some areas on campus and there are no alarm posts around campus, but video cameras placed beside some buildings are a good idea.

Alumni: Anne Murray ("Snowbird" songstress), Dalton Camp (journalist), Bliss Carman (poet), Fredrik Eaton (former shop owner), J.D. Hazen (politician), George E. Foster (former finance minister and ambassador to the League of Nations).

they test rats' intelligence with. Lady Beaverbrook Residence is located right next to the Engineering building and so tends to be full of engineers.

One final option might be the seven-story apartment building Magee House (which is right next to McLeod House)—it is also owned by the university, and tends to attract international students and their families, so it might not be accessible to most undergrads.

Off-campus living can be cheaper if you can find enough people to room with, but getting up to campus in the winter months can be hazardous to your health on the colder days.

NIGHT LIFE While UNB did have a reputation for being a real party school (at one point being given David Letterman's stamp of approval on The Late Show), Fredericton isn't really blessed with a whole lot of variety when it comes to watering holes and other non-school recreational choices.

Campus-wise, the only place that is really worth visiting regularly is The Social Club. Located on the top floor of the Student Union Building, it offers both cheap drinks and loud music. It does also have a slight "meat market" feel to it, but that could be part of its charm. Admission is by membership only (or as a signed-in guest), and they sell out fast at the

A Word to the Wise:

1. Get your partying out of your system early and then concentrate on the academic side of things—you'll be glad of it when you are trying to upgrade your GPA for applying to law school or medicine.

2. Live in residence if you want to experience the whole social aspect of university life, but stay off campus if you are penny pinching.

3. Attend the different cultural events on campus and expand your worldly experiences.

4. Read *The Brunswickan* and listen to CHSR-FM to find out what is going on on campus.

5. Make the most of the warm weather because you'll long for it when the cold winter days arrive.

beginning of the year. The only other bar on campus is The Cellar, down in the basement of the SUB—it has been open for three years now, and has lost money each and every one of those years. But it somehow remains open, and offers a quiet alternative for those unwilling to leave campus. It also features live bands from time to time, and that is a good reason to keep an eye on it.

Most of the notable bars are located in a relatively small area in downtown Fredericton—a boon to those who want to go bar hopping. If you are looking for an atmospheric pub, The Lunar Rogue is the best the town has—it is just as popular for its choice of beers and whiskies as it is for its Nacho Night every Tuesday. Less authentic but almost as popular is Dolan's, an Irish pub (of sorts) where you will inevitably be bombarded with either live or recorded Celtic music. Those looking for the best beer in town will enjoy a visit to Picaroon's, a bar with its own microbrewery and a variety of ales to tempt more discerning palates.

If you like to dance, then Fredericton really isn't the place for you. There are the usual trashy nightclubs (Sweetwaters in particular fits this category), a country bar (The Rockin' Rodeo), and one "real" dance club (The G Spot) where a DJ gives it more of a rave feel. But that's about it. Fans of live music will find themselves in a similar predicament—the availability of gigs in town seems to go in a cycle, and we are at a low at the moment. There will always be a few concerts on campus, but they tend to be unadventurous and the rest of the town appears to feature the same local musicians every weekend. Still, check out Rye's Deli, The Chestnut, and The

Dock and you could be pleasantly surprised. And there's always the chance of an all-ages show at assorted venues around town—keep an eye open for posters when roaming the downtown areas.

ON FREDERICTON

Fredericton is a lushly picturesque city of around 50,000 people. The city is cut in half by the Saint John River, with the south side being where you'll spend almost all your time because it not only contains the university campus, but also all the shopping sites you'll ever need. At one time it was called "The City of Stately Elms" because of the many elm trees lining the street. Disease has unfortunately taken its toll on the trees, but there are still enough of them that the city has a distinct green tinge to it when viewed during the summer months. And plenty of oxygen, too.

It is a friendly city that is still small enough to make walking the perfect way to explore your new surroundings. There are a decent number of restaurants and shops in the downtown area, and the walk along The Green to the wonderful Beaverbrook Art Gallery is the perfect way to spend a Sunday afternoon. A weekly social highlight in town is the Boyces Farmers' Market (which happens every Saturday), where you can not only stock up on locally grown vegetables but also buy a variety of foodstuffs from many different cultures—the samosas are well worth trying.

Fredericton is very rich in all things arty—from galleries to live dramatic productions to movie productions, there is always something artistic happening in town. Theatre New Brunswick is based at the city's Playhouse, and offers several plays during the year, with special rates for students on preview nights. Those who enjoy independent movies will find The Capital Film Society a godsend—the movies are shown on campus, and again student rates are offered. Every September, Fredericton hosts the Harvest Jazz & Blues Festival, with all kinds of concerts—a lot of the gigs feature local artists that play in town quite frequently, but there are always a few bigger or more interesting names that are worth seeking out.

It can feel a little isolated at times because the nearest city of any size is Halifax, and that is about a five-hour drive away. Being the capital city of the province doesn't necessarily mean it is going to be the biggest, but it is a good point to start exploring the rest of the province if you have access to a car—Fundy National Park and the Saint John River Valley are both good places to start.

St. Thomas University

By Sally Cogswell

Priding itself on being a leader in liberal arts education, with the largest arts enrollment in Eastern Canada, St. Thomas University is a small, Catholic institution that welcomes students of all faith backgrounds and seeks to provide a comfortable learning environment, where liberal arts ideas and values are put into action. St. Thomas University has deep ties to two New Brunswick communities. Originally founded in 1910 as a high school in Chatham, St. Thomas became a university in 1934 and in 1964 relocated to the "top of the hill" of the campus it shares with the University of New Brunswick in the province's capital of Fredericton. The close proximity and shared agreement between STU and UNB allow St. Thomas students the best of both worlds—an intimate small school environment as well as access to additional courses, services, and facilities through UNB. St. Thomas University is a student centred community—the faculty, staff, and administration demonstrate a genuine concern for students, their academic progress, and their well-being.

The St. Thomas campus consists of seven buildings and a beautifully landscaped, cobblestone courtyard. Over $6 million has been spent over the last five years on construction and renovations to our campus and the changes have definitely been for the better. The main administration building, George Martin Hall, is located in the centre of the campus and is easily recognizable by the steeple on top. This building is a hot spot for student activity, housing most of the administrative offices as well as the Admissions Office, and a combined office for the Registrar and Financial Services. The cafeteria used by residence students and the university chapel are also located in this building. Edmund Casey Hall is made up mostly of classrooms and faculty offices. Holy Cross House, which sits next to the Leroy Washburn Field (a practice field that includes a basketball court, a gazebo-like structure for aesthetic purposes, and a large marble ball whose use is unknown) has a unique design, holding the Social Work and Native Studies departments, classrooms, a large conference room, and four residence wings (two on each end of the building). Sir James Dunn Hall, opened in January 1994, is the busiest building. It contains the Student Affairs Office, the Computer Lab, the Black Box Theatre, a cafeteria (that

has a Tim Horton's for those who need a good blast of caffeine on their way to class), as well as a basement full of classrooms. Vanier Hall and Harrington Hall, the two largest St. Thomas residences, house about 200 residents each. A new addition to campus in the spring was the completion of the J.B. O'Keefe Fitness Centre. The Athletics Office is located here as well as new fitness facilities complete with large shower/locker rooms, free for the use of all full-time St. Thomas students. St. Thomas students also commonly frequent two buildings shared with UNB—the Harriet Irving Library, a five-floor library for Arts, Business, and Education students on campus, and the Student Union Building, home to the St. Thomas Student Union, the two campus bars, the campus radio station CHSR, and *The Aquinian* (the STU student newspaper).

CAMPUS CULTURE

Anyone walking around the STU campus might notice the abundance of women. The female to male ratio at St. Thomas is approximately 69% to 31% (gentlemen, pack your bags!). This ratio does not seem to harm the social lives of St. Thomas students since UNB has more men. St. Thomas students range in age anywhere from 17 to 65 years young and the St. Thomas Adults Returning to School or S.T.A.R.S. program offers peer support to students returning to studies after time off.

STU and UNB are friendly neighbours, sharing many resources and student services, but students are also aware of the friendly rivalry that exists between some STU and UNB students. Could it, perhaps, be related to a mysterious theft of a beaver mascot head? Or maybe they are simply envious of St. Thomas's supreme location at the top of the campus?

Just in case you ever need an excuse to party, St. Thomas observes two "special" days in addition to other holidays— January 28 is the Feast Day of St. Thomas Aquinas, the patron saint of St. Thomas University, and February 11 is Chancellor's Day (classes are cancelled on Chancellor's Day).

Looking for something to do in your spare time? Never fear, there are many possibilities to chose from. Anyone interested in athletics, playing or spectating, at either the varsity or

Vital Statistics

Address: P.O. Box 4569, Station A, Fredericton, New Brunswick, E3B 5G3

Admissions office: (506) 452-7700

Website: www.stthomasu.ca

Total enrollment: 2,251

Male-female ratio: 31 to 69

Average entrance grades: Arts: 65%

Tuition fees: Arts and Social Work: $2,960 (one of the lowest tuitions in the Maritimes!); Journalism: $2,960 + $100 lab fee; Education: $4,500; Post-Degree Social Work Program: $6,000; Transition Year Program for International Students: $10,000; part-time students pay $324 per three credit hours.

Residence fees: Double rooms range from $4,210–$4,360 and single rooms from $5,170–$5,320, depending on whether the base meal plan or the enhanced meal plan is

chosen. Residence students are also required to pay a refundable caution and key deposit of $60 and a $40 house dues which supports initiatives planned by residence house committees.

Percentage of students in residence: 25% of all full-time STU students live on campus. Many others party there.

Percentage of out-of-province first-year students: 37%

Financial aid: St. Thomas University operates a generous scholarship program, funding both university entrance awards for incoming first-year students and in-course scholarships for continuing St. Thomas students. About 20% of first-year students are offered entrance scholarships, many of which are renewable awards. Both the university and the Student Union offer a number of bursaries to students in financial need, and the student aid

office can assist students needing information about applying for student loans or financial aid. STU commits over $400,000 each year to an employment program which creates student jobs on campus.

Co-op programs: All arts programs have a co-op option.

Services for students with disabilities: The Student Affairs Office offers assistance to students with disabilities and the entire campus is wheelchair accessible.

Aboriginal students: Native Student Council; programs for Native students.

Student services: Academic, personal, and career counselling; Campus Ministry's chaplaincy team; daycare; Employment Services; the Student Health Clinic; Information Help Centre; International Student Advisor; ombudsperson.

intramural level, can contact the Athletics Office for more information on how to get involved. STU has an active Drama department organized under Professor Ilkay Silk. The St. Thomas Student Union is always looking for students to hold council positions, volunteer to serve on committees, and help with special events, and they also fund a number of clubs and societies that students may join. Interested in journalism? Get involved with CHSR or *The Aquinian*!

Orientation has changed for the better at St. Thomas. Focusing on the "welcoming" part of orienting new students to campus, the university's Student Union and Residence House Committees plan a number of great activities for students during Frosh Week.

ACADEMIC ISSUES
The Bachelor of Arts degree program is the cornerstone of all academic programs at STU. While St. Thomas University specializes in liberal arts, it also offers professional programs in Education and Social Work, and applied arts programming in Criminal Justice, Gerontology, and Journalism. In addition to courses taught at STU during the normal academic year, STU offers inter-session and summer-session courses taught by extension in

Miramichi, and an International Exchange program that allows St. Thomas students the opportunity to study abroad in countries such as Malta, Chile, and Argentina. STU students are also eligible to take courses at UNB for credit and a number of STU and UNB professors teach courses on both campuses. St. Thomas has approximately 2,000 full-time students as well as approximately 250 part-time students. St. Thomas also inherits a number of transfer students from other academic institutions each year. The average class size at STU consists of 35 students. This small class size affords students and professors an informal learning atmosphere and the opportunity to know each other well. All students (including first-year students) are given the opportunity for early registration and this means an end to long lineups.

St. Thomas University welcomes both students of proven academic ability and those who show a potential for academic success. A number of academic support services are in place for all students, including an annual series of academic workshops known as the "Step Ahead Program," a system of one-on-one faculty advising, and free tutoring for St. Thomas students. An Academic Information Fair is held every year during Orientation Week to help new students make informed decisions about their course of study. Career coun-

In a Nut Shell

The university in a phrase: "At St. Thomas University, we're getting large enough that we can't always remember your name, but we're small enough that we're always embarrassed when we can't" (a quote attributed to our Registrar Larry Batt by other St. Thomas staff).

Best thing about the university: One of the best things about STU—its size! You are treated like a person, not as a student number! Student input is valued and student leadership encouraged.

Worst thing about the university: No Coke on campus! STU and UNB have an exclusive deal with Pepsi. Also, the Bank of Montreal has a monopoly on campus banking.

Favourite professors: M. Clow (Sociology); Rev. J. Dolan (Religious Studies); P. Malcolmson (Poli-Sci); B. Ouellette (Social Work); N. Rio (Spanish); I. Silk (Drama).

Most popular bird courses: Religious studies with Father Dolan; Spanish 100—say adios to a bad grade.

Hot spots to study on campus: The cafeteria in Sir James Dunn Hall.

Quietest spots to study on campus: Harriet Irving Library.

Need for car and parking availability: You don't *need* a car to get around the campus or the city, but it is definitely a bonus if you want to cruise around the Maritimes and to the States. Parking costs $75 per vehicle per year. Fredericton Transit makes bus travel easy, cabs are cheap, and sidewalks and crosswalks are plentiful for pedestrians, so commuting to campus will not be difficult.

Sexually speaking: Ultra-conservative attitude towards sex (part of STU's good ol' Catholic tradition).

Fraternities/sororities: They don't exist here.

Athletic facilities: The Lady Beaverbrook Gymnasium, the Education Gym and the Aitken University Centre, and the new J.B. O'Keefe Fitness Centre; swimming pools, handball and squash courts, a dance studio, an indoor jogging track, tennis courts, gymnastic and martial arts facilities, skating rinks, outdoor sports fields, and three fully equipped gyms right on campus.

Library facilities: STU and UNB students share the Harriet Irving Library. Sign up for a tour and learn how to use the computer system and navigate around the library to find the books you need.

Computer facilities: STU offers state-of-the-art computer labs where students can type assignments, use e-mail, and surf the Internet for free (the only charge is 10 cents a page for laser printing). All students receive a computer account and have free online access to library catalogues, the Internet, and e-mail.

Weather: Beautiful and picturesque fall; lots of snow, slush, and cold spells in the winter (the campus is usually covered in snow from November to March); balmy springs; warm but humid summers.

Safety on campus: Safewalk and Safedrive programs operate at night for students concerned about travelling around campus. UNB security patrols the campus both by vehicle and on foot.

Alumni: Greg Byrne, New Brunswick minister of Justice; Stompin' Tom Connors (honorary degree); Sheree Lee Fitch, author; Michael Humes, VP of the American Hockey League; David Adams Richard, novelist; Dawn Russell, dean of Dalhousie University's School of Law.

---

selling is available to students at the Career Resource Centre, a shared service with UNB, and this is especially helpful for students who have not yet decided what to do after their BA. Both the Registrar and the Student Affairs Office offer support to students with learning disabilities.

As a part of its commitment to discovering new approaches to the study of liberal arts, St. Thomas has developed the Aquinas program as an option for first-year students. The Aquinas program is an interdisciplinary program that explores the connections between disciplines, linking them together in a thematic approach. Examples are this year's "Gender and Society: Sex, Lives, and Videotapes," "Ideas that Matter: An Introduction to Thoughtful Reading," and "Truth in Society." Another new innovation is the new

Co-op Arts program which incorporates three paid work terms into an Arts degree so students gain practical work experience while they learn.

REZ LIFE Finding suitable student housing in Fredericton is not a problem for STU students. Students wishing to live in residence can choose from four residences— Vanier Hall which houses 200 women, Harrington Hall which houses two floors of men and one floor of women (not co-ed), Holy Cross House which houses approximately 70 women, and the newly acquired "Forest Hills Property," formerly Keddy's Motel, will allow St. Thomas to offer residence rooms to an additional 150 students each year. STU

A Word to the Wise:

1. Make the most out of your four years in Fredericton. Study hard, make friends, see the town! Enjoy what Fredericton and St. Thomas University have to offer.

2. Be nice to people–especially your professors, classmates, university support staff, student employees, and the reference librarians at the Harriet Irving Library. This will benefit you in the long run.

3. Get to know yourself if you don't already. Learn to like what you see.

4. Organize a schedule that is right for you. Take morning classes if you are an early bird. Schedule around TV shows you just *have* to watch so you won't skip classes. Don't take on too many extracurricular activities. Remember, you are here for academic reasons!

5. Learn to ignore the arts jokes engineers toss your way. Remember that a liberal arts education will instill in you skills like critical thinking and a desire for learning that you will have for a lifetime and no one can ever take away.

students can also apply for UNB residence if they wish and there are small numbers of UNB students who choose to live in residence at STU.

Since the number of single rooms is limited and students are awarded them on the basis of a point system, it is fairly rare for first-year students to get single rooms. Rooms are assigned on a first-come, first-served basis, so if you are interested in residence, apply as early as possible! Residence offers students life in a community within a community—residence is a great place to meet people, especially if you are new to Fredericton. It is also very convenient for students travelling a fair distance. After you are assigned a room, you just need to show up, suitcase in hand. While the rooms may not be huge, it is amazing how much stuff students can fit into them. Unfortunately, our residences do not have elevators, so bring loved ones along to help you move in. Each house is equipped with special wheelchair-accessible rooms, and students with special medical needs should inform the Student Affairs Office when they apply. Each residence has an elected house committee and is staffed by a team trained in First Aid, CPR, and

student issues. The team consists of a Residence Coordinator and several proctors and is supervised by the Student Affairs Office. All STU residences are security buildings equipped with intercoms at the front doors so guests can call to be admitted. STU publishes a residence handbook that is updated yearly with new information and sent out to all residence students so they will know what to expect. Cafeteria food is provided by Aramark and the meal plan is very flexible and student friendly.

Students wishing to live off campus can contact either the off-campus housing office, shared with UNB, or the Student Affairs Office for a list of available student housing. Watch for notices in local newspapers or contact landlords at some of the various apartment complexes in the city. Finding a place to live will not be a problem, but the earlier you look the more successful you will be in getting exactly what you want.

NIGHT LIFE

There are two bars on campus: the College Hill Social Club (found upstairs in the SUB) and The Cellar (in the SUB basement). Student Union nights at The Cellar attract great crowds! Fredericton now has minimum drink prices set by law, but this does not stop students from having a good time. Most of the other bars in town can be found downtown on King, Queen, and York streets, but there are a few others uptown and on the north side as well. To list the bars frequented by students: ALL OF THEM! Different student groups have their preferred watering holes, so you may have to just give them the ol' college try once you arrive. Drink responsibly, though—puking your guts on the sidewalk in front of the bar is not cool!

ON FREDERICTON

Home to two universities and over 15,000 students, Fredericton is a very student friendly city and offers its 50,000 residents lots to see and do. There are four malls, three within walking distance of the campus, for those who like to shop or hang out at the mall. Empire Theaters has an eight-screen theatre in Regent Mall and there a number of arcades and video stores close to campus. Most pizza places deliver free to campus in the evening and there are a number of cool places to eat and drink in the city, like the Diplomat, Mexicali Rosas, the Hilltop, Keystone Kelly's, the Rogue, and the list goes on and on. Odell Park is great for park strolls and nature hikes, and if you want a big cone of ice cream, Tingleys is the place to go. On Saturdays, there is a farmer's market downtown.

University of Prince Edward Island

By Karen Rawlines

Nestled in Canada's cradle of confederation, the University of Prince Edward Island, as it is known today, is a young and growing, up-and-coming institution, which has been sustained by the smallest province in Canada for 30 years. While Bryan Adams was buying his first real six string at the five and dime in 1969, UPEI was being founded as the result of the amalgamation of Prince of Wales College and Saint Dunstan's University. For over 150 years, however, post-secondary education on the Island existed in other forms, such as Central Academy and St. Andrew's College. The newly conceived UPEI was created to provide a non-denominational facility that could benefit all Islanders.

The petite campus is clean and grassy, and aesthetics are generally consistent among the brick buildings that dot the small property. Ivy climbs a number of these constructs, lending a traditional feeling to the campus despite its relative youth. Main Building is among the few well-aged structures which, in their maturity, seem to exude the residual wisdom of alumni. More recent additions to the campus, such as Duffy (Science) and Kelley (Business) struggle to continue the brick, ivy league theme with their late sixties/early seventies design, but for most students, the initial clash of old and new somehow dissolves after a few months. The biggest hiccup in the stately brick trend is the university's Chaplaincy Centre at the heart of the campus, looking like a Lego house that ran out of blocks, though it is still reasonably quaint. For adventurous types, the Robertson Library eases into the bank of a hill and acts as a temptress for ambitious climbers who occasionally scale the sloping roof and explore the campus from its two-story climb or spy on the studious through skylights. The source of greatest pride in terms of edifices is the big, red barn—wittily monikered "The Barn"—that houses the UPEI Student Union Centre (which reads as USUC). The Barn makes students swell with pride, and becomes the living room they always wanted, complete with beer-saturated carpet, eau de beer gently wafting throughout the area, and a bar where beer is sold. Unfortunately, The Barn is slated to retire soon, and will be replaced by a new student union building that bares an uncanny resemblance to a train station.

UPEI buildings benefit from a mandatory building fund donation that all students make (it's included in student fees). These donations are put towards the renovation or construction of buildings, and the perks of this initiative are easily seen, as in the case of Main and Cass. Other valuable donations have made the modern KC Irving Chemistry Centre a reality. The Young Canada Games Centre (a.k.a. the fieldhouse) hosts UPEI's varsity Panthers' athletic action, and is also a relatively recent addition of high quality.

CAMPUS CULTURE

The high percentage of students who are Islanders makes the campus more than a little homogenous—but not in a bad way. Students from away amuse themselves for the first bit by exploiting the original islanders' accents which suddenly seem so different (slippery is usually "slippy") and see how many mainland students titter with giggles as they ask PEI'ers to say H_2O or to spell "hat." Most UPEI folk don't become mired in the realm of student politics or other events that require an excessive output of energy. Small conglomerates of quasiradicals try their hands at changing the world via Student Union, student press or radio, the theatre society, and varsity or intramural sports. Still others dabble in activities of the extracurricular ilk such as the campus women's centre, WUSC, or debating. The strongest ties seem to be made by the department societies, such as the Biology Club or the Business, Soc/Anth, and English societies. Each department at UPEI has its own lounge, and it's here that the social academics tend to invest most of their time in the form of lounge lizard. The couches and chairs of these spaces never seem to be vacant, and come exam and essay season, the lounges are teeming with the harried and the haggard. It's not likely a safe environment for a

Vital Statistics

Address: 550 University Avenue, Charlottetown, Prince Edward Island, C1A 4P3

Admissions office: (902) 566-0439

Website: www.upei.ca

Total enrollment: 2,718

Male-female ratio: 39 to 61

Percentage of out-of-province first-year students: 19%

Cut-off grade for admissions: Arts: 76%; Science: 82%; Commerce: 78%; Engineering: 84%

Tuition fees: $3,331

Residence fees: Room $2,300–$3,252; board $2,340–$3512; room and board $4,640–$5,764 (double occupancy/14-meal plan). 40% of residence spaces allocated by lottery. 60% of residence spaces reserved for first-year students.

Percentage of students in residence: 14%

Co-op programs: Internships available for Business students

Financial aid: 56 renewable scholarships, full tuition, capped at $3,000; 75 non-renewable entrance scholarships of $1,000 and $1,500 available for first-year students. Once accepted, students have access to a wide variety of scholarships and awards.

Facilities for students with disabilities: Services for Disabled Students

Student services: Career Development Centre, Chaplaincy, Counselling, Daycare Centre, First-Year Advisement Centre, Health Centre, International Student Services, Learning Assistance Centre, New Student Orientation

panic-stricken first year, but the situation breeds empathy, and, in rare cases, what comes close to compassionate assistance from peers who know what you're going through.

ACADEMIC ISSUES

UPEI's small size means that most classes keep to an intimate atmosphere, highlighting a personalized experience—one which most students find beneficial. Professors learn and remember not only your names, but your personalities, aptitudes, and other trivia. The casual interactions many students and professors enjoy eventually create a comfortable classroom environment. Professors are approachable. They notice when you're sleeping in class, or altogether absent, and while some mind less, others will follow up with an e-mail to investigate the situation. Your prof can be your best friend on this campus, and it's a good friendship to forge. Over the years, they will become more than educators, but advisors, confidantes, and teammates on the intramural court.

The Atlantic Veterinary College is one of the country's few schools for animal medicine, and thus acts as one of UPEI's primary draws and recruitment benefits. Every year, throngs of students begin their post-secondary education at UPEI in hopes of making their way through the hallowed halls of the AVC in a few years. Not all will hang on to make it, and even fewer of these bother applying. By the time third or fourth year rolls around, a large proportion of the aspiring Biology majors who proclaimed to be "pre-vet" students in their first year aren't anymore, having switched into another faculty, or in some cases, switched to another university. The lure of the Vet College is a strong one, but not all hang on to the dream for the long haul.

UPEI is primarily geared towards the needs of undergraduate students, but just recently indoctrinated its first PhD degree, and Masters' degrees in Science are also available in some disciplines. The school offers undergrad education in Arts, Science, Education, Music, Engineering, Business Administration, Veterinary Medicine, and Nursing. The school continues to develop new programs in addition to these, and has recently celebrated the first classes of graduates in Computer Science, Adult Education, Foods and Nutrition, Family Science, a two-year post-degree Bachelor of Education program, and a Bachelor of Business Administration featuring an internship. The diminutive scale of the school does not lessen the quality of education received at UPEI. Biology and Psychology are among the most popular departments on campus, along with English and Business. Biology and English, in particular, fare extremely well when representing the school at Atlantic Undergraduate conferences. Unfortunately, the university's small size does restrict some class offerings, making the more popular and appealing electives often difficult to get into. Some disciplines offered at UPEI are in keeping with

In a Nut Shell

The university in a phrase: It's a province. It's an island. It's a university.

Best thing about the university: Small classes, profs not only know your name, they get to know your personalities and aptitudes.

Worst thing about the university: The lack of student involvement in extracurricular activities.

Favourite professors: D. Adams (Accounting); D. Bulger (Philosophy/Political Science); A. Ferris (Business); N. Kunjundzic (Philosophy); C. Lacroix (Biology); G. Lindsay (English); C. Ryan (Psychology); B. MacLaine (English), R. Lemm (English), S. Murray (English), R. Haines (Chem), Boudreau (Psych), R. Kurial (History).

Most popular bird courses: University 100, Computer Science 111, Music 104.

Hot spot to study on campus: The Impressions Cafe (commonly and nostalgically called "the Pit").

Quietest spot to study on campus: Basement of the Robertson Library in a vacant classroom.

Most social spots to study on campus: The Pit in the Robertson Library.

Need for car and parking availability: There are no buses, but most places in Charlottetown can be reached by a $5 cab ride. Anything beyond city limits needs wheels. Parking is around $50–$60 for the year, and a big number of students need to drive, so there's a lot of complaining about the hike to class from the parking lot (but it's not really that bad).

Sexually speaking: Many students come to UPEI with their high school sweethearts, so a lot of people are taken. Remember, reputations are easy to acquire and not easy to change.

Fraternities/sororities: There aren't any at UPEI.

Athletic facilities: The Sports Centre houses indoor facilities including aerobics, fitness and weight training, racquetball, and squash. Outdoor field hockey/rugby and soccer fields, softball diamonds, tennis courts, volleyball.

Library facilities: Library includes electronic catalogue, CD-ROMs, and Internet-enhanced reference area.

Computer facilities: Information Technology Education Centre with demonstration area for students. Desktop and room-based video conferencing available. All students provided with Novell LAN, with over 225 microcomputers available in public and departmental microcomputer labs. Twenty classrooms equipped with data/video projection. Three mobile units available from audio visual services.

Weather: It's cold. It's windy. It's sunny. It's rainy. It's an island. It's Maritime weather. Learn how to layer.

Safety on campus: SafeWalk program, and flashing blue lights and two-way communication system in former dimly lit areas of the campus.

Alumni: Journalist Mike Duffy; singer/songwriter Lenny Gallant; former premier of PEI Joseph Ghiz; author L.M. Montgomery.

---

some of UPEI's strongest themes, such as the Business Administration degree specializing in tourism, and other courses offered via UPEI's L.M. Montgomery Institute.

REZ LIFE Residence life at UPEI is different from that of many other Atlantic campuses. The bulk of the student population is native to PEI, and so most either live at home, or find a place to call their own off campus. Students from away usually stay in residence, if only for their first year. The residences include Marian Hall (an all-male residence), Bernardine Hall (all female, with one co-ed floor), and Blanchard Hall (an apartment-style residence). The first two are generally used as stepping stones for students new to living away from home. Particularly in their first year, residents will be nurtured by the communal lifestyle and by each other. As is the case for most other universities, students who live in residence are making valuable connections that often last a lifetime. The small num-

ber of residents on hand and the fact that the campus is situated on the outer edge of the city, can make the rez experience a stifling or frustrating one. Most will choose to test the off-campus waters at some point. Living in the residence system does provide some luxuries in the form of rather modern digs, particularly in the case of Bernardine Hall, which offers rooms that have adjoining bathrooms, and a sink in every room—something that will be envied by rez cohorts on other campuses. Marian is a multipurpose unit, which is adjacent to the university's health centre and, ironically, the daycare. Blanchard tends to have some climate control troubles in the winters, but many still prefer the chance to cook their very own Kraft Dinner. Overall, the rez students are a rather overlooked set in the eyes of the rest of campus, perhaps because the cozy atmosphere is not yet well understood. Those on the inside mostly enjoy it, calling it home and stomaching the cuisine of the neighbouring Wanda Wyatt dining hall, and proud to have their own slate of activities, councils, and lifestyle.

NIGHT LIFE

Again, a small city does somewhat impose limits, and in this case, the grandeur of a night life sees its magnificence restricted. Still, it's not all moonshine and bootleggers when weekend comes around, as Charlottetown has a number of decent pubs and licensed establishments. The flagship of the lot is the Myron's compound: a relatively sprawling bar offering a watered-down Electric Circus flavour for those who just want to shake their money makers to the tune of Captain Morgan and Alexander Keith's ale. There's also a cabaret where touring talent often stop (April Wine comes a lot), a number of little nooks and crannies with couches, and a restaurant. The whole compound is loud, and expensive, but for some, it has a cliché, this-is-university and I-love-my-student-loan feel. Over time, most will outgrow this phase, and try to make it to Myron's a mere couple times a week, if at all. Others abandon the good ship drinky-drinky completely and sip coffee intellectually and discuss deep things elsewhere. Another hotbed of activity for the thirsty and dry alike is the university pub, the Panther Lounge, housed in the beautiful Barn. Generally described as a big rec room for the wayward. The lounge is rarely empty—be it a few dedicated attendees during a break between classes watching the big-screen televisions, or a capacity crowd at a major event such as the St. Patrick's Day Pub, Hallowe'en Pub, or the secret "drink the barn dry" event held at the end of each semester. For the more relaxed sect, there is a host of coffee houses and low-key pubs and restaurants, such as Baba's Lounge (upstairs from Cedar's Eatery) and Cedar's Eatery (downstairs from Baba's Lounge), and Rye's. Trivia nights at The Barn and at other establishments are also extremely popular. No matter what the spur of the moment may dictate, most hotbeds of activity can be reached by foot, or by a $5 cab ride that will take you pretty much anywhere in the city. Since there isn't a bus system, cabs will become important, as will friends with chariots of fire.

ON PEI

Beyond the harsh cultural and social stereotypes the Island province has endured, there exists a community that is very much alive—one that has developed beyond potatoes, Anne of Green Gables, and the legendary red dirt. For a city housing roughly 30,000 inhabitants, Charlottetown is as big as little can be, whether it's considered the world's finest self-contained tourist trap or the planet's greatest floating spud. The Island is nothing short of being absolutely unique in its circumstance and character. As a capital city, Charlottetown is privy to perhaps more urban commodities than elsewhere on the Island. This town boasts an independent cinema, spades of cafés and restaurants, and every other modern luxury a modern tourist could anticipate or desire. However, the business knows its market and the winter months begin with a yawn as sites which were happening and hep during the summer close earlier during the long off-season, or often hibernate throughout the snowy months.

There are no beverages in cans on PEI, save for a few delinquent products which have somehow infiltrated. In first year, cans are the biggest treat a CFA (come from away) can be blessed with. However, as years pass, bottles become irreplaceable as a mode of ingesting any potable—potent or otherwise—and anything else just isn't quite the same...especially when bottles are cashed in for lucrative deposit refunds, something very handy come laundry time. All things considered, Charlottetown is not really a university town, despite having its main drag named University Ave. Although the city can often seem very quiet and suffocating if one is trapped on campus, the virtue of living in a petite province should not be overlooked. The sights and sounds, the colours and the shapes of this clod of red dirt are beyond reproach. Charlottetown is the big little town that brings in tourists from as far as Japan who hope for a glimpse of Anne's house, and the tiny city where the Fathers of Confederation brought together their vision of a country. What can be mistaken for sleepiness is actually serenity, a peaceful beauty that begs to be explored. An education at UPEI is not complete without visiting the national park to see the unique dune systems at Greenwich, or Cavendish's red sand beaches. There is something calming and natural about the Island, perhaps because it is calm and natural. Should the feeling of isolation seem insurmountable, the recently constructed engineering wonder of the Confederation Bridge means that it is never permanent, and a quick trip to another Maritime province (although expensive with the one way $35 bridge toll) can often cure itchy feet. Those who require constant action à la Bruce Willis movies might be better off elsewhere; those who have at least a red grain of patience (or are looking to find one) will appreciate the predominantly rural culture of the Island.

Memorial University of Newfoundland

By Leigh Borden

Memorial University of Newfoundland was founded in 1949, the successor to Memorial University College, which was established in 1925. The university is the largest in Atlantic Canada, with approximately 12,000 full-time and 2,000 part-time undergraduate students and 1,600 graduate students. A perfect university for diversity in programs and locations, Memorial University has four campuses. The main campus is located in St. John's, the capital city of Newfoundland. This campus has the greatest student population and number of programs. Sir Wilfred Grenfell College, located in Corner Brook, Newfoundland, is a lovely small liberal arts and sciences college specializing in Theatre, Visual Arts, and Environmental Studies. The university's other two campuses are located in Harlow, England, and on the island of St. Pierre, a French territory off the coast of Newfoundland. Both of the international campuses are fantastic places to acquire educational experiences in a foreign context.

Newfoundland is the perfect locale for marine studies. Affiliated with Memorial University is the Fisheries and Marine Institute. This world-class facility offers degree, diploma, and certificate programs in everything from Naval Architecture to Nautical Science to Marine Environmental Studies. Equipped with the latest and best marine technology, the Marine Institute is a world leader in marine and oceanographic research.

Architecturally, the main campus of Memorial University is, for the most part, quite simple. Most of the buildings were completed in the 1960s, and so display a not-quite-attractive modern look. However, two new and very attractive buildings are in progress. A Field House (sportsplex) will be started soon and a new Student Centre will be opening in January 2000. The campus is being revitalized by the development of these new facilities. Cosmetically, Memorial is improving day by day.

CAMPUS CULTURE

A somewhat homogeneous student body populates Memorial University. Most of the university's students are Newfoundlanders; however, the proportion of out-of-province and international students is quickly increasing. There's always a place for any student at Memorial. Traditional Newfoundland friendliness combined with common ideas and interests make the clubs and societies on our campus very active, successful, and fun. Some of the largest and most active clubs and societies are the Chinese Students' Association and the Scholars' Association, with over 200 members. There is also the Debating Society, whose national competition performances have been stellar, the various academic societies (e.g., English, Biology, Engineering) who have finally succeeded in creating some semblance of school spirit on the campus, and a variety of other political, social, and academic groups are inspiring the entire university community.

In St. John's, campus media attracts a great number of aspiring writers and broadcasters. The student newspaper, *the muse*, is regarded as one of the best campus newspapers in Canada. It publishes weekly during the fall and winter semesters and biweekly during the spring semester. CHMR-FM, the campus radio station, has approx-

Vital Statistics

Address: P.O. Box 4200, Station C, St. John's, Newfoundland, A1C 5S7

Admissions office: (709) 737-8000

Website: www.mun.ca

Total enrollment: 15,504

Male-female ratio: 42 to 58

Percentage of out-of-province students: 2%

Percentage of international students: 2%

Cut-off-grade for admissions: 70%

Tuition fees: $110 per credit hour; $330 per course; $1,650 per semester.

Residence fees: $672 (double room/semester); $830 (single room/semester); $1,223 (14 meal plan/semester)

Percentage of students in residence: 6%

Co-op programs: Business Administration, Engineering, Physical Education, Applied Social Psychology, Social Work

Facilities for students with disabilities: All buildings on campus are accessible. The Glenn Roy Blundon Centre offers assistance to students with disabilities in the form of elevator keys, notetakers, special seating or desks, etc. MUN Disability Information and Support Centre is funded by the Students' Union and operates by students, and provides advocacy and a peer support network for students with disabilities.

Student services: Student Health, Counselling Centre, Student Housing and Food Services, General Student Services, Student Development, Student Recruitment, International Office.

imately 140 volunteers during the fall and winter semesters. At CHMR, they'll teach you to operate the board and help you develop and broadcast your own show. Both *the muse* and CHMR provide students with excellent training for careers later in life. In fact, many alumni are very famous Canadians—for instance, Bob Cole of CBC Sports was a volunteer at CHMR-FM!

ACADEMIC ISSUES

As MUN is the only degree-granting institution in Newfoundland and Labrador, it serves a special function to the residents of the province. Memorial has the responsibility of educating the people of Newfoundland and Labrador and researching and studying the unique facets of Newfoundland's environment, culture, and society. This characteristic makes Memorial a special and unmatched place to learn.

Funding at Memorial University is tight due to cuts in transfer payments from the federal government; however, after an intensive three-year fundraising campaign, the university is now able to replace some worn facilities and, happily, significantly increase the number of scholarships available to both undergraduate and graduate students. And while small programs in the arts have been scrutinized as being too expensive to maintain, the university has resisted cutting any of the small but fantastic programs such as Russian Language and Literature.

Memorial has one of the best professor-to-student ratios in Canada. First-year Psychology is the only large (200+) class at the university; in all other programs, the class sizes are among the smallest in Canada. In particular, first-year classes have been deliberately kept small, ensuring the best learning environment for the student.

Some programs at Memorial, such as the BComm (co-op) and Psychology, have highly competitive entrance requirements. Many frustrated students spend semester after semester taking pre-requisites and hoping that this time, they'll get in. Restricted enrollment and sometimes unconquerable wait-lists are some of the most problematic issues for students at MUN.

As one might expect, the faculties of Business Administration and Engineering and Applied Sciences are the best funded at the university. The extra support, of course, tends to come from the private sector. Both these faculties are very large and extremely popular to new students (somewhat to the detriment of the faculties of arts and science). However, a new concurrent degree program, BA/BComm (co-op), is proving to be an extremely desirable (if exhausting) option for a number of students.

REZ LIFE

Residence at Memorial comes in two forms: traditional residences for men and women, and apartment-style residences for those who have completed their first year (four single bedrooms and a kitchen per apartment). Paton College, as the 10 traditional residence houses are collectively known, houses approximately 900 students, mostly in

In a Nut Shell

University in a phrase: Committed to excellence in teaching, research, and scholarship, and service to the general public.

Best thing about the university: Small classes.

Worst thing about the university: Course wait lists.

Favourite professors: Noreen Golfman (English); the only civilian ever to be appointed to Scotland Yard and author Elliot Leyton (Anthropology); A. Staveley (English); C. Youé (History)

Most popular bird course: Anthropology 2260—War and Aggression

Hot spots to study on campus: QEII Library reading rooms, Health Sciences Centre Library, The Breezeway.

Quietest spots to study on campus: Quiet study areas in the QEII library.

Need for car and parking availability: Not many parking spots available. If you don't have a car, don't worry. St. John's isn't that big.

Sexually speaking: Many opportunities for sexual encounters in St. John's—as long as you're straight. St. John's is severely homophobic.

Fraternities/sororities: There aren't any frats or sororities at MUN.

Athletic facilities: Gym, weight rooms, and squash courts. Aquarena neighbours the campus.

Library facilities: Queen Elizabeth II Library has 1.6 million volumes and approximately twice that in micro-material holdings.

Computer facilities: Easy access to a computer—if you can find MUN's computer labs. Certain courses offer computer-learning labs.

Weather: Temperature is fairly mild. Bring an umbrella and expect rain—lots in winter.

Safety on campus: The Students' Union operates a Walksafe program that is well used and helps students feel at ease.

Alumni: Alan Doyle, John Fraser (Master of Massey College), Bob Hallett, Sean McCann, Rex Murphy (CBC commentator), Darrell Power (Great Big Sea)

---

double rooms. They're not large, but you can stow an incredible amount of stuff in all those drawers and shelves. Four of the houses are single sex: three for women and one for men. The remaining six are co-ed.

Nowhere near as wild and unrestrained as once they were, residences at Memorial are still great fun. In Paton College, you can count on lots of parties, regular Thursday nights at the Breezeway, and a super environment for making loads of friends. Each semester, the 10 houses each hold cabin parties and boat tours, and of course, the ever-popular "House Day." Each house chooses a Saturday early in the semester and spends the day together partying, playing foolish games, welcoming first-year students, and trying to outdo other houses in spirit (and volume!). The evening usually culminates in a trip to some downtown dance bar.

Food service is not terrible at MUN. The Main Dining Hall, open during the fall and winter semesters, offers one vegetarian and two meat entrees at lunch and dinner every day. All Paton College residents eat there.

Residence life ought to be a part of everyone's university experience. Memorial's residences are fun and some-

times a little wild, but are also excellent places for learning and making friends in a new and possibly scary environment.

NIGHT LIFE

For many Memorial students, the first St. John's bar they ever visit is the infamous and lauded campus bar, The Breezeway. This bar, owned and operated by the Students' Union, is about to move to its third, biggest, and best location in the new student centre. The Breezeway is home to many students. As an added bonus, Breezeway regular beer and drink prices are way cheaper than anywhere else in town (at time of printing, $2.30/local beer and $2.40/drink). Thursday and Friday nights are favoured by patrons. Be prepared, though, lineups usually begin by 9:30 or 10 p.m, so come early to avoid the wait. The first and last days of semesters are even worse, so act accordingly.

St. John's has the most bars and pubs per capita of any city in Canada, so never is there a

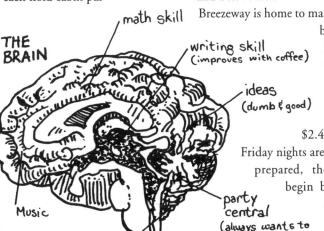

THE BRAIN

math skill

writing skill (improves with coffee)

ideas (dumb & good)

Music

party central (always wants to take over the rest of the brain)

sexuality (yeah! it's pretty low brain activity)

shortage of places to go. Dance bars like Trapper John's, the Sundance, Turkey Joe's, and Kelly's offer your typical trendy, Top-40 dance hits, with a nice mix of retro tunes. Junctions is a great alternative bar, usually featuring some great local rock bands. O'Reilly's and the Blarney Stone have live Irish music—you can be sure that these bars will always be crowded, lively, full of dancers, and a really super time.

St. John's also has a number of pubs featuring snacks, beers on tap, and a comfortable, friendly environment. Favourites of MUN students include Bitters (the Graduate Students' Union pub), Big Ben's, and the Guv'nor's Pub. Bitters is located on the north side of campus in Field Hall. Big Ben's and the Guv'nor are within a five-minute walk from campus. Downtown, the Ship Inn and the Duke of Duckworth are two favourite pubs. The Ship Inn often features live music and readings by local authors. Both are very popular among a varied group of people. You'll never find either of these pubs filled with all young people, or all old people. The crowd is always diverse, and that is, of course, what makes them interesting places to be.

> "Such is the nature of this city: windy, fishy, anecdotal, proud, weather-beaten, quirky, obliging, ornery, and fun."
>
> Jan Morris, *Saturday Night*, March 1989.

ON ST. JOHN'S

If you are looking for a city that's friendly, happening, attractive, and homey, St. John's is your best bet. St. John's is the oldest city in North America, and that history envelops all aspects of life here. Culturally, there are innumerable events—festivals, exhibits, concerts, theatre, and so much more. St. John's is rarely boring or lacking something interesting and unusual to do. The city is quite beautiful, with its unique architecture, lush green parklands, and somewhat wind-battered landscape. Hiking, sea kayaking, climbing, canoeing, fishing, swimming, and whale- and bird-watching are all common hobbies of residents of St. John's. Some of these activities are within walking distance—others are just a short drive away.

St. John's is a safe city by Canadian standards. Crime rates are fairly low. The Memorial University campus is very safe as well. All in all, one may feel comfortable on St. John's streets.

The city and province are among the best places to live in Canada. The weather's not bad, everything one would want is available, and the people can't be beat. It's an ideal place to pursue post-secondary education, and as many students feel, St. John's is a great place to be.

Terms to Know

Aggie: The term given to students who are majoring in Agriculture at the University of Guelph, or somewhere out west. These are generally friendly people with a decidedly natural bend. They have been known to prefer Wranglers to Levis.

Anti-calendar: Course and professor evaluations by students for students published each year. A very handy piece that for many becomes the bible of academic study for the year ahead. Be smart and get one, it'll make life much easier.

Apathy: A lack of student involvement and lack of student activism.

Artsie: A nickname given to students in Arts programs. Often can be seen wandering around campus with philosophy texts and poetry journals in ink-stained hands, looking slightly lost. An excellent and kind specimen of humanity.

Bachelor's degree: A first degree awarded by a university after three of four years of full-time study. A fancy piece of paper that has your name on it, the university's seal, and superpowers, too. It puts more money in your pocket (statistics show a correlation with university study and higher salaries).

Bird course: a.k.a. basketweaving, joke, or rubber courses. These courses are usually easy and students take them to boost their GPAs. See **GPA**. No, there isn't really a course on basketweaving.

Bursary: A financial award given primarily on the basis of financial need, although academic excellence and extracurricular activities are also taken into account. Bursaries are usually non-repayable, which means you don't have to pay them back, which means they are an excellent way of filling your pocket.

If you're in need, do look into the bursaries offered by your university.

Calendar: A university publication that lists admission and program requirements, information on degree programs, course descriptions, and important dates and deadlines. The university calendar is also often filled with bits of advice from students at the university, tips, and even coupons for restaurants and stores around campus.

CEGEP (Collège d'enseignement général et professionnel): After high school, students from Quebec complete a two- or three-year diploma which prepares them for university or a trade school.

Certificate program: A university program that is usually one year in length.

Christmas graduates: Students who can't hack a certain course, or university for that matter, and drop out around exam time before the winter holiday break.

College: 1. A post-secondary degree-granting institution. 2. A part of a university that serves as a home base. It offers academic counselling, programmes and/or residence accommodation, and special student services. Colleges were originally formed to alleviate the sense of anonymity that is prevalent in larger universities. Your college can become your social hang-out, your residence, and your identity while at university.

Compulsory course: A course that you need to take, and pass, in order to complete your minor/major.

Convocation: a.k.a. graduation, the black gown, the procession, and the large white envelope containing your degree.

Co-op program: A program that allows students to combine academic learning with real-life work experience. Students alternate on-campus academic study terms with off-campus paid work terms in a field directly related to their area of study.

Credit: A unit of an academic program earned toward a degree by successfully completing a course. By the end of third or fourth year many students can be seen fervidly counting their credits in order to ensure graduation is possible.

Department: A subdivision of a faculty. See **Faculty**.

Diploma: Usually awarded on the basis of one or two years of study at an undergraduate level. Some diplomas are offered at the graduate level.

Doctorate: A degree ranking above the Master's degree.

Don: a.k.a. floor-fellow or resident assistant (RA) An upper-year student who lives on your floor (in your hall or your house) in residence and acts as an activity planner, guidance counsellor, and voice of reason in the chaos of day-to-day residence life. Dons can answers your questions about rez life, campus life, and life in general. They're also a great way of getting to know people in university who are a bit older.

Drop/add date: A specific time period when students shop around for courses. If you drop a course during this period, that course will not count on your transcript and you will get back 100% of your fees for that course.

Elective: Any course you take that is not required. The credits you receive for elective courses count towards your degree, but they do not count towards your major/minor.

Faculty: 1. The teaching staff of a university. 2. An academic subdivision of a university that is normally larger than a department. For example, a Faculty of Science may include the departments of Biology, Botany, Chemistry, Physiology, and Zoology.

Freshman fifteen: Refers to the 15 or so pounds that many freshman pack on simply by eating the compulsory residence food of your meal plan—dessert, second helpings, snacks between classes, junk food, grease, cholesterol, etc. You have

no control, so it's not your fault. Just be sure to pack sweatpants with elastic waist bands.

Frosh: To some, a politically incorrect way of referring to first-year students. Freshman, freshperson, first-year. However you spell it, it means *you* in your first year of university. Wear it proudly.

Frosh Week/Orientation Week: Normally a week-long orientation that is jam-packed with fun and wacky events organized by older students to make the frosh feel welcome. Events include campus and city tours, pub crawls, barbecues, ice-breaker activities, and much more. Frosh Week is one huge party. Words of advice: Watch out for engineers. Bring a flask or wineskin. Wear crappy clothing.

Gender-neutral: Politically correct use of language. For example, saying humankind instead of mankind and not calling women "girls."

(Student) Ghetto: An area of the city where a high proportion of students live, usually within close distance to the university campus. Here you'll find apartments and houses that are usually rented out for cheap rates and are occasionally a bit run-down. In general, though, this is a great place to live once you've outgrown rez life.

GPA (Grade Point Average): Your academic average is based on the grades you attain and is calculated at the end of each academic term. Your GPA does not recognize the amount of time spent studying for an exam (that you failed in the end anyway), nor does it take effort into account. Your Cumulative GPA (CGPA), on the other hand, is calculated using your entire academic record and it's what really counts. It is often used by universities to separate the sheep from the goats. Your CGPA is the main factor in deciding scholarships and admission to some programs, professional faculties, and graduate schools.

Graduate: After you complete your undergraduate degree, you can hide from the "real world" and continue with graduate studies. Graduate programs lead to postgraduate degrees and diplomas.

Granolas (granola eaters): A label given to students who wear Birkenstocks with wool socks, who snack on bean products, and who are generally concerned with the environment, deforestation, and endangered species. Excellent people.

Homecoming: Usually in the fall, a social event in which a university's alumni return to relive the nostalgia of days gone by. Homecoming Weekend festivities often include a football game and lots of drinking. Queen's and Bishop's Homecoming weekends are legendary.

Honours: Indicates a higher degree of specialization in your major and is usually awarded after four years of full-time study in your Bachelor's degree program.

Incidental fees: a.k.a. Student services fees, ancillary fees. These are extra costs that pay for access to student services and athletic and recreation facilities.

Inter-library loans: Access to other university libraries. You can find out if a copy of the book you want/need is anywhere nearby.

Inter-session: Time off (a vacation) from school between academic terms. Universities usually shut down during this period (e.g. Winter Break).

Intramurals: Sports organized by and for the regular student body.

Liberal arts: A well-rounded general education that combines arts, humanities, music, social science, and science.

Major/minor: A facade you put on for three or four years to trick others into thinking that there is actually a purpose to your studies. A major program indicates a higher degree of specialization, with a number of courses from one area of concentration; a minor indicates a lesser degree of specialization from one area. You usually have to declare your major(s)/minor(s) in your second year of university study. A major/minor is something that many people switch two, three, or sometimes more times before graduation.

Master's degree: A degree pursued by students who have already received a Bachelor's degree. Students can attain this degree by taking courses and passing exams, and/or by conducting research and presenting a thesis.

OAC: Ontario Academic Credit. Can't get into university without 'em.

Ombudsperson: A university official who offers impartial and confidential advice and assistance with any campus complaints or grievances.

OSAP (Ontario Student Assistance Program): Loans through the Ontario Provincial Government which provide financial aid to students based on demonstrated need, taking into account two main factors: (1) family and personal resources, and (2) the cost of tuition.

Politically correct: The language of the average educated university person. Politically correct means you know the difference between African Canadian and black, Asians and Chinese, and all kinds of other subtle bits of language that shows respect for people's individuality and culture.

Prerequisite: A course you need to pass before you can register into a particular course or program.

Prof: Short form for *prof*essor. They're not called "teachers" anymore. A prof is a fountain of knowledge who rambles on and on about their field of expertise, often getting off track. Also considered to be a part-time judge, jury, and executioner when it comes to the fate of your GPA. Act accordingly.

Program: A series of courses that lead to a degree, usually taken over three or four years of full-time university study.

Pub crawl: A boozefest where you and a whole bunch of people hop from pub to club to bar to drink and be merry.

Reading Week: a.k.a. Slack Week or Spring Break. Most universities give their students a week off, usually in mid to late February. Most students drink, fly south, party, and sleep during this period, although it is rumoured that some have actually used this time to catch up on studying and computing assignments.

Registrar: The Registrar's Office is responsible for admissions, student academic records, academic counselling, and university timetables.

Rez: Short for residence, rez, *res*idence, get it? The reason many people decide to go to university. Rez is a social, high-traffic, noisy place where you can do anything but sleep and study. Enjoy.

Rezzie: A nickname given to students living in rez. These creatures often emerge for early morning classes pyjama clad, and yawning, with wacky hair and sleep gooped into the corners of their eyes, Treat them kindly, but remember: Do not to feed the animals.

Rush: The time of year when members of a fraternity or a sorority recruit new members, nicknamed "pledges" or "rushes," into their fold, who then must try to secure a pledge of membership from the fraternity or sorority.

Safewalk/Walksafe: A program offered by the university that provides student accompaniment in and around campus after dark so students can get around safely.

Scholarship: A financial award granted to students on the basis of academic merit.

Section: The same course offered at different times.

Student body: That's you. Once you've entered the hallowed halls of universitydom, you become the student body. Whether that means artsie, science geek, sports nut, trendoid, or whatever, wear it well.

Student ID number: Each student at the university is assigned a unique identification number. You are normally given a handy-dandy photo ID card along with the ID number that you usually need to write exams, access library resources, use athletic facilities, vote in student elections, etc.

Students' Union: a.k.a Student's Association, Student's Society, Alma Mater Society. These are names for student governments. Members are elected by the students.

TA (teaching assistant): A graduate student who assists professors in medium- to large-sized classes. TAs grade papers, answer questions on course material, and help students who are feeling lost—don't be afraid to ask for help.

Teleregistration: You can register for courses through a computerized voice system. All you need is a touch-tone phone and quick-trigger finger reflexes. Hint: To guarantee you get into all the courses you want, the first second that the phone lines open for registration, dial the number and keep your finger on the redial button until you get through.

Transcript: A record that lists courses that you are currently taking and have taken (pass or fail), along with your course marks and GPA.

Tutorials: A small discussion group that meets with a professor or TA once or twice a week to discuss course material.

Undergraduate: A student registered in a program that leads to a Bachelor's degree, a first professional degree, a certificate, or a diploma.

Varsity sports: Individual and team sports that are offered at the competitive level through CIAU (Canadian Interuniversity Athletic Union).

Contributors . . .

Ayesha Adhami wrote the piece on Saint Mary's University.

D. Peter Akman is a double major graduate in English and Communications. He was also an All-American member of the SFU Varsity Swim Team and was the first swimmer to complete his degree in the expected four-year allotment. As well as swimming and scholastics, Peter also worked for the writing centre as an academic tutor. Peter will be taking a one-year sabbatical from his studies before returning in the year 2000 to attain his Master's in Journalism with the goal of working for a large television station as a reporter.

Luigi Aloia is currently enrolled in his third year of Political Science at Lakehead University. He is loving every minute of it.

Leigh Anne Baker gave up her international touring and outdoor life as a Canadian National Team Freestyle Skier to attend Queen's Commerce and has never regretted it. She fully admits that she chose Queen's because she came up for Homecoming and had an amazing time hanging out and partying in the village. She would like to thank Kristen Taylor and Wendy Franks for reading her piece and offering suggestions.

Barrett Lincoln Bingley was born in Ottawa but moved around a lot as a kid and ended up living all over Canada, finally settling in Victoria, BC. He did a year in the Writing program at the University of Victoria. In the middle of the winter semester, he decided to switch career tracks entirely and apply to the Royal Military College of Canada. He was accepted in the spring of 1998. He survived BOTC I, Recruit Term, and all of the other wonderful surprises of first year, and is currently a second-year Officer Cadet (OCdt) at RMC in 7 Squadron. He is on the varsity karate team and is taking a degree in Military and Strategic Studies with an Economics minor. Once he has graduated and received his commission, OCdt Bingley hopes to be an officer in the Infantry and spend time on UN and NATO missions.

Leigh Borden is a fourth-year Honours English Literature student at Memorial University of Newfoundland. She has been involved with the Students' Union at MUN for three years, and is currently the president. After graduation in May 2000, Leigh hopes to pursue graduate studies in English Literature and Education.

Mae Cantos is currently in her third year at the University of Waterloo. She is working towards her Honours Bachelor of Science in the Health Studies co-op programme, with a minor in Gerontology and an option in Pre-Health Professions (it's gonna be a jam-packed diploma!). When she's not busy academically, she spends her time teaching aerobics, cheerleading, working for Campus Rec, or chairing Student Ambassador Association meetings. She would like to thank everyone who has made UW an experience to remember and a remembrance to experience.

Chen Chekki attained his BA in 1997, and was a member of the Clifford J. Robson Excellence in Teaching Award committee at the University of Winnipeg. He is now a council member on the board of the U of W Alumni Association, and serves as Editor in Chief for publications such as *The Uniter* (the official student newspaper of the University of Winnipeg), and the Undergraduate Liberal Arts and Science Review journal.

Jason Chow wrote the piece on McGill University. He is in his final year at McGill, majoring in English Literature and History. Originally from Medicine Hat, Alberta, he moved to Montreal to attend McGill in 1996. Jason is presently the Coordinating Editor of the *McGill Daily* and plans on pursuing a career in journalism.

Sally Cogswell is from Centreville, New Brunswick. She completed her BA at St. Thomas University in 1996 and her BEd in 1997. She is currently working on her Masters in History at the University of New Brunswick.

Lisa Drysdale is an interdisciplinary grad student studying English and Gender Studies at the University of Northern British Columbia. She has about one and a half more years to go, then will go on to a PhD. Lisa spends most of her time ardently pursuing her education, building websites, and drinking coffee.

Joshua Dunford recently graduated from Trinity Western University with a degree in Biology. He has now changed directions to pursue his passion for graphic design and photography and he believes that "orange is the colour of the new millennium."

Rebecca Earle is a fourth-year Biology major/Nutrition minor student at Acadia University. She chose Acadia because it's in a small town and it's just like her own hometown, New Glasgow, Nova Scotia. The biggest thing that she learned since attending Acadia is that "university is not about what you have learned, but about the friends that you make along the way." Rebecca dedicates her piece on Acadia to her friends. When she has spare time, she volunteers at the local hospital at home, enjoys aerobics, downhill skiing, travelling, singing, and spending time with friends and family. Rebecca plans to stay in Canada and study medicine, or nursing.

Michael Edwards originally hails from Scotland, but has made Canada his home since 1992. He has been involved with *The Brunswickan*, the student newspaper at the University of New Brunswick, for longer than he cares to remember or admit. In his spare time he writes for several other publications, including *Exclaim!,* and collects music obsessively.

Brent Evans is a graduate of the Lakehead University Bachelor of Education program as well as the Kinesiology program. He has spent the last five years at Lakehead and has enjoyed every minute of it.

Ed Garinger has been involved in all facets of Nipissing University life (he can attest, the walls are thin), from playing the lead in the drama entourage production, to being a member of the varsity volleyball team, to bartending at the campus pub, to the coup de gras, becoming Student Union president. He has studied a myriad of subjects, but hopes he'll garner enough credits to be considered for an English degree, which will hopefully parlay into some sort of teaching, writing, or "horse whispering" career. Future aspirations include a 57 Mustang for his father, a rafting adventure for his mother, a date with Pamela Lee for his brother, and last but certainly not least, a straw shack somewhere in the South Pacific for himself.

Andrea Gordon is presently enrolled in a BA programme at Bishop's University. She is also the current acting President of the Bishop's University Students' Representative Council.

Maggie Greyson started her "formal education" at Western University but left after first year. She got involved with the Fine Arts Students Alliance for fun her first week at her new school, Concordia University. Since then her fun has included publishing the first and second annual *Fine Connections*, fine arts directories for visual and performance artists. After five years of university Concordia will be sad to see her go into the "real world." She takes with her a Design for the Theatre degree. Maggie hopes to marry her desire for ultimate relaxation with the need to be creative in a money-making scheme soon in the future.

Caitlin Hayward is a fourth-year student studying Political Science, and is originally from Toronto. She is currently weighing her future options, debating between grad school or a life as a North Atlantic surf bum.

Tyler Hellard is currently a senior at St. F.X. majoring in English. He is also the editor of the university newspaper, the *Xaverian Weekly*, and does freelance work for the *Halifax Chronicle Herald*.

Sean Junor is entering his fifth year of studies at the University of Saskatchewan pursuing a four-year honours degree in Political Science. In 1998–99, he served as vice-president (Government Affairs) for the University of Saskatchewan Students' Union and in 1999–2000 was elected president. He enjoys playing hockey, watching baseball (which he finds to be very relaxing), and keeping himself informed about the political comings and goings in Canada. He looks forward to travelling after finishing his undergraduate degree and then working on his Master's degree in Political Science. After that it is anyone's guess as to where he may end up.

James Kirkpatrick was born and raised in Kingston, Ontario. He graduated from the University of Guelph with a Bachelor of Landscape Architecture with Honours in 1999. He served on Residence Council for two years, as Residence Assistant for one year, as well as a campus Safewalker for one year. James worked in the university's Power Plant for two years and in the university library for one year. He was also a member of the Landscape Architecture Student Society for two years. James has literally seen every square inch of the campus in his four years at Guelph.

Jon Koch wrote the piece on the University of Lethbridge. A native of Brooks, Alberta, Jon will be graduating from the University of Lethbridge with a BA in Political Science and History in December 1999. Jon is a former Students' Union Executive, and at the time of publication, was serving as Copy Editor with the student newspaper, *The Meliorist*.

Tannys Laughren graduated from Laurentian University in 1996 with a BComm. She has been business manager for the Students' Association at Laurentian (since 1998) and has been involved in student politics for several years, with an emphasis on the financial side. Tannys also works part-time for the Commerce Department at LU as a teaching assistant, serves on several boards including the YWCA, and the board for CKLU FM, the student radio station. Tannys would like to thank the people who assisted in the Laurentian piece: Jamie Wylie, LU SGA president (BA in English) and very involved in residence council (president and vice-president); Bryce Collins, Residence Life Coordinator for 1998–99 (Bachelor of Phys.Ed.); and Kevin Predon, Residence Life Coordinator for 1999–00 (Bachelor of Social Sciences).

Colin MacMillan helped write the piece on St. Mary's University.

Kris Magliaro is a Bachelor of Science graduate (Psychology) of UCCB (1998). He wrote a weekly column for the *Cape Breton Post* from September 1998 to March 1999. The title of the column was "Student's View at UCCB," and it dealt with all facets of life at the university from a student's perspective. He has also recently been accepted into the BEd. program at the University of Maine at Fort Kent for the fall of 1999.

Travis Mason is currently in his fourth year at Brock University pursing his Honours BA in English Language and Literature. He enjoys reading, writing, listening to music, cycling, camping, and cool weather. After completing his honours year, which includes a thesis paper, he plans to go away for graduate studies in Canadian Literature. He hopes to earn his MA and eventually a PhD on his way to teaching at the university level.

Sarah Mayes wrote the piece on the University of Ottawa. Sarah is a fourth-year student in the Honours English program at the University of Ottawa who is tired of telling people she does not go to Carleton. She currently serves on the editorial board of *Bywords*, a poetry journal affiliated with the English department, and considers herself a part-time poet. Sarah is a native Torontonian who loves living in downtown Ottawa, but after three winters there lives in fear of the first snowfall. She

hopes to head to a milder climate out west after graduation to do graduate work.

Lorraine McMeekin graduated from York University in June of 1999 with a Bachelor of Arts in Philosophy. During her years at York, she was involved in various student organizations. Lorraine sat on the Bethune College Council for two terms as the External Affairs Representative and on the York Federation of Students as the Bethune College Representative. She was also actively involved with the creation of the Food F.O.R. York Food Bank. Lorraine is now attending Centennial College as a student in the Corporate Communications program.

Michele Murphy is a fourth-year PRC student at Trent University. Originally from Thornhill, Ontario, she has truly made Peterborough her home and is sad as well as excited at the prospect of moving on. She'll probably come back often just to go to The Only Café. After leaving Trent, she will be attending Queen's for teacher's college. Her time at Trent has been fantastic. She has met many incredible people, and learned much about herself and the world. Peter-Patch is a special place, and it will always be close to her heart. All you really need is Tofu, Perrier, and the Pork…

Amy Patterson wrote the piece on the University of British Columbia. Amy is a twenty-something Vancouverite who graduated from UBC in 1998 with a BA in Women's Studies and Religion and Literature. Recently, with partner and Sweet Pea the cat in tow, she has temporarily relocated to Toronto and is currently attending York University for a Master's in Women's Studies.

Cornelia Ratt is German, 29 years old, married, and has two cats. After finishing high school, she briefly attended Bonn University to study English Literature, but quickly decided that she wanted to study in an English-speaking country. She came to Canada in 1993 and moved to Regina where she received her honours degree in English from the University of Regina in 1997, and her Master's in 1999. Right now, she is beginning her doctoral program at the University of Saskatchewan in Saskatoon. Apart from literature studies, she works as a translator, model, and actress.

Karen Rawlines graduated from UPEI in 1999 with a Bachelor of Science degree. She spent two years as editor-in-chief of the student newspaper, *The Cadre*. Karen is a poet, fiction writer, and freelance journalist, and plans to study journalism at the University of King's College this year. She calls the Maritimes home.

Greg Severight is a graduate of the Lakehead University Outdoor Recreation program. He has spent the last four years at Lakehead and has enjoyed every minute of it.

Rob South is a fourth-year Economics major at the University of Calgary. Additionally Rob minors in both Political Science and Communications. He is presently the President of the Students' Union. Other campus activities have included writing for *the gauntlet*, being a student safe-walker, and being the Executive Director of the U of C Amnesty International Association. Future plans have Rob either going to law school or working for an NGO.

Tanya Spencer is a third-year Neuroscience student at the University of Alberta. She loves NCAA basketball and *Buffy the Vampire Slayer*. Tanya's plans for the future include grad school and/or med school, and a research career.

Katy Sternbergh graduated from McMaster in May 1999 with a Bachelor's degree in Political Science. She is currently spending the next year working full-time as the Executive Editor of Mac's official student newspaper, *The Silhouette*. Katy has wanted to pursue a career in journalism ever since she discovered it was a popular alter ego for superheroes. Due to contractual obligations, Katy is unable to reveal her own superhuman powers at this time.

Gavin Tong has a BSc. in Microbiology from the University of Victoria. He has been living in Victoria for four years and plans to finish off one more year doing an environmental health audit on UVic as part of the University of Victoria Sustainability project, playing Ulti, and livin' large. Gavin would like to thank Sue Bel, a.k.a. LB, for all her help and, of course, all his friends.

Monique Trottier completed a four-year honours degree in English in 1997. She started her Master's in English and is working on a creative thesis. She moved to Vancouver last year and is completing her Master's in Publishing this December. So yes, two Master's.

Ryan Ward has just completed his Bachelor of Arts in Political Science and History at Carleton University. He served on the University Senate, New University Government, and Carleton University Students' Association and is now working for the Policy Planning Division of Foreign Affairs and International Trade. For the past nine years, he has been a writer, editor, photographer, and desktop publisher for various newspapers across Ontario. He aspires to be a sports broadcaster or journalist and to run for political office in the upcoming future.

Robin Whittaker graduated from Wilfrid Laurier University in 1999 with a degree in Honours English with a Theatre Major and Co-op Option. He was Managing Editor of the *Laurier Cord* in 1997–98 and wrote, directed, and stage-managed plays with Laurier's University Players and the Laurier Theatre Collective. He has published a book of poetry entitled *Happen Stance*, and is continuing his education as a Master's student in Theatre.

Jill Wilson wrote the piece on Brandon University. She is currently enrolled in the undergraduate program there.

About the Editors . . .

Christine Ibarra is completing her final year at the University of Toronto studying Physiology and French Translation. (What a combination!) Bilingual in French and English, she has travelled to the pyramids in Egypt, the Parthenon in Greece, the cathedrals in Russia, the Eiffel Tower, the Louvre in France, and beyond. Born and living the big-city life in Toronto, Chris enjoys alpine skiing in the winter and English riding in the summer. Chris plans to pursue a career in law.

Blair Trudell is a nomadic student who has attended Dalhousie University, Université d'Aix-Marseille in France, and has currently landed at the University of Victoria, where he is completing a BA in Political Science. His ambitions include: at least one tenure as the prime minister of Canada, a captaincy with the Toronto Maple Leafs, and getting up before 9:00 a.m. He has vowed to quit smoking despite several unsuccessful attempts and has become increasingly more paranoid about the coming of the new millennium—which has done nothing to curb his habit.